Michael Haneke

Michael Haneke

The Intermedial Void

Christopher Rowe

NORTHWESTERN UNIVERSITY PRESS
EVANSTON, ILLINOIS

Northwestern University Press
www.nupress.northwestern.edu

Printed in the United States of America

10 9 8 7 6 5 4 3 2 1

Library of Congress Cataloging-in-Publication Data

Names: Rowe, Christopher, 1978– author.
Title: Michael Haneke : the intermedial void / Christopher Rowe.
Description: Evanston, Illinois : Northwestern University Press, 2017. | Includes bibliographical references and index.
Identifiers: LCCN 2016055007 | ISBN 9780810134607 (cloth : alk. paper) | ISBN 9780810134591 (pbk. : alk. paper) | ISBN 9780810134614 (e book)
Subjects: LCSH: Haneke, Michael, 1942– —Criticism and interpretation.
Classification: LCC PN1998.3.H36 R56 2017 | DDC 791.4302/33092—dc23
LC record available at https://lccn.loc.gov/2016055007

♾The paper used in this publication meets the minimum requirements of the American National Standard for Information Sciences—Permanence of Paper for Printed Library Materials, ANSI Z39.48–1992.

CONTENTS

ACKNOWLEDGMENTS

This study began at the University of Melbourne, where it and its author benefited incalculably from the scholarly guidance, enthusiastic encouragement, and intellectual generosity of the brilliant Justin Clemens. Its evolution into its present form was in no small part motivated by encouragement—and excellent critical feedback—from Robert Sinnerbrink and Gregory Flaxman. My thanks to Gregory are also due for his instrumental role in connecting me with the excellent staff of Northwestern University Press and in particular to Michael Levine, who has been a pleasure to work with at every stage of this process.

I would also like to extend my sincere gratitude to Brian Price for providing essential advice and generous support over the past few years; to Călin-Andrei Mihăilescu for being an unfailing source of inspiration and immoral support; and to the anonymous readers of this manuscript for their attentive, informed, and highly valuable comments.

Essential financial support for this project was provided by the Social Sciences and Humanities Research Council of Canada, both in the form of an International Doctoral Fellowship and a Postdoctoral Fellowship. The latter was hosted by the University of Toronto's Cinema Studies Institute and very helpfully facilitated by Charlie Keil and Corinn Columpar, whose support is also gratefully acknowledged. Donald Ainslie and John W. Marshall were also instrumental in helping to find me an office in the most beautiful university building I've ever seen—much less had the pleasure of working in—at University College.

And finally, my unending gratitude and love are offered to my family for their patience, wisdom, motivation, and kind support. This work, and its author, remain humbly dedicated to them.

Introduction

✦

Haneke and the Media Question

Michael Haneke's films provoke and disturb because they expose us to the media that structure contemporary existence in the postindustrialized world; they use cinema as a means of manipulating these mediated gazes and actions to profound artistic and emotional effect. Simultaneously evoking both a sense of distantiation from and an intimate resubjectification to these perceptual and performative mechanisms, Haneke's oeuvre reconfigures the function of the cinematic image, and hence the cinema's very system of representation, in crucial ways. Because of this, his films tend to elide description and analysis based on conventional critical and theoretical frameworks. They instead invite more innovative readings that problematize established categories such as spectatorship, genre, narrative realism, and medium specificity itself. What follows is a series of theoretical interpellations with Haneke's oeuvre that rethink his films' powers of expression along different axes, departing from the viewpoints of those who define his films purely as works of cinema that function solely within modes of cinematic spectatorial engagement. In the process, I will explore the question of what it means to conceptualize cinema less as a medium bound to its own set of audiovisual codes and conventions and more as a medial and intermedial assemblage that presents—as Haneke consistently does—a multiplicity of distinct formal, perceptual, and affective encounters with different medial interfaces.

Indeed, although he maintains a consistent aesthetic of realism, emotional and moral complexity, and philosophical and conceptual rigor—as well as a place among the most respected of European art cinema auteurs[1]—Haneke has nonetheless produced films that confront the very structures and premises of noncinematic media through their embodied presentation within the films themselves. Rather than simply referencing, satirizing, or explicitly commenting upon the effects of these other medial forms, Haneke's films obtain relationships with nonfilmic audiovisual material at a primary level of mimetic expression. Furthermore, his films cannot be identified as hybridized or synthesized medial texts; instead they draw together these disparate media forms while maintaining the discursive and representational disjunctions separating them. Thus, for instance, the use of television as a visual backdrop in all of his present-day narrative features—and particularly in *Der siebente Kontinent* (*The Seventh Continent*; 1989) and *71 Fragmente einer Chronologie des Zufalls* (*71 Fragments of a Chronology of Chance*; 1994), his first and third cinematic works—incorporates the other medium not as a mutual image that supports the narrative and discourse or extends the visual palette of the film. Television remains instead utterly incommensurate with and intrusive upon cinematic representation. This mimetic disjunction is likewise maintained, implicitly or explicitly, throughout his oeuvre, even as other media assume significant roles in the films' narratives and modes of expression. These media include, but are not limited to, the following: video in *Benny's Video* (1992), *Funny Games* (1997 and 2007), and *Caché* (*Hidden*; 2005); photography in *Code inconnu* (*Code Unknown*; 2000); genre movies in *Funny Games*, *Code inconnu*, *La pianiste* (*The Piano Teacher*; 2001), and *Caché*; recorded sound and music in *Code inconnu*, *La pianiste*, and *Le temps du loup* (*Time of the Wolf*; 2003); video games in *71 Fragmente* and *Funny Games*; and literary voice in *Das Schloß* (The Castle; 1997), *La pianiste*, and his literary adaptations for television. The aporetic and multifaceted relationships between film and these other media in Haneke's work will inform my definition of *intermediality* as the staging of *productive disjunctions* between the medium of film and these other media.[2] In Haneke's strategy of medial fragmentation, cinema does not come to "represent," "deconstruct," or otherwise implicitly master other media, but rather to establish irresolvable spatiotemporal discontinuities between these forms of expression, producing mimetically fractured yet profoundly affective and evocative images of thought. The culmination of Haneke's formal practice of intermediality is *Caché*, in which the film itself and the videos that appear within the film are presented as both incompossible and indistinguishable and together constitute an unprecedented innovation of the expressive potential of the moving image.

An important antecedent for this theoretical framework is the philosophy of Gilles Deleuze, including both his film theory and his highly evocative considerations of the problematic interrelationship between film and electronic media.[3] In effect, I will argue that Haneke's work—in an extended project that reaches its apotheosis in *Caché*—constitutes a new intermedial permutation of Deleuze's crystalline time-image. This notion will most likely appear somewhat controversial to those closely subscribing to Deleuze's Bergson-inflected philosophy of the cinematic image, which positions the time-image as the realization of cinema's capacity to express pure virtualities that could not be more different from the largely simplistic narrative and representational-referential systems of television and other commercial media. Yet such an approach has a clear foundation in Deleuze's texts on cinema: for instance, a question posed near the end of *Cinema 1* (1983)—"how can the cinema attack the dark organization of clichés, when it participates in their fabrication and propagation, as much as magazines or television?"—prompts

Deleuze to posit that it is the very presence of such clichés in cinema that "allow[s] certain directors to attain a critical reflection which they would not have at their disposal elsewhere."[4] Anticipating a major theme from the second *Cinema* text, the philosopher invokes the power of the cinematographic image to resist the representational structures of conventional and commercial media from within this system itself. From this perspective, Haneke's incorporation of, for example, a televised "power ballad" performed by Meat Loaf into the harrowing scenes of familial suicide in *Der siebente Kontinent* can be characterized as a profound critical gesture, whereby the very shallowness of the TV program is rendered troubling, if not deeply distressing, in juxtaposition to the film narrative.[5] Yet this propensity toward cliché only scratches the surface of the problems facing us in the contemporary audiovisual regime that cinema finds itself within, just as this potential for critical reflection only hints at the expressive possibilities brought into play by Haneke's practice of intermediality.

A seemingly more dire state of affairs is presented by Deleuze at the conclusion of *Cinema 2* (1985). Here Deleuze makes the following remarkable—though not often remarked-upon—statement regarding the relation of film to other media forms: "The electronic image, that is, the tele and video image . . . had either *to transform cinema* or to replace it, to mark its death."[6] In the confrontation between cinema and other audiovisual media, Deleuze implies, more is at stake than the former's aesthetic primacy; the encroachment of electronic media as the defining mode of perceptual engagement with the world at large presents a direct threat to the cinematic image as a mode of apprehending, much less resisting, contemporary sociopolitical reality. According to Deleuze, while cinema offers images of thought through which we may obtain the means of conceptualizing, and ultimately believing in, "this world, as it is,"[7] we have ample reasons to be skeptical of the idea that electronic media are capable of producing or maintaining anything like the intellectual and aesthetic richness of movement- and time-images.[8] In place of any genuinely affective or conceptual image of the world, these media offer only the "nullity" and "radical ineffectiveness" of information, and Deleuze goes on to state quite plainly that "[t]he life or the afterlife of cinema depends on its internal struggle with informatics."[9] Thus, as D. N. Rodowick observes in the introduction of *Gilles Deleuze's Time Machine* (1997), Deleuze's *Cinema* books are not solely concerned with the artistic and signifying potential of the film image: "Deleuze is quite sensitive to the ways in which contemporary culture is becoming fundamentally an audiovisual culture. For him, the semiotic history of film is coincident with a century-long transformation wherein we have come to represent and understand ourselves socially through spatial and temporal articulations founded in cinema, if now realized more clearly in the electronic and digital media."[10] In *Cinema 2* in particular, then, Deleuze highlights the resonance of the cinematographic image with our contemporary experience of collective reality (or unreality)—"the link between man and the world"—even at the level of perception: "The modern fact is that we no longer believe in this world. We do not even believe in the events which happen to us, love, death, as if they only half concerned us. It is not we who make cinema; it is the world which looks to us like a bad film."[11] Deleuze's implication, as Rodowick points out, is that the aesthetic potential of cinema to produce affirmative images of lived events is being continually subverted by the abundance of "bad films" and other aesthetically empty audiovisual forms. Television, video, online content, and other postcinematic screen media—what Deleuze collectively refers to as "informatics"—have instead come to define the world we inhabit, undermining artistic images through their circulation of empty, repetitive representations of reality that diminish our capacities for conviction and affirmation; that neutralize, rather than support and extend, the perceptual and affective energies of lived experience. But this is not necessarily all that they *can* do.

Should one uncritically accept Deleuze's bleak portrait of the current state of affairs, which is so similar to the visions of theorists such as Jean Baudrillard, Guy Debord, and Paul Virilio, among many other of his contemporaries? Or do commercial cinema and new media forms possess certain possibilities for self-reflection, and for encounters with beings and events, that are in many respects comparable to those of the art-cinematic images and the expressive material of other traditional art forms? A primary aim of this text will be to analyze the intermedial structures present in Haneke's cinema in order to launch a series of theoretically informed inquiries into these very questions, with the goal of reapproaching the issue by framing it through the perspectives of more nuanced modes of media theory, which diverge in important respects from the art-critical and continental-philosophical traditions informing the views of Deleuze and his contemporaries. Ironically, I will be using Deleuzian theory as the grounds for my own intermedial and "media-philosophical" approach, using the philosopher's thought to temper his rather broadly stated analysis of the social and intellectual ill-effects of informatic media. However, my intentions remain true to the spirit of his exhortations, as I will find in Haneke's films evidence of the longed-for aesthetic transformation mentioned above, whereby electronic media, far from announcing the death knell of the cinematic image, provide new potentialities for its expression of lived experience and, ultimately, for a revitalized mode of cinematic realism. To use specifically Deleuzian terms, in Haneke's oeuvre the cinematographic image enters into a mutual becoming with electronic media via a shared "plane of immanence," a plane that must be qualified as intermedial.

Before examining this theoretical approach in more detail, however, yet another level of irony must be addressed: in many respects my framework also tends to align itself against Haneke's own stated views on the matter, which generally adhere to a position similar to those of Deleuze and his critical contemporaries. In his essays and interviews, the director draws a clear distinction between art films—i.e. those of the type that he makes himself—and commercial cinema and television. Film and other audiovisual media, in Haneke's outlook, are art forms only *in potentia* until they can uncover a means of attaining artistic self-reflection, which is characterized as the defining stylistic and aesthetic mode of artistic modernism. Haneke states his position unequivocally at the conclusion of his essay "Violence and the Media" (1998): "Yes, I would go so far as to speak of medial ART only when it contains this act of text-based self-reflection, an act that has long become a *sine qua non* condition of all other forms of modern art."[12] Elsewhere, in an interview with Franz Grabner, Haneke further clarifies this point, indicating that a film lacking this type of self-reflexivity is indistinguishable in function from the mechanisms of social control that Deleuze associates with television and electronic media: "For film to be a form of art, it must assume an aesthetic-moral responsibility to reflect the questionable and dangerous nature of its manipulative means in its own work."[13] Such strict distinctions between art and commercial media would seem to cripple my proposed intermedial framework from the outset: the very subject of my study is against me! Yet it is also clear that Haneke's assertions do not preclude the use of such "manipulative" media forms in the service of artistic self-reflection. Indeed, Haneke's use of postcinematic media—no less than the presence in his films of high-cultural texts such as works of literature, musical compositions, painting, and art photography—are often vectors for his employment of a "modernist" mode of self-reflexivity.[14] Put differently, there is rarely, if ever, a sense that these other media objects or systems compose a kind of audiovisual pastiche, and their presence is instead grounded in an artistically meaningful, though often ambiguous and elusive, structure. Before proceeding to elaborate on my Deleuze-inflected media theory, then, it will be necessary to give a more detailed account of the intermedial schema of Haneke's works.

Haneke's Intermedial Schema

Haneke's films demonstrate, with admirable clarity and rigor, that our general acceptance of an integral, systemic, and substantive notion of "The Media" is untenable and fundamentally misleading. In this respect, the concept of The Media, in the sense of a continuous and at some level homogeneous "mediascape," resembles those other well-worn and by now presumably discarded universals, History and Reality, in new dress. An implicit belief that print, photography, recorded sound, radio, cinema, television, and video somehow constitute a unified plane of reference or representation is equally as problematic as the classical presumption that empirical time and space constitute experientially stable, measurable, and verifiable planes of existence. Yet such an understanding of media generally persists in contemporary culture, largely due to two factors: the fact that these disparate media can be mechanically, electronically, or digitally mass-produced and widely disseminated in a similar manner to one another, thus ensuring their ubiquitous influence on our attentions and perceptions; and the apparent ability of computer and communications technologies to reproduce individual instantiations, and even aggregates, of any and all of these media. Consequently, there also persists the almost ineluctable idea of an evolutionary sociohistorical progress through which one form technically overtakes and undermines another, an idea that was already encountered in Deleuze: the implication that the cinematographic image succeeded the printed word as a means of apprehending lived experience, only to risk being succeeded in turn by television and video, and so on.[15] Our continued subscription to this logic is clear from the fact that we presuppose, whether anxiously or enthusiastically, that our variously sized computers and screens will render (or have already rendered) all of our previous media technologies obsolete. Underlying any such assumption is a technical-evolutionary model of media relations whereby any media object—whether visual image, recorded sound, or written text—is transposable to another medium with only negligible alteration or adaptation. Haneke, however, reinvests the question of the medium and its contents with a fundamental force of difference that resists any simple interpretations of one medium representing, replacing, or reframing another. His films thus complexify the relations and associations we perceive, or create, between diverse media forms by preserving the irreconcilable perceptual and sensational differences that persist between each respective system of negotiations between subject and medium. This practice is the very definition of intermediality, a concept that will require further elaboration in order to differentiate its aesthetic and theoretical usages, both of which will figure into my approach.

The term "intermediality," which is gaining currency in English-language scholarship, has long been in use in Western European media studies, particularly in Germanic scholarship (where it is rendered *Intermedialität*). Intermediality in its present usage is relatable both to the aesthetic category of "intermedia" and to a theoretical framework derived from Julia Kristeva's critical model of intertextuality. As Yvonne Spielmann points out, such variance in the term's employment has led to a certain ambiguity as to its definition and meaning:

> The understanding of the phenomenon described as intermedia shifts in different discourses. . . . [I]ntermedia is a conceptual term. It should be applied in the first place to a specific type of transformation between different media. Secondly, intermedia indicates the structure of the transformation that is effected by a collision of elements taken from different media. Furthermore, it is an aesthetic device to be identified in the media arts. To conclude: I suggest using the term

> intermedia on three levels, that it is a transformation category, a structural term, and an aesthetic device.[16]

While the next section will focus more on the theoretical potential the term holds for considering the structures of transformation (and transformations of structures) informing media studies and media philosophy, I will first examine its potential for describing Haneke's aesthetic practice. This use of the word "intermedia" as an aesthetic definition is largely associated with Dick Higgins's essay "Intermedia" (1965; expanded in 1981). Higgins himself traces the word's provenance back to an 1812 essay by Samuel Taylor Coleridge, where it appears, according to him, "exactly in its contemporary sense." Intermedia are defined by Higgins as works of art that "fall conceptually between media that are already known" rather than conforming to a single "pure" medium.[17] Higgins points out that intermedia must, on this basis, be distinguished from works of "mixed media"—that is, works that combine different *physical* media, such as oil paint and gouache, into a single image. As examples of *conceptual* differences characteristic of intermedia, Higgins cites Marcel Duchamp's ready-mades, which are indeterminately situated between identifiable artistic media, such as sculpture and performance art, and perhaps even exceed any categorical definition of art itself: "The ready-made or found object . . . suggests a location in the field between the general area of art media and those of life media."[18] The intermedial work's crossing of conceptual categories—even to the extent of encompassing both art and nonart—appears ideal as a means of defining many of Haneke's films, which similarly incorporate two identifiably disparate "artistic" media, such as photography and cinema in *Code inconnu*, or incorporate "artistic" and "nonartistic" media forms, such as cinema and television in *Der siebente Kontinent* and *71 Fragmente* or cinema and video in *Benny's Video*, *Funny Games*, and *Caché*. The significant presence of electronic and informatic mass media in these films troubles our acceptance of them as works belonging to a "pure" cinematic medium (itself a highly suspect category), yet they remain equally unacceptable as unified works of cinematic "mixed media." It is much more useful to conceptualize these films as works of intermedia, in that they transgress or even erode the boundaries separating different art forms and even artistic and nonartistic media.

Immediately, however, this aesthetic model elicits a number of potential problems. To begin with, the terms "intermedium" and "intermediality" present themselves as redundancies. If a medium, in the most general sense of the word, is that which provides a conduit between two other things or between two extremes of a common substance, then a medium is by definition already "intermedial." Intermediality, generally speaking, should refer to a function or attribute of any and all media. As Eckart Voigst-Virchow similarly notes, while still acknowledging the usefulness of the designation, "[t]he term seems tautologous as it duplicates the 'in-betweenness' of both the terms 'medium' and 'inter.' "[19] Thus, one seems to be forced to reify the notion of a given medium in and of itself; that is, to render it a relatively static and stable—or "pure," in Higgins's words—entity, but without allowing it to devolve into a strictly materialist definition (which would invalidate its conceptual value and thus the distinction between "intermedia" and "mixed media"). An index of difference must be upheld between media in order for intermediality to obtain relevance, but this approach appears to presuppose either that media are fixed and unchangeable concepts or that they are permutations of a unified, tautological representational structure, pointing us back toward an overdetermined notion of the "mediascape." In what sense, then, is the prefix "inter-" in intermediality valid if it is in fact being applied either to a totalizing abstraction or to mutually incommunicable categories? Must one conceive of a new medium with which to negotiate between these conceptually and formally distinct media, which are themselves already *between* other entities (image and viewer, past and present, sender and receiver, etc.)? What is between the in-between?

The short answer to this last question, for the purposes of this text, is: "Nothing." But this "nothing" is so obvious that it becomes itself almost perceivable, almost palpable. Intermediality, in this approach, is a decidedly nonintuitive term that refers not to a positive spatiotemporal or conceptual interconnection but rather to a *negative* sensory plane or *void* between—and even within—different media. In the presently dominant, overgeneralized notion of the mediascape, disparate medial texts and forms have been increasingly perceived as being enfolded within one vast informatic substance, each thus becoming eminently capable of operations of communication and exchange with one other. All media would thus be intermedia.[20] Haneke's films, however, express a consistent thematic and formal counterargument to this idea, highlighting instead the profound *gaps*—in knowledge, cognition, intellectual and emotional communication, mediated and lived experience, and ultimately subjectivity itself—which arise out of our continual engagement with diverse and disconnected media. Dramatically, these gaps are often explored through narrative and performance, particularly in his early Glaciation Trilogy [*Vergletscherung-trilogie*]: *Der siebente Kontinent*, *Benny's Video*, and *71 Fragmente*. In these films, characters struggle in the midst of personal, familial, generational, and social breakdowns in communication that undermine their capacities to express understanding, love, and compassion, and these breakdowns are implied to be proportional to their level of interaction with various media, and with television in particular. Furthermore, Haneke exposes the films' spectators to these media directly and thus, in very important respects, *independently of* cinematic representation.

Formally, Haneke's depiction of other media consistently indexes the absolute mimetic difference between film and the other medium, as opposed to implicitly presenting film as a "master text" capable of containing and controlling the modes of expression of other media. As Georg Seeβlen, one of the most astute commentators on Haneke's work, points out, Haneke's camera intentionally exposes the attenuations of and disconnections within sensory experience that are both integral to film and unavoidable in the encounter between film and other audiovisual media: "Very different from the camera in mainstream cinema, it refrains from trying to overcome the mundane limitations of perception through tricks, instead describing precisely these limitations of perception, the reduction of the perceptual field. When the camera looks at a switched-on television, it disappears into it."[21] The television screens that appear so frequently in Haneke's oeuvre are never simply relegated to the background of the mise-en-scène and tend even to actively resist the cinematic frame imposed on them, to engage the camera, and by extension the spectator, in *televisual* rather than *cinematic* terms. Hence, the simultaneity of two utterly distinct modes of medial expression within a shot or scene—the cinematographic and the televisual—must be considered an *intermedial* rather than a medial problem, since its analysis must include at least three terms: the film frame, the television screen, and the intermedial incommensurability of these two phenomena, the *void* instituted by the very *absence* of a common medium of expression to unite them.

This theoretical framework is, as mentioned above, rather unintuitive, since it involves—to state only the most obvious implication—an understanding of the cinema screen not only as a frame for the cinematic image but also as a site for multiple noncinematic media that invite different modes of spectatorial suture. Yet this approach has not been entirely unknown in cinema—one could, for instance, point to much of the work of Jean-Luc Godard as a sustained engagement with similar intermedial strategies. Furthermore, one could cite any number of individual instances of intermediality from cinema whose effects are comparable to Haneke's.[22] Yet Haneke's films nonetheless offer a unique and sustained perspective on such intermedial relations and nonrelations, since these relations are not only constitutive of the films' audiovisual structures on a mimetic level but also of their thematic and aesthetic concerns. In other words, Haneke does not simply include noncinematic media in his films' image systems for stylistic purposes; his films are fundamentally definable according to the multitudinous interrelations between narrative events, artistic images, and informatic referents that are instantiated by these intermedial gaps themselves. The conceptual implications of this representational strategy are profound and will be explored in detail throughout this text. Suffice it to say, for now, that Haneke's films enable a perspective on the functioning of electronic mass media that largely eludes us in our firsthand engagement with these technologies. In this way, the director confronts an aesthetic problematic that is perhaps best identified in the systems-theoretical approach of Niklas Luhmann in *The Reality of the Mass Media* (1996). Luhmann laments "the lack of an adequate reflexive theory" of mass media, a theory rendered practically unobtainable by the fact that our continual deferral to—and reentry into—a mass-mediated view of reality instantiates a perceptual system wherein "the distinction between the world as it is and the world as it is observed becomes blurred."[23] The "transcendental illusion" thus generated by mass media—within which we have long been ensnared, according to Luhmann—seems to preclude the possibility of observing mass media's direct effects on our observation; that is, unless we innovate some means of (or medium for) observing the effects of this already-mediated observation of the world: "What is needed in order to resolve this paradox of the confusion of two worlds is imagination or creative ideas which refer reflexively to the state of the system [of observation] just reached, but which are not determined by it."[24] In order to counteract the deterministic influence of mass-mediated perception, then, it is necessary to create a method of approaching this spectatorial system without defaulting to the representational conditions of these media themselves, and thus subscribing, unavoidably, to their reconstitutive worldviews. Haneke's films generate a particularly effective perceptual and affective countersystem to that of the mass media, one which contravenes and almost parodies electronic media's audiovisual structures (or outright parodies them, in the case of *Funny Games*), but nonetheless upholds a strict, even severe, cinematic relation to actuality and lived experience. For this reason, one must conceptualize Haneke's aesthetic in terms of a renovated mode of cinematic realism or, better still, of *intermedial* realism. Let me briefly contextualize the stakes of this argument.

It has long been acknowledged that realism should not be understood simply as an attribute of certain technologies of representation, whether or not one ascribes to these an indexical relationship with lived conditions or experiences of seeing and hearing. For instance, Marshall McLuhan notes in "Media Log," his collection of aphorisms, that "[p]hotography and cinema have abolished realism as too easy; they substitute themselves for realism."[25] This point resonates still, as evidenced by a remark made by W. J. T. Mitchell many years later, in response to general suspicions surrounding the assumed ease of manipulability, and therefore inherent "untrustworthiness," of digital photography: "Realism is not built in to the ontology of any medium as such."[26] Yet, uncoupling the concept of realism from any given "medium ontology," one is faced instead with an unfixed principle and, consequently, a continually evolving series of strategies for vouchsafing an identifiably realist orientation and aesthetic. Realism is in this estimation never definable strictly as a property of a given stylistic approach or medium, but instead must be continually renegotiated in relation both to sociopolitical actuality and to representational-technological possibility. Such an understanding of realism is set forth by Jean-Louis Comolli, in his influential essay "Machines of the Visible" (1971), in terms of a retroactively instantiated gap between human perception and technological representation—in other words, from the very impossibility of these two ever fully coinciding. Resembling in this sense Luhmann's paradox of mass-mediated and lived worlds of perception (as well as Deleuze's definition of cinema as a mode of belief in the world), Comolli's definition of cinematic realism is primarily founded not on the medium's increasing capacity for verisimilitude but on the spectator's diminishing capacity to be courted and coerced by illusion. Cinematic realism thus functions according to a core mechanism of subjective doubt and disavowal rather than of objective resemblance to the world:

> The mechanic magic of the analogical representation of the visible is accomplished and articulated from a doubt as to the fidelity of human vision, and more widely as to the truth of sensory impressions.
>
> I wonder if it is not from this, from this lack to be filled, that could have come the extreme eagerness of the first spectators to *recognize* in the images of the first films—devoid of colour, nuance, fluidity—the identical image, the double of life itself. If there is not, in the very principle of representation, a force of disavowal which gives free rein to an analogical illusion that is yet only weakly manifested by the iconic signifiers themselves?[27]

The capacity of cinema to produce a realistic image of the world, in Comolli's interpretation, has from its earliest history up to the present been based less on the representational properties of the medium than on its manifestation of a persistent gap in lived perception, a mistrust in our capacity to fully believe our eyes.[28] Each technical "improvement" in cinema's history—including depth of field, synchronized sound, color, 3-D, and higher frame rates, to name but the most obvious enhancements—is offered as a remedy for a perceived insufficiency in cinema's representation of reality, when in fact its function is to defer a mistrust that persists with regard to our own capacity to register reality *im*mediately, as objective experience. Hence, the question of realism—whether posed as a narrative, representational, or stylistic concern—is inextricably linked in the cinema to technological more so than aesthetic innovations, since these address more directly the crux of the "analogical illusion" that manifests our self-doubt as perceiving subjects. As Lev Manovich points out in *The Language of New Media* (2001), with reference to Comolli's essay, "[s]o theorized, realistic effect in the cinema appears as a constant sum in an equation with a few variables that change historically and have equal weight."[29] In what way, then, does Haneke's intermediality supply a new permutation of this equation of cinematic realism?

We will proceed by arguing that the intermedial system that is instantiated in Haneke's cinema relaunches, as opposed to remediates, the perceptual gap that motivates realist innovations and interventions, as though answering a void with another void. The "sum" of cinematic realism—framed by Manovich as the addition of a techno-medial innovation to a perceptual gap displaced onto representation—is thus reconfigured in Haneke's practice as the force of *difference* produced by two mutually negating medial values.[30]

In other words, Haneke does not subscribe to the deferral or displacement of the ever-evolving problem of disavowal onto the film medium itself according to an additive logic of technological advancement, thereby identifying a gap in cinematic representation (its lack of depth, sound, color, a spatial z-axis, etc.) as the locus of a disjunction between perception and representation that can be repaired technologically. Nor does he simply move in the opposite direction, proceeding toward a realist aesthetic by stripping away certain elements of film narrative and representation to reach an ascetic minimum that mirrors actual (mundane) experience.[31] Haneke instead stages a lateral intervention into cinematic representation—exposing its limits along with those of noncinematic media—with the simultaneous effects of signaling the constructedness of the cinema's "analogical illusion" and of expressing the power of the cinematic image to contextualize and resist the other, more ubiquitous (and in Haneke's view, more pernicious) modes of technologically mediated perception to which we are subjected. Haneke's films thus subscribe to a mode of realism that refers, first and foremost, to the *un*reality that underpins our collective experience, if not our very existence, as spectators. The gaps in our mediated perceptions open up not onto some notion of an accessible immediate real, but rather onto other incommensurable forms of mediation, and hence the individuals he presents as film characters are themselves subject to the representations and effects of television, video, and so on. Because of this, it is not possible to give an adequate account of Haneke's realist aesthetic without first defining the complexities instituted by the modes of intermediality that precondition its consistencies and inconsistencies.

It may of course be argued that a theoretically sound definition of what constitutes a medium and its relation to other media would itself account for what has here been termed intermediality. Yet such a definition of media is elusive, at least insofar as it would be applicable to Haneke's work.[32] As Brian Price and John David Rhodes point out in their introduction to the essay collection *On Michael Haneke* (2010), for instance, current critical perspectives on the mediated image offer a largely ineffectual theoretical model through which to explore the director's realist-representational strategies:

> Haneke's work suggests to us the insufficiency of theories of the image that tend predominantly to questions of medium specificity and the cognitive and moral effects of the moving image, the effects of media *as* media. . . . If the notion of medium is at all appropriate to Haneke's work, it will need to be broadly expanded, allowed a wider berth in which we might come to understand the term not simply as a set of properties unique to any one art or mode of communication but also as something that *stands between*.[33]

In *Benny's Video*, *Funny Games*, and *Caché*, in particular, Haneke stages his aural and visual imagery in such a way as to deliberately interrupt and fragment the signifying chain that would connect the perceptual field of the spectator to that of the characters within the film. In these films, and to some extent in all of his work, he does not offer images as medial objects to be viewed but rather as signifiers both of what is viewable or representable and of what is unrepresentable; he utilizes the film image "as a site of relay and deferral."[34] Perhaps, then, the expansion of the concept of the medium as such, as called for by Price and Rhodes, is achievable through a reconsideration of how a medium is defined relative to spectatorial perception. In the next section, I will explore the possibility of such a definition as a key through-line in post-McLuhan media and communication studies and examine the degree to which a specifically Deleuzian reading of this concept of the medium clarifies its relevance to Haneke's intermedial realism.

A Deleuzian Media Theory

We have already introduced Deleuze's position regarding the conflict between the cinematographic image and electronic or informatic media—his position being that the latter threatens to subvert the former, and that there is a need for cinema to transform itself in order to retain its potential to provide artistically oriented models for belief in the world. The philosopher expands on this position in the essay "Letter to Serge Daney" (1986). Here, Deleuze asserts, in agreement with Daney, that we have no means of assessing televisual imagery on the basis of the film image, since television fulfills a much more overtly sociopolitical function—"a function of control and power"—and possesses no discernible aesthetic comparable to that of cinema.[35] Television's aesthetic potential is in this consideration almost completely untapped, and it produces instead a redundantly informatic image of the world, one that is cinematic only to the extent that it emits the aesthetically empty image of "any film at all."[36] Deleuze repeats—and in even stronger terms than he had at the conclusion of *Cinema 2*—that cinema must respond to television's "social engineering" with its own medial and imagistic transformations:

> Cinema ought to stop "being cinematic," stop playacting, and set up specific relationships with video, with electronic and digital images, in order to develop a new form of resistance and combat the televisual function of surveillance and control. It's not a question of short-circuiting television—how could that be possible?—but of preventing television [from] subverting or short-circuiting the extension of cinema into the new types of image.[37]

Deleuze's exhortations remain compelling today, as informatics and digital image media—if, indeed, the digital can be said to produce an "image" as such—have altered the production, distribution, and mode of engagement not only of film but also of photography, print, home video, and recorded music. However, whether or not cinema as an art form in general has responded to electronic media's increasing dominance in public consciousness with new types of image—or with, as Deleuze puts it in *Cinema 2*, "as yet unknown aspects of the time-image"[38]—remains debatable. While both mainstream and art cinema continue to be influenced by television and new media at a number of levels of expression, there have been relatively few films that directly confront the function of informatic media while providing a genuine image of thought in the sense Deleuze describes. It is not a question of thematically exploring or stylistically referencing the conditions of media saturation that have come to define contemporary representation, as, for example, in the manner of Oliver Stone's *Natural Born Killers* (1994), David Fincher's *Fight Club* (1999), or Edgar Wright's *Scott Pilgrim vs. the World* (2010). Rather, such an image's engagement with electronic media would be immanent to its very expressive potential. This Deleuzian model, I assert once again, is eminently applicable to Haneke's intermedial aesthetic, and the work of the philosopher is likewise highly valuable for any theorization of intermediality (and, as we shall see, is often cited by scholars who employ the term). But does this imply that Deleuze may himself be considered a media theorist?

Not so. To cite but one prominent example of Deleuze's lack of interest in defining the medium itself as a category, one might refer to his essay "Cold and Heat" (1973), which concerns the paintings of Gérard Fromanger. It is highly significant that when describing the work of this artist, who frequently uses photographs as bases or "canvases" for his paintings, Deleuze scarcely acknowledges this aspect of his artistic practice. Indeed, Deleuze never refers to "intermedia" or "mixed media" when discussing Fromanger's work, much less making anything of this dual mediation conceptually.[39] His views on Fromanger's work are instead completely taken up with a set of expressive relations between color, figure, and other elements. Even though he makes a central reference to—and even titles his essay after—a media-theoretical schema set out by Marshall McLuhan, Deleuze pointedly elides any questions of medium-specificity and instead focuses all of his attention on the affective-expressive qualities of the paintings and their actual or nascent powers to activate spectatorial thought and sensation. Deleuze locates a set of disjunctions in Fromanger's work, to be sure, but these are annexed to questions of sensation rather than forms of image media; his concern is with "the system of secondary colours which organizes on the contrary the *disjunctions* of hot and cold, a whole reversible play of transformations, reactions, inversions, inductions, heatings and coolings."[40] Only when invoking McLuhan directly does Deleuze so much as refer to the notion of a medium, and he does so in order to premise his own thoughts regarding the play of mutually opposed yet interdependent forces that are manifested by and within art itself: "As McLuhan demonstrates, when the medium is hot, nothing circulates or communicates except by virtue of the cold that governs all active participation, of the painter in his model, the spectator in his painter, the model in its copy. What counts are the perpetual inversions of 'hot' and 'cool' in which the hot chills the cold, the cold heats the hot: heating an oven by heaping up snowballs."[41] Taking McLuhan at his word, Deleuze utilizes the terms "hot" and "cool" as intensities that circulate along all of the trajectories through which art finds dynamic expression: in its creation, spectatorship, reproduction, and so on. These intensities do not define a given work, or a given medium, within an either-or regime of identity but rather manifest themselves as forces or flows propelled by one another as contraries. Fromanger's art—like anything worth designating "art," in Deleuze's reckoning—evidences such an energetics, laying claim to these circuits of intensity and sensation.

Of course, one could quite easily accuse Deleuze of misapplying McLuhan's concepts of "hot" and "cool" media, which were originally borrowed from jazz parlance as a way to designate the disparate levels of audience participation requisite for a medium to function effectively. A medium is considered "hot" if it addresses a sensory channel in "high definition" and "cool" if the spectator or listener is tasked with supplying additional sensory input to effectuate its expression: "Hot media are, therefore, low in participation, and cool media are high in participation or completion by the audience."[42] Deleuze, ignoring the medium-specific and differential application of the concepts of "hot" and "cool," transforms the application of these terms and, by bringing them to bear on the work of a single artist, appears to reformulate McLuhan's medium-oriented project of classification.[43] Indeed, one could similarly accuse Deleuze and Félix Guattari of misinterpreting McLuhan's definition of electric light as "a medium without a message" in *Anti-Oedipus* (1972): "This seems to us to be the significance of McLuhan's analyses: to have shown what a language of decoded flows is, as opposed to a signifier that strangles and overcodes the flows."[44] Deleuze and Guattari's reading, like Deleuze's in the Fromanger essay, again characterizes and utilizes McLuhan's media theory as a mode of thinking in relations and potentialities rather than through defined categories. McLuhan provides for them a means of circumventing rigidified sign systems and thus an avenue for understanding capitalist production as, quintessentially, the production of *codes* that commodify languages, materials, representations, and subjects alike. In other words, Deleuze and Guattari do away with the notion of a medium in advance, focusing their attention instead on forces and flows that could be considered sub-, super-, or transmedial in that they underpin, transcend, or multiply the formal categories we defer to when conceptualizing media, including material and technological bases as well as informational, representational, or signifying systems. As media have been subjected to formal analysis for practically the entire history of media studies, this approach would likely strike most as highly unorthodox, if not outright incoherent, but it is also refreshingly unconstrained by dogma or doxa.[45] Furthermore, it is arguable that Deleuze's radicalization of McLuhan's formulas clarifies and extends a highly important theoretical strain in media studies that too often goes unexplored. Deleuze offers a compelling, though highly unconventional, approach to the fundamental question of how the channels through which both artistic expression and informatic communication flow actually operate—that is, not simply within their own independent systems but also between themselves and the audience or receiver. He thus lends philosophical rigor to any such conceptualization of media. More particularly, Deleuze's work has a great deal of potential value for the theory of intermediality, which also aspires to reframe the way one understands the mutual (trans)formations, as well as the subjective effects, of media as highly complex and dynamic systems. This is not to say that Deleuze would have embraced intermediality as a conceptual framework; rather, it is to say that intermediality would do well to embrace Deleuzian philosophy, and the fact that many theorists of intermediality have done so (as we shall see presently) is highly encouraging.

Before outlining my Deleuze-inflected conceptualization of intermediality, however, it will be necessary to briefly recapitulate the relevant theoretical current in media studies, wherein the question of technological mediation is inextricably intertwined with the problem of sensory perception. In the previous section we encountered, via Comolli, the idea that an aesthetic of realism utilizes the gap that inheres between the evidence of our senses and the compelling view of the world reproduced through technical means. In media studies in general, the formation of perceptual continuities and discontinuities in the indeterminate zone of the "in-between"—between subjects, between subject and world, between immediate and remote sensory phenomena, and so on—is directly addressed, whether in terms of McLuhan's definition of media as "extensions of man" or in Friedrich Kittler's characterization of the contemporary subject as something like an apparatus or coupling exploited by information networks. In order to understand this theoretical current, it is necessary to mention the pathbreaking work of the Toronto School of media and communication scholars in the 1950s and 1960s, which was initiated by the insights of Harold A. Innis.

After having explored the crucial role played by natural resources such as fur, timber, and fish in the historical-economic development of Canada, Innis in his later career turned his attention to a very different resource that played, if anything, an even more critical role in the formation of nations and empires: their communications media. In his seminal work *Empire and Communications* (1950), Innis argues that the media employed by a given political regime were instrumental in securing the extensivity of its governable territory in space as well as the endurance of its cultural-religious principles in time. Specifically linking the power structure of a given empire to its creation, or exploitation, of new systems of communication, Innis devises a means of defining a historical epoch not only according to its social attitudes and the events that shaped and maintained its political structures, but also according to forces that took effect *in between* the offices of power and its outposts, *in between* the rhythms of its quotidian existence and the periods of upheaval and conflict it endured, and *in between* the interests of government and the beliefs of the citizenry. To assess the rise and fall of empires according to the minutiae and ephemera of their bureaucratic and religious systems is a nebulous foundation for academic inquiry indeed, and Innis fully acknowledges the difficulties inherent in making media themselves into the object of a study itself mediated by systems of thought and communication:

> The significance of a basic medium to its civilization is difficult to appraise since the means of appraisal are influenced by the media, and indeed the fact of appraisal appears to be peculiar to certain types of media. A change in the type of medium implies a change in the type of appraisal and hence makes it difficult for one civilization to understand another. The difficulty is enhanced by the character of the material, particularly its relative permanence.[46]

Two important consequences of this passage, and of Innis's approach as a whole, immediately present themselves, which one could call the twin conundrums of medial likeness and difference. The first asserts that media are the slipperiest of concepts or phenomena to grasp, since the means we have of grasping them are always already mediated—for example, how can the significance of the innovation of writing be assessed when we are still immersed in a form of scholarship that is expressed through writing? The second conundrum concerns the immense difficulty involved in understanding a civilization in terms of its own dominant media if these differ from ours—is it possible, for example, for a literate culture to comprehend the social and perceptual characteristics of an oral culture? The "bias" of our own communications systems, and in particular the dominance therein of spatial extensivity over temporal duration, emerges in full force whether we turn the lens of scholarship toward another culture or our own. Hence Innis, in illuminating the inestimable importance of the medial in-between in one's understanding of a given civilization, simultaneously signals the monumental problems inherent in taking up this line of inquiry. Additionally, of course, his approach raises significant questions regarding the nature of the media systems that define contemporary societies, particularly the vast cultural changes being wrought by the comparatively recent emergence of electronic communications such as telegraphy and telephony, radio, and television, and the ongoing explosion of mass cultural phenomena such as cinema and the popular press. Taking up these questions directly, Innis argues that modern communications are becoming increasingly, and perhaps irrevocably, biased in favor of spatial dissemination and thus temporal impermanence, and calls for increased attention to the pitfalls of this tendency toward the end of *Empire and Communications*: "The ability to develop a system of government in which the bias of communication can be checked and an appraisal of the significance of space and time can be reached remains a problem of empire and of the Western world."[47]

Following Innis's death in 1952, the individual who most ardently undertook the task of continuing and extending this mode of inquiry was Marshall McLuhan. Indeed, his debt to Innis cannot be underestimated and is professed by McLuhan himself in his introduction to the 1964 reprint of Innis's essay collection *The Bias of Communication*: "I am pleased to think of my own book *The Gutenberg Galaxy* (University of Toronto Press, 1962) as a footnote to the observations of Innis on the subject of the psychic and social consequences, first of writing and then of printing."[48] McLuhan indeed reframes Innis's media studies project as a new means of understanding the psychosocial tendencies that he considers dominant in post-Renaissance Western culture. In *Understanding Media*, McLuhan goes on to use these tendencies as a basis for measuring the stakes, and consequences, of the fundamental societal shift from print media to telecommunications, a medial transformation instrumental in what he sees as an overturning of the West's collective, and longstanding, visual-perceptual bias. In McLuhan's work, then, the determining political-historical role that Innis ascribes to media is instead applied to the experiential level of human action and sensory perception, and media studies is cast as a major new hermeneutic framework for the study of human nature, perhaps the first such inquiry to be introduced since Freudian psychology: "In the sense that these media are extensions of ourselves—of man—then my interest in them is utterly humanistic. All these technologies and the mechanisms they create are profoundly human."[49] Like his colleagues at the University of Toronto, as well as numerous other scholars,[50] McLuhan defines media primarily as avenues for extending the potentialities of human perception, interaction, and endeavor. Moreover, this anthropocentric approach posits media not simply as an interim or channel between messages sent and received, but rather as sites of diverse modes of production. According to this model, in other words, media do not merely transmit a priori sense data, images, messages, ideas, and so on; on the contrary, these phenomena are actively and diversely shaped and produced by the media themselves. In the same interview quoted above, McLuhan states this very clearly: "Most people have the idea of communication as something matching between what is said and what is understood. In actual fact, communication is *making*."[51]

McLuhan's fundamental realization that media constitute sites of production prefigures many other subsequent analyses in media and communications studies. One finds a similar approach, for example, in Stuart Hall's influential essay "Encoding/Decoding" (1980), which states the following at the outset:

> Traditionally, mass-communications research has conceptualized the process of communication in terms of a circulation circuit or loop. This model has been criticized for its linearity—sender/message/

> receiver—for its concentration on the level of message exchange and for the absence of a structured conception of the different moments as a complex structure of relations. But it is also possible (and useful) to think of this process in terms of a structure produced and sustained through the articulation of linked but distinctive moments—production, circulation, distribution/consumption, reproduction.[52]

Hall goes on to define mediated communications as entailing a set of "material instruments—its 'means'—as well as its own sets of social (production) relations" that must ultimately be "translated—transformed, again—into social practices if the circuit is to be both completed and effective."[53] In other words, it is impossible to discount the role of actual social production and practices if one is to understand how media and communication function, even if this necessitates the complication of one's understanding of the *in-between* as something more than simply a given channel through which pass preexisting and independently conceived data. Consequently, media cannot be defined merely as spatiotemporal circuits of transmission, but must instead be conceived as processes that encompass extensive and practically irreconcilable assemblages that include some or all of the following: human perceptions, artificial representations, material instruments, material or electronic transmitters, human or nonhuman coders and decoders, human-to-human social relations, human-to-machine technological relations, and any number of space-time relations or permutations. And all of these (sense-) relations must be acknowledged before one engages in any consideration of the nature and effects of the images and information being conveyed. How can one possibly formulate a straightforward definition of a "medium," then, based on the variety of factors that must necessarily be encompassed by such a definition? The best approach is perhaps to refrain from even attempting to essentialize the concept of the medium as such, in the interest of maximizing its usage for describing forces and forms that as yet exist only *in potentia*. Siegfried Zielinsky offers such an interpretation of the term in his impressive media-archaeological study, translated into English as *Deep Time of the Media* (2002), and is worth quoting at length:

> My archaeology makes a plea to keep the concept of media as wide open as possible. The case of media is similar to Roessler the endophysicist's relation to consciousness: we swim in it like fish in the ocean, it is essential for us, and for this reason it is ultimately inaccessible to us. All we can do is to make certain cuts across it to gain operational access. These cuts can be defined as built constructs; in the case of media, as interfaces, devices, programs, technical systems, networks, and media forms of expression and realization, such as film, video, machine installations, books, or websites. We find them located between the one and the other, between the technology and its users,

> different places and times. In this in-between realm, media process, model, standardize, symbolize, transform, structure, expand, combine, and link. This they perform with the aid of symbols that can be accessed by the human senses: numbers, images, texts, sounds, designs, and choreography. Media worlds are phenomena of the relational. The one or the other may be just as plausible from the way the objects are looked at as the bridges and boundaries that have been constructed between or around them. However, it is not my intention to place a limit on the multitude of possible linkages by pinning them down.[54]

Media studies has, since Innis, approached its central point of inquiry as something like an inconceivable "subject-object." This entity encompasses, and thus always remains beyond, our very reckoning or formulation, which would be, in any case, always already mediated by some system of knowledge or expression. In this consideration, a medium possesses no independent ontological claim, being always relational and processual, a point reinforced by Joachim Paech, a theorist of intermediality, who states that the problems inherent in defining a medium are only avoided "if one ceases to inquire ontologically into the being of the medium."[55] This fact alone appears to justify an intermedial approach to the very concept of media and helps to account for the fact that a medium only becomes perceivable as an object for investigation when we are subject to multiple and diverse media forms as an everyday fact, as McLuhan himself suggests in the essay "Myth and Mass Media" (1959): "Today, when ordinary consciousness is exposed to the patternmaking of several media at once, we are becoming more attentive to the unique properties of each of the media."[56] There is no perspective from which we can access or assess *all* media as such, but we can gain some particular knowledge of, and resistance to, the effects of one medium by reframing it through another, in the manner of Haneke's cinematic works' "framing" of noncinematic media.

Yet even though I have opened up the definition of media as widely as possible, and have acknowledged the diversity of the products and processes it encompasses, I still face a seemingly intractable problem for media studies, one that I argue stands to be remediated by applying a Deleuzian philosophical framework. This problem is best expressed by the critically important objections to McLuhan's theories made by Friedrich Kittler. While acknowledging the immense debt media studies owes to McLuhan, and to Innis before him, Kittler points out that the model employed by the Toronto School is deeply flawed due to the anthropocentric picture of technological development it offers:

> [McLuhan's] unquestioned assumption that the subject of all media is naturally the human is methodologically tricky. For when the development of a medial subsystem is analyzed in all of its historical breadth,

> as the history of optical media is being analyzed here, the exact opposite suspicion arises that technical innovations—following the model of military escalations—only refer and answer to each other, and the end result of this proprietary development, which progresses completely independent of individual or even collective bodies of people, is an overwhelming impact on senses and organs in general.[57]

Kittler's stated counterposition to McLuhan, then, consists of the assertion that media are essentially ahumanistic and technological, and media studies must consequently also subscribe to this premise. This characterization of McLuhan's theoretical project as thoroughly humanist is certainly justifiable—McLuhan himself states as much in the "*Hot and Cool* Interview" previously quoted—and Kittler's criticism takes into account the important fact that McLuhan does not consider media as simply extending the reach of the senses but also of "amputating," and thus numbing and altering, human perceptual capacities. Kittler maintains, however, that in the age of mechanization, information technology, and computing, the sense ratios of a human subject cease to even register as factors in communications media, and the utter marginalization and obsolescence of the organic being he often refers to as "so-called Man" is, practically speaking, a foregone conclusion. Thus, in his preface to *Gramophone, Film, Typewriter* (1986), Kittler famously states the following:

> What remains of people is what media can store and communicate. What counts are not the messages or the content with which they equip so-called souls for the duration of a technological era, but rather (and in strict accordance with McLuhan) their circuits, the very schematism of perceptibility. . . . At the moment of merciless submission to laws whose cases we are, the phantasm of man as the creator of media vanishes. And it becomes possible to take stock of the situation.[58]

Any human dimension media could formerly have been said to possess is overwritten, in Kittler's view, by developments in informatics, which have far outstripped the capacities of organic interfaces and cognition. Media are no longer extensions or outerings of our perceptions in this situation; on the contrary, our perceptual apparatus is merely an appurtanance for media systems that function according to speeds and networks whose extensivities and effects we cannot begin to comprehend. As Geoffrey Winthrop-Young points out, this realization seems to amount to a fundamental difference between the two theorists: "Unlike McLuhan, Kittler does not feel the need to squeeze all of media through the bottleneck of the human sensory apparatus."[59]

What Kittler has proposed is a Copernican turn in media studies that corresponds to a new era in media technology, which has itself left the formerly central figure of the so-called human far behind. Yet this proposal of a fracture between what one could term a sensory-subjective schema and an informatic-asubjective schema for understanding media is perhaps misplaced, and not just because Kittler continually raises the specter of the "so-called human" throughout his work, even if only to dismiss it. Rather, this division seems to present something of a false problematic from the perspective of a Deleuzian approach to media studies. Deleuze's philosophy is, in fact, capable of accommodating all of the fundamental facets of media theory that I have identified so far, including its intrinsically relational (i.e. *in between* and systems-oriented) approach to questions of historical and sociopolitical formations; its definition of media as processes of production, though of potentialities rather than materialities; and its tendency to invoke the transformation, marginalization, or outright effacement of the perceiving (human) subject.

Indeed, taking Deleuze's overt statements about humankind's relationship to media technology at face value, even a careful reader might be forgiven for siding the philosopher either with McLuhan or with Kittler. Like the former thinker, he seems to understand technology from a clearly anthropocentric perspective: "An evolutionary line going from man to tool, and from tool to technological machine, is purely imaginary. The machine is social in its primary sense, and is primary in relation to the structures it crosses, to the men it makes use of, to the tools it selects, and to the technologies it promotes."[60] Yet one can also already sense a Kittlerian bent in this passage, particularly in his suggestion that the social machine "makes use of" men rather than the reverse. Indeed, Deleuze clearly shares Kittler's notion—likewise derived from the famous final passage of Foucault's *The Order of Things* (1966)—that informatics de-centers and even de-composes the classical human subject:

> We must take quite literally the idea that man is a face drawn in the sand between two tides: he is a composition appearing only between two others, a classical past that never knew him, and a future that will no longer know him. There is no occasion either for rejoicing or for weeping. Is it not commonplace nowadays to say that the forces of man have already entered into a relation with the forces of information technology and their third-generation machines which together create something other than man, indivisible "man-machine" systems? Is this a union with silicon instead of carbon?[61]

But I must also add that McLuhan speculated along these lines as well and did so prior to Foucault's "face drawn in the sand" image. In the essay "Culture Without Literacy," which appeared in the first issue of *Explorations* (1953), McLuhan states that "[h]istory has been abolished by our new media," and consequently raises the following possibility: "May not the upshot of our technology be the awakening from the historically conditioned nightmare of the past into a timeless present? Historic man may turn out to have been literate man. An episode."[62] Thus, to suggest that one may side either with Kittler, in whose consideration media override and impact the senses, or with McLuhan, in whose consideration media extend the central nervous system, is to establish an oversimplified or even false dichotomy. But it is a dichotomy that still persists, as evidenced by Winthrop-Young's comments above and also by Caroline A. Jones's characterization of the two thinkers as representatives of opposing positions at the outset of a 2010 essay:

> Media theorists can argue (as with Kittler) that the senses are an effect of media or (with McLuhan) that mediating technologies are "extensions" of man. These two approaches—technological determinism (the body senses change radically with mediation) versus what we might call naturalization (the senses are grounded in the body and merely "extend" their reach through mediating technologies)—stage the senses in a crucial area for determining the effects of mediation on understanding.[63]

Jones's distinction indicates what is perhaps the primary reason for the perception that McLuhan's media theory cannot do without a central position for the perceiving subject, the same subject with which Kittler dispenses with such alacrity: if media are extensions of the senses, then there must remain an embodied subject to which these are connected; if, on the other hand, media and their interfaces determine sensory data, the subject no longer serves any such grounding or centralizing function.

Yet, given the common tendency of both media theorists—and Deleuze (and Foucault)—to dissolve the classical concept of the historically situated human subject, it would appear that this conceptual gesture is a consequence not of a side taken in an extended debate but rather of *relational*, as opposed to subject- and object-oriented, thinking. Media studies is the art of thinking relationally, and thus it tends to elide the categories that other modes of thought rely on, including the central concept of the embodied human being. Deleuze is the philosopher who—both alone and in his collaboration with Guattari—has taken this mode of thinking to perhaps its greatest and most radical extremes. It is Deleuze who presents us with the simple empirical formula that implicitly or explicitly informs all media theory—"*Relations are external to their terms*"—and who best elaborates on the world picture that emerges through this realization: "If one takes this exteriority of relations as a conducting wire or as a line, one sees a very strange world unfold, fragment by fragment: a Harlequin's jacket or patchwork, made up of solid parts and voids, blocs and ruptures, attractions and divisions, nuances and bluntnesses, conjunctions and separations, alternations and interweavings, additions which never reach a total and subtractions whose remainder is never fixed."[64] This description provides a basic overview of the dynamic world of forces that is summoned forth by relational thought, the world that Foucault similarly conjures up when he defines power, in "The Subject and Power" (1982), as "an action upon an action, on existing actions or on those which may arise in the present or the future."[65] As Deleuze points out in his book on Foucault, this implies the following: "Power has no essence; it is simply operational. It is not an attribute but a relation: the power-relation is the set of possible relations between forces."[66] For Foucault—as for Deleuze, McLuhan, and Kittler—the primary function of technologies and media of communication is not to exchange messages between subjects or beings but rather to activate and modulate these forces: "Relationships of communication imply finalized activities (even if only the correct putting into operation of elements of meaning) and, by virtue of modifying the field of information between partners, produce effects of power."[67] Power is not definable simply as an extension of an individual's will or desire, for subjects do not preexist power relations; rather, relations of power preexist—and constitute—subjects. The study of power relations is thus, for Foucault, a study of how the subject is objectified; in other words, how "human beings are made subjects."[68] Deleuze, however, arguably goes even further than Foucault, eschewing the concept of objectification in his definition of subjects in favor of that of machines, a totally relational perspective best expressed with Guattari at the outset of *Anti-Oedipus*: "Producing-machines, desiring-machines everywhere, schizophrenic machines, all of species life: the self and the non-self, outside and inside, no longer have any meaning whatsoever."[69] What is conventionally considered an enshrined self that relates to other selves via various modes of expression and communication becomes, in Deleuzo-Guattarian thought, only another process of production, an "unfixed remainder" of social power relations. In Deleuzian terms, media—like the unconscious[70]—are *factories* that, in the process of producing the machines through which we cannot but function, also produce our selves. There is consequently no need to choose between a McLuhanistic sensory-subjective schema and a Kittlerian informatic-asubjective schema in media theory, since underlying both are the same Deleuzo-Guattarian machinic assemblages of production. But what, conceptually speaking, do these media-machines produce?

When one references McLuhan's dictum that "the 'content' of any medium is always another medium," one should always emphasize the quotation marks around the word "content" along with the almost paradoxical nature of the assertion. What possible objective relationship could exist between media such that one could "contain" another? McLuhan's formula only obtains meaning if one reads it nonobjectively and nonliterally. McLuhan follows up his initial statement with examples and clarification of this counterintuitive relationship: "The content of writing is speech, just as the written word is the content of print, and print is the content of the telegraph. If it is asked, 'What is the content of speech?,' it is necessary to say, 'It is an actual process of thought, which is in itself nonverbal.' [. . .] For the 'message' of any medium or technology is the change of scale or pace or pattern that it introduces into human affairs."[71] Writing, according to this approach, "contains" not graphic symbols but speech, which itself "contains" not utterances but thought, and so on. There is no "space"—actual or conceptual—in any of these media for words themselves. Words are formed or produced only as a consequence of the relations between the medium and its users and between one medial system and another; words are quite naturally what we attend to in our engagement with these media systems, but this is because they are the products of these written or spoken communications, as opposed to something like their "building blocks." McLuhan therefore implies that one should never confuse what a medium *communicates* or *produces* with the notion of a priori *content*; the images or texts we associate with a given medium are largely, if not entirely, independent of the medium itself. In this sense, communication and production are one and the same process. If I prefer to use the notion of "production" above "communication," it is because I affirm that there is always an *excess* produced by a given medium, stemming from the medium itself autonomously of what is ostensibly communicated or represented. Thus, I assert that even if representation can be conceptualized in terms of a given medium or media, the medium cannot in turn be conceptualized in terms of representation. While it initially appears obvious that film produces images, or that speech produces words, it must be understood that these do not emerge from a reserve of images or words "internal" to the medium, since a medium does not possess internality, properly speaking. Additionally, it would be incorrect to specify that a medium is a strictly *re*productive process, even though reproduction and representation are quite clearly major mediatic functions.[72] In order to understand what is produced by media, I must turn to what Deleuze and Guattari, in *What is Philosophy?* (1991), consider the constitutive components of artistic expression itself, namely the *percepts* and *affects* which combine to form *sensation*. Let us use the medium of cinema as a case study in this mode of production, both because it is a medium to which Deleuze's philosophy devotes a great deal of specific attention—along with literature and, to a lesser extent, painting—and because it is the primary medium dealt with in this text, through Haneke.

It is worth recalling that *What is Philosophy?*, as Paola Marrati asserts,[73] can be considered a direct sequel to Deleuze's *Cinema* books in a number of important respects. Indeed, the antepenultimate sentence of *Cinema 2* directly alludes to the imminent publication of this text: "[T]here is always a time, midday-midnight, when we must no longer ask ourselves, 'What is cinema?' but 'What is philosophy?' "[74] This reference is bookended by two propositions which, I argue, allude to the specific problems arising from a consideration of film as a medium (just as earlier in his conclusion Deleuze had presented the struggle for supremacy between film and television or video as a problem specific to the relationship between modes of belief in the world rather than to images themselves). The first proposition concerns the inability of cinema to express its own concepts: "Cinema's concepts are not given in cinema. And yet they are cinema's concepts, not theories about cinema." The second proposition—the concluding sentences of the book—concerns the unaccountability of cinema's concepts within any medium-specific theoretical framework: "Cinema itself is a new practice of images and signs, whose theory philosophy must produce as conceptual practice. For no technical determination, whether applied (psychoanalysis, linguistics) or reflexive, is sufficient to constitute the concepts of cinema itself."[75] Essentially, Deleuze argues that cinema creates, or at least initiates, *sui generis* concepts, but that these concepts are neither given "in cinema"—by the medium—nor in any medium-specific or technical theories of the cinema. Of course, Deleuze and Guattari will go on to argue in *What is Philosophy?* that no work of art—and, by extension, no medium-specific theory—produces veritable concepts, since "[t]he concept belongs to philosophy and only to philosophy."[76] From where, then, do cinematic concepts arise, if cinema itself (for all of its artistic potential) possesses no inherent philosophical power? Deleuze might argue that cinema's concepts are modifications or transformations of Henri Bergson's concept of the image, the philosophical premise of the cinema books.[77] As Bergson notes in *Matter and Memory* (1896), "the photograph, if photograph there be, is already taken, already developed in the very heart of things and at all the points of space."[78] The medium of photography—like that of film—does not *create* such an image, since its immanent existence (however inaccessible to us as such) remains independent from any medium; rather, the medium detaches a percept from the world and simultaneously introduces a set of potential affective engagements with it. Even if this is the case, however, the "new practice of images and signs" that Deleuze refers to cinema as instituting, and that necessitates philosophical investigation, remains uniquely cinematic. That is, it is instantiated by the medium of film to which Deleuze alludes, by the event that makes possible this medium and is made possible through it. This is very different from the idea of using works of cinema to illustrate philosophical ideas, as Slavoj Žižek inarguably does, for example; rather, Deleuze seeks in cinema a different conceptual configuration than that available to linguistic expression, as he points out in his interview "The Brain is the Screen" (1989): "Every work has its beginning or its consequence in the other arts. I was able to write on cinema not because I have some right to reflect on it, but because certain philosophical problems pushed me to seek out the solutions in cinema, even if this only serves to raise more problems. All research, scholarly or creative, participates in such a relay system."[79] The film medium is a site of possibilities or potentialities that do not preexist it except perhaps in a partial conceptual history. But this approach toward cinema as a pre- or proto-conceptual phenomenon has not yet rigorously distinguished film as a medium from the cinematic image as a mode of artistic thought.

Deleuze and Guattari imply that a work of art achieves aesthetic autonomy and depth independently of its material medium of expression by "preserv[ing] in itself . . . *a bloc of sensations, that is to say, a compound of percepts and affects*."[80] Percepts are independent of any perceiving subject, just as affects are independent of any feeling or affected subject; both of these phenomena, and the sensations they comprise, "exist in the absence of man": "The work of art is a being of sensation and nothing else: it exists in itself."[81] While Deleuze and Guattari are scarcely interested in defining a given medium as such, then, they are nonetheless highly interested in defining the asubjective, autonomous, and substantive "material" that renders artistic expression possible. I am, of course, deriving a definition of "the medium" from the writings of Deleuze and of Deleuze and Guattari that is not explicitly identified as such in their work. However, in their opposition to the conceptualization of art in representational terms, their philosophy presents an implicit idea of the medium that is particularly suited to engaging with Haneke's intermediality, which exhibits its own vexed relationship to questions of representation. A passage from *Francis Bacon: The Logic of Sensation* (1981), Deleuze's work on the Irish painter, perhaps best encapsulates this distinction between representation and sensation as I am applying it: "The violence of sensation is opposed to the violence of the represented (the sensational, the cliché). The former is inseparable from its direct action on the nervous system, the levels through which it passes, the domains it traverses: being itself a Figure, it must have nothing of the nature of a represented object."[82] Some might assert that Deleuze presents sensation—which is repeatedly described in the Bacon text in terms of its "direct" or "immediate" action on the nervous system[83]—as an unmediated phenomenon; I assert, on the contrary, that the production of sensation is the *primary* function of media. The percepts and affects that constitute blocks of sensations are themselves non-imagistic and nonrepresentational; they are instead forces and becomings that circulate in the relational, machinic systems that Deleuze often refers to as "planes of immanence." Thus, beings of sensation are always already mediated, in that they are coextensive with the material through which they find expression, even up to the flesh of the human body itself: "In short, the being of sensation is not the flesh but the compound of nonhuman forces of the cosmos, of man's nonhuman becomings, and of the ambiguous house that exchanges and adjusts them, makes them whirl around like winds. Flesh is only the developer which disappears in what it develops: the compound of sensation."[84] I thus submit that a medium is anything—material or virtual; simple or complex; organic, electronic, or digital—that produces or "develops" percepts and affects, the dynamic forces that are formed into sensational configurations by works of art. Media neither create nor contain beings of sensation themselves, since clearly not all media products are definable as art, but they do provide the assemblage or nexus point of "raw" percepts and affects that enables art—or, even more simply, sensation—to come into being.

As Deleuze and Guattari suggest in the above passage, flesh is something like the proto- or ur-medium, the primary "developer" for potential sensations. This perspective accords with McLuhan's definition of media as "extensions of man" in an actual somatic configuration, as "organs" or "appendages" connected to the central nervous system that launch us into new forms of physical, mental, and perceptual activity.[85] Yet, while McLuhan's model implies the existence of an embodied subject as a center for this phenomenon, Deleuze and Guattari put forward the idea that "it is the *flesh* that . . . is freed from the lived body, the perceived world," going on to state that the flesh undergoes an "intermingling" with the world itself wherein "flesh of the world and flesh of the body . . . are exchanged as correlates."[86] In other words, there is no need to posit, as McLuhan does, that there is a "center" in the nervous or sensational system from out of which media extend. Sensation does not rely on an organic brain for its existence, much less a human one; the brain instead functions like a screen onto which sensation is projected. The electronic media that McLuhan is so fond of comparing to an externalized brain are flesh enough to mediate all manner of sensation. One recalls in this regard the repeated slogan of David Cronenberg's *Videodrome* (1983)—"Long Live the New Flesh"—as well as the film's depiction of the McLuhan-esque media theorist Dr. Brian O'Blivion (Jack Creley), whose body has died, yet who nonetheless maintains a presence throughout the events of the film via the video recordings he has made of himself before succumbing to cancer.[87] Here, video itself assumes the role of "new flesh" within what Fredric Jameson terms—in the interpretation of the film he offers in *The Geopolitical Aesthetic* (1992)—"a landscape of media objects now endowed with a delirious life and autonomy of their own."[88] While Kittler would tend to associate such autonomy largely with a postindustrial condition of electronic and digital media—an ongoing revolution that began with a trio of inventions: gramophone, film, and typewriter—Deleuze and Guattari convincingly argue that works of art, as beings of sensation, have always attained independence from their creators or receivers. Media, as nonorganic "flesh," the "developer" of raw compounds of percepts and affects, are by this definition both material *and* immaterial, imagistic *and* informatic. Indeed, this conceptualization of media actively undermines such distinctions, along with any framework that approaches the notion of medium strictly from the perspective of representation.

But how precisely does one make the leap from raw percept/affect compounds to the complex beings of sensation that are termed works of art, the realization of the medium's potential, while still preserving a notion of the medium itself? Deleuze, as I have noted, is not even interested in doing so, and hence tends to defer to the concept of a medium as such only when discussing modes of information communication that remain—by his own reckoning and others'—non-imagistic and nonartistic in constitution and function. But when doing so, he nonetheless notes the presence of other forces underpinning the informatic bias these media evidence. The popular press, radio, television, video, video games, and computer interfaces thus can be said to secure a basic affective engagement seemingly detached from their potential to communicate even information, much less artistic images, and thus still may be defined primarily in terms of sensation. However, this sensational payload would suggest a much less complex compound of percepts and affects than that required to support the sensational figures transmitted by artistic works. It is this phenomenon that Deleuze refers to in his essay on Godard's television series *Six fois deux* (1976). Television (and, by and large, all informatic media), he states, transmits a redundant and repetitive affective injunction—"Watch this!"—over and above any informational component:

> Language [on television] is a system of commands and not a means of information. On television: "Now for some entertainment . . . the news will follow shortly . . ." In fact the hierarchies of information theory need to be reversed. Information theory implies a maximum of theoretical information; then at the opposite pole it puts pure noise, interference; and between the two, redundancy, which detracts from information but puts it on a higher level than noise. It's the other way round: at the top you should put redundancy as the transmission and repetition of orders and commands; below that information, always a minimum requirement if commands are to be understood. And below that? Well, there would be something like silence, or stammering, or a cry, something which would flow under redundancy and information, which would make language flow and still make itself understood.[89]

The percept (of information) is never completely free of the affect (of compulsion), then, in that all media vouchsafe some form of affective suture at a fundamental level. Thus, in the compound model Deleuze outlines above, any informational percepts are always already sandwiched between an overriding affect of command and the underpinning flow of anticipative "silence," "stammering," or "a cry" carrying its own pseudo-evental affective force.[90] This latter point is particularly interesting, given that at this lowest level of expression there seems to be only a semiotically and representationally empty propulsive force. In *What is Philosophy?* it is made clear that not only do all material media carry both perceptual and affective charges—they list "the smile of oil, the gesture of fired clay, the thrust of metal, the crouch of Romanesque stone, and the ascent of Gothic stone"[91]—but that "even the void is sensation. All sensation is composed with the void in composing itself with itself, and everything holds together on earth and in the air, and preserves the void, is preserved in the void by preserving itself."[92] Thus, the static of the empty television screen lacking a signal—as presented, for example, at the conclusion of *Der siebente Kontinent*—remains a transmitter of potential sensation, even if it is also pure audiovisual noise. The void is a force that mobilizes percepts and affects while itself retaining bare affective attractors.

Two points remain to be made before moving on to my exploration of intermediality as a conceptual framework for navigating the relational and production-oriented definition of media systems that I have developed thus far.

The first is to note that my application of Deleuze's and Deleuze and Guattari's concept of sensation to cinema—a gesture that Deleuze does not himself perform, preferring in his *Cinema* books primarily to elaborate a semiology of the Bergsonian image—is in no way a wholly original one, even if I have focused more on its significance for media studies in general than most others have.[93] Approaching cinema as a mode of sensational or sensual thought-expression has become a major current in contemporary film theory, and a number of scholarly works have used Deleuzian philosophy as a foundation in this regard, most notably Laura U. Marks's *The Skin of the Film* (2000), Barbara M. Kennedy's *Deleuze and Cinema: The Aesthetics of Sensation* (2000), and Martine Beugnet's *Cinema and Sensation* (2007). The insights of these scholars and the highly interesting readings that they have consequently produced of significant films and auteurs need not be rehearsed in this text; suffice it to say they and other scholars have developed and will continue to develop major avenues into the understanding of cinema and cinematic spectatorship in terms of sensation and of multisensory interfaces. Doing so, they extend Deleuze's project of thinking through cinema, as Gregory Flaxman points out in his introduction to *The Brain is the Screen* (2000): "[T]he image is a collection of sensations . . . that we cannot simply re-cognize and that we encounter, as such, at the very limit of the sensible. Sensations possess the capacity to derange the everyday, to short-circuit the mechanism of common sense, and thus to catalyze a different kind of thinking; indeed, sensations are encountered at a threshold we might call the 'thinkable.'"[94] My own interests lie along a different path, however, and involve the application of Deleuze's new possibilities for thought less to cinematic images and more to the intermedial frameworks to which they can give rise, a distinct but related field of inquiry that will be discussed in more detail in the following section.

The second point to highlight is that what I have characterized as a nascent media theory in Deleuze's writings also includes a political component that has not thus far been emphasized. For Deleuze and Guattari, the capitalist socius functions on the basis of code, in particular on a de- and recoding of the flows of desire that circulate in the dynamic relational systems discussed above. In this model—which echoes the theory outlined by Stuart Hall in "Encoding/Decoding"—mass media can be considered an especially effective machine for the production and distribution of codes that constitute and drive the socioeconomic machines of consumerism, in a manner that is termed, in *Anti-Oedipus*, *axiomatic*.[95] Deleuze and Guattari point out that such axioms are definitively nonlinguistic—"Capitalism is profoundly illiterate"[96]—and that the machines of private industry instead manufacture and distribute "floating images" that necessitate and invite decoding on the part of the spectator-consumer:

> [T]hese images do not initiate a making public of the private so much as a privatization of the public: the whole world unfolds right at home, without one's having to leave the TV screen. This gives private persons a very special role in the system: a role of *application*, and no longer of implication, in a code. . . . [O]ne must not think that it replaces the socius, the social machine, with an aggregate of technical machines. The difference in nature between the two types of machines persists, although they are both machines in the strict sense, without metaphor. Capitalism's originality resides rather in the fact that the social machine has for its parts technical machines as constant capital attached to the full body of the socius, and no longer men, the latter having become adjacent to the technical machines . . . .[97]

The sociopolitical ramifications of Deleuze and Guattari's characterization of informatic media are thus profound and should always be borne in mind. In what follows, however, I will focus on the subjective-sensory processes by means of which these forces take effect much more so than the wider political implications of their functioning, as it is this intimate perspective that is consistently, and uniquely, uncovered by Haneke's intermedial schema and its realist aesthetic.

Having outlined the widest possible definition of media and media studies, then, I will proceed to concentrate my inquiry on the particularities of intermedial dynamics, with a renewed attention toward the affective energies and perceptual effects that unfold in encounters between media systems.

Affect, Intermediality, and the Void

In the previous section I derived from Deleuze and Guattari a wider definition of media as diversely patterned compounds of raw perceptual and affective forces that form assemblages of sensation. Deleuze and Guattari also conceptualize the void between media as both possessing its own sensational charge and acting as a structuring element in these compounds. Intermediality, as manifested in Haneke's oeuvre, was earlier similarly qualified as rendering sensible the void between different media. In Deleuzo-Guattarian terms, then, this mode of intermediality produces percepts and affects that accord less with the idea of the medium as a "new flesh" than with the gaps defining and enabling an encounter *between* beings of flesh and other machines, an enfolding of bodies of sensation into an emergent aesthetic, perhaps even a potential artistic medium. Haneke's use of intermediality thus uncovers percepts and affects *particular to the void between media*, a void that one confronts on a daily basis in contemporary life and that has infiltrated contemporary cinema to a significant extent.[98] As already pointed out, intermedial percepts necessitate a multiplication of the modes of engagement that a viewer experiences relative to the medial "content" of a Haneke film, wherein television assumes a televisual—and thus, broadly speaking, an imageless and informatic—perceptual mode irreconcilable with that of film. Yet one must also account for the percepts that obtain within the void itself, a void between and within media that is often signified by Haneke's use of black "spacers" and other audiovisual motifs.[99]

Affectively, a very different case presents itself via an intermedial conceptual framework. If one were to approach intermediality as a symptom of postmodernity, for example, one could defer to what Fredric Jameson identifies as a collectively experienced "waning of affect" endemic in all forms of medial production, a phenomenon that stems from the lack of an embodied perceptual self or center within the multiplicity of media forms that our senses inhabit.[100] Indeed, this perceived problem has frequently been cited as a consistent theme in Haneke's work, with his first films—especially the "Glaciation Trilogy"—often described as confronting this state of "affectlessness" directly.[101] Yet under what circumstances can affect itself be conceived of as absent or diminished? One could index such an idea to the psychological phenomena of dissociation and desensitization, wherein a subject attains a condition of impassivity relative to situations and experiences in which a normal or expected emotional reflex does not manifest itself. But this remains a problem of subjective reception and reaction, a problem that would have to be posited via a concept of a collective consciousness—and, moreover, a mass consciousness that is descending into a fugue-like state—in order to manifest itself on the sociopolitical and mass-cultural levels. Furthermore, Jameson's notion of the "waning of affect" is not, as it is so often characterized, a matter of the simple dissolution or degradation of emotional response, whether obtaining expression in mediated or unmediated situations. Rather, it describes the replacement of an embodied or personified model of affective engagement with a different existential or experiential situation:

> As for expression and feelings or emotions, the liberation, in contemporary society, from the older *anomie* of the centered subject may also mean not merely a liberation from anxiety but a liberation from every other kind of feeling as well, since there is no longer a self present to do the feeling. This is not to say that the cultural products of the postmodern era are utterly devoid of feeling, but rather that such feelings—which it may be better and more accurate, following J-F. Lyotard, to call "intensities"—are now free-floating and impersonal and tend to be dominated by a peculiar kind of euphoria[.][102]

These ideas—the redefinition of affect as disembodied force or "intensity" rather than internal "feeling," and of a persistent euphoric character to one's interactions with media forms—suggest the presence of other strata of affective forces not immediately reconcilable with a purely subjective model of medial engagement, either direct or indirect.

Instead, the primary experience of intermediality—the differential relation between the "old flesh" of the body and the "new flesh" of media—presents not simply separate perceptual-affective modes of engagement relative to a single embodied subject but rather irreconcilable subjectivities instituted by different media,[103] along with a pronounced affective force of euphoria arising from this very disjunction itself. Intermediality, as is often noted, is a derivation of the term intertextuality; what is less often acknowledged is that the concept thus necessarily enfolds the philosophical notion of *intersubjectivity* as well. As Julia Kristeva, originator of the concept of intertextuality, stated in an early essay titled "Word, Dialogue, and Novel" (1966), a given text does not simply pass from author to reader along a dialogic "horizontal axis" but also incorporates an intersection with other texts along a coexistent "vertical axis": "Any text is the absorption and transformation of another. The notion of *intertextuality* replaces that of intersubjectivity, and poetic language is read as at least *double*."[104] The logic of this intellectual maneuver—which Kristeva attributes to Mikhail Bakhtin—is not substitutive but rather additive: "Bakhtinian dialogism identifies writing as both subjectivity and communication, or better, as intertextuality. Confronted with this dialogism, the notion of a 'person-subject of writing' becomes blurred, yielding to that of 'ambivalence of writing.'"[105] Subjectivity is multiplied in this theoretical model, ceding its pride of place—in other words, its centrality and self-identity—to a polyvalent and polyphonic network of semantic-semiotic doublings necessitating collective social practices of encoding and decoding. Hence, when the intermedial theorist Ágnes Pethő points out that "intermediality is not textual in nature" and therefore "argue[s] for the necessity of re-defining both mediality and intermediality as something entirely divorced from models of 'text,' 'texture' and 'reading,'"[106] she is speaking against a rather narrow definition of Kristeva's concept. If one understands intersubjectivity as encompassing more than just the notion of interlocution, then it is not difficult to perceive intermediality as a mutation of intertextuality that brings an intersubjective dynamic back to the fore. Furthermore, intermediality reinvests this intersubjective axis with sensual and sensational components that are not typically associated with linguistic structures of expression. It is thus significant that Pethő goes on to differentiate medial from textual relations in the following terms:

> So while "reading" intertextual relations engages our intellectual capacities, "reading" intermedial relations requires, more than anything else, an embodied spectator: film cannot be denied to be a profoundly sensuous experience in many ways. Intertextuality operates with intellectual constructions: we read a text and associate other texts, intertexts with it; we activate our memories of texts. However, if we think of a medium . . . as a sensual interface in our world perceived with all the richness of our senses, even "reading"

> a written text becomes no longer a mere intellectual endeavour but a multi-sensual experience. . . . "Sensing" the intermediality of film is therefore grounded in the (inter)sensuality of cinema itself, in the experience of the viewer being aroused simultaneously on different levels of consciousness and perception.[107]

Such intermedial-intersubjective enfoldings occur, in this consideration, both between and within a given medium. What I wish to stress, as a complement to this idea of sensual interface, is that the notion of an embodied spectator does not preclude the notion of a *dis*embodied spectator; on the contrary, it necessitates such a figure. Just as intertextuality promoted the structure of language itself—conceived of at that time as the essence of thought—above the figure of the author, intermediality must conceptually extricate media's production of sensation from the figure of the embodied spectator-subject. In short, the intersubjective interface itself, as opposed to the body, becomes the locus for the affects and percepts composing the "media subject."

This model is perhaps most clearly evident in the medium of video games, wherein the actual body of the player is no longer the center of nervous sensation; it is instead part of an input and output mechanism coding, in "real time," the various stimuli and responses required for continuous play. Here, the virtual player-character (who may or may not be represented on-screen but is totally "immersed" in the game space regardless) becomes the primary focal point not only for the action of the game but for the affective charge of these actions; the virtual player-character is not an extension but rather a *displacement* of the player's sensorium. As Robbie Cooper's *Immersion* project demonstrates,[108] the face of the player barely registers emotion during the act of play (unless immersion is temporarily broken) and seemingly registers even less as the gameplay intensifies. The affective response in the play experience is not absent but rather seems to be almost wholly deferred to the virtual self of the player-character.[109] Additionally, the sense of self-disconnection experienced by the video game player seems in itself to carry a positive affective force or *jouissance* that partially or fully overrides the expected emotional responses to the often violent spectacle offered on the screen—"the medium is the massage," to quote McLuhan's later slogan.[110] While we seem to have little trouble assembling disparate *perceptual subjectivities* into a seemingly unified, if uncanny, experience—perhaps because this active assemblage of percepts resembles our normal combining of disparate input from our unique senses in any given experiential situation—the *affective components* of these subjectivities are not integrated or mixed but *overcoded* instead. Thus, even if the average viewer would not strictly differentiate between the moving image percepts presented by, for example, film and video, each medium still exerts a distinct affective charge that must be accounted for. The effect of this layering of affective subjectivities is generally interpreted in terms of an overall decline in affective response. In contradistinction to this, one can perceive in the current intermedial climate not a paucity but a *superabundance* of affective power. This interpretation, however, is premised on one's acceptance—following Deleuze and Guattari (and, to some extent, Jameson)—that affects are not internal "subjective" phenomena but rather external forces and intensities. The contemporary spectator or media subject is not "disaffected," then, but rather "over-affected" or "auto-affected," affected primarily by media as such rather than by their representational or informational "contents."

Throughout his oeuvre, but particularly in his early trilogy, Haneke presents characters whose continual affective engagement with the omnipresent media of radio, television, and video has largely overwritten their capacity for firsthand emotional expression and interpersonal connection. This situation is restaged for the film viewer through the director's presentation of and emphasis on intermediality itself, and his utilization of the affective-sensational power of the void that obtains between different media forms. The culmination of this practice, as previously stated, is *Caché*, wherein the imperceptible intermedial void between the film itself and the videos within the film forms the core of the film's expression of an affective experience of shame.[111] Emotion and affect in Haneke's films are at times directly represented and performed by the characters, to be sure, but nonetheless Haneke arguably never resorts to a direct staging of affective power through traditional cinematic or melodramatic means, such as via musical scores and editing, though he parodies such conventions in *Funny Games*, *La pianiste*, and *Code inconnu*. In the majority of his films, affect instead emerges along a transversal, intermedial axis, playing out in this void space. In order to better understand this process, however, intermediality as a theoretical model should be inflected with a Deleuzian philosophy of relations.

It is not difficult to align the emergent theory of intermediality both implicitly and explicitly with Deleuzian thought. Implicitly, because intermediality is premised upon the idea that relations precede and shape, yet retain independence from, their terms. Jens Schröter, in "Discourses and Models of Intermediality" (2011), suggests such a direction when he assigns the intermedial an almost protoplasmic status that assumes priority over "pure" media, asserting that "it is not individual media that are primal and then move towards each other intermedially, but that it is intermediality that is primal and that the clearly separated 'monomedia' is the result of purposeful and institutionally caused blockades, incisions, and mechanisms of exclusion."[112] Difference is, in this consideration, a primary force rather than a secondary attribute derived from a juxtaposition of two pregiven objects or phenomena. Media remain dynamic and free-flowing intensities possessing potential more so than formalized expressivity, at least until the latter is imposed on them by social convention or institutional control. A similar notion is offered by André Gaudreault and Philippe Marion in their essay on intermediality titled "A Medium is Always Born Twice . . ." (2005). Here, the authors characterize the passage of a given genre or mode of expression from its earliest existence as a "proto-medium" to its "second birth" into its own status as medium in terms of taking on its self-recognition and self-reflexivity as overt themes:

> At this stage the proto-medium reveals hardly any self-awareness as a medium, the self-awareness of a fully fledged and stable medium. . . . But during this stage there is evidence of a sort of reflexive commotion, an unrestrained disorder, which derives from an anxiety around its uncertain identity. Some manifestations of this phenomenon are [early comics innovator Rodolph] Töpffer's constant *mises-en-abîme*, the large number of self-referential films made during the period of early cinema, and what we might call Nadar's reflexive reflections on photography.[113]

According to this model, a medium passes from a state of "spontaneous intermediality"—in which the nascent medium borrows heavily from other media forms out of necessity—to one of "negotiated" or "subjugated" intermediality in which its own status as medium becomes decisive and recognizable regardless of the interrelationships it forms with other media.[114] In these considerations, as in numerous other intermedial approaches to the question of origin, the dynamic "in-between" state of a medium precedes any notion of its independent identity or existence. This approach implicitly corresponds to Deleuze's empirical mode of investigation, which is perhaps most plainly stated, with Parnet, in *Dialogues*: "Substitute the AND [*et*] for IS [*est*]. A *and* B. The AND is not even a specific relation or conjunction, it is that which subtends all relations, the path of all relations, which makes relations shoot outside their terms and outside the set of their terms, and outside everything which would be determined as Being, One, or Whole. The AND as extra-being, inter-being."[115] Intermediality implies that the only way to understand media—both their origins and their effects—is through such a gesture, prioritizing the relational power they manifest over and above the question of their constitutive being.

By taking up this approach to the study of media, intermediality is capable of lending academic consistency and coherence to the diversely expressed but highly important work of media theorists such as Paul Virilio, Joseph Vogl, and Peter Sloterdijk, all of whom articulate the development and effects of media through predominantly relational conceptualizations. To give but a small sampling of their insights, which are highly relevant to Haneke's work as well, Virilio, in *The University of Disaster* (2007), maintains that "visual and acoustic sensations, far from complementing each other, in fact meld in a magma, in the indistinctness of an 'art without end,' an art without head or tail, in which audiovisuality achieves the chaos produced by the derealization of the art of seeing and knowing."[116] The current media saturation, then, forces a recognition of a ubiquitous "chaosmos" of sensation that ceases to extend or create any singular or stable sensory configuration, as was the purpose and function of traditional artistic media. Joseph Vogl favors, as does Deleuze, thinking with and through modes of becoming rather than being, and particularizes this approach with respect to media studies in his essay "Becoming Media: Galileo's Telescope" (2007):

> What media are and what they do, how they work and the effects they create, their places in cultural and social practices, their specific roles as cultural technologies, not to mention the concept of medium itself—none of this can be reduced to a simple definition, template, or set of facts. In this respect, media analysis is not simply about communications, devices, and codes but also about media-events. These are events in a particular, double sense: the events are communicated through media, but the very act of communication simultaneously communicates the specific event-character of media *themselves*. Media make things readable, audible, visible, perceptible, but in doing so they also have a tendency to erase themselves and their constitutive sensory function, making themselves imperceptible and "anesthetic."[117]

Understanding media as sets of dynamic and self-erasing perceptual force relations, Vogl privileges an evental rather than an objective approach that is consistent with both Deleuzian thought and with intermediality. Lastly, I wish to cite Peter Sloterdijk's reconfiguration of humanism and anthropology as media questions, as most succinctly expressed in his essay "*Actio in Distans*: On Forms of Telerational World-Making" (2012), wherein Sloterdijk's aim in exploring "what media do to other media" is to evoke "a sense of the connection between interapparativity and intersubjectivity; here the decisive factor is how new 'tele-functions' can modify the form of subjectivity."[118] By treating the human brain not as the seat of a self-recognizing subject or nervous center but rather as a biological media apparatus, Sloterdijk erases the distinctions that could be made between technological and organic media systems: "Brains are media for what other brains do and have done; one intelligence serves as the release-stimulus for another, triggering its autonomous functioning. As with language and emotion, intelligence is not a subject but a milieu, a system of resonances."[119] In all such considerations, one is unable to treat either a given medium or a given individual in isolation; one can only consider the medium or individual within the conjunctions and systems that form between individuals, between individuals and the media they use, and between these media forms themselves. A strikingly similar mode of thinking emerges in the work of these theorists that is consistent with Deleuze's overall philosophical project and with intermediality as a means of capturing and putting into perspective this state of affairs.

It is thus of little surprise that a number of proponents of intermediality cite the work of Deleuze specifically as a theoretical resource. For instance, Bernd Herzogenrath, in his introduction to the collection *Travels in Intermedia[lity]* (2012), refers to Deleuze's philosophy of immanence as expressed in *The Logic of Sense* (1969) as a model for apprehending the forms and effects of media as revealed by an intermedial perspective:

> [M]edia are nothing but these machineries of sense-production, and the rhizomatic interconnections among the various media are what constitute the field of intermedia[lity]. Intermedia[lity] is thus the "media-version" of the plane of immanence, of that fractal surface—which is not to say that *first* there are different media, and *then* there is intermedia[lity]: this rhizomatic intermedia[lity] is the quasi-ontological plane underlying all media, out of which the specific media that we know percolate, so to speak.[120]

The other essays in the collection bear out this premise, particularly Julia Meier's "Genuine Thought is Inter(medial)," in which she uses Deleuze and Guattari to "argue that the virtual 'space in-between' has the potential to create genuine thought as an *event* within the concentrated form of intermedial artwork."[121] Taking their cues from Deleuze, such approaches unfold an array of potential directions for intermedial inquiry that are largely closed to conventional media studies, which tend to focus primarily on constructing definitions of individual media in isolation from—and in contradistinction to—one another, thus privileging identity over difference. These Deleuze-inflected approaches remain largely undeveloped, however, and moreover do not adequately address the critically important question of the disjunctions themselves—the voids and gaps—whose crucial importance in this ecosystem of medial difference must be acknowledged. Virilio, to be sure, is readily able to identify these voids and locate their source in our medial disembodiment, but he assigns them a negative connotation:

> Not only is the "full body" of the earth vanishing before our eyes, but our own body is also becoming blurred and afflicting us with an unprecedented "disorder," a paralysis (or autism) which leaves us still *where we were*, with an imposing ponderous mass, while the loss of the full body of being is carrying us towards the void. This "void," moreover, has nothing in common with the gap to be found in "real" space, since it is the void of a *virtual* environment, of a space-time whose techniques of telecommunication are at once the beginning and the end.[122]

Yet what is a source of anxiety for Virilio becomes that of an affirmative power in Deleuze's philosophy, as such a void is seen as part of the desiring-machines that erase the distinctions between self and other, subject and object:

> But who has you believe that by losing the co-ordinates of object and subject you lack something? Who is pushing you into believing that indefinite articles and pronouns (a, one), third persons (he, she) and verbs in the infinitive are in the least indeterminate? The plane of consistence or of immanence, the body without organs, includes voids and deserts. But these are "fully" part of desire, far from accentuating some kind of lack in it. What a strange confusion—that of void with lack.[123]

As we proceed with our inquiry into the intermedial voids that emerge in Haneke's cinema, let us approach all such gaps we encounter in this Deleuzian spirit—in other words, not as an occasion for marking a loss or lack, but instead as mechanisms for potentializing new perceptual and affective configurations relative both to the spectator and to the characters within the films. Ultimately, what will arise out of this approach are both new modes of apprehending cinema, along with other media forms, and a means of gauging Haneke's unprecedented artistic and aesthetic achievements.

Having defined my conceptual model of intermediality and the means it gives us of approaching Haneke's films from an alternative aesthetic perspective, my study will now apply this model directly to the director's work through a series of close readings of the films themselves. The chapters that follow proceed through relevant examples of intermediality in Haneke's filmography in roughly chronological order but also by grouping the films according to the nonfilmic media with which they negotiate. Each chapter will seek to reveal a different aspect of the director's critical and thematic treatments of media while simultaneously modulating the application of my conceptual model appropriately. In chapter 1, the important role played by television and other commercial media in *Der siebente Kontinent*, Haneke's film debut, will be read via an exploration of these media as productive not of images but rather of "non-images" relative to cinema's image system, and via a consideration of the void thereby instantiated by the copresence of the image and "non-image" in the work. The signaletic material of home video will be analyzed through chapter 2's readings of *Benny's Video* and *Funny Games*, which emphasize the mimetic, subjective, and potentially ethical problematics the newer medium elicits in comparison with film. The differently fragmented temporal, aural, and visual structures of the events presented by television, film, and photography will form the subject of chapter 3, which focuses on Haneke's two "choral" films *71 Fragmente einer Chronologie des Zufalls* and *Code inconnu*. In chapter 4, which concerns Haneke's literary adaptations for television as well as his sole cinematic adaptation, *La pianiste*, I will take a different approach to the question of intermediality, and of adaptation itself; the chapter will demonstrate how film and novel may be considered separate intermedial structures that differently negotiate, but nonetheless share, a common medium: voice. The final chapter will be devoted to *Caché*, in which the affective experience of shame conditions the culmination of Haneke's intermedial strategies, wherein cinema and video become both indistinguishable and profoundly different, thus forming a veritable intermedial "time-crystal." Diverse though they may appear, these approaches to the films of Michael Haneke will consistently return to the aspects of the director's work that strike me as his most significant contributions to contemporary cinema: his commitment to eliciting and expressing the perceptual and affective voids introduced by competing audiovisual media into Western society's defining condition of spectatorship; and his commitment to affirming the unique power of cinema to provide a perspective on this state of affairs, even to the point of founding a new intermedial aesthetic of realism.

Chapter 1

✦

The Non-Image

Der siebente Kontinent

In his monograph *Michael Haneke*, Peter Brunette refers to *Der siebente Kontinent* as the director's "first feature-length film made for theatrical distribution."[1] This ungainly description underscores the fact that Haneke had already been a writer and director of television movies for over fifteen years before releasing his remarkably assured cinematic debut. In fact, there is no clear demarcation between Haneke's career as a director for television and as a *cineast*, as he continued to make movies for Austrian television after the release of *Der siebente Kontinent*, writing and directing three feature-length television productions in the 1990s—*Nachruf für einen Mörder* (*Obituary for a Murderer*; 1991), *Die Rebellion* (*The Rebellion*; 1993), and *Das Schloß* (*The Castle*; 1997)—as well as a television production of his theatrical staging of Mozart's *Cosí fan tutti* (2013). In all, if one counts his two-part TV movie *Lemminge* (*Lemmings*; 1979) as a single work, Haneke directed twenty-two features between 1974 and 2014: eleven of them for television and eleven for the cinema. Of the television works only *Das Schloß*, the adaptation of Franz Kafka's novel, was subsequently released theatrically and purportedly against Haneke's wishes.[2] Thus, even if I had limited the scope of my study of the director's work to include only his theatrical releases[3]—which would be akin to omitting most of *Dekalog* from a study of Krzysztof Kieślowski or *Twin Peaks* from a study of David Lynch—I would have faced a problem specific to Haneke. Many of the director's films implicitly or explicitly invoke a critique of television, a medium that, in his words, contributes to a widespread social "crisis" centered around "our collective loss of reality and social disorientation."[4] Yet Haneke's early development as a filmmaker is inextricably tied to his television productions. While there is no reason to consider Haneke's televisual works as substantially different from his films in a narrative or thematic sense,[5] at issue is the aesthetic orientation and technical disposition of television as opposed to film and the perceptual intersections and deviations the director has derived from these oppositions. It is this fundamental aesthetic divergence that Haneke alludes to when he clearly characterizes cinema as a veritable potential art form and television (as well as its ally, commercial cinema) as a tool of distraction and distortion of reality. Haneke frequently makes comments to this effect in interviews: "[C]inema still has the capacity, I think, to let us experience the world anew"; "What you see on the [television] screen is enough to make you very depressed!"; "TV films . . . can never really do what a theatrical movie can do."[6]

Haneke's shift toward cinema may have been motivated by considerations other than aesthetic preference, though. In his 2007 *New York Times* profile of Haneke, John Wray notes that *Der siebente Kontinent* was developed as a theatrical feature "only after having been rejected by a German television station." Wray goes on to speculate that this rejection was likely due to the film's depressing story line, which chronicles the daily lives of a family of three—father, mother, and young daughter—who in the film's final act systematically destroy all of their material possessions and commit group suicide.[7] Whatever the reason for the switch to a different medium, the origins of the production are telling with regard to the film's unique style, which combines visual tropes and accelerated editing derived from television programs and commercials with decidedly cinematic techniques such as long takes and the minimization of dialogue. Television, however, also takes root in the image system of the film itself as an entity that informs the means through which the viewer engages with the film, and as an entity that defines the interactions between the characters and their narrative milieu. This reading of *Der siebente Kontinent*—which runs somewhat counter to Haneke's statement that the film is less concerned with "the phenomenon of television" than later films like *Benny's Video* and *Funny Games*[8]—posits a deep internal disjunction wherein the film image and television's audiovisual output actively undermine each other's primacy as signaletic material. In other words, from the outset of his career as a filmmaker, Haneke incorporated the intermedial difference between television and film into his very mode of expression at a fundamental level. The incommensurability between these two media additionally contributes to one of the most overt thematic concerns in *Der siebente Kontinent* and in Haneke's later films; one that Roy Grundmann aptly refers to as "a pervasive crisis of vision" that manifests itself through both the relationships between the characters and their presentation to the viewer.[9] The TV signal, in its opposition to the film image, represents both a source of this crisis and its external manifestation, a perceptual black hole indexing the intermedial void between televisual and cinematic regimes of representation.

The term "non-image" is employed in this chapter to describe essential aspects of *Der siebente Kontinent*'s image system, including its depictions of television. This word choice is not meant to imply that the "animated poster" of the Australian beach, the television screen, or the black-screen "spacers" that punctuate the film lack affective or signifying power. On the contrary, even when filled with total blackness and silence the screen continues to signify, to command attention and invite affective suture, and to retain the pressure of preceding and anticipated image percepts. However, it is ultimately impossible to situate the spacers, the poster image, and television itself within the parameters of the film's mimesis. Each remains, albeit in a different way, unaccountable as an element of cinematic representation. Yet the designation "non-image" is also not meant to suggest a specifically dialectical relation between two distinct forms of image production. The term is instead intended to highlight Haneke's staging of profoundly different audiovisual phenomena that introduce gaps or voids into the film's perceptual field. These gaps arise from the absolute incongruency of image and non-image—the fact that, despite their exhibition on a single screen in a common time frame, they seem to belong not just to different films but also to completely different systems, or media, of expression. The employment of these antonyms will index the degree to which Haneke's use of intermediality reflects a profound absence that is unrepresentable via conventional cinematic imagery alone. In a thematic sense, then, the non-image indicates the pervasive sense of loss, particularly loss of vision, with which the lives of the characters are imbued and the acts of destruction and suicide that constitute the characters' final (and perhaps only possible) actualization of this loss. The perceptual and affective crisis initiated by the intermedial void in *Der siebente Kontinent*, which culminates in the use of television during the film's final scene, thus denotes a state of affairs that impinges upon—and ultimately comes to define—the audiovisual fields of the characters and spectators alike.

Non-Image One: Long Cuts

In *Michael Haneke's Cinema: The Ethic of the Image*, Catherine Wheatley refers to "a binary image system operating within [*Der siebente Kontinent*], a system linked to questions of time."[10] She identifies the two parts of this binary as "episodes" and "moments": the former are the longer and more developed sequences that retain a sense of narrative coherence, though they remain largely hermetic with respect to one another; the latter are the fragmentary shots that "are without explanation, often without dialogue, and which seemingly have no internal narrative structure."[11] While Wheatley's attention to narrative leads her to focus on the temporal aspects of this image system, another clear differentiating characteristic emerges in the spatial dimensions of each type of scene. The "episodes" offer somewhat conventional framing, while the "moments" tend to depict objects in close-up, typically when they are being used to perform rote or repetitive actions, without including establishing shots of the situations or countershots of the faces of those performing these actions. Along with recalling a mode of framing used by Robert Bresson, most notably in *Pickpocket* (1959), the accelerated cutting and the close-ups of hands, feet, and objects that characterize these "moments" are intended to evoke televisual montage and framing, particularly that of TV advertising. Haneke himself makes this association clear:

> From an aesthetic standpoint, much of the film could be said to resemble television advertising. I have many reservations about television, but saw a use for its style here. If *The Seventh Continent* had been made for television it would have failed totally in my view. But in the cinematic setting, a close-up of shoes or a doorknob takes on a far different sense than a similar shot in TV, where that style is the norm. This was a very conscious choice, since I wanted to convey not just images of objects but the objectification of life.[12]

This comment regarding the presumable failure of the film's aesthetic impact had it been produced for television is telling: it identifies the stylistic mode of such "moments" as one of high irony, the use of such televisual tropes highlighting the very disparity between the spatiotemporal dimensions of television and those of the film image. The influence of the accelerated rhythms of television on popular film (including that of the hyperaccelerated rhythms of music videos) has long and often been acknowledged. In *The Medium is the Massage* (1967), for instance, Marshall McLuhan and Quentin Fiore point out that then-recent films such as *A Hard Day's Night* (1964) and *What's New Pussycat?* (1965) "would [have] prove[d] unacceptable as mass audience films if the audience had not been preconditioned by television commericals to abrupt zooms, elliptical editing, no story lines, flash cuts."[13] *Der siebente Kontinent*, however, only relays such televisual tropes in order to estrange them internally through their juxtaposition to profoundly antitelevisual techniques: namely the long take and the "long cut."

As Raymond Williams asserts in his influential study *Television: Technology and Cultural Form* (1974), television is best conceived of not as a medium for the ordered transmission of discrete units of text but rather as a "planned flow, in which the true series is not the published sequence of programme items but this sequence transformed by the inclusion of another kind of sequence [advertisements], so that these sequences together compose the real flow, the real 'broadcasting.'"[14] In other words, the program one is viewing—whether news, sports, sitcom, or soap opera—is inseparable from the commercial advertising blocks interspersed throughout the transmission in a supplemental flow, and the interruption of either flow is anathema to the medium.[15] Haneke's use of the art-cinematic aesthetic of long takes, which linger on scenes of little or no movement or rote repetitive action, is thus overtly oppositional to the rhythms and temporalities typical of television even as it references other aspects of the medium. Taken together, these different series—"episodes" and "moments"—constitute an arrhythmic internal flow as well as a seemingly self-divided aesthetic, both of which challenge the expectations of viewers accustomed to such modes of expression only as independent phenomena. Even before the television screen itself enters the picture, then, *Der siebente Kontinent* has admitted the televisual into its image system, if only to establish a mutual subversion of the modes of spatiotemporal and spectatorial engagement proper to each medium.

Even more profoundly oppositional to televisual flow (and to the continuity of cinematic montage as well), however, is the director's use of "spacers"—moments in which the screen cuts to black and the audio goes silent. Along with being the most obviously identifiable non-images proffered by the film—Libby Saxton, for instance, uses the specific term "non-images" in reference to these blackout shots[16]—the recurrent spacers further complexify the film's audiovisual field, utilizing black screens and silence not simply as gaps or bridges between sounds and pictures but as productive signaletic material with specific thematic implications. While Haneke would go on to use such spacers in his later films *71 Fragmente* and *Code inconnu* as well, they serve a distinctly different function in *Der siebente Kontinent*. To begin with, *71 Fragmente* and *Code inconnu* both use spacers of a uniform duration, two seconds each, suggesting that they follow a definable rhythm that is largely independent from the scenes they separate.[17] The black screen time in the former film demarcates the titular fragments and enforces their disconnectedness; this effect of fragmentation applies to the latter film as well, though in *Code inconnu* the spacers also function to draw attention to the single-take presentation of most of its scenes by making each cut palpable. In *Der siebente Kontinent*, however, the spacers are employed not only between but also *within* scenes, and their durations are variable—from less than one second to several seconds in length. Wheatley assumes that "the spacers in *Der siebente Kontinent* were cut in proportion to the length of each 'scene' . . . so the spacer is longer at the end of a longer episode, very short at the end of a brief moment," but this is not correct.[18] A very short scene is at times followed by a spacer of several seconds, while longer scenes are often followed by brief spacers. Rather than transitioning between the film's narrative-temporal blocks, then, the spacers seem to institute gaps within the film's audiovisual field itself.[19] What, then, do these gaps signify, and what is the purpose of their variation?

Haneke himself states that the duration of each of the spacers—which he refers to as "black shots"—"corresponded to the *depth* of the preceding scene. If there was a lot to think about in the sequence, I made the black last longer."[20] In this consideration, the suspension of the audiovisual assumes the potential to negotiate a temporary space for spectatorial self-reflection. Haneke's comment suggests that the black screens are fields for the *mental afterimages* of the preceding scenes, the absence of on-screen images forcing an introspective component into the film's reception that mitigates the unceasing flow of image-percepts experienced in the act of film viewership. This interpretation bears a close resemblance to the model proposed by Raymond

Bellour in "The Pensive Spectator" (1984), though Bellour applies this mode of reception to still photographic images inserted into film, the insertions thereby achieving "effects of suspension, freezing, reflexivity, effects which enable the spectator to reflect on what he/she is seeing."[21] In Bellour's view, still images serve to activate in the spectator an awareness of filmic temporality by halting its expression through movement: "[The photographs'] relative stillness tempers the 'hysteria' of the film. . . . Though drawn more deeply into the flow of the film, the spectator is simultaneously able to reflect on it with a maximum of intensity."[22] The spacers, however, do not simply suspend *movement* within the film image through the insertion of a materially and temporally different medium (the photograph) but rather temporarily negate the presence of the imagery itself. Libby Saxton thus goes a step further in her analysis of the function of the spacers, seeing them less as fields for reflexive spectatorship than as means for the temporary disavowal of film's audiovisuality; in effect they are almost an antimedium: "The temporarily empty, dark screen implies an ethical gesture of refusal, a withdrawal from the ubiquitous 'visuel' and its regime of permanent visibility. Like the televisual snow which terminates the flow of images in *Der siebente Kontinent*, the repeated interruption of the image chain in *Code inconnu* disrupts those processes of bodily sense-making on which cinema habitually relies."[23] The connection made by Saxton between the static-filled television screen and the spacers is significant, as both function as a sort of representational negative space or vacuum in relation to the film image, imposing themselves directly on the image system at a fundamental perceptual level.

The spacers, then, serve several related functions in *Der siebente Kontinent*: establishing a reflexive field for the viewer with respect to both the mimetic and temporal materiality of the film; marking the formal difference between art cinema and television/commercial cinema by introducing gaps and stops (which have no correspondence to temporal gaps within the narrative) into the flow of imagery; and integrating non-images directly into the image system of the film. This last function, in particular, serves to indicate that the film's audiovisual structure is profoundly compromised. The self-instituted relation of images and non-images in *Der siebente Kontinent* not only calls attention to the film's constructedness but also actively undermines its own spatial and temporal continuity and audiovisual integrity. This practice is thus oriented toward a specifically intermedial mode of expression and viewer reception, one in which the perceptual limits of the medium are confronted and exceeded, and new affective and reflexive potentialities are uncovered. The affective charges particular to the void of the non-image—culminating in nihilism, hopelessness, and despair—will be explored in greater detail in the following sections. It is notable, however, that from the film's outset affect is generated by Haneke intermedially through the appropriation and distortion of the stylistics of television advertising, signalled by his use of delimited framing and black spacers. As Marshall McLuhan's colleague

Edmund Carpenter pointed out long ago, advertising is clearly counterpoised to most other forms of television programming in such an affective sense:

> The child is right in not regarding commercials as interruptions. For the only time anyone smiles on TV is in commercials. The rest of life, in news broadcasts and soap operas, is presented as so horrible that the only way to get through life is to buy this product: then you'll smile. Aesop never wrote a clearer fable. It's heaven and hell brought up to date: Hell in the headline, Heaven in the ad. Without the other, neither has meaning.[24]

By refusing to frame the faces of the family members—which in any case are almost certainly not radiating the happiness of their commercial counterparts—Haneke lays bare the underlying anxieties propelling the televisual cycle. The spectator and the consumer alike are denied the relief of the smiling face, and in place of this affect-image what is offered is only palpable silence and darkness. Along with acting as sites for pensive reflection, then, the spacers are increasingly revealed as sublimations of spectatorial anxiety, negative signifiers of our medial disorientation that ascend to the surface of the screen like oil slicks on water.

In *Der siebente Kontinent*, the two other aspects of the film that best resonate with this reading of the spacer as non-image are the poster image of Australia, a recurring motif, and the television screen in the film's finale. Both of these can similarly be qualified as non-images, though in a different sense from the spacers; although they are likewise incommensurable with the film's medial field, they are nonetheless integral to the film's diegesis. In other words, while the spacers address the zone of film spectatorship exclusively, being perceivable by the filmgoer yet completely distinct from the milieu of the film, the poster image and television screen both emerge from within the film's narrative and mimesis, even if they do not remain circumscribed by these spatiotemporal parameters. Thus, the poster and television screen overtly relate to the perceptual fields of the characters and the film viewers alike, problematizing the degree to which the two can be differentiated and potentially desubjectivizing both character and filmgoer.

Non-Image Two: Poster of an Undiscovered Country

The title *Der siebente Kontinent* is a direct allusion to Australia, which has two interrelated points of reference within the film. The country is depicted, early in the film, in a wall-sized tourism advertisement that the camera lingers on as the family exits a car wash, the poster showing a rural beach and mountain setting with the words "Welcome to Australia" garishly printed in red letters in the top right corner of the image and "Australian Travel

Agency" in smaller letters in the lower left. Although there is no indication of the family even noticing this advertisement in the opening scenes, the image will reappear at crucial points in the film as a moving film image accompanied on the sound track by crashing waves and the cries of gulls, and it is suggested that the scene is a subjective dream or fantasy image experienced by Georg. A second, verbal reference to Australia is made in the final third of the film in a scene set at a bank: Georg and Anna are withdrawing their life savings as cash (which will be flushed down the toilet in a later scene), and when asked by the teller why they have decided to withdraw their savings so abruptly, Anna replies that the family is "emigrating to Australia." This use of Australia as a euphemism for collective suicide recolors our perception of the tableau of the poster, bringing it into symbolic association with death. Hence, a number of interesting potential relations circulate in and around the poster.

As Haneke indicates in a video interview with Serge Toubiana, the picture on the tourism advertisement presents an impossible convergence of land and ocean that is produced through a superimposition of separate images, with the waves washing onto the shore seeming to pass through the mountains in the background (see figure 1).[25] The composite image is not especially jarring when viewed as a still photo in an advertisement but takes on an unsettling unreality when presented as a moving image: the shot is irreconcilable with Australia as a place, or indeed with any real place. As Marc Augé points out in *Non-Places* (1995), there is an inherent falsity in all such depictions of "tourist destinations," which produce and present "imaginary places: banal utopias, clichés."[26] Here, though, the image of "Australia"—the non-image of a non-place—is further interpretable as a sublimation of nihilism. Christopher Sharrett thus suggests that the unreal landscape, in the context of the family's actions, "introduces altogether unanticipated questions about the nature of utopia, suggesting that the quietude of death may constitute a satisfactory promised land in the mind of the suicide."[27] This specifically psychological reading of the image's significance, however, does not quite account for the ways in which the ad is incorporated into the image system of the film.

The poster is first reframed as a moving image at the end of part one of the film, appearing on-screen immediately after Anna has tucked Evi into bed and turned out the light, in a cut not preceded by a spacer. The jarringly discontinuous image lingers for about twenty seconds, at which point it cuts to the couple's bedside table at night as Georg's hand reaches out to turn on the light. Anna asks, "What is the matter?" "Nothing," Georg replies, but the light remains on and we hear him breathing heavily offscreen, as though recomposing himself. The subjective or psychological status that could be assigned to the beach image based on this presentation—it is strongly implied that we have glimpsed a nightmare Georg has had—is undermined in the image's three subsequent appearances, which are offered with little context and no suggestion of its being an imagined vision (although its final

Figure 1: A poster advertisement of Australia becomes an uncanny moving image. *Der siebente Kontinent* (Michael Haneke, 1989).

appearance is ambiguous in this regard). Significantly, the third time we encounter the image is immediately following the death of Evi. The moment Georg switches off the television set, on which Meatloaf is performing the power ballad "Piece of the Action," rather than capturing the TV screen's transition to blankness the film cuts to the shot of "Australia" for several seconds. The beach scene thus marks the disappearance of the television image as much as it marks the death of the child—it can be seen as representing, in other words, not a vision so much as an *absence* of vision. The fact that the composite image presents an impossible spatial relation between mountains and sea is thus appropriate, as it indicates that a singular and subjective viewpoint is not implied by the shot, that it cannot be traced back to any actual or embodied visual perspective. This loss of the dyadic subject-object or seer-seen relationship is enforced by the visual dynamics and rhythms of the film, where the close-up and spacer fragment and desubjectify the visual, spatial, and temporal consistency of the film's milieu, as well as in the eye and sight motifs that pervade its narrative and mise-en-scène.

Indeed, most critical studies of *Der siebente Kontinent* note its symbolic and explicit references to an atrophying of visual power. Roy Grundmann points out that the film "uses eyesight and the lack thereof as narrative ploy and metaphor," while Vicky Lebeau describes the film's repeated depiction of downturned gazes as "an aversion that speaks . . . of estrangement, of introspection and perhaps of a kind of blind seeing."[28] The motif is quite clearly conveyed by the film's story: Anna is an optometrist, and a close-up of her customer's eye being scanned by a machine early in the film is accompanied by the customer's anecdote about her poor vision being a punishment for taunting a bespectacled girl as a child. At the same time, Evi feigns blindness at her school, a ploy apparently inspired by a newpaper story about a little girl who is "blind but no longer lonely" ["*Blind—Aber nie mehr einsam*"]. The film's attention to the mechanics of vision as a defining mode of subjectivity, then, is largely conveyed through the breakdown of vision and hence of interpersonal and interaffective exchange. *Der siebente Kontinent* presents a situation in which the gaze is scarcely ever directed toward others but is instead riveted to the machines and media that command spectatorial attention: the car wash, the cash register, advertisements, the television.

The film viewer is likewise implicated in this phenomenon, as the opening scene makes abundantly clear. Georg and Anna are initially presented facing away from the camera and in an attitude doubling that of the spectator, their attention fixed on the brushes and spraying water of the car wash visible through the windshield of their automobile. The scene is an inverse of the opening of *Caché*, wherein that film's bourgeois couple Georges and Anne will occupy an offscreen space that doubles that of the spectator by virtue of their common subjective point of view. *Der siebente Kontinent*'s opening does not carry the same self-reflexive shock, however, as it is not a shared subjectivity but rather a shared *objectification* that connects characters and viewers.[29] The scene parodies the spectator's habitude and gaze, withholding the faces of the protagonists and offering instead still figures arrested by the mechanism within which they are enmeshed. This mechanism indirectly implicates the film viewer as well, and within the same image chain: Georg and Anna are watching the car wash's giant brushes, and we are watching them watch the giant brushes. The infection of the moving film image by the poster image marks the consummation of this relationship between viewer and character, who are subjected to, and desubjectified by, this image in precisely the same way. Indeed, Jean Baudrillard, in *Simulacra and Simulation* (1981), connects such billboard images explicitly to the undecidability between the contemporary consumer's role as the subject or object of surveillance. It is this inherently repressive process of signification "that huge billboards express by inviting you to relax and to choose in complete serenity. These billboards, in fact, observe and surveil you as well, or as badly, as the 'policing' television. The latter looks at you, you look at yourself in it, mixed with the other, it is the mirror without silvering (*tain*) in the activity of consumption, a game of splitting in two and doubling that closes this world on itself."[30] If the Australian beach is a vision of the utopian non-place of death, then, it is not a vision that is sought out by the characters so much as one that seeks them out and lures them in; it is the predetermined outcome of an image system that revolves around a fundamental emptiness divorced from any subjective or objective representation of reality: the "image" that stands in for an absolute non-image. Baudrillard, in fact, qualifies all advertising in these terms, as "the empty and inescapable form of seduction."[31]

In *The Vision Machine* (1988), Paul Virilio offers a strikingly similar analysis of advertising imagery that extends its relevance to Haneke's film. Noting the same "inversion of perception" that is so striking to Baudrillard, Virilio describes the typical poster ad in the following terms: "Behind the wall, I cannot see the poster; in front of the wall, the poster forces itself on me, its image perceives me."[32] He then characterizes this effect in terms close to that of a camera-and-screen apparatus, albeit one in which the camera gaze is emitted by the very image that appears before us in the ad, a *virtual*—that is, extradimensional—camera gaze that is all the more powerful for the very banality of the image it projects on and into us:

> The graphic or photographic quality of the advertising image, its *high definition* as they say, is no longer a guarantee of some kind of aesthetic or precision, of photographic sharpness etc. It is merely the search for a stereoscopic effect, for a third dimension. This then in itself becomes what the message projects, a commercial message of some kind that strives, through our gaze, to attain the depth, the density of meaning it sadly lacks. . . . The phatic image that grabs our attention and forces us to look is no longer a powerful image; it is a cliché attempting, in the manner of the cineframe, to inscribe itself in some unfolding of time in which the optic and the kinematic are indistinguishable.[33]

Virilio here implicitly invites, as Deleuze explicitly does in an essay cited in the introduction, a revised understanding of McLuhan's terminology: the medium that constitutes the message of the ad image is not photographic but kinematic—that is, a temporal image, one in movement or flux, that is usually attributed to cinema and television—and in this specific sense it is both a "hot" *and* "cool" medium. To the extent that it is (actually) a photograph, it is "hot," arresting the gaze and demanding attention; to the extent that it is (virtually) a moving image, it is "cool," demanding that we invest our perception in it in order to lend it spatial dimensionality and temporal animation via our own gaze. Yet the image provides no aesthetic or intellectual return on this perceptual investment and therefore only circulates what Baudrillard describes earlier as an empty, yet inescapable, "seduction" of our attention. It is as though, in the case of the advertising image, the "content" of the medium of photography becomes the medium of television, or perhaps a drastically cooled-down form of commercial cinema. In optical terms, this inversion of medial content translates to an inversion of perception, a reversal of the seeing-nonseeing dyadic that Virilio uses to define a collective "vision machine" the installation of which in contemporary culture has only been furthered by advances in telecommunications and computing: "Blindness is thus very much at the heart of the coming 'vision machine.' The production of *sightless vision* is itself merely the reproduction of an intense blindness that will become the latest and last form of industrialization: *the industrialization of the non-gaze.*"[34] Haneke's cinematic animation of the poster's non-image of Australia is in this sense an actualization of its virtual role in the industrialization of nonseeing. In fact, the poster trumps all of the other motifs of blindness and loss of vision that pervade the film and does so by offering a direct audiovisual experience of this effect, one that does not (like the spacers) simply entail the withholding of audiovisual material. Instead, the poster presents a sublimated blindness that obtains within and through visuality itself, via its inversion of the traditionally understood relationship of seer to scene. The poster itself takes the active role in the visual exchange, its void-scene gazing—like Friedrich Nietzsche's abyss—*into* the spectator, overcoding their perceptions with the optical power of its own cliché. This inversion effectively preconditions and foreshadows the film's presentation of the non-image signifying the vision machine itself: the television screen.

Indeed, the final appearance of the moving poster bears out Baudrillard's and Virilio's connection of the poster to the surveilling television screen, with the latter emerging as the dominant force in the image system of the film. In a sequence that will be analyzed in greater detail further down, *Der siebente Kontinent* ends with a rapid montage of previous shots from the film displayed over a recurring shot of a television screen that emits only the static of a receiver without a signal—visual "snow" and aural noise. During the final appearance of the beach, which is the last image we see apart from an extreme close-up of the televised snow, the sound track does not switch to the ambient sounds of waves and bird cries. Instead it retains the unnatural hiss of the television set. A number of related interpretations of this sound bridge are possible: the idea that there is no real distinction between the visual static on the television and the beach scene, both being non-images empty of content, fostering blindness rather than sight; the idea that the utopian vision of death has been corrupted, its signal-to-noise ratio pushed into the latter extreme, revealing its true nature as a media construct rather than a utopian vision; and the idea that television's mode of perception has in fact defined, determined, or bled into every visual relation within the film, including the abstract relation between the beach scene and the film image, with respect to the spectator's and the characters' subjectivities. It is this third possibility, which directly reveals the deeper intermedial strategies at play in the film, that will be explored in the next section.

Non-Image Three: Television

I have already noted the direct contrast between the image systems of *Der siebente Kontinent* and of most television programming with respect to the use of the spacer, which offers some respite and reflexive space in the film that implicitly oppose the continuous flow of audiovisual material proffered by television. Roy Grundmann is thus able to convincingly assert that the film directly utilizes "TV's superficial visual wealth [as] a negative coefficient . . . to the characters' lack of insight into their lives [and] to their lack of vision of the future."[35] In this consideration, TV functions as an inverse spacer, offering a plenitude of visual material that stands in opposition to the perceptual void that seems to enfold the characters. But there is another way to interpret the signifying presence of television than by juxtaposing its "visual wealth" against the characters' metaphorical blindness. From an intermedial perspective, the television screen is a foreign installation in the film's mimetic system that affects *all* its visual relations in a fundamental sense. To begin with, material on television—in particular the static-filled screen at the end of the film—obtains a status that is neither subject nor object but rather the source of a purely abstract gaze without origin or termination. Television allies itself with objects and individuals indiscriminately. Indeed, it has been pointed out that much of *Der siebente Kontinent* is filmed from the "viewpoint . . . of objects,"[36] which is telling with regard to its largely asubjective camera gaze and mise-en-scène and its mimicking of the mechanics of television advertising. A sort of inorganic life is imbued into these objects via close-ups and editing, of the type that is most recognizable in television commercials when the products are literally animated: a bottle of mouthwash swinging through a jungle like Tarzan, a talking piece of breakfast cereal, anthropomorphized foam shoes that literally massage their owner's feet, and so on. In the representational regime of commercial television and cinema, it is implied that objects are accorded a status that exceeds even fetishism and is in fact equal, or superior, to that of the consumer. Moreover, the film suggests that this regime has infiltrated lived experience, with the characters' existence being utterly enmeshed with, and even subordinate to, that of the objects they possess. For this reason, the family cannot kill themselves without also destroying their possessions, nor can they destroy their possessions without also killing themselves. Referring to the actual reported event that inspired the film's plot, Haneke states that it was this aspect that attracted his attention in the first place: "What really interested me was not that there was a family that committed suicide because, sad as it is, there are a lot of those. What I thought was fascinating was that there was a family that goes out and commits suicide, but before they do so, they destroy everything they possess. I thought that was a good metaphor for our situation."[37] Haneke associates this act with the German expression "Destroy what destroys you" ["*Macht kaputt was euch kaputt macht*"],[38] but in the film itself the sense of this statement is ironically and tragically undercut, as the same gesture enacts the destruction of the self as well as of the objects motivating that destruction. If one considers television to be the source of the breakdown of the subject-object and seer-seen relationships, ultimately the gesture also fails to acquire the force of a cathartic release, as the television is seemingly the only object in the family's home to escape destruction. But in what sense can one account for the role of television itself in this self-destructive regime? What affective power, what perverse vitality, does it possess such that it is the sole "survivor" of the household?

There is an intriguing piece of dialogue toward the end of the first section of the film, spoken by Anna's brother Alexander as the family settles down to watch an awards ceremony on TV after dinner, that gives us a clue as to the medium's significance in this regard. Alexander comments that his and Anna's mother—whose recent death has left him emotionally and mentally shattered—had, just before passing away, commented that she "wonder[ed] what it would be like if people would have a screen [*Monitor*] instead of a head so everybody could see their thoughts." Georg and Anna show no visible reaction to these words, their eyes remaining fixed on the television as it cuts from the TV set to close-ups of the faces of Anna, Georg, and Alexander in turn, illuminated only by the flickering light of the screen. The ironic significance of the statement is apparent in the presentation: the faces of the characters fail to register anything apart from the reflection of the screen, suggesting that were we to see their thoughts we would find nothing beyond what is already displayed on the television screen they're viewing. In other words, they already possess monitors in place of heads. A number of theoretical determinations of television offer similar conclusions: Edmund Carpenter, for example, comments that "We don't watch TV; it watches us: it guides us."[39] Fredric Jameson, further elaborating on such a phenomenon, states the following apropos "machine time," the dominant form of temporality of video and commercial television: "[I]ts machinery uniquely dominates and depersonalizes subject and object alike, transforming the former into a quasi-material registering apparatus for the machine time of the latter and of the video image or 'total flow.' "[40] This notion of the viewer transformed into a receiving device for television's stream of informatic "content" is expressed in even stronger terms in *Simulacra and Simulation*, wherein Baudrillard contrasts television with cinema, a medium that remains capable, to his mind, of supporting actual images: "Nothing of any of this in the 'TV' image, which suggests nothing, which mesmerizes, which itself is nothing but a screen, not even that: a miniaturized terminal that, in fact, is immediately located in your head—you are the screen, and the TV watches you—it transistorizes all the neurons and passes through like a magnetic tape—a tape, not an image."[41] Television is in this consideration not even productive of images, and therefore the television viewer is incapable of perceiving anything like images. The concept of television is not founded, as the concept of film generally is, on the basis of the image, but rather on the basis of the interface. The experience of watching television, then, is not definable in terms of perceiving subject and perceived image. Instead, the screen on the device becomes the screen in one's head, producing a singular relation: a televisual subject-object.[42]

The profound difficulty involved in conceptualizing television arises out of this inability to identify an objective basis for the medium's visual material without factoring in the perceptual field of the viewer, which completes the apparatus. This problem presents itself in any attempt to bring television's form and content into an integral disposition—to posit, in other words, an "aesthetics" of television. As a phenomenon defined by its effect, which is one of flow over and above anything resembling veritable images, television's medial field bears far more conceptual importance in its definition than in virtually any message it has to offer.[43] Stanley Cavell acknowledges this in his essay "The Fact of Television," the title of which is itself an admission that very little can be stated about the medium with assurance, other than "the sheer fact that television exists, and that this existence is at once among the most obvious and the most mysterious facts of contemporary life."[44] Cavell approaches television via the very mode of perception it entails, stating that while film is a medium for *viewing*, television is a medium of *monitoring*:

> [T]he mysterious sets, or visual fields, in our houses, for our private lives, are to be seen not as receivers, but as monitors. My claim about the aesthetic medium of television can now be put this way: its successful formats are to be understood as revelations (acknowledgments) of the conditions of monitoring, and by means of a serial-episode procedure of composition, which is to say, by means of an aesthetic procedure in which the basis of a medium is acknowledged primarily by the format rather than primarily by the instantiations.[45]

Cavell thus arrives at something like an "aesthetic" of television by completely subordinating its content to its function, basing the success of its programming not on what is being represented but on how well its visual field conforms to the perceptual-affective disposition of monitoring. Cavell does not go as far as Baudrillard, who asserts that *we* in fact are being monitored *by* the television sets in our homes, but he does characterize television as utterly different from film in terms of its audiovisual and temporal dynamics. The cinema screen reflects representations of other space-times that retain the potential to form images; the television screen operates like a conduit for what Cavell terms "a *current of simultaneous event reception*."[46] Cinema draws the viewer and the image into a common—albeit heterotopic and multisubjective—space, while television annihilates the distance separating viewer and action within its unceasing flow of percepts and its attendant affect of compulsion to watch. The cinema screen is the receiver of the projected film image, which is then offered up to the gaze of the filmgoer; the television screen relays its audiovisual content directly to the viewer, who is the actual receiver in this apparatus.

It is precisely these differences that emerge when *Der siebente Kontinent* stages, in its final sequence, a direct intermedial encounter between cinematic and televisual pictures, and it is significant that the film does so after emptying the televisual apparatus of all but its bare receptive and signaletic fields: the dying Georg stares blankly at a television that emits, as previously described, only the audiovisual static indicating the absence of a signal. The film conveys, in this way, the pure and empty subject-apparatus relationship defining televisual spectatorship, its viewer (almost) completely lacking consciousness and the screen (almost) completely lacking audiovisual content. The scene begins with a medium profile shot of Georg—recumbent on the bed, propped up by the headboard and totally motionless, with the corpses of Evi and Anna lying next to him—staring at the television; it then cuts to a shot/reverse shot matching Georg's face and the TV screen, both in medium close-up, followed by a tight close-up on Georg's face. The camera then appears to adopt Georg's point of view with a medium shot of the television, the screen of which is slightly skewed and misaligned in relation to the cinema screen, as it is resting unevenly on a pile of debris (see figure 2). The sequence that follows intercuts flashes of images from earlier parts of the film with increasingly closer shots of the television screen, accompanied by the rising volume of the television's hiss on the sound track; the film ends on a shot of the television screen completely filling the cinematic frame in extreme close-up. The edges of the television screen are no longer visible, and the film screen is dominated by the non-image of the visual static. The montage of intercut images speeds up—multiplying and decreasing in individual duration—each time the film cuts away from the television: the first cutaway is a shot of the brushes in the car wash through the windshield; the second, a flash of the bodies from the accident scene covered in plastic from the end of part two; then the cutaways become increasingly erratic sequences of much briefer shots, including a sequence of shots of the dying fish from the family's destroyed aquarium, Anna's face in various emotional states, cash register displays and the downturned gazes of store clerks, the face of the man whom Georg replaced at his workplace, and Evi's wide-eyed, impassive face; and finally the moving poster image of Australia is viewed for several seconds before the final close-up shot of the television and a cut to a black screen. The film then ends with scrolling text that briefly outlines the discovery of their bodies, their burial, and the fact that Georg's parents do not accept their deaths as a suicide and demand a police investigation.

The most obvious interpretation of these evocative images is that they are drawn out of Georg's memory, a cinematic rendering of the concept of one's life "flashing before one's eyes" in the moments preceding death. Indeed, the selection of images is strongly suggestive of this, since all are drawn from scenes that include Georg (sometimes from situations involving Georg exclusively, such as the shot of the former manager at his workplace), from a perspective that could reasonably be assumed to be his, and also because his own face is not featured in any of the cutaway shots. The point of view thus rests decisively with Georg thoughout the scene, with respect to the recurring shot of the television screen and the shots from past scenes in the film.[47] There is a profound shift here from the perspectival techniques used throughout

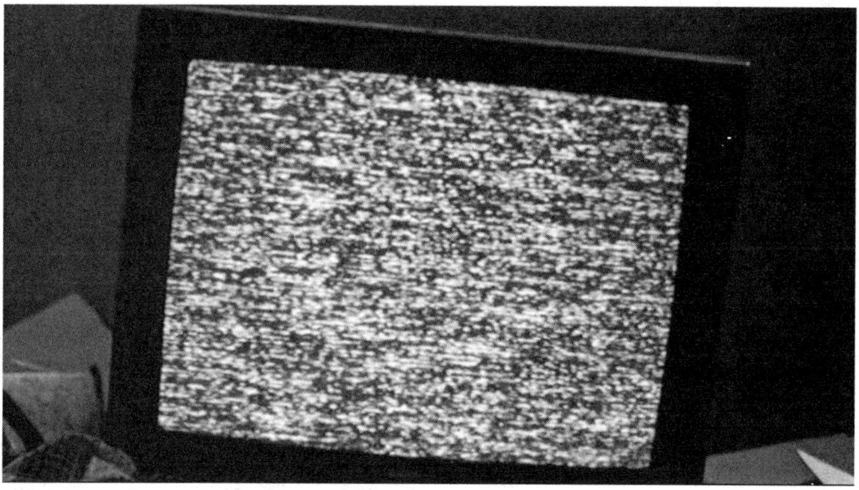

Figure 2: The static-filled television screen seems to return the gaze of the dying Georg. *Der siebente Kontinent* (Michael Haneke, 1989).

the rest of the film, which radically desubjectivize the characters. It is as though Georg is recovering his subjectivity in the moments before his death by recalling fleeting images of life experience, but the television responds by continually pulling him back into its mediatic field all the more insistently. Indeed, there is a strong suggestion in the shot/countershot between the dying man and the television set, staged at the beginning of the scene, that Georg's gaze is somehow being answered by that of the television screen. This not only connects with Baudrillard's and other theorists' idea of the television monitor's surveillance of the spectator, but also with the idea that the televisual medium is actively influencing the dynamics of image and non-image in the scene. The progressively larger television screen virtually imposes itself onto the pattern of cutaway shots, its presence continually interrupting the emergence of the cinematic memory-images. It is arguable, furthermore, that the acceleration and increasing brevity of the flashback shots denote the shots' conformity to a mode of perception specific to television, which Haneke characterizes in his interview with Sharrett as "accelerat[ing] our habits of seeing."[48] Even emptied of content, then, the televisual apparatus remains decisive in shaping the perceptual fields of subject and spectator, the film's images—no less than Georg's mental images—being impacted by the intermedial configuration the film introduces into the situation. In this presentation, television is implicated in the end of conscious existence no less than the overdose of narcotics Georg ingests—indeed, here we have a depiction of the medial narcosis forewarned of by theorists such as Virilio, who in a 1990 essay states, quite plainly, that "these new electromagnetic technologies will ruin us and literally kill us; television's so-called *real* instant only ever being that of the sudden disappearance of our *immediate consciousness*."[49] Georg's memory-images, which are simultaneously film images, are reorganized, recomposed, and finally annihilated by television.

The final scene of *Der siebente Kontinent* depicts a direct encounter not only between human and televisual perception, then, but also between film and television media, and this latter relation is more complex than it would at first appear. Meghan Sutherland, whose essay "Death, with Television" is one of the few critical works on Haneke that includes a detailed analysis of this scene, aptly defines the gradual subsumption of the film screen by the television screen as a "mise-en-abyme . . . creating the dizzying reproductive effect of a screen-within-screen."[50] The concept of mise en abyme implies, however, a mutual reflection or a recursion that has its basis in representation, whereas in the ending of the film the television screen does not offer any form of image production and thus does not enter into any reflexive exchange with the film image or with film as a medium (as the filming of a cinema screen might). The fact that the TV screen is depicted as slightly skewed with respect to the film screen is also subtly suggestive of this lack of a recursive or self-reflexive image chain. The frames of the television and film screens never quite coincide, and thus there is no connotation of undecidability between the contents of the frame (the film image) and the frame itself (the film screen).[51] Instead, the television screen functions less as the "content" of the cinema screen and more as what Deleuze qualifies in the second chapter of *Cinema 1* as a radical "out-of-field" (*hors-champ*), a presence that "cannot even be said to exist, but rather to 'insist' or 'subsist,' a more radical Elsewhere, outside homogeneous space and time"[52]—a concept that will be revisited when discussing *Caché*. Rather than implying an "offscreen" space-time, the screen being associated with a delimited planar segment of Cartesian space, the television screen introduces an anomalous element into the audiovisual field of the film from *within* the cinematic frame. The non-imagistic audiovisual field of the television is profoundly *other* to that of the film screen, and its effect could be likened to that of a black hole's gravitational effect on space-time, warping and ultimately subsuming the film image itself along with the consciousness of Georg, the diegetic viewer. The conjunction of film and television screens does not denote a mise en abyme, then, but an abyss of another kind, an emptiness standing in for the absolute *non*conjunction of image and non-image. It is a manifestation of the intermedial void *par excellence*.

The definition of a non-image could indeed best be expressed as that which is *both on-screen and out of field*. The black spacers, the poster image, and the television screen in *Der siebente Kontinent* are each circumscribed by the cinematic frame, but they remain absolutely discontinuous with the audiovisual system and perceptual field of the film. In this sense, the non-image fundamentally enforces the chain of signification within the film surrounding the film's motif of loss of vision as well as its thematic treatment of both mutual alienation and self-alienation and their sublimation in an extended act of destruction and suicide. But the void instituted by the intermedial relation between image and non-image also carries out a distinct function in relation to the film spectator, whose perspective remains superior to that of the characters, if only marginally in many considerations. The arrhythmic temporalities conveyed by the black spacers, the imposition of the asubjective poster image, and, above all, the direct invasion of the filmic image by the televisual static at the film's end all destabilize the representational system of the film in such a way that the spectator experiences totally different forms of medial engagement with these images and non-images, respectively, to disorienting effect. However, I would argue that rather than undermining the affective investment in the film—thus encouraging detached intellection or emotional distantiation on the part of the viewer—the film posits a decentered spectatorial position wherein we encounter a multiplicity of medial forms and intermedial interstices that potentialize new modes of affective experience vis-à-vis the film. *Der siebente Kontinent* thus confirms that, at the very outset of his filmmaking practice, Haneke uncovered a means of reconfiguring filmic and nonfilmic media in his work and of utilizing the expressive force of the intermedial gaps exposed by these new configurations. In *Der siebente Kontinent*, he employs these means in such a way that the realist impact of the narrative is heightened rather than diminished. In his next film, *Benny's Video*, Haneke applies this approach to the medium of home video, situated within the context of a very different thematic and representational treatment of violence that will culminate in the notorious *Funny Games*.

Chapter 2

✦

The Film of the Video

Benny's Video and *Funny Games*

One of the explanations given in the previous chapter for the difficulty of conceptualizing television was the distance separating components of its apparatus: unlike the film strip, projector, and screen mechanism, television's monitor relays a signal originating from a location utterly displaced from the presumably domestic space of viewership. Home video (which I will henceforth refer to simply as "video"), however, brings both the mode of capture and that of display into a common situation and apparatus, thus negating the separation between recording and screening that one finds in the film medium. This property of video media, combined with the format's potential for easy temporal manipulation (through actions such as freeze-frame, fast-forward, rewinding, etc.), profoundly distantiates video from film, a disparity analogous to the difference between film and television. Yet a crucial difference between television and video also presents itself: television's medial schema has been primarily defined in terms of informatic flow and the subsumption of the viewer's subjectivity within a condition of monitoring. One can therefore characterize television's spatiotemporal character, as Mary-Ann Doane does, in terms of "presentness" or "liveness" and the annihilation of distance, as opposed to film's commonly received temporal mode of "pastness" and alternate spatiality.[1] Video, however, potentializes a state of absolute proximity, and even self-proximity, in both spatial and temporal terms. The video medium is capable, in other words, not only of recording and displaying its own immediate surroundings, but also of displaying its own display—of including, among its represented objects, even its own mode of representation. Paul Virilio, at the outset of *Polar Inertia*, expresses the implications of this shift in representational capacity in the following terms:

> Even the old 35 mm cine-camera has had its eyepiece viewfinder replaced to advantage with a screen that actually displays the recorded images.

> How can one fail to see here the essential characteristic of video technology: not a more or less up-to-the-minute "representation" of an event, but *live presentation of a place* or an electro-optical environment—the result, it would seem, of *putting reality on waves* by means of electro-magnetic physics.[2]

Video's mediatic field brings the categories of sensible reality and audiovisual representation into such close association that they veer toward interchangeability, toward expression as a common (wave-)physical substance. This is the specific intermedial problem confronted by Haneke in *Benny's Video* and *Funny Games*—the crisis of sense perception instituted by video's audiovisuality, as opposed to the film image, and the spatiotemporal aporia this initiates. One of the most direct illustrations of this phenomenon, however, comes not from Haneke's films but from Mel Brooks's Star Wars spoof *Spaceballs* (1987). Before confronting video's significance in demonstrating the limits of representational violence, then, let us examine its potential for comedy.

Spaceballs was released soon after the commercial sale and rental of VHS (Video Home System) cassettes of theatrical films had become standard practice and imagines a future where the process has reached a new peak of efficiency. Hence, the film's villains Dark Helmet (Rick Moranis) and Colonel Sandurz (George Wyner) attempt to ascertain the whereabouts of the protagonist by viewing an "instant cassette," which Sandurz describes as a "new breakthrough in home video marketing" that puts the VHS tape of the film into stores "before the movie is finished." After starting the videotape and fast-forwarding through the standard Federal Bureau of Investigation warning, the opening credits, and earlier scenes from the film, the video arrives at the exact moment in the film that the characters occupy, and a mise en abyme enters the mise-en-scène: the video monitor in the center of the frame displays an infinite recursion of other monitors, all playing the sequence of the film we are currently viewing (see figure 3). The wonderful exchange between the characters that ensues is worth presenting in full:

> DARK HELMET: "What the hell am I looking at? When did *this* happen in the movie?"
> COLONEL SANDURZ: "*Now*. You're looking at *now*, sir. Everything that happens now is happening *now*."
> DH: "What happened to *then*?"
> CS: "We passed *then*."
> DH: "When?"
> CS: "Just now. We're at *now* now."
> DH: "Go back to *then*."
> CS: "When?"
> DH: "Now."

Figure 3: "Everything that happens now is happening *now*." Colonel Sandurz (*right*) explains to Dark Helmet the concept of viewing, on video, the part of the movie that they are currently filming. *Spaceballs* (Mel Brooks, 1987).

CS: "Now?"
DH: "Now!"
CS: "I can't."
DH: "Why?"
CS: "We missed it."
DH: "When?"
CS: "Just now."
DH [pauses]: "When will *then* be *now*?"
CS: "Soon."[3]

This ludic dialogue captures something endemic to video's absolute temporal and spatial self-presence, which is the profound difficulty—or perhaps impossibility—of reconciling its medial representation of the present space-time with our actual experience of it. Video's capacity to represent its own representation as it is recorded introduces an informatic feedback loop into a given situation, creating a unique crisis for the spectator, who is simultaneously the viewing subject and viewed object and thus is caught within an infinite perceptual-representational chain. As previously stated, this can be considered an actualization of the mise en abyme effect that has long been identified within other forms of representation, but never literalized before video (unless one qualifies the effect of holding one mirror up to another); video, which is always potentially self-representational, mimetically occupies the edges of an audiovisual abyss. Furthermore, Dark Helmet's consternation—evident in his demand to know what he is viewing and when it took place, his refusal to accept that it is happening "now," and his command to "go back to *then*"—indicates the specifically temporal problematic that defines video's self-representation: its exposure of the vanishing point of our perceptual experience of the present.[4] There is no position from which the subject in time can grasp the present moment as it occurs; any frame of reference for the utterance "now" must be either proleptic or retroactive, actually signifying the immediate future or past. Dark Helmet and Colonel Sandurz's apparently nonsensical exchange—"When will *then* be *now*?" "Soon."—is in fact quite correct, given this conception of time: the immediate past (*then*) is only experienced as the present (*now*) the instant after its occurrence (*soon*). The great irony of video is that its mediated representation of the present is closer to the temporal void of the ever-elusive moment *between* past and future than our own seemingly unmediated experience of present time. Video is, in this specific temporal sense, a medium for immediacy. It directly exposes the temporal gap separating the present moment and its apprehension, the gap that we necessarily dismiss in our own time-perception, and thus positions itself more closely to "real events"—including events of violence and death—than the film image. Haneke's own incorporation of video into his films privileges and exploits this capacity of the newer medium.

The films by Haneke that specifically explore the implications of the video medium are *Benny's Video*, *Funny Games* (including Haneke's 2007 American remake of the film, *Funny Games U.S.*), and *Caché*. This last film will be the subject of its own chapter, since it utilizes video and surveillance in a completely different manner than the previous films, applying video's defining system of representation to a conceptualization of shame and its affectively charged temporalities. *Benny's Video* and *Funny Games* must also be distinguished from one another in their particular uses of video representation, which (as with television in *Der siebente Kontinent*) inform not only the narrative and diegetic elements of the films but also their thematic concerns and audiovisual modalities. *Benny's Video* is specifically concerned with the problematic proximity of video to real experience and its effect on the subjectivity of the adolescent Benny (Arno Frisch), whose act of violent murder and the chain of representations it unleashes create a crisis in his self-image that also extends to his family situation. *Funny Games*, however, is a dark parody of a specific subgenre of horror or thriller, the "home invasion" film[5]; the parody reveals the film's implicit connection to video and video game violence in metanarrative terms, via a single shocking sequence and the self-reflexive subjectivity of "Paul" (Arno Frisch in the original; Michael Pitt in the remake). In spite of these differences, the films' respective treatments of video equally highlight the presentness of the medium to itself—focusing, in particular, on the effects of video's temporal mode on perception and subjectivity—and thereby index the intermedial fractures that emerge between video and film representation.

Video and Violence

The title of *Benny's Video* is significant in that, rather than focusing on the character of Benny or his crime, it emphasizes the means through which the central crime is recorded, displayed, discovered, and possibly inspired. Benny is consistently presented in the film as being emotionally and morally dissociated from the act of murder he has perpetrated, his behavior following the crime being enigmatic and ambiguous, and so the video of the incident (as well as subsequent videos Benny makes of himself and his parents) is not just the best but perhaps the only testament to the murder.[6] Video mediates the crime at every level of the film narrative: the pretext for the girl visiting Benny's apartment is to see his array of video equipment and home video footage; the killing is carried out in a way that strongly echoes the slaughter of the pig in the video the pair views, using the same weapon and means (when we see the girl's corpse it is clear that Benny's final, lethal shot of the bolt gun is to the back of the girl's skull, the point at which the pig is shot in Benny's video); the viewer witnesses the incident only through video, as the film camera rests on the output monitor of the video camera in Benny's bedroom for the entire sequence; Benny's "confession" of his crime to his parents consists of him playing this video on the television while they are watching the evening news; the parents' own complicity in covering up the crime is established via a video of their conversation that Benny presents to the police; and so on. The film's opening also signals that its mode of representation is skewed toward video, as the first shot to appear on-screen is the video of the killing of the pig, footage that is rewound so that the animal's death can be replayed in slow motion, at which point the screen cuts to static. This sequence is significant for a number of reasons, among them its demonstration of the temporal manipulation to which video is readily subjected and of the relationship video has to reality, the actual on-screen death of the pig underscoring the sense of stark realism we tend to associate with raw video footage, as opposed to fictional film's carefully staged and framed mimesis.[7] At the end of the sequence the title of the film and the name of its director are displayed in bright red capital letters superimposed onto a screen filled with visual and aural static, which Peter Brunette described, we recall, as "Haneke's universal signifier for the medium as such, as pure form."[8] Like the title, this opening suggests that the true subject of the film is not what is captured by the first video (or the subsequent videos) and is not even Benny, the presence behind the camera, but rather the medium itself.

The visual and aural static that signals the termination of the opening video here clearly refers back to the presence of the same at the ending of *Der siebente Kontinent* and, like Haneke's previous film, suggests that a nonfilmic medium has infiltrated the work's very mode of representation. In *Benny's Video*, this infiltration is unambiguous from the outset of the film (as opposed to *Der siebente Kontinent*, where television's entry into the film is made explicit only during the final scene). However, the overall sense of internal estrangement that characterizes the representational strategies of the earlier film—including the black spacers and the juxtaposition of televisual close-ups and quick cuts with long takes—is far less prominent in *Benny's Video*.[9] As a film it offers less resistance to video than *Der siebente Kontinent* does to television, though this can be attributed as much to a flexibility in the mimetic structure of video as to stylistic considerations on Haneke's part. As Yvonne Spielmann points out in her remarkably detailed study of the medium, video as a system of representation differs from film in that it has no fixed cinematic space for display, and differs from television in that it is not presented collectively or in a regular sequence of programming: "There can be no particular place and no fixed dispositive sequence for the generation, transmission, and display of electronic representations of visuality. Instead, video contains multiple audiovisual possibilities for transforming audio and visual signals."[10] This lack of a definable video *dispositif* is deeply related to video's spatiotemporal mode of absolute presentness; this "video presence" insinuates itself into the film's image system in ways that demonstrate the remarkable flexibility of the video medium. While *Der siebente Kontinent*'s erratic shifts in time frame and radically delimited mise-en-scène are factors of the profound contrast between the film image's visual and temporal rhythms and television's audiovisual content, in *Benny's Video* the video sequences do little to disrupt the film's temporal and spatial rhythms. There are no black spacers and few disconcerting jumps between rapid- and long-take montage. The video sequences are, to be sure, clearly demarcated from the film itself—the former are characterized by a different image quality and amateur framing and camera movement—yet the transitions to videos within the film are smooth, often not involving a cut at all. Generally, the videos are presented via close-ups of monitors within the film, which then often dominate the entire cinematic frame, but these representations tend to supplement, rather than undermine or estrange themselves from, the film narrative. Even when videos present previous events from the film's narrative, including the murder, the nature of the medium itself accounts for these reinsertions into the film's time frame, in keeping with Haneke's avowed refusal to employ cinematic flashbacks.[11]

Yet this immediacy of video, the very quality of the medium that allows it to insinuate itself into virtually any situation, tends to problematize any understanding of it as a form of image making. In one of the most famous theorizations of the medium, "Video: The Aesthetics of Narcissism," Rosalind Krauss thus characterizes video not in terms of an image technology but rather a particular subjective-perceptual situation: "This is why it seems inappropriate to speak of a physical medium in relation to video. For the object (the electronic equipment and its capabilities) has become merely an appurtenance. And instead, video's real medium is a psychological situation, the very terms of which are to withdraw attention from an external object—an Other—and invest it in the Self."[12] Video's capacity for self-representation is collapsed into its definition, but only through its projection onto a given subject, who also becomes the object of representation. In fact, this conception of the "video aesthetic" subordinates representation almost entirely to the mode of visual experience that characterizes narcissism: reflection. While representation-as-reflection provides an intriguing theoretical premise for video's capacity for immediate visual feedback and self-representation, the Narcissus model adopted by Krauss and many subsequent theorists is burdened by our received associations with the myth, namely vanity and self-obsession. These problematic associations, in relation to Benny's unique subjectivity, will be discussed in the next section; the ideas of reflexivity and narcissism are introduced here to approach the complex differences between the representations of film and video that are interrogated in Haneke's film, particularly in the presentation of the act of violence around which the plot revolves.

Like television, video cannot be categorized with photography and film as an image-based medium; similarly, video offers a "non-image" in relation to film. Spielmann is very clear about this distinction:

> [E]ven if compatible characteristics of recording can be discerned in both of the analog media—film and video—a relevant material difference in the status of the technical images remains. The electronically recorded "image," which is then transferred to a display medium and mostly projected onto a screen, deserves this designation only on condition that the continuous flow of the signals, through which an electronic image can be evoked, is kept in mind. In tune with its unstable and incoherent character and in the interest of precision, I, therefore, suggest separating the transformative characteristics of video anchored in the signal processes conceptually from the entity of the image limited in space/time, perhaps as "tableau," surround, or "frame."[13]

Electronic media, whose visual component is referred to by Spielmann as "pictoriality"—a term denoting "flexible, unstable, nonfixed forms of the image"—instead of "imagery," is clearly informatic rather than imagistic in its perceptual disposition and technical basis.[14] In a very real sense, Spielmann asserts, video consists of the organization and reorganization of pure noise into visible and audible information: "video in its radical media form has to be actually allotted to the category of noise rather than to a consistent type of image."[15] Lev Manovich likewise supports an informatic, as opposed to imagistic, understanding of displays such as radar and television, which relay information in real time: "What this means is that the image, in a traditional sense, no longer exists! And it is only by habit that we still refer to what we see on the real-time screen as 'images.'"[16] The audiovisual static that ends *Der siebente Kontinent* and opens *Benny's Video*, then, can signify both an absence *and* a plenitude of televisual or video information, as this noise is the raw informatic material out of which is translated identifiable pictorial and audio signals. Spielmann also notes that sound and picture share a common basis in this uniform audiovisual noise; thus, the visual and aural components of video do not preexist their output on the monitor: "we see and hear how lines are bent and spacing between image lines is changed."[17] Sound input can be in fact be registered visually, as shifting lines or colors, and vice versa; this "interchangeability of audio and video signals" is indicative of the profound paradox underpinning the video apparatus and its popular understanding.[18] The medium of video is at once considered one of the most immediate and "realistic" modes of representation and yet is simultaneously one of the most nebulous and protean; its relationship to perceived reality—to actual configurations of light, bodies, and sounds—is entirely incidental to its output. Being composed solely of electronic information, video can in fact be generated internally and without the use of a camera.

It is indeed video's incidental nature, coupled with its ability to simultaneously receive and reproduce its signal, that makes the form so eminently capable of self-representation. This is likely what prompts so many comparisons between the video apparatus and the mirror: neither offers any inherent *resistance* to its visual input. This is not to say that video's reproductions are not transformative, since the medium's output is qualitatively transfigured in dimensionality, intensity, temporality, and form relative to its input. Until high-definition digital video was introduced, the medium presented to us relatively degraded visual likenesses of real-world objects and events, particularly in comparison with film—thus its designation as a "cool" medium in McLuhan's categorization. Video's primary advantage over film, however, rests in the apparatus's capacity for perpetual monitoring and voluminous recording and in its production of a seemingly endless chain of audiovisual representation. The structure of *Benny's Video* draws on this aspect of the medium superbly, presenting a series of interrelated videos that support and advance the plot almost independently of the film image. Nearly every major plot point involves a viewing situation that leads to a new video recording, which in turn leads to another viewing, then another recording, and so on: The viewing of the pig video catalyzes the video of the murder of the girl with the same weapon. Then, Georg and Anna's viewing of the girl's killing prompts their discovery of Benny's crime and their decision to dispose of the girl's corpse, ostensibly to protect their son. Near the end of the film, it is revealed that Benny has recorded his parents' self-incriminating conversation, and he screens the footage for the police as evidence of Georg and Anna's crime. In the film's final shot, the security cameras and video monitors at the police station record and display the parents' arrest and their ambiguous and tense encounter with Benny following this revelation. Were these videos screened in isolation from the film images, one can imagine, the basic plot structure of the film would remain largely intact.

Video is indeed present at every prominent event in the story; during the key scene of the girl's murder and its immediate aftermath, video is the sole means by which the film presents the incident, blurring the boundaries separating the mimetic content of the videos within the film from the content of the film itself. The disorienting opening, in which the pig killing video is shown, blurs these lines as well. This aspect of *Benny's Video* prompts Vinzenz Hediger, in his analysis of the film, to comment that "[v]ideo . . . threatens film's epistemic privilege."[19] Such an assertion, while interesting in itself, is very nearly beside the point; film scarcely contests video's claims to expository or epistemic priority in *Benny's Video*. It is in fact the intermedial relationship *between* film and video, rather than any agonistic confrontation involving the two media, that sustains their mutual expression of an act of violence and its aftereffects. Furthermore, just as the intermedial void obtaining between film and television in *Der siebente Kontinent* indicates the impossibility of understanding the act of collective suicide even as the void serves as the clearest manifestation of this act, the interrelationship of film and video here indexes the *unrepresentability* of violent murder even as it "represents" the unthinkable act itself.

The scene in which violence and video converge most explicitly in the film is of course the protracted murder of the unnamed girl, presented in the film as occurring "live," in a single long take, yet mediated completely through the video monitor that the film camera comes to rest upon immediately after the first shot is fired by Benny. Haneke describes the scene as follows: "[T]he viewer does not get to see the murder—it takes place almost exclusively offscreen and we can only hear what's happening—instead the viewer can only see a TV set and on this TV set, which is showing the adolescent murderer's room, which he himself is recording with his video camera, there is nothing to be seen: it is only our fantasy—spurred on by the noises—that enlivens the screen."[20] The director's interpretation of the scene's psychological impact, as well as the visual-ethical strategy that underpins it, is emblematic of a great number of similar considerations of offscreen violence in Haneke's oeuvre that similarly discount or ignore the added element of the video recording and representation within this particular scene.[21] Other than its signaling to the viewer that the act is being recorded (and utilizing the monitor as a novel way of relegating the violent act itself to offscreen space), the scene is not generally considered in substantially different terms from similar murders in *Funny Games* and *Le temps du loup* that also occur in the visual out-of-field but do not indicate the presence of other forms of mediation in the diegetic space.[22] And yet, I argue, the film's depiction of the video monitor during the murder substantially alters the nature of the act, even if the violence is not represented on-screen via video any more than via film. In terms of visual association, for instance, the presence of video during the murder of the girl recalls the presentation of the actual death of the pig in the video that opens the film (which Benny and the girl view just before the murder).

As Michael Lawrence points out, "By prefiguring the killing of the girl with the killing of the pig, Haneke's film brings the real (the death of the pig) into an overdetermined narrative relationship with a simulation of reality (the death of the girl)."[23] The film is, in effect, co-opting the correlation that video has obtained with media representations of actual violence and death—both internally, in connection with the video of the pig, and more generally, in television news footage of war zones, acts of terrorism, rioting, natural disasters, and other such events (some of which are featured in a news broadcast that Benny watches with his parents earlier in the film). Thus, video violence decisively diverges from the simulated violence of fictional films, which Benny himself describes as involving "ketchup and plastic." Peter Brunette comments that the shift in attention to the video monitor during the girl's murder amounts to "the substitution of the representation of violence for the 'real' violence";[24] however, what propels the scene is not *a* representation of violence, but rather the represent*ability* of violence and the fact that video has become much more closely associated with representations of "real" violence than narrative film. In this sense, the added level of mediation through the monitor within the film does not distance the viewer further from the represented event; on the contrary, it brings the fictional murder closer to immediate (or "unmediated") "reality" via the medium of video.

Haneke's strategy of intermedial expression in *Benny's Video*, then, is substantially different from his strategy in the staging of violent events in offscreen space in other films, though both bring to bear questions of presence and absence as they relate to documenting reality. There are in fact a number of potential criticisms of the more or less prevalent idea that Haneke stakes out a higher ethical position than commercial cinema by not "representing" acts of violence in his films. One is that relegating the acts visually to the proximal out-of-field but making them audible and subsequently presenting us with the blood and corpses remaining in their aftermaths does not in any way constitute a "nonrepresentation" of violence. As Brunette observes, the sounds of screaming and weapons being used is in fact "a kind of 'immediate' representation . . . that doesn't rely on codes or signs as much as visual images do."[25] Another major criticism of the strategy is that the confinement of violent acts to offscreen space generally only applies to *simulated* or fictitious violence and death. Haneke quite often depicts real acts of violence on-screen, albeit in very specific forms: the killing of animals and the "documentary" violence of television news footage. Along with the killing of the pig in this film, Haneke's cinema features the actual on-screen deaths of fish (*Der siebente Kontinent*), a horse and goat (*Le temps du loup*), and a rooster (*Caché*). Additionally, as mentioned above, many of his films feature television news footage of actual conflict and violence, and *Benny's Video* presents a particularly interesting instance of the characters' reactions upon viewing such a broadcast. As Benny and his mother watch footage of an Austrian race riot and a bombing in the former Yugoslavia, much of which is presented via a close-up of the television screen, Georg enters the room. He asks Anna, who appears intently absorbed in the program, what is happening in the news, and she replies, "Nothing." When he asks again, she repeats, "I don't know. Nothing." This mirrors Georg's response in *Der siebente Kontinent* after being questioned about his apparent nightmare involving the moving poster image. Perhaps, like that other non-image, television here presents us with a perceptual void, an affirmation of nothingness that renders "nothing" an appropriate and affirmative response rather than an evasion of the question. Inundated with media representations of actual human violence, it is implied, the viewer cannot situate her- or himself so as to reconcile television's contents with real events, or even with information about such events.[26] Catherine Wheatley thus interprets Anna's replies as evidence of television's effacement of the past, its foreclosure of any real engagement with reality, through its temporal mode of liveness, reiterating Mary Ann Doane's assertion that "television thrives on its own forgettability."[27] Brunette similarly considers the exchange an indication of "a developing Haneke critique of the empty form of television news that endlessly repeats itself with apparently different content each time, but whose fixed formal structure prevents any real difference—and thus, real communication—from appearing."[28] Such interpretations fall easily into step with the previous chapter's account of television as non-image. However, there remains an interesting dichotomy that presents itself in this scene's relationship to the murder video, whereby Anna's situation as a viewer of actual violence who nevertheless sees "nothing" directly opposes the film viewer's (and later, Benny's parents') situation with respect to the video of the murder, which visually represents "nothing" and yet conveys some sense of the "reality" of violence. At the root of this seeming contradiction is the issue of the representability of violence, particularly within the media of video, television, and film.

There is an intriguing remark made by Oliver Speck in his book-length study of Haneke, *Funny Frames*; the author posits that the director "restores the violence that is always already present in representation."[29] If one provisionally accepts this assertion—and overlook the seemingly self-contradictory notion that something "always already present" may be "restored"—then the next proposition would be to identify where and how this violence of representation comes about. Is the violence inflicted upon the original object of representation by means of the apparatus of representation itself, or is it inflicted upon the viewer of the representation by its authors or producers? The first approach could loosely be termed "iconoclastic," its violent character resulting from a violation of objects' and beings' natural or inherent resistance toward being "recreated" mimetically. The second approach might be called representation's "sociopsychological" violence, though of course it drastically predates this contemporary discourse; it perceives a violation of the viewer's sensibilities through the inherent danger of mistaking the represented for the real, or at least of bringing the two into an unstable relationship.

Needless to say, the first approach has largely fallen out of favor, in Western culture at least, while the second remains an acceptable proposition and is in fact often used to account for Benny's actions in studies of Haneke's film. Both approaches locate violence in a violation of the realm of the real, and of the subject's genuine being-in-the-world, by the representational; the inherent violence of representation is revealed as a breaking of taboo, in this case the taboo of disturbing the sacrosanct dimension of the real. Yet most discourse regarding violence and representation remains centered around the representation of violence rather than the violence of representation, which suggests that violence itself—as an unmistakably real phenomenon—shares the real's almost sacred dimension. That is, violence, as an intrusion on the domain of the real (hence there being a general violence of representation), is not simply the defining characteristic of the breaking or violation of taboo; "real violence" also attains its own "sacred" status, inherently resisting and defying simulation. A specific approach to the representation of violence, then, would be to identify a violation, by representation, of violence itself, of violence as a fundamental, existential-ontological facet of the real. Furthermore, this self-reflexive approach would be premised on the fact that violence is characterized by qualities that are not only themselves unrepresentable but also define the very limits of representation—namely, pain and death.

In *The Body in Pain* (1985), Elaine Scarry conceives of pain as the foundation for affirmation and denial, albeit a foundation that simultaneously marks out an absolute distance between self and other: "So, for the person in pain, so incontestably and unnegotiably present is it that 'having pain' may come to be thought of as the most vibrant example of what it is to 'have certainty,' while for the other person it is so elusive that 'hearing about pain' may exist as the primary model of what it is 'to have doubt.' Thus pain comes unsharably into our midst as at once that which cannot be denied and that which cannot be confirmed."[30] The utter presence of pain to the subject experiencing it is its defining quality—as Scarry puts it, "the most crucial fact about pain is its *presentness*"[31]—and as such it not only articulates the gulf of experience separating beings whose existences are otherwise shared, but also highlights the impossibility of pain's representation, as it allows no medium of communication for or reproduction of itself or its attributes.[32] Pain remains a uniquely situated affect that evokes in an observer a range of responses, from sympathy to discomfort to excitation. This affective indefinability of pain, which turns upon a number of vastly different intersubjective and power relations, in turn deeply influences and contextualizes our perception of violence.[33]

Thus, while the purpose, or at least the tangible result, of violence is the infliction of harm rather than pain (the intentional infliction of pain over and above harm being the province of torture, a specialized mode of violence), pain is the aspect of violence that anchors it in the unfolding of the present and confirms its effects. Violence, Scarry implies, is neither accountable nor recollectable and only enters a given situation *im*mediately, as event. What, then, are we viewing in a scene from a film, television program, video game, or video that we identify as "violent," and is there a substantial difference between viewing a representation of actual violence and viewing one of simulated violence? As I have stated, Haneke willingly depicts the former but scarcely ever the latter, implying that it is in fact simulated violence that carries a more powerful representational taboo and thus constitutes a greater obscenity, though dominant cultural mores would suggest that the reverse is true. The point that Vivian Sobchack makes about on-screen death also applies to violence in general: "whereas death is generally experienced in fiction films as representable and often excessively visible, in nonfiction or documentary films it is experienced as confounding representation and exceeding visibility."[34] The justification for the medial representation of simulated violence is, quite obviously, that no actual harm has been committed to obtain it, yet it is for this very reason, Haneke's approach implies, that the simulation of violence is a greater sacrilege: a "representation" of actual violence presents us with the very *unrepresentability* of actual pain and death, whereas simulated violence carries the presumption that violence *is* representable, that it can be staged independently of pain and harm. That is, simulated violence violates not only the sacred space of the spatiotemporal real, but also the sacredness of the unique, unrepeatable, and terrible event of violence itself.[35]

Because it does not represent the narrative's fictional violence directly (in visual terms at least), Benny's video preserves a sense of the obscenity of violence and death, the latter of which is referred to by André Bazin as "the unique moment par excellence."[36] Video, of all existent media, brings representation closest to the present moment (through the near-simultaneity of recording and reproduction) and to its own apparatus (through its potential for self-representation, or what others have identified as reflexivity). These factors would suggest that video has the greatest potential of any medium to isolate or extract the properties of a unique event from its actual spatiotemporal situation, just as photography is able to extract from movement the poses that completely elude the perception of the subject in time. And yet video, like film before it, has demonstrably failed to capture the *event* of death, only in fact confirming its utter unrepresentability. An understanding of this confirmation of unrepresentability was slow to emerge in film and media theory. For instance, Bazin proposed that film is capable of formerly unthinkable acts of obscenity:

> [T]wo moments in life radically rebel against this concession made by consciousness: the sexual act and death. Each is in its own way the absolute negation of objective time, the qualitative instant in its purest form. Like death, love must be experienced and cannot be represented . . . without violating its nature. This violation is called obscenity. The representation of a real death is also an obscenity, no

> longer a moral one, as in love, but metaphysical. We do not die twice. In this respect, a photograph does not have the power of film; it can only represent someone dying or a corpse, not the elusive passage from one state to the other.[37]

Subsequently, however, it was demonstrated that this "elusive passage" of death itself eluded even a recording that extracted twenty-four poses per second from a dying body. Sobchack notes this fact with respect to experiments in filming death that culminated in

> always disappointing post hoc attempts to "find" and "see" the *exact* moment of death in nonfiction films through a close inspection of every frame recording the event. Such spatial and temporal dissection echoes several of Zeno's paradoxes that, in dissecting space and movement into their component "objective" parts, undo the experience and achievements of both—and, in relation to the present discussion, this dissection "undoes" what was merely the illusion of the representation of death to leave us with the continuing mystery and unrepresentability of its actual fact.[38]

The opening of *Benny's Video* echoes such an attempt to pinpoint the exact moment of death: the killing of the pig is replayed in slow motion and paused directly after the shot from the bolt gun, as if Benny is attempting "to locate the exact split second of death," a moment on the tape that represents not the still-living animal or its corpse but the event of death itself.[39] The exercise appears, of course, to be as futile in video as it is in film.

Video does offer a different perspective from film, however, in that its material representation is not imagistic but rather informatic and signaletic, and thus it does not parse time into a series of photographic instants, one of which would theoretically coincide with the "unique moment" of death. Video's "fluid pictoriality" does not segment time;[40] instead, it electronically represents a given audiovisual situation that always exists in an unfinished form, in the midst of being "written" to the monitor. Thus, a "freeze-frame" of a video is a different entity than a frame of film, as it depicts an incomplete stage of information transmission rather than an instantaneous, temporally delimited image. It would stand to reason, then, that the precise moment of death would be identifiable in some part of the video at some stage of its signal process. Yet death remains fundamentally elusive to any endeavor to locate it visually as a temporal singularity, even in video, simply because it is not a part or component of a given space-time and therefore cannot be identified among any space-time's contents after the fact. Instead, death remains an event that changes the situation itself, irreversible and thus unrepresentable. Death fails to obtain within any part of video's data set, and the medium demonstrates that the event of death comes to pass not *between* instants—such as between the frames of a filmstrip—but rather *outside* of the sensible or representable elements of a given situation. Deleuze alludes to this unrepresentability of death in *The Logic of Sense*, stating the following:

> For example, the perception of death as a state of affairs and as a quality, or the concept "mortal" as a predicate of signification, remain extrinsic (deprived of sense) as long as they do not encompass the event of dying as that which is actualized in the one and expressed in the other. Representation must encompass an expression *which it does not represent*, but without which it itself would not be "comprehensive," and would have truth only by chance or from outside.[41]

The actual event of dying, Deleuze states, cannot occupy the same plane as representation, but representation must nonetheless somehow encompass this impossible fact of death or doom itself to incompletion and incomprehensibility.

The primary strength of Haneke's presentation of the murder in *Benny's Video* is that, by relegating the visual signifiers of violence and death to the out-of-field, its signifying structure adopts a position indicative of the very extradimensionality of death, which is always in excess of the sensible—and hence the representable—field of a given situation. The medium of video itself, with its maximal relation to the present in temporal terms and to representational realism in spatial terms, provides a limit test for the extent to which violence may be represented without positive signifiers—in other words, in and through its very unrepresentability. In their introduction to the essay collection *On Michael Haneke*, Brian Price and John David Rhodes approach such an understanding of *Benny's Video* and extend it to the director's work as a whole:

> The ethical dynamic at work here exists instead in the relay between the images we see and the images we do not see or, more accurately, between the images we see and the activities that have not been represented as images. The image, therefore, becomes a site of relay and of deferral—not a site of lack in a Lacanian sense, but a mode of deferral in which we are pointed to another site, one that could nevertheless at any moment be rendered obscenely, pornographically.[42]

The visual field continually defers violence-as-obscenity to another site, a site that is never reached in Haneke's films (with the notable exception of the act of suicide in *Caché*, which will be discussed in chapter 5). The existence of this site, though, is paradoxically affirmed more strongly in its nonrepresentation than it would be if it entered the visual field. Thus, it is the intermedial void between film and video that provides the affective and signifying structure for what Bazin terms, in reference to death, a "metaphysical obscenity":

something that is never admitted into a given visual or discursive field—accessible through representation—because it defies the sensible register of existence itself.[43] The associations that obtain between video and death in Haneke's film, then, utilize the medium of video not only as an index of realism in representation but also, in relation both to film and to actuality, as an index of absolute *nonrepresentability*.

Benny's Video places its titular medium at the center of the film's plot, its sensible field, and its thematic and theoretical approach to the question of violence and representation. It is not difficult, therefore, to consider the eponymous character somewhat incidental to the film and its central act of violence; as Maximilian Le Cain puts it, the video apparatus "steals the act from Benny, so to speak."[44] Benny's enigmatic and ambiguous agency and subjectivity, as presented within the film, tend to point toward a relatively simplistic interpretation of the character, an interpretation that belies the complexity of his unique position vis-à-vis both the video apparatus within the film and the film itself. This simplified view of Benny holds that the character remains unaware of the differences between reality and representation—or, rather, the differences between the film he is *in* and the videos he views and creates *within* the film. In fact, as will be discussed in the next section, Benny's situation within the intermedial schism between film and video is far more complicated than this, and challenges our associations with respect to both media as they relate to actuality, action, and (self-) perception.

Benny and Narcissus

The most common position adopted by those who seek correlations between actual violent behavior and representational media focuses on the manner in which such forms of entertainment erode or threaten a subject's "reality principle." It is said that, for a desensitized consumer, exposure to simulations of violence has the effect of making such representations indistinguishable from real violence, thus increasing the possibility of the consumer's violent response in actual situations or conflicts. A great number of critical responses to and interpretations of *Benny's Video* attribute the protagonist's act of murder to just such an effect. To cite just a few examples: Brigitte Peucker states that Benny "cannot distinguish between simulations and the real"; Mattias Frey echoes this interpretation, asserting that "Benny is unable to distinguish between the actual and the virtual or the real and the mediated"; Robin Wood similarly posits that "the constant environment of violence in sound and image has blurred any distinction between the real and the fabricated"; D. I. Grossvogel notes that Benny acts "as if the image were both the only reality and its exculpation"; and so on.[45] Though clearly ubiquitous in connection with the film—as in any reportage of actual cases of violence even tangentially related to violent media—the theory that represented violence provokes an acute weakening of the reality principle in a given subject is both syllogistic and premised upon a conflation of at least two distinct problematics.

The inability to distinguish reality from representation is a completely different phenomenon than the heightened levels of aggression that some theorize are an effect of exposure to violent imagery in media. Furthermore, the neoplatonic problem of the confusion of reality and representation has a plethora of potential consequences, with violence to oneself or another being a relatively small, though serious, facet that is not necessarily connected to the emulation of the violent behavior of a fictional character. To take a much different fictional character than Benny as an example, Don Quixote, who confuses fantastical romances with reality, causes himself a great deal of harm by acting out the most virtuous and high-minded of roles, that of the knight-errant; to draw on any number of actual examples, a young boy who breaks a leg attempting to fly off of his roof like Superman or gives himself a hernia by attempting to lift a car like the Hulk has not committed an act of violence, but has still brought harm upon himself by emulating a fantastical character. These imitators have not acted immorally but have simply chosen the wrong attributes of their respective fictional heroes to apply to actual behavior. They emulate unreal abilities—flight, super strength, and the martial prowess to combat monsters—rather than moral virtues (chivalry, a sense of justice, or courage, for example). A great deal of the rhetoric directed against media texts that have a perceived negative or violent influence upon impressionable minds has to do with the fact that the characters with whom impressionable minds may identify are considered morally objectionable, rather than with the work's objectively violent content. To cite an obvious illustration of this point, Mel Gibson's *The Passion of the Christ* (2004) contains graphic depictions of torture and bloodletting, but it is understood that the many parents who took their children to the film would have expected the children to identify with Jesus, who submits to flagellation and crucifixion for the salvation of mankind, rather than with the Roman soldier wielding the whip.[46]

The main weakness of the theory of correlation between violent media and violent behavior is that it considers both the identification with aggressive or violent characters and the confusion of representation and reality as manifestations of a single problem. In Benny's case, though he is shown watching the video of a violent film—the self-consciously schlocky and parodic Troma film *The Toxic Avenger* (1984; directed by Lloyd Kaufman and Michael Herz)—and views the pig killing video immediately before the murder is committed, he does not in any way meet the criteria set out by the theory of correlation. There is no aggression in his act, no model for his action presented in any other media within the film (unless it is the offscreen farmhand who slaughters the pig), and no evidence that he lacks the capacity to distinguish between real and simulated violence, as he even explains to the girl during the film viewing scene that the violence is faked using "ketchup and plastic." Even in the absence of such elements, however, there is a deep connection between Benny's actions and the video apparatus that mediates his perception of reality, and this connection is much more profound and complicated than an apparent inability to differentiate the real from the represented. As Roy Grundmann aptly puts it, "Benny may be desensitized, but he is not duped. He knows perfectly well that video is not reality. The point is, he still prefers video."[47]

Benny's perceptions are indeed to a large extent mediated by video. For instance, while the window shades in his bedroom are permanently drawn, a video camera pointed through a gap in the curtains delivers a live feed of the street view to a monitor. His social interactions are depicted as being similarly mediated: he is present at two gatherings that his sister hosts at the family's apartment, but we never *see* him there since the parties are presented via the videos he records, and he is the one holding the camera. Benny's modes of interaction with the world hold implications not for his ability to perceive reality, though, but for the structure of his subjectivity, the manner in which he orients himself in his milieu. As Fredic Jameson states, film is a uniquely desubjectivizing medium with respect to the viewer, an effect that in video extends also to the videographer:

> Interesting analyses (mostly from a Lacanian perspective) have been offered in recent film theory of the relationship between the mediation of the filmic machine and the construction of the viewer's subjectivity—at once depersonalized, and yet still powerfully motivated to reestablish the false homogeneities of the ego and of representation. I have the feeling that mechanical depersonalization (or decentering of the subject) goes even further in the new medium [of video], where the auteurs themselves are dissolved along with the spectator.[48]

Benny occupies the decentered "center" of a system of representation that implicates him both as the videographer and as the viewer without embodying or including him as either. In fact, video appears to suppress or negate Benny's self-image in an almost literal sense; the only indications we have of Benny's presence in the early videos are when individuals being videotaped acknowledge him in some way—Georg irritably waving him away in the pig killing video, the winner of his sister Evi's "pilot game" showing him the cash he has amassed—and such gestures pass through Benny and instead seem directed at the viewer(s) of the videos. Behind the video camera, Benny is already a post hoc viewer of the situation even as he records it, and he is present within the situation only as a kind of faceless observing presence. Significantly, Benny himself does not appear in any of his own videos until after the murder has taken place, and signs of his growing self-awareness begin to emerge. This uncoupling of the self and the visual field—and its attendant desubjectivization of the videographer—is endemic to video, making it all the more puzzling that the model of Narcissus is so often invoked when conceptualizing the video apparatus and also appears in certain assessments of Benny's character.

As previously noted, the term "narcissism" in its most general and widely understood sense suggests extreme vanity and self-obsession, particularly as it relates to one's own image or appearance. However, Krauss's influential essay on "the aesthetics of narcissism" approaches the model in a more psychologically sophisticated manner. The perceived potential for immediate reflexivity in the video apparatus—and the way this potential is utilized in early works of video art—is linked to an imbalance between representation and the real wherein the represented or reflected image of the self is never fully differentiable from the embodied subject:

> [T]he nature of video performance is specified as an activity of bracketing out the text and substituting for it the mirror-reflection. The result of this substitution is the presentation of a self understood to have no past, and as well, no connection with any objects that are external to it. For the double that appears on the monitor cannot be called a true external object. Rather it is a displacement of the self which has the effect . . . of transforming the performer's subjectivity into another, mirror, object.[49]

In applying a similar model to Benny, by way of Baudrillard's concept of a mediatized Narcissus, Mattias Frey posits that the adolescent Benny is pre- or non-Oedipal. In other words, the character does not individuate according to a sexual schema but rather through an enactment of the represented violence that video and television inundate him with. He thereby consummates an autoerotic relationship using the medium that he perceives as fostering his subjectivity, his ego-representation, and his "libidinal" power: "If the Oedipal myth in its various hetero- and homoerotic forms functions to reproduce the idea that human subjectivity is sexually realized in the bonded, love relationship, then the Baudrillardian Narcissus myth as found in *Benny's Video* instructs Benny that mediated, digitally manipulable violence is the 'authentic' experience in a 'me' world without connections, so why not 'see how it is'?"[50] The crucial problem with this attribution of narcissism to Benny's situation—or, indeed, to the entire aesthetic of video—is that it forces one to locate and identify a subjectivity or self-image *within* the representation. While this is not difficult in the works of self-interaction and autoportraiture that Krauss cites as examples, the credibility of this interpretation is strained in Frey's account of Benny's motivations: "Benny wants to be the agent in a killing, but more importantly, he wants to *see* himself on his monitor killing, he wants to be able to rewind, slow-down, and edit the act on his console. For Benny, the experience of this after-the-fact 'virtual reality' is even more dramatic than the actual deed itself . . . e.g. he spends much more time viewing and re-viewing the video than cleaning up the body."[51] If Benny had actually wanted to videotape and subsequently view himself killing the girl, though, he has decisively failed—the video depicts him on-screen only as he runs past the camera to grab more ammunition for the bolt gun, pleading for the girl to stop screaming as he does so. Also, when he eventually replays the video for his parents—a video that is clearly unedited—he appears visibly agitated and looks away from the screen when the girl's screams begin, although his parents' attention remains riveted to the video. Benny is shown in the interim watching the video recording he made of himself after the murder, but when he rewinds this video he leaves the room before the murder begins to play itself out in reverse. Benny does, then, videotape and view himself, but this form of interaction with video evidently occurs as a result of, rather than as a motivating factor for, the murder. If one proposes to ascribe narcissistic tendencies to Benny and interpret such tendencies—along with the video apparatus itself—as having a role in the murder, then one must adopt a different approach to the idea of narcissism both in relation to video and to Benny.

In *Understanding Media*, Marshall McLuhan also uses the Narcissus model in direct connection with a condition of media saturation, but in a very different sense than Krauss, Baudrillard, and other theorists. For McLuhan, the myth presents a situation not of self-love or autoeroticism but rather of self-misrecognition: "[T]he wisdom of the Narcissus myth does not convey any idea that Narcissus fell in love with anything he regarded as himself. Obviously he would have had very different feelings about the image had he known it was an extension or repetition of himself."[52] Instead—and in direct contradistinction to the models described above—McLuhan's Narcissus experiences a profound *dissociation* from his own image that is premised upon an "autoamputation" affecting the subject's sensorimotor schema and perceptual field. This amputation, which forestalls the irritation or discomfort resulting from an amplification or overstimulation of sensory power, is comparable to that brought about by the stimulus of audiovisual media: "Such amplification is bearable by the nervous system only through numbness or blocking of perception. This is the sense of the Narcissus myth. The young man's image is a self-amputation or extension induced by irritating pressures. As counter-irritant, the image produces a generalized numbness or shock that declines recognition. Self-amputation forbids self-recognition."[53] *Benny's Video* could almost be considered a parable with this moral or theme, a restaging of the Narcissus myth with an inversion of the central visual motif: rather than a reflecting pool giving back the unrecognized self-image of the subject, Benny has the monitor and speakers, which give back to him the mediated percepts that have been divorced from his immediate sensory experience and dissociated from his embodied self. Benny's direct sense perceptions have been overwritten by the audiovisual apparatus, which is attractive in its malleability and capacity for repetition but delivers an immensely impoverished sensory experience. Benny-as-viewer has superseded Benny-as-seer, and in fact the character, as initially presented in the film, seems to have relinquished his immediate subjective sensory capacity almost entirely. He does not mistake the representations in fictional films for reality and would not fail to recognize himself in such a representation (which is actually where he recognizes himself most fully), but *he has mistaken the gaze of the camera for his own gaze and the microphone for his own ears.* Benny has "amputated" his capacity for direct sensation—for firsthand perceptual and affective experience—from his body and allowed it to take up residence in a new medial apparatus. He has adopted the "new flesh" of the video medium. The film traces the process of Benny's gradual reconnection to direct, embodied sensory experience—his resubjectification—following his tragic encounter with the reality of the girl's murder, which he tells his father he did "to see what it's like."[54] What he has previously lacked—and what Narcissus lacked, in McLuhan's interpretation—is a subjective center through which to process or "develop" these audiovisual percepts and their concomitant affective strata.

The immediate aftermath of the murder presents several image-motifs signaling Benny's crisis of subjectivity, with such images standing in for an almost total lack of affective response on Benny's part. Benny goes to the kitchen, drinks a glass of water, eats a cup of yogurt, uses the toilet, and—after emptying the girl's backpack in what appears to be an ultimately unsuccessful attempt to identify her—does his homework in his room while listening to very loud rock music, with the television and monitor also switched on and the corpse remaining on the floor. He then methodically cleans his bloodstained bedsheet (which he had covered the body with) in the bathtub, moves the corpse to his closet, and mops up the blood that has pooled on the floor, but is interrupted in this activity by a phone call from his friend Ricci. The conversation that ensues is unrevealingly banal—strikingly so, given the recent events in Benny's life—but the viewer begins to witness a change in Benny at this point. He is nude, having disrobed to avoid getting blood on his clothes, and as he speaks on the phone he glances at the wall of the dining room, which is covered with dozens of framed prints or posters of well-known paintings and photographs (along with a few vintage advertisements).[55] Prominently placed among the reproductions (ironically, considering its title) is a sizable poster of René Magritte's *La reproduction interdite* (*Not to be Reproduced*, 1937; see figure 4), which depicts a man looking into a mirror but encountering a representation of his own painted image rather than his reflection, whereas a book (Edgar Allan Poe's *The Narrative of Arthur Gordon Pym*) is reflected normally.

When the camera returns to Benny's face in close-up, he is visibly uncomfortable, almost nauseous-looking, and he lowers his gaze to another set of

Figure 4: A pseudovideographic subjective relation was visualized by the artist decades before the electronic apparatus was realized, profoundly affecting Benny. René Magritte, *La reproduction interdite* (*Not to Be Reproduced*, 1937). Copyright Museum Boijmans Van Beuningen; used with permission.

pictures.[56] He then shifts his attention to the right, toward a large mirror. At this point, Haneke inserts a subtly unsettling shot: Benny appears to be facing and looking directly into a mirror, but the film camera that captures this viewing situation is not present in the apparently reflected image. This effect is achieved by having the camera shoot Benny frontally, framing him within the shot by a white border, and moving the phone and his wristwatch to his right hand (as well as rearranging the desk and other furniture accordingly); Frisch effectively becomes a stand-in for his own reflection (see figure 5). Looking at himself in the mirror, Benny notices a bloodstain just above his hip and appears affected by the discovery. Immediately after this self-encounter Benny videotapes himself smearing the blood over his torso, then he turns the video camera on the girl's corpse.

The idea of self-discovery pervades these sequences, and in this moment Benny seems to gain some form of awareness of his physicality, his own sensory field, and his subjectivity. The effect of this knowledge is ambiguous, however, and it prompts him only to place himself within, rather than behind, the apparatus of representation; video remains a mediator between subject and percept. The Magritte painting offers a particularly compelling figuration of Benny's relationship to himself, all the more so for its being

Figure 5: In a subtly subversive trick shot, Benny appears to look at himself in a mirror, and perceives the bloodstain on his torso. *Benny's Video* (Michael Haneke, 1992).

immediately followed by the "mirror" shot: the artwork presents a mirror that represents rather than reflects, while the cinematic shot presents, via visual tricks in staging and continuity editing, a representation that simulates a reflection. Magritte's absurdist piece provides a startlingly relevant visual figuration both of video and of its determining effects on Benny's relationship with himself, since the malfunctioning mirror within the painting, like a video monitor, repeats the man's image solely as viewer, without offering any change in perspective or encounter with oneself.[57] In fact, if the mirror in the painting also repeated *itself* in its "reflection," it would present precisely the mise en abyme effect that we see in the shot from *Spaceballs*, the epitome of video self-representation. The mirror in *La reproduction interdite* is, from a certain extradimensional perspective, *doubly* reflective, reappropriating the normal catoptric visual circuit and offering what is already a reflection of the reflection, as if another mirror behind the figure is being re-reflected in front of the figure yet somehow occupying the entire surface. Indeed, the concept of video as a doubly reflective medium is suggested by Raymond Bellour, whom Spielmann cites as a revisionist of Krauss's "aesthetics of narcissism": "For Bellour, the nature of the video image derives from the narcissistic mirror situation in such a way that the autoportrait is a *multiple reproduction of the mirror image*, and shows *a doubling of the body and its reflection*."[58] Video may be considered a reflective medium, then, but only insofar as this reflection is always already *doubled* and thus forecloses a direct visual encounter between the subject and his or her own image. In this sense, the seemingly paradoxical title of Magritte's painting is literally enforced by the video apparatus, and the self-encounter of the subject is excluded from the visual field. When Benny sees himself in the mirror, nude and marked by the blood of the girl, it is a revelation not just of his physicality but also of a mode of perception wherein the self is included and embodied rather than rendered transparent, faceless, disembodied, and desensitized.

Benny's encounter with his reflection can easily be interpreted in terms of a return to a Lacanian mirror stage, and thus a return to a symbolic structure of reality centered around subjectivity.[59] In this sense, he has shifted away from video as a desubjectifying medium and toward a reflexive self-image that he continually reencounters from that point on in the film. Regarding this motif, Peter Schwartz points out the proliferation of reflective surfaces the film places in proximity to Benny but draws very different conclusions as to their significance: "Throughout the film, Benny is bracketed by semi-reflective surfaces of metal or glass, often doors. . . . The boy's relations to self, to the world, and to others . . . are a house of mirrors, translucencies, transparencies, opacities, and simulacra."[60] It should be noted, however, that these mirrored surfaces are largely absent from the film prior to the murder scene, and hence come into play as indicators of Benny's newly discovered subjective self-relation more so than as images of his disembodiment. The fact that Haneke presents the initial mirror image using the film camera as one pole in the self/image dyad is intriguing in this respect: the camera here assumes the position of what amounts to an *absolute* point of view shot, replacing Benny's physical presence entirely even as he seems to encounter his own figure in the mirror. The film camera implicitly lays claim to a greater flexibility of perception than video is capable of adopting; in narratological terms, the film camera can be "first person" or "third person," whereas the home video camera is always "first-person-as-third-person," relegating the videographer to the exterior space of viewership even during the act of recording a given situation (as the earlier quote from Jameson also suggests; see note 48). It is almost as though Benny is scarcely a seen and seeing presence in *Benny's Video* until after the murder and his encounter with his self-image, at which point he presents himself both to the mirror and to the film camera, in the same gesture, and gains a filmic body at the same moment he gains bodily self-awareness. This is not to say that Benny's embodiment changes the representational structure of the film, but rather that the representational "conundrums" surrounding Benny and his actions, as Vivian Sobchack puts it in a different context, "become intelligible and find their provisional resolution not in abstraction but in the lived body's concrete and active 'sense-ability.'"[61] The grounding of representation in actual sense-experience is portrayed, via film rather than video, as the component that Benny has previously lacked in his immersion within this audiovisual apparatus. Significantly, after viewing the pig video Benny is asked by the girl whether or not he has ever seen a real corpse, and he confesses that at his grandfather's wake he was held up by his father to look into the coffin but closed his eyes. Although he is able to distinguish representations of real violence from fictional violence, and real corpses from fictional ones, Benny is unable to connect such representations with any sensation derived from firsthand experience, even a simply visual one. His unmediated encounter with violence and death—and subsequent encounter with his self-image—prompts him to videotape himself, first touching his own body, then touching the corpse of the girl he has killed, which he rolls over to reveal her face.[62]

The murder and its aftermath, then, provide a pathway from representation to reality via the embodiment of sensation, the primary developer without which media fails to communicate or represent any aspect of subjective or lived experience—any direct engagement with percepts and affects—least of all the unrepresentable qualities that define pain, violence, and death. This, in fact, is what Haneke cites as the inspiration for the film in his interview with Serge Toubiana:

> I was often asked, "What triggered this film?" I remember answering . . . [that] it's something Benny says in the film when his father asks him, "Why did you do that?" And he answers that he wanted to know what it's like. It's a sentence I read once in a magazine that told the story of a crime committed by a boy . . . I don't remember anymore. It was a boy who killed another child or something like that. When the police interrogated him, that was his answer. And I was shocked by that. And for the next two or three years, I collected articles of that kind. And that sentence came up again several times. "I wanted to know what it's like." For me, those are the words of a person who's out of contact with reality. When you learn life and reality only through the media, you have the sense that you're missing something. I'm missing the feeling of reality. If I see only a film, only images, even images of reality, a documentary, I'm always outside. For once I wanted to know what it's like.[63]

Benny's Video juxtaposes the disparate media of video and film in order to evoke an intermedial concept of the phenomenal difference between representation and reality. Simultaneously, and in a related gesture, the narrative theorizes the effects that an encounter with actual violence would have on a desensitized and distantiated individual: resubjectification, self-awareness, and a realization of the experiential underpinnings of representation. Finally, with Benny's act of turning his parents over to the police, the film puts forth the possibility—though it remains ambiguous and unconfirmed—of Benny's development of an ethical component of perception and representation. This last point will be further explored with reference to *Funny Games*, which can be considered in many ways a continuation and expansion of this nascent element in *Benny's Video*.

Funny Games and Medial Ethics

Through my examination of Haneke's treatment of media and violence in *Benny's Video*, I have suggested that the spatiotemporal void that obtains between video representation and actuality conveys the utter immediacy and unrepresentability of pain and death. Thus, Haneke's use of the intermedial relationship between video and film at the moment of the film's central event of violence "represents" the violent act better than any simulated on-screen representation could. Furthermore, subtle changes in Benny's presentation and actions in the wake of this event indicate crucial developments in the character's subjectivity. Benny does not reject the video medium following the murder, but he does begin to renegotiate its relationship to actuality, particularly its relationship to his self-image and bodily self-awareness. If one interprets the ending of the film along the same lines, it would appear to be an extension of Benny's individuation—an indictment of and rebellion against his parents' bourgeois value system, or even against the structure of family itself, and an effectuation of some form of justice for the victim via the exposure (through video) of their complicity. Yet this reading, like practically any one could apply to Benny's gesture, remains deeply ambiguous and troubling. Do Georg and Anna deserve such condemnation, given that they claim to have been motivated by a desire to protect their child in their decision to cover up the murder? Is there an intentionally ethical dimension to Benny's having turned them in, or do his actions betoken the opposite: the boy's persistent state of immaturity, amorality, and even sociopathy? Haneke's depiction of this plot turn seems designed to sustain such ethical questions rather than provide answers for them, and the divergent readings of the film that I have cited indicate that viewers have drawn a range of individual conclusions regarding the moral focus of the film, both in general and with regard to its intriguing central character.

When Haneke set out to make *Funny Games*,[64] which once again concerns the deeper relationships between youth violence and media engagement, his casting of the lead actors seems intended to add still another level of moral ambiguity to *Benny's Video*. Arno Frisch, the actor who played Benny, takes on the role of "Paul," the cheerful psychopath who leads the torture and murder of a bourgeois family. This family's patriarch Georg is played by Ulrich Mühe, who performed as Benny's father in the earlier film. Haneke states that the casting choice was an "inside joke," a qualification that implies that some (likely ironic) significance can be attributed to the actors' presence.[65] But the casting is not the only meaningful link between the films. *Funny Games* can be connected to *Benny's Video* through its similar employment of self-reflexive moments—although here they are more pronounced and metafictional in nature—that are based in an intermedial relation between film and video. As so many interpretations of the film's strategy, including Haneke's, attest, *Funny Games* brings to the forefront the notion of an ethics

Figure 6: "Paul," the main perpetrator of the torture and murder that constitute the film's titular "games," shares a glance and wink of complicity with the spectator. *Funny Games* (Michael Haneke, 1997).

of representation that remains latent in *Benny's Video* and the character of Benny; this ethics becomes focused squarely on the film spectator, the actual consumer of its violent imagery. After examining this interpretation of *Funny Games*, I will investigate the ways in which this ethical question is situated with reference not only to video but also to two other medial configurations the film draws upon: genre and the video game.

In her monograph, Catherine Wheatley puts forth a well-developed, if somewhat presumptuous, theorization of Haneke as a preeminently ethical filmmaker. She is careful to point out that "[h]is cinema is not didactic, but it is educational, for it asks the spectator questions and places them in a position whereby they are able to make up their own mind about the possible answers."[66] The films that most fully embody this mode of spectatorship for Wheatley are *Funny Games* and *Caché*, with the former film provoking this spectatorial stance via its parody of its own ostensible genre—the "home invasion" thriller—and Paul's direct provocation of the spectator. Thirty minutes into the film, Paul looks directly into the camera, smiles, and winks (see figure 6). Later, when outlining the terms of the most important "game" he wishes to play with the family, a bet as to whether or not they can survive for twelve hours, he turns toward the camera and addresses the audience directly, asking "What do you think? Do you think they have a chance of winning?" and questioning "whose side" the viewer is on. As Wheatley points out, through such gestures "Paul does not merely acknowledge the audience as spectators, but he also accuses them of being his very *raison d'être*."[67]

The purpose of such Brechtian maneuvers, as Haneke himself avows in the Toubiana interview, is to cast the film viewer as the "accomplice" of the killers and then to "chastise" the viewer for this role.[68] Shocking the spectators out of their hermetic space of voyeurism, his intention is to make them conscious of their desire for violent spectacle and hence of their complicity in, and victimization by, the film's representation of torture and murder. In short, as Haneke rather bluntly puts it, he attempts "to rape the viewer into independence."[69]

The moral inflections inherent in this approach arise from the dialectical relationship between the spectator's normal affective investment in "violent" media and the spectator's self-conscious detachment from the spectacle such metafilmic gestures induce, as stated clearly in an earlier essay by Wheatley: "From the moment that the spectator is positioned as a moral agent, instinctive response and rational response are dialectical, combining to induce moral sentiment. Haneke thus mobilizes a tension between emotion and reason that perfectly echoes the Kantian conception of how the moral law is felt."[70] Wheatley's interpretation of *Funny Games*' ethical dimension relies on a double play of identification: the audience members are estranged from the fiction by being forced to identify with the antagonist Paul, yet they are also forced at an intellectual level to identify with *themselves* as spectators. Hence, the spectator assumes a moral agency when confronted with the *im*morality of Paul, whose consciousness is presented as being both internal and external to the narrative—he is a character within the film and yet also shares with the viewer an awareness of the fact that the events are staged as spectacle. The viewer's voyeuristic *jouissance* is thus countered and inverted by Paul; we are caught out as willing participants in the family's suffering, even if it is "only a movie." In Wheatley's model, then, our affective engagement with the film—our sympathy for the family and antipathy toward the killers—comes directly into conflict with our consciousness of the fictionality of the narrative, and we seek a moral basis or recourse for our objection to this development.

As provocative as this model is, it relies on narrative more so than medial considerations, reifying the events of the plot and the audience's identification with Paul (or the rejection thereof) even as these elements are presented as representational constructs. To enter into any such direct identification with a central character becomes, as Fredric Jameson points out, a "fatally moral or moralizing" proposition.[71] Any expectation that our absorption into or enjoyment of a work is based on the relatability of its protagonist, who is conceived as a vehicle for the spectator's self-image or ego-representation, *presupposes* a relatively simplistic moral value system. Such notions of audience identification return us to the Quixote problem mentioned earlier in this chapter—partial (moral) exemplification of fictional role models is positive, yet total (delusional) exemplification is negative. Thus, all fictional works are charged with upholding a pseudodidactic ethical function while simultaneously signaling their distance from lived experience. For Jameson, this narrative-psychological model of identification should be replaced by one that accounts for the medial apparatus itself and our situation within it. Hence, there is a conceptual advantage with alternative spectatorial-psychological models such as the Lacanian suture, "in which 'identification' is less the effect of some a priori harmony between my own ego and some external representation of the identity or personality of another, than rather my mesmerization by the empty place of 'interpellation,' for instance, by the returning gaze, from the open screen, of the shot/reverse shot as that empty place becomes ambiguously associated both with myself as spectator and with the other character/interlocutor."[72] In this consideration, the screen is not simply the site of "encounters" (moral or otherwise) between preexisting identities, whether viewer or character, but rather an intriguing and destabilizing emptiness—a productive void—through which new subjective and intersubjective potentialities can be formed.

Marc Vernet, in his important essay "The Look at the Camera" (1983), puts forward a similar perspective. Vernet defines the traditional interpretation of the look as follows: it "attacks the spectator's voyeurism by putting the space of the film and the space of the movie theater briefly in direct contact" and thereby affirms an interlocutional "I/You" between character and viewer.[73] Yet this assumption that the in-camera look's effect holds in all cases—"as if this cinematic figure were homogeneous and unique"[74]—is insufficient for explaining the diversity of its employment, as evidenced, for example, within different genre-specific contexts such as comedies, musicals, and pornography. Paul's look into the camera need not denote a direct exchange of gazes between viewing subjects, then. Instead, it can be understood as an invitation to the audience members to renegotiate the terms of their investment in the representation; it is a violation of the audience's genre-specific expectations and their proper tonal and stylistic presentation as much as, or more so than, it is a violation of the viewing situation and the audience's moral (non-)identification with the film's characters.[75] *Funny Games*' metafilmic gestures are thus additionally intermedial to the extent that, in Stanley Cavell's words, "a genre is a medium."[76]

Indeed, although inserted into an especially harrowing thriller, these asides to the audience resemble, more than anything else, moments from classic sound-film comedies: Oliver Hardy's glances to the audience as he is seeking sympathy for having to put up with Stan Laurel's idiocy; Groucho Marx's remark to the audience that they should think of making a quick trip to the lobby rather than having to sit through Chico's singing lesson in *Horse Feathers* (Norman Z. McLeod; 1932); and of course the mugging and asides to the camera performed by Bugs Bunny, Daffy Duck, and others in any number of the Warner Brothers animated shorts of the 1940s and 1950s. Predictably, Haneke suggests that such moments in *Funny Games* were inspired by his childhood experience watching one such madcap comedy, namely Tony

Richardson's screen adaptation of Henry Fielding's farcical novel *Tom Jones* (1963):

> "Suddenly, about a third of the way through the film," Haneke told me, "the hero, played by Albert Finney, stops in the middle of a chase scene, turns to face the camera—in other words, the viewer—and addresses a few offhand remarks to the audience. Nothing especially racy, but by that simple gesture he shocks the viewer into self-awareness." Though he didn't know it at the time, that moment marked a loss of cinematic innocence that would indelibly mark every film he went on to direct. "After 'Tom Jones,' I began to look behind the mirror, so to speak—to see the cinema with different eyes, and to distrust the storytellers, who claimed to be serving up real life. But my hunger for stories was stronger than ever—I wasn't sure what I was looking for from cinema, but I knew it would have to offer the magic of my first moviegoing experiences without turning me into a passive, voiceless victim of the story—which is to say, of the people behind the story. I wanted movies that enchanted me without exploiting me."[77]

In spite of Haneke's conveniently explanatory anecdote, the question remains as to why we find direct address acceptable as a trope in comedic cinema and seemingly insupportable in the context of a dramatic genre. A possible explanation presents itself, however, if one understands comedy and drama as mediators of fundamentally different modes of affective and perceptual engagement. Film comedy, as Vernet points out, retains a strong connection to vaudeville and burlesque traditions. These attractions are staged with an awareness of a "Third Party" in whose view the humor is played out; this is in fact an essential component of comedy. To be "laughable" is to be potentially laughed *at* from some external perspective. Moreover, the audience whose perspective supplies this comedic element need not necessarily correspond to the *actual* audience in the theater. Thus, for Vernet, film comedy's "behind the scenes look is not destined to the spectator as individual, but rather to a much larger and more abstract entity, the public as a whole or, in an even greater way, to the entire universe taken as a witness for the look."[78] The look into the camera—quintessentially, Oliver Hardy's look—is in this sense an alternate manifestation of the appeal to a divine witness for one's folly and misfortune, the heavenward look of "why me?" On the other hand, dramatic and especially horrific cinema generally derive maximal effectiveness from being staged in extreme isolation from external or public view, so that the performers remain fully immersed in their own pressurized affective situation, lacking any reprieve by, or even means of appealing to, an external agency. In short, drama thrives on intimacy. Hence, the viewer of dramatic genres occupies a privileged position with respect to the on-screen events—a position that is utterly excluded from the action, even in an abstract sense, and to which it is easy to ascribe voyeuristic overtones.

By staging an intermedial intersection between comedic and dramatic genres—applying as he does the tropes of the former to a situation characteristic of the latter—Haneke performs a violation not simply of the zone of spectatorship but also of the medial-representational propriety governing both genres. If one wishes to ascribe an ethical motivation to this violation by referring to the represented events, then it appears that the viewer has been delivered a comeuppance for experiencing a morally questionable "enjoyment" of violent spectacle. What defines the ethical register of viewership, though? Is every act of viewing represented violence a morally reprehensible one, or can one only establish anything like an ethical dimension by referring back to the perceptual and affective structure of a given genre? Perhaps morality, in the context of viewing a film, is not present in the form of an autonomous moral agency brought to bear by each individual filmgoer. Rather, the very conventions of genre seem to constitute a social contract, and it is this contract that determines the ethical value set brought to bear on film narrative and spectator alike. To this extent, "moral engagement" is a variable of the genre-as-medium—a functional derivative of the medium's "message"—and Haneke's intermedial distortion of this ethical code is the primary or only moral infraction that can be identified in *Funny Games*: Haneke has violated the ethical code of genre itself. One can push this interpretation further still, however, by applying to *Funny Games* the notions of video and violence that were developed in the earlier part of this chapter, particularly as they pertain to the film's most startling metacinematic gesture.

In a highly intriguing reading, Scott Durham concludes that *Funny Games* presents the question of violence without any reference to lived reality and therefore addresses violence as an exclusively mediatic construct:

> What is foregrounded in *Funny Games* is not a distance between the forms of social life and the forms of its representation but the Baudrillardian Möbius strip that leads from the "fictions" of the media to the media themselves as a social and institutional power. The media thus appear in this film as the ultimate perpetrators of its violence. . . . In this light, the killers appear within the diegetic world of the film at once as "artifacts" of the media and as their delegated representatives within that subsidiary world. In *Funny Games*, the violence of the characters is secondary to a primary violence of the media, from which it derives.[79]

Paul and his accomplice "Peter" are most assuredly presented as constructions rather than as realistic subjects, as they do not even possess veritable identities within the context of the film. Their names, for one thing, are variable: they address one another, alternately, as Peter and Paul, Tom and

Jerry, and Beavis and Butthead. Also, at one point in the film Paul begins to invent different back stories for Peter to account for his criminality, and both stories—the first of a cruel childhood and sexual abuse, the second of bourgeois anomie—seem to be accepted by Peter in turn as though true. As Daniel Frampton notes, "Peter almost seems to be Paul's creation—he cries when Paul gives him a deprived and abused background, then smiles thankfully when he is given a privileged back story."[80] Paul and Peter's actions toward the family, then, seem determined simply by the roles they play in the genre film rather than through any sense of them as characters with a priori identities. Most telling of all, however, is the moment in the film that aligns Paul decisively with the medium of representation itself. Near the plot's climax, during a particularly brutal game in which Georg is being tortured offscreen, Anna gets hold of a shotgun and shoots Peter dead. Shocked yet undeterred, Paul locates the family's remote control, uses it to rewind the film itself to a point just before this event occurs, and then prevents her from grabbing the gun when the scene is replayed. From this temporal manipulation, via controller input, one can infer that the film's mode of representation is primarily aligned with the video as opposed to the cinematographic apparatus. It also becomes clear that Paul's consciousness is external to both the temporal and spatial coordinates of the narrative, since he alone appears to be aware of this reversal, just as he alone seems capable of bringing about the absurd and absolute medial violence of this time-axis manipulation. Or rather Haneke is only capable of staging this act of medial violence through the unaccountable story- and machine-operator designated "Paul."

The gesture of rewinding the diegesis demonstrates that the most important of the film's titular games is the "video game," in more than one sense of the term. First of all, the rewinding signifies that the intermedial relationship between film and video in *Benny's Video* has been ontologically reversed in *Funny Games*. In the earlier film, the cinematic medium retains narrative, if not mimetic, priority over that of video, since it dictates the course and status of events as singular and irreversible, even if their video representations are reversed and replayed within the film. In the case of *Funny Games*, the obscene reversal of death and the restaging of the scene indicate that video has assumed priority over and control of the film's narrative as well as its mimesis. This being the case, video's temporal repeatability and malleability completely undermine the ontological and epistemological basis of the film image and serve not to undo the act of violent retribution we have just witnessed but to reinforce it at a metafictional, if not metaphysical, level. Oliver Speck thus describes Haneke's practice of doing "violence to the medium itself, as illustrated by the infamous rewinding of the film in *Funny Games* that truly violates the film."[81] The rewinding of the murder forces the film image into the configuration of the video non-image: the event has taken place *on-screen* and *out-of-field*; that is, the act is revealed, after the fact, to have been committed within the spatiotemporal void separating film from video. By consigning the violent event to intermedial oblivion, Haneke's film replaces the representation of violence with a more profound, but also more abstract, "violence of representation" that was referred to in a quote by Speck at the start of this chapter. Brian Price similarly identifies this and other such moments in Haneke's films—such as the revealing of blood on the television screen, signifying the murder of the couple's child Schorschi—as "disinformatic images," since they follow "the representational logic of pain."[82] Through the employment of such images, according to Price, "Haneke identifies media as a structure of power predicated on the creation and subsequent quieting of someone else's pain."[83] In this consideration, violence and pain form the deeper perceptual and affective structures of these modes of entertainment media, the continual, empty repetition of cycles of represented and representational violence sustaining the continual relay of informatic and disinformatic audiovisual feedback in a zero-sum game.

In another sense, though, the film image's subordination to video presents a figuration of the medium of video games. Paul's act of rewinding the film is the equivalent of returning to a save point in a computer game, and he is able to repeat his actions with the added knowledge of what will transpire in one potential sequence of events. As Alexander Galloway points out, in the case of video games "time and space are mutable within the diegesis in ways unavailable before. Games have the luxury of being able to exist outside real, optical time. Games pause, speed up, slow down, and restart often."[84] Unlike works of film, electronic gameplay requires actions to unfold in different configurations within the same overall milieu and this temporal flexibility does not substantially alter the form of the work itself. Narrative film, however, is not only necessarily temporally linear as an expressive medium but also static with respect to its content each time it is viewed. Speck also points out this aspect of the film, stating that its antagonists are "able to manipulate the diegetic world and restart as if they were players of a video game."[85] *Funny Games*' violation of filmic mimesis thus aligns it with the medium of video games, an association that is signaled within the dialogue in the remake, as Wheatley points out: "It is telling that amongst the very few script changes that *Funny Games U.S.* sees are a number of references to gaming culture: Paul's opening gambit to George upon returning to the house is 'Player One, Next Level'; his final declaration before killing him is to tell Anna 'You've failed . . . Game over.' "[86] In fact, one could see the remake itself—as well as the narrative's other suggestions of the repeatability of the young men's game—as evidence of this relation to the newer medium.

Funny Games presents itself as but one iteration of a series of games played by Paul and Peter. As the film begins we see the pair playing golf with a neighboring family, and only later do we realize that this family has been enduring the same physical and psychological torture to which the characters we are following are subjected over the course of the film. The film ends as yet another game begins, this time playing out with a third family living across the lake whose members have been introduced earlier as friends of Georg and Anna. From this perspective—of the "narrative" as a selection from continuous and minimally variable blocks of gameplay—even the shot-for-shot remake could simply be considered a new iteration, or perhaps localization, of this game using different performer-players.[87] Price refers to this aspect of the film, then, when he states that "one can say that *Funny Games*—no matter which version one sees—is itself about the remake."[88] The film prefigures its own reproduction by highlighting, from the outset, its own ability to be reiterated as part and parcel of its intermedial alignment with the nonfilmic media of video and video games. Perhaps the majority of Haneke's filmography falls into step with this consideration, as his film narratives so often consist, at one level, of experimental variations on contemporary bourgeois family life, the minimal difference between its figures being implied by his always naming the central couple some cultural-linguistic variation of Georg and Anna.[89] In this manner, Haneke's cinema subtly undermines its own often disturbing narrative content in order to draw attention to a much more troubling effect: the fact that film itself is reverting to the temporality and reiterative ability characteristic of video.

In *Benny's Video* and *Funny Games*, then, Haneke posits a direct and profoundly complex relationship between the subject of violence, as represented by media, and the violation of the subject by media itself—that is, of both the subjects within these films and the spectator. Video is for Haneke the most violent of media, not simply because it "represents" so well the unrepresentable phenomena of pain and death. There are indeed abundant reasons for this attribution: video rips holes in our visual fields (mise en abyme); it annihilates individuals and their perceptions (desubjectification and depersonalization); and it tears asunder the natural course and experience of events (time-axis manipulation). From one perspective, the cinematic image scarcely survives its intermedial encounter with the informatic non-image of video; from another, however, the vitality of the cinematic image is all the more strongly affirmed in this encounter, its aesthetic power allowing it to shift and reshift perceptual registers while continuing to engage and challenge character and spectator alike as affective and even potentially ethical agents. In the next chapter, I will explore what is revealed when Haneke traces the effects of such medial transgressions and transformations less on the individual subject than on society at large.

Chapter 3

✦

Audiovisual Fragmentation and the Event

71 Fragmente einer Chronologie des Zufalls and *Code inconnu*

All of the films examined in the previous chapters have approached the question of medial engagement—and, in particular, its profound influence on perception, affect, subjectivity, and violence—via the structure of the nuclear family. *Der siebente Kontinent*, *Benny's Video*, and *Funny Games* all present domestic spaces and familial relationships that are catastrophically infected by destructive forces either existential (*Der siebente Kontinent*), internal (*Benny's Video*), or external (*Funny Games*).[1] Moreover, in each film these forces are inextricably tied to the various media that circulate between the outside world and the largely hermetic spaces of the domicile, or, in the case of video, within the spaces themselves. Thus, these films explore social milieux in an age of media saturation largely, if not exclusively, through what Haneke refers to as the "longitudinal sections" of the family structures.[2] The director goes on to differentiate this approach from that of *71 Fragmente einer Chronologie des Zufalls* (*71 Fragments of a Chronology of Chance*), which instead "presents a cross-section through the hierarchy of society,"[3] a narrative strategy he employs again later in *Code inconnu: Récit incomplet de divers voyages* (*Code Unknown: Incomplete Tales of Several Journeys*). As the title of the former film and the subtitle of the latter suggest, this presentation gestures simultaneously toward narrative and nonnarrative configurations of subjects, spaces, and temporalities. While each film maintains a sense of chronological progress and a consistency of character and situation, each also refuses to acknowledge any direct causal relationship between actions and events or to convey any sense of conventional narrative closure. Additionally, both films employ, between scenes, the black spacers used in *Der siebente Kontinent*, to the similar effect of introducing gaps in the films' audiovisual integrity and narrative-representational continuity. These non-imagistic fractures further communicate the pervasive sense of fragmentation that defines the perceptual fields of the films. However, the diegetic and extradiegetic relationships to television and other media that *71 Fragmente* and *Code inconnu* develop are markedly different from those characterizing Haneke's debut film, and so present divergent modes of fragmentation implying disparate sets of effects. Before more closely inquiring into these specific and often subtle differences, though, I will outline the director's own justifications for this unintegrated aesthetic approach as well as Roy Grundmann's pertinent critical interpretation of Haneke's employment of fragmentation in these particular films.

Upon its initial release in Austria, *71 Fragmente* was accompanied by a program that included an essay by Haneke—itself quite fragmentary in structure—described as a set of "notes to the film." Here, Haneke is clear about his aesthetic intentions from the outset:

> The title attempts to convey the conception of the film as precisely as possible. In the literature of modernism claim[s] of [the] holistic representation of reality have long been abandoned. Since Kafka at the latest, the fragment has unavoidably been at the basis of apprehending reality and is considered a crucial part of cognitive practice.
>
> Only in film, the most recent and potentially most modern form of art, the manner of thinking continues on the level prevalent in the nineteenth century. Whether naively or cynically, but in any case with financial success, the comforting illusion prevails that the world can be completely described and thus explained. My film and its title take issue with this view and attempt to dismantle this attitude.[4]

Haneke's approach in this film—which equally applies, as the director himself avers, to *Code inconnu*[5]—is qualified as an attempt to analogize or transpose the structure of literary modernism onto film, as a counterprogram to the naive forms of representational realism underpinning most commercial cinema. By means of its very ambiguity, Haneke goes on to state, fragmentation shifts the burden of interpretation more directly onto the spectator, who is left not only to account for the connections between the situations and actions the film depicts but also to reflect on the very principles of selectivity and continuity that inform mainstream filmmaking:

> By telling the story in [this] manner . . . a film can be irritating and also productive. As soon as spectators find themselves alone with the questions posed by the story, without instructions for ready interpretation, they feel disturbed and begin to assemble their defenses. A productive conflict, I would think. The more radically the answers are withheld, the sooner they will have to find their own. And this process of denial, I believe, can be applied to all aspects of film as an artificial product.[6]

Haneke's aesthetic of fragmentation (in the director's own account, at least) thus carries specific hermeneutic implications both at the level of story, by withholding information related to character motivation and plot, and at the level of representation, by introducing more or less controlled gaps or rests into the image flow. These gaps destabilize the fundamental audiovisual logic defining the cinematographic illusion, potentializing new modes of expression and of spectatorial engagement. In this sense, fragmentation fulfills a number of the non-image's functions that were explored in chapter 1. The perception that *71 Fragmente* is essentially an extension of the fractured montage employed in *Der siebente Kontinent*, albeit applied to a social milieu that extends far beyond the familial household, would hence be quite acceptable. Yet, in spite of their stylistic similarities with Haneke's debut feature, *71 Fragmente* and *Code inconnu* evidence clear aesthetic and narrative departures from *Der siebente Kontinent*, as well as from one another. This differentiation is best approached, firstly, with respect to the films' relationships to sociopolitical actuality and, secondly, to their own statuses as medial objects.

In an essay titled "Between Adorno and Lyotard: Michael Haneke's Aesthetic of Fragmentation," Roy Grundmann's account of Haneke's representational strategies in *71 Fragmente* and *Code inconnu* offers a direct reflection on the differing philosophical and aesthetic frameworks informing the films' formal gestures toward fragmentation. Grundmann perceives the earlier film as bearing out a definably modernist, or Adornian, perspective toward contemporary sociopolitical actuality, whereas the later film reflects a more postmodernist approach in line with Jean-François Lyotard's theorization of contemporaneity:

> Generally speaking, *71 Fragments* represents the world as a shattered totality that finds its just and honest representation in scattered, disjointed scenes of loss, destruction, and dysfunction. In *Code Unknown*, destroyed coherence is recast as uneasy, chafing heterogeneity, which the film dramatizes in scenes depicting the incommensurability of speaking positions, and which is visually rendered by a camera that, while moving fluidly, is keenly aware that justice towards the individual is impossible.[7]

Interestingly, Grundmann's conceptualization of the films' philosophical frames of reference—that of, in the Austrian film, a modernist melancholia brought about by the palpable absence of centrality or meaning, as opposed to the French film's self-definition as an acentered, postmodernist multitext—is seemingly at odds with the films' respective incorporations of other medial forms. *Code inconnu* remains focused on the historically modernist media of filmmaking and photography; it includes scenes of characters watching television, for example, but never captures the television screens themselves in close-up, as has been Haneke's style in his other films up to this point. *71 Fragmente*, though, is overtly defined by an engagement with new media, as it incorporates televisual news reportage directly into its mimetic structure. If one accepts Grundmann's assertion of *Code inconnu*'s aesthetic of postmodernism relative to *71 Fragmente*'s modernism, then, one must assume that these sociopolitical frames of reference have been established independently of, or in contradistinction to, the films' respective engagements with other audiovisual media. However, an intermedial approach could account for the differences between the films' modes of fragmentation without indexing them to either modernist or postmodernist aesthetics in terms of the realist sociopolitical perspective each film offers. As Grundmann himself points out, in these films "form . . . remains connected to contents, but it also becomes contents unto itself";[8] fragmentation not only determines the means by which narrative-representational expression is enunciated but also comes to constitute the very substance of these expressions themselves. Put succinctly, *both* the fragments *and* the gaps delimiting them are equally qualifiable as medial "content"—as mutually and individually productive of percepts and affects—in configurations through which form and content become indiscernible.[9] In this manner, Haneke's fragmented films present a mosaic—one composed of sense and non-sense, image and non-image, communication and miscommunication, and reality and its medial reproduction—as the defining condition of lived experience in the contemporary urban spaces of postindustrial societies.

In this chapter I will approach these two films' differential modes of fragmentation via an exploration of the intermedial disjunctures between cinema and television in *71 Fragmente*, followed by a media-specific reading of *Code inconnu*'s diegetic incorporation of filmmaking and photography, with a particular focus on the cinematic relationship between sound and visual imagery exploited thereby. In addition to attempting to differentiate the modes of fragmentation that these distinct media elicit, these readings will seek to negotiate the films' respective gestures toward realism by examining how events themselves are conceptualized and mediated through cinema, television, and photography respectively. In this way, Haneke's ongoing concern with cinema's ability to generate an artistically and intellectually viable image of the world will be assessed not according to an a priori notion of reality and its "true" representation, but instead according to the temporal definition and the perceptual and affective fields that are brought to bear upon cinematic, televisual, and photographic concepts of the event.

Televisual Fragmentation

As mentioned above, *71 Fragmente einer Chronologie des Zufalls* stylistically follows Haneke's two previous films, *Der siebente Kontinent* and *Benny's Video*, in its depiction of television. In these three works, the camera closes in on the TV screen in such a way that the cinematic frame is substituted for that of the monitor within the film and thus essentially presents the foreign medium *as such*, even as the televisual medium is decontextualized and self-estranged by the cinematic apparatus. In *71 Fragmente*, however, the television footage is presented directly to the spectator without diegetic context. The news reports usually do not derive from a viewing situation within the film, in other words, but are mimetically coextensive with the film itself. This footage functions, in part, to provide a chronological frame for the film, the plot of which is divided into a series of individual days with on-screen dates (in a manner reminiscent of *Der siebente Kontinent*'s "one day per year" temporal structure, although encompassing a much smaller time frame), and each day begins with an excerpt from a highly convincing simulation of a television news program detailing the state of global events on that day: the five dates are October 12, 26, and 30, followed by November 17, and finally December 23, all in 1993. The juxtaposition of the events of the film against the mass media–reported global events of the news broadcasts foreshadows a convergence of the two, which is also signaled from the film's outset by text that appears on-screen prior to any other visual image: "On Dec 23, 1993, Maximilien B., a 19-year-old student, killed three people in a Viennese bank. Shortly after that he shot himself in the head."[10] The film's self-definition as a "chronology of chance" rather than as a conventional narrative is thus undermined to a significant extent by its opening text and by the anticipatory temporal framework this statement institutes with respect to the film's timeline. While it posits the connections between events and character actions as being completely aleatory, the film nevertheless plots a course to a preordained outcome through its temporal orientation. In retrospect, this singular and terrible event directly or indirectly affects all of the characters whose lives and circumstances are revealed in the fragments preceding this climax. Hence, even if the film appears to elide causal and logical connections between its discursive sections, the individual actions it depicts constitute a temporally ordered sequence leading inevitably toward a climactic event. Though by no means conventional in its plot development, *71 Fragmente* is nonetheless conceivable as a narrative or sequence of interrelated narratives.

In its fragmentary visual structure, however, the film bears a definite resemblance to the aforementioned television news reports, a resemblance that connects the two media independently of their shared timeframe and eventual convergence. Indeed, the film presents itself as possessing certain formal similarities to a news segment, albeit one that is unfolding much more slowly than and with far different representational content from most broadcast news. Studies of the film often cite this fact: Maximilian Le Cain, for instance, describes *71 Fragmente* as "without doubt the most intelligent and powerful study yet by cinema of television."[11] He then asserts that its strategy of fragmentation is "importantly analogous to the way in which information is conveyed in short clips on television news programmes."[12] A possible interpretation of this analogy is that the film complements the fragmentary montage of its simulated news segments with a decelerated and de-sensationalized series of similarly structured episodes and shots, the presentation of which also, significantly, lacks the news reports' voice-over narration or reportage. In so doing, Haneke's film provides a cinematic counterprogram to and implicit metacommentary on the informatic television news media it references and depicts. This view accords well with Haneke's expressed critique of commercial film and television, as stated in his notes to the film:

> Contemporary film editing is most commonly determined by the practices of television-timing, by the expectation of a rapid flow of information. Apart from its visual attractiveness, a picture is [there] to provide linear information which can be quickly consumed and checked off. Video clips and commercials have established the benchmark for timing. They offer the most persuasive guarantee for sanitized emotions, that is, for sterility.
>
> However, emotions as well as experience have to do with time. As soon as time becomes manifest in a film, it disturbs the spectators who are used to a fast pace, especially if the pictures concern matters which they have learned to suppress. At first they react with irritation, then they are bored and finally annoyed—the classic sequence of a defensive reaction. If one has the courage to put them through this ordeal, they will in the end come to face the condition with which they are confronted in picture and sound. As a result, the contents once again will become felt, instead of being merely registered as information to be checked off.[13]

Haneke perceives mainstream cinema as having adopted the accelerated rhythms of television in order to meet the expectations of spectators conditioned to absorb a plenitude of information that lacks all but the most superficial affective resonance. In opposition to the definably televisual approach of privileging only the recognition of successive on-screen objects or of actions within a flow of the same, then, Haneke's ponderous and deliberately disconcerting style is intended to appeal to and even elicit a differently engaged and more deeply affected contemporary viewership. Haneke thus even details the psychological effects of this process on a typical filmgoer.[14] The recurring news reports, which also bookend the film, are emblematic of sensationalistic information-based media, and the film sets out to reconfigure the spectator's perceptual and affective engagement with the audiovisual material incessantly and fleetingly disseminated by television and inherited by commercial cinema. In this interpretation, then, the film adopts the formal qualities of television news only to subvert and realign them according to the tenets of art-cinematic realism, an effect achieved largely by simply extending the temporal dimensions of their presentation.

In this consideration, *71 Fragmente* would constitute a work of intermedial polyphony, each medium highlighting the other's uniquely fragmented modality and imbuing the other with new affective and perceptual potentialities. Indeed, this is the conclusion that Le Cain reaches in his oft-cited reading of the film. It is worth quoting at length Le Cain's interpretation that the film's final fictional news report is an overtly humanistic, even uplifting, statement on the director's part:

> After the student has cracked up in a bank and gone on a killing spree that ends in his suicide, an incident which involves most of the film's characters, the film switches to a simulated news report of the killing in which witnesses express their horror and incomprehension. Haneke then boldly moves on to real news stories such as the war in Sarajevo and Michael Jackson's alleged child abuse. Perhaps the most obvious interpretation of this device would be a pessimistic one—that real lives and real people so easily become just another news story in a parade of media images, the actual state of their lives becoming lost as they—like the family at the end of *Benny's Video*—become subject to an uncomprehendingly impersonal image system. That, in a world already saturated with images, they become just another image.
>
> Yet the miracle of *71 Fragments of a Chronology of Chance*, its "healing" aspect, is that this conclusion also has the opposite effect: it re-humanizes the other non-fictional news stories, makes the predicaments they bear witness to suddenly seem very close and real. As the film progresses, the viewer becomes emotionally engaged with one individual story after another from one different part of society after another: the smallest units of the narrative. In the bank massacre these small units cohere into one large unit. Having trained the viewer to engage with small units and brought him or her to understand their ultimate agglomeration, by inserting the large unit into the context of the news programme he is making it a smaller unit and beginning the process once again with the news programme as the new large, encompassing narrative unit. In this way we come to perceive the woman interviewed on the streets of Sarajevo or, for that matter, Michael Jackson with the same intimacy as the fictional characters we have come to know and care about. Haneke has succeeded in reaffirming the common humanity of the subjects behind the images that assail us each day, counteracting the desensitization brought about by media overkill. Just as we thought that his mosaic was completed, he revealed that it was in fact endless, capable of expanding in all directions, encompassing all the narrative fragments that make up all the lives in the world.[15]

Le Cain's compelling reading of the film perceives a mutual reinforcement of the respective expressive powers of film and television media. The film as a whole, described here as the "large unit" of narrative fragments (and seeming to encompass the excerpts from the news program as smaller fragments),[16] is subsequently inserted into the final news excerpt as one of *its* segments. This short segment, in turn, is reconfigured as a "small unit," a monad-like encapsulation of the film narrative that becomes, due to the open-ended format of television news, endlessly expandable into other potential films. Thus, the news program is invested with the affective and aesthetic gravity of art cinema, supplying added emotional depth and resonance to its nominally informatic material. In Le Cain's reading, *71 Fragmente* effects a convergence of cinematic and televisual modes of narrative fragmentation and hence a convergence of cinematic and televisual modes of realism. By implicitly referring back to the film's nuanced and ultimately tragic affective power, which stands in direct contrast to the clinical presentation of the event and of its human toll in the news report, the reportage gains in dramatic-realistic texture and dimension. This dimension is subsequently and by association imparted to the reports that follow, which concern the conflict in Sarajevo and the first Michael Jackson child molestation scandal. Additionally, in a reverse exchange, one could consider the film itself to have been retrospectively invested with the urgency and proximity to present time that define and sustain televisual realism, drawing the narrative fragments closer to mass humanity, to the territory and temporality of everyday spectacle.

Le Cain's interpretation of the film's transition into news report acknowledges the overt differences in the temporal and audiovisual dispositions of televisual and cinematic media, as well as the distinct affective and perceptual modes of engagement that each medium invites, but nonetheless perceives a positive conceptual synthesis between the two forms that expands the depth and scope of both. Yet, if one approaches this intuition of *71 Fragmente* through the perspective of intermedial difference, as developed up to this point in this text, a problematic aspect of his reading presents itself. Le Cain's interpretation assumes the existence of a shared representational basis between film and television and thus depicts their apparently common points of reference as capable of bridging the profound perceptual and affective gap separating the two media. The characters within the film must remain "characters" in the simulated television broadcast, even as they are rendered equivalent to Michael Jackson and the citizens of Sarajevo, and the event that warrants televised news coverage must stand as identical with the climax of the film's fragmented narrative. In Le Cain's view, the filmic subjects and the film's narrative are admitted wholesale into the news report's presentation of the shooting, if only from the perspective of the spectator, who has witnessed the event and its actants as rendered in both media forms. In other words, the film and the news report within the film are considered to be continuous and cotemporal with each other, not only to the extent that both refer to a shared world, with specific individuals and events in common, but also in the fact that the narrative of the film remains implicitly expressed in the informatic presentation of the shooting on television. As noted above, the overtly atypical fragmentary structure of the film narrative—which Le Cain has identified as "importantly analogous" to the structure of television news—appears to support this synergetic interrelationship. What insights might obtain, however, in an explicitly intermedial consideration of the void between the film and the news reports within the film? Specifically, what primary differences and discontinuities between filmic fragmentation and televisual fragmentation are indicated by *71 Fragmente*?

To begin with, even if *71 Fragmente* resembles, in its manner of construction, a slow-motion TV news report, it lacks the cyclical aspect that defines the presentation of the televisual segments. The news program follows a strictly ordered sequence, the repetition of which is highlighted by the film: the shot of the anchor addressing the camera to introduce the next segment; a short pan left, to allow room for a small graphic to appear as a visual cue for the segment; a brief pause before the program cuts to the footage assembled for the segment and the offscreen voice of the reporter picks up the story; and, immediately after the reporter signs off, a cut back to the studio as the anchor resumes the position screen center and introduces the next segment. Even if the assemblage of footage within the segments themselves is registered as fragmentary, then, both the continual presence of a voice on the sound track—either the anchor's, the reporter's, or that of an individual interviewed within the news clip—and the repetition of nearly identical transitions into and out of these segments sustain the overall consistency and continuity of the program flow. The film itself, by contrast, marks the transitions between scenes only with the blank and silent spacers and largely withholds visual and vocal cues such as establishing shots, apart from the dates that appear on-screen after a transition to a new temporal setting. In a definite sense, then, the filmic fragmentation differs rhythmically from that of the televisual; the audiovisual fragmentation of the news segments and that of the film are structured according to distinctly different tempos and inflections, and hence Haneke describes the film as having "a contrapuntal form as a whole."[17] The film and the news report thus remain utterly incommensurable until they converge in their points of reference at the close of the film, when the circumstances and effects of the shooting—which the film has explored through a measured alternation of image and non-image, sound and silence—are rendered via the vocal discourse, cyclical structuring, and temporally attenuated visual fragments of a simulated television news report. The representational contents of the film and those of the news reports have been ostensibly united; nonetheless, the two media continue to operate on utterly different wavelengths, problematizing any narrative bridge that one could propose to construct between the two. If one perceives a collaboration between the two media that is in service to a more expansive vision of the world, perhaps this will be revealed less through surface similarities in their respective modes and rhythms of fragmentation than through the identification of some other force drawing the cinematic and televisual fragments together within a larger structure. In other words, rather than admitting the news reports into the film's narrative and then admitting the narrative in turn into cyclical media reportage, one may instead posit a type of flow that encompasses both narrative and informatic materials while preserving their mutual incommensurability.

As Margaret Morse indicates in her insightful and influential studies of TV news, television's departure from cinematic convention can be understood in terms of a distinction between *story*, a mode of enunciation in which the recipient remains removed from the events described, and *discourse*, an inclusive enunciation with the potential for exchange and dialogue: "The cinema presents itself as story—its screen segregates the incommensurable realm of the story with its 'impression of reality' from the realm of the audience with its relations of proximity and potential for discursive exchange. Television, despite the amount of drama which appears on it, is a strongly discursive medium."[18] The direct address to the viewer, which is ubiquitous on television but rare in conventional filmmaking, indicates this distinction, enforcing as it does the idea that television as a medium occupies the position of a "quasi-subject" that shares the viewer's chronotope, even if any actual exchange is necessarily simulated. Morse provides a concise interpretation of this almost uncanny state of affairs in the essay's conclusion: "Our relation to television can be summarized as one in which a medium structured to prevent dialogue with the other in our society has developed a fictional form of dialogue; television cannot satisfy our desire for subjectivity, but it can displace it. It caters to both our desire for mastery and pleasure in identification as well as our wish to share in subjectivity through recognizing and being recognized by others as a 'you.'"[19] Television's discursive position—its disposition toward intersubjective exchange in form and structure if not in fact—places at its disposal a profound capacity for sustained spectatorial engagement. The mode of address employed by television, Morse argues, plays a role in the medium's attractive force that Raymond Williams's concept of anticipative temporal flow is unable to account for in and of itself.

In her essay "An Ontology of Everyday Distraction," Morse refines her argument regarding television's *dispositif* by identifying two coextensive representational-discursive functions in television. She characterizes one as *passage*—the sense of transition from one space or subject to another in a manner cognate with intersubjective discourse and akin to Williams's concept of flow—and the other as *segmentation*—the marking off of discrete units of space-time that gesture away from discourse and toward the pseudofilmic modality of story. Taken together, these factors vouchsafe televisual continuity even if the content itself is spatiotemporally discontinuous and marked by sudden diegetic shifts:

> The basic dualism of televisual representation . . . helps to explain why, despite its segmentation into unrelated items, television is *not* commonly perceived as fragmented, but rather is experienced as unified and contained. Nor is that coherence achieved simply by virtue of "flow" or the juxtaposition of items on the same plane of discourse. The duality of *passage* and *segmentation* in physical as well as represented space is related in turn to the dual planes of language, the engaged discourse of a subject in passage and the disengagement of stories from the here and now of the subject.[20]

Within a news report, then, the studio space from which the anchor directly addresses the spectator both visually and vocally is the primary space of intersubjective discourse, whereas the footage of war zones and other sites of newsworthy events at a remove from this intersubjective exchange are qualified by Morse as "story spaces." These two modes of space together constitute the segmentation of the program. Furthermore, the passages between these spaces are clearly signaled by vocal and visual cues, which are structured according to predefined repetitions and rhythms. Thus, even as segmentation presents a visually and representationally fragmented view of the world—a view that, between programs, can easily shift from factual to fictional (or encompass both, as does most "reality" television)—the continual presence of a unifying discourse that provides passage between and through the segments preserves a sense of cohesion. In the case of the news, as in sports programs and certain other television genres, this discourse is sustained by on- or offscreen voices that rarely cease throughout the duration of the program.[21]

In *71 Fragmente*, the film's segmentation into fragments is not counterbalanced by such an effect of coherence, other than the overall gesture toward narrative chronology mentioned above. Indeed, as in *Der siebente Kontinent*, the film's punctuation by imageless and silent spacers registers as a specifically countertelevisual mode of expression. However, the film does establish a coherence and rhythm of sorts not by its own means but by admitting the discursive effects of television into its image system. As Roy Grundmann points out, television in *71 Fragmente* is neither diegetic nor extradiegetic but rather, in his words, "supradiegetic: it functions as an external divider between some of the film's narrative fragments, but it also links several of the film's individual narrative strands by constituting their protagonists as television's public, whereby it assumes a diegetic presence within the frame."[22] This linking function that Grundmann refers to assumes particular significance at a key point in the film: after having turned himself in to police custody, the Romanian boy Marian is shown being interviewed, via a translator, as part of a television news report concerning illegal immigration. We initially come across this program when it is viewed by the elderly man, the father of the bank teller, at which point (in a gesture typical of Haneke's films) the camera moves in to frame the television screen in close-up. When the camera withdraws once again, though, it no longer occupies the space of the elderly man's living room but has imperceptibly transitioned into the home of the bourgeois couple seeking to adopt Anna, who are also viewing the program. Rather than having been separated by a spacer, the two disparate fragments—and the situations of the characters they depict—have been "bridged" by the shared experience of television viewing.[23] Haneke's intentions in employing television as a connector between fragments in this manner are ambiguous, as the TV screen serves as a means of closing the diegetic and mimetic distance separating the segments and yet also thereby attains an inherent association with the spacers as a form of noncinematic non-image. The television screen, in short, simultaneously overcomes and reinforces the film's fragmentary structure. Yet this very fact points toward an intermedial reading of *71 Fragmente*: while the news segments impart to the film as a whole a sense of rhythm and momentum—acting in this way much like the studio space and anchor to which the news program continually returns in order to reinforce its discursive coherence—the film nonetheless continually registers the profound gaps between these media. Thus, even though at one level the film appeals to the news reports to help maintain its sense of chronological progress and contribute to its overall structural cohesion and sense of closure, it is highly problematic to perceive in this surface effect evidence of a representational or conceptual union of film and television. In fact, the supradiegetic transitions from film to television indicate an even more profound effect of fragmentation than that which is achieved in the pattern of image-spacer-image: the spacer indicates only a spatiotemporal gap within the film's mimesis, while the television screen *fractures the mimesis itself*. Rather than staging a direct play of presence and absence via the withholding of audiovisual material, *71 Fragmente* utilizes the changeover to another medium to fragment the very consistency of the film, to fragment both its imagery and the connections that obtain between those images. By imposing a different form of audiovisual content, the televisual fragments the very mode of fragmentation at the film's disposal.[24]

Yet it could still be argued, with Le Cain, that the simulated news segment displayed at the end of the film, which encompasses an event within the film narrative, goes against this intermedial reading. Here, it is demonstrated that the television segment and the film are grounded within a common milieu, and therefore—leaving aside their obvious formal differences—there must be some degree of overlap in their respective perceptual fields. In short, both the filmic and the televisual segments represent a single event that occurs within a shared realist plane of existence. The issue thus hinges on narrative film's and television's respective means of conceptualizing and representing the event, and whether the singularity of the event transcends the differences inherent in the perceptual and affective assemblage each medium brings to bear.

The Televisual Event

In a statement left largely undeveloped, Scott Durham alludes to a conceptual union of filmic and televisual fragmentation in terms of the latter's offering a structure for the event of the shooting that the film is not capable of providing on its own narrative terms: "To be sure, Haneke is mocking the arbitrary unities imposed by the narrative forms of network news. But he is also implicitly acknowledging that his own disassembly of these unities presupposes and depends upon them. For they occupy, in our mental representation of the otherwise unrepresentable event, the empty center around which its fragments orbit."[25] The section that follows will similarly posit that television possesses a means of conceptualizing the event that film does not, and that such means are essentially void from the perspective of representation. However, unlike Durham, I will argue that this informatic expression of the event cannot be reintegrated into the film's narrative or representational strategies, either as a phantom "mental" representation or as a missing center (a concept that is also invoked in Grundmann's reading of the film as a work of modernist fragmentation). This impossibility of integration is due to television's utter incommensurability with cinema in temporal terms.

Television, I have posited, is an aggressively informatic medium. As Walter Benjamin famously attests in "The Storyteller" (1936), information constitutes a form of communication that is a "stranger" both to traditional storytelling and to the novel, to narrative itself in fact.[26] The inimical relationship between informatic and narrative discourse is, in Benjamin's analysis, a result of information's inability to establish connections between events that are independent of a given event's intrinsic plausibility or understandability. Information is thus defined by its "already being shot through with explanation"; by contrast, "it is half the art of storytelling to keep a story free from explanation as one reproduces it," and "the psychological connection of the events is not forced upon the reader. It is left up to him to interpret things the way he understands them, and thus the narrative achieves an amplitude that information lacks."[27] The connective tissue between events in a narrative context, then, may remain enigmatic and therefore highly compelling, whereas from the perspective of information intereventel connections must remain not only verifiable but also expunged of any ambiguity. If one once again compares the fragmentation of *71 Fragmente*'s narrative to that of its simulated news programs, one senses in the film segments the presence of this alternative amplitude Benjamin describes. For example, a number of unexplained but intriguing potential connections can be made between Maximilian B.'s act of violence and the various forms of social and psychophysical conditioning he is subjected to: standing in line for food service at his university; practicing his table tennis swing against a ball-dispensing machine; and, just before the massacre, being thrown to the ground by a fellow customer when Maximilian attempts to cut into line at the bank in order to pay at the petrol station (where his car is blocking a service pump). Without directly explaining the student's actions, such episodes unveil a set of alienating and deindividualizing circumstances similar to those experienced by the family in *Der siebente Kontinent*, and suggestive of certain disturbing psychological or existential effects brought about by life in a postindustrial consumer society. The reporter of the "news story," however, somehow makes a factual assertion out of the indefinable motivations and circumstances leading to the massacre: "The reason for these absurd killings is unknown. In any case, it is clear that he was not trying to rob the bank." This statement is supported by a clip from an interview with the petrol station attendant, who simply declares, in response to the reporter's inquiry into the reasons for the killing spree, "No idea. I do not know. This is madness."

The stark contrast between the evocative intereventental amplitude of the film narrative and the information offered by the news report is exceedingly evident. Indeed, the aleatory definition given in the film's title may be read as directly antithetical to the uncompromising logic of causality and factuality that is characteristic of information media, rather than as in opposition to a sequential narrative structure. On television, uncertainty and doubt form the basis for positive statements ("It is not known . . .") until new information emerges ("It is now known . . ."). The obvious initial point of distinction that presents itself between narrative discourse and informatic discourse, then, is the degree to which the factuality of the event confronts the spectrum of possible relationships that are obtainable between it and other events. Haneke's film enforces this distinction between these two modes. In the informatic news report, the truth value of the event is only admitted as self-explanatory, in accordance with verifiable logic and common sense, and therefore the massacre is deemed "absurd" and unknowable, an act of "madness." The film's narrative, by contrast, exposes the event to a myriad set of connections to other events and circumstances that, though potentially arbitrary and contingent, remain compossible with it, providing a "causality field" of sorts.[28] It is arguable, as well, that the contrast between narrative and information is not one defined by an opposition of fiction to documented reality—indeed, an actual occurrence may be narrativized just as a fictional work may be presented informatically[29]—but rather by film's and television's respective views of the world and their respective temporal situations. If one conceives of the film image as situated, like the photographic image, within a temporal mode of pastness—as Raymond Bellour observes, "[w]e are beginning to realize that the cinema is a gigantic theater of memory, open and metamorphic"[30]—then one must oppose this to television's proximity to present time.

Mary-Ann Doane considers television's defining characteristic, in direct opposition to film and photography, to be "an insistent 'present-ness'—a '*This-is-going-on*' rather than a '*That-has-been*,' a celebration of the instantaneous." Such a temporal disposition maximizes television's situation with respect to what we generally refer to as "current events," which become the primary points of orientation for the medium: television "organizes itself around the event."[31] In fact, although she cites Morse's assertions of televisual discourse and flow, Doane considers the temporal alignment of televisual information to be the source of television's cohesion and ideological power: "[T]he ideology of 'liveness' works to overcome the excessive fragmentation within television's flow. If television is indeed thought to be inherently 'live,' the impression of a unity of 'real time' is preserved, covering over the extreme discontinuity which is in fact typical of television in the U.S. at this historical moment."[32] If a fragmented film is temporally disposed to resemble an incomplete memory image whose gaps are registered as a sort of Proustian "lost time," then television avoids any sense of this gapping or loss by annexing its mimesis to the unfolding of events more or less concurrent with the "real time" of the viewing experience. The sense of present time with which television is invested provides the medium with its greatest force of affective attraction. According to Doane, this force supersedes representation as a factor in the medium's view of the world: "Television does not so much *represent* as it *informs*. Theories of representation painstakingly elaborated in relation to film are clearly inadequate."[33] This preference by the medium for a sense of presentness over and above any represented space, object, or duration is attested to by the play of visibility and nonvisibility at work in the medium. *71 Fragmente* exemplifies this aspect of the televisual exceedingly well via the bank massacre footage offered in the simulated news report. The film depicts the events leading up to the shooting, the shooting itself (although Haneke of course relegates the site of injury and death to offscreen space), and its immediate aftereffects. The news report, however, replaces any representation of the event itself with evidence of its aftermath: the bodies of the slain being removed from the bank, police officers investigating the scene of the crime and interviewing witnesses outside, the bloodstain on the lobby floor. Doane refers to footage of this kind as constituting a "simulated vision" of the event: "What becomes crucial for the act of reportage . . . is the simple gesture of being on the scene, *where* it happened, so that presence in space compensates for the inevitable temporal lag."[34] Even as it defines the entire informatic discourse and temporality of the medium, then, the event as encountered through television remains largely ineffable, even as its reality is factually affirmed.

Doane's conceptualization of television is exemplary of a number of similar theories of the medium, some of which have already been invoked in this study—Stanley Cavell, for instance, had previously defined the "material basis of television" as "a current of simultaneous event reception."[35] What makes Doane's study especially relevant to the implicit critique of television I uncover in *71 Fragmente*, however, is the fact that she provides a theoretically sound account for a particularly troubling aspect of television and new media that is often referred to without elaboration in the work of other media theorists. We recall Rodowick's characterization of Deleuze's

Cinema books as responses to a state of affairs in which the statuses of film theory and the film image are becoming displaced by media devoid of artistic-imagistic potential: "[A]s this culture becomes more televisual and as society becomes one of control marked by the flows of information . . . the disciplines of mass communications—marketing, design, advertising, and information technologies—lay claim to the title of *concepteurs* as the creators of 'events.' "[36] Rodowick is joined in this view by theorists such as Raymond Williams, who, in his study of the medium, finds that, due to a variety of factors of presentation and selection, "the televisual impression of 'seeing the event for oneself' is at times and perhaps always deceptive."[37] Baudrillard takes a similar position regarding the televisual event when he states that "TV . . . cools and neutralizes the meaning and the energy of events"; Doane likewise refers to "the tendency of television to banalize all events through a kind of leveling process."[38] In all such critiques, television and other informatic media are portrayed as deficient in their ability to impart a sense of social or historical value and intellectual and emotional weight to the events they communicate, instead relativizing the importance of all affairs by subjecting them to the same repetitious and temporally ephemeral cycles of programming. Doane, though, convincingly argues that these effects do not result from deficiencies in television's ideological apparatus, but rather from inescapable facets of the temporal mode through which television mediates the event. Moreover, as Doane affirms, there emerges in the TV medium an ambiguity regarding whether the event's significance is such that it merits television coverage, or whether the fact of its receiving media coverage imparts significance to the event irrespective of its innate importance.[39] Television's temporal alignment with the passing present, she argues, is itself both the source of the medium's affective interest and the primary reason for its inability to invest a deeper meaning or significance into the events around which it is structured. The ephemerality and equivalency of TV's informatic perspective on the event are indistinguishable from the temporal disposition of the medium itself.

Such a criticism of television, then, points to both an inherent disposition of the television medium and a much more general philosophical and epistemological problem—namely, the perception of events as discrete incidents that, in their buildup, occurrence, and aftermath, organize linear time into past, present, and future. This philosophical problem may be identified as the problem of succession, which Deleuze, in *Cinema 2*, poses in the following way: "If the present is actually distinguishable from the future and the past, it is because it is presence of something, which precisely stops being present when it is replaced by *something else*. It is in relation to the present of something else that the past and future are said of a thing. We are, then, passing along different events, in accordance with an explicit time or a form of succession which entails that a variety of things fill the present one after another."[40] Because we define the present time in terms of the presence of an event or events that unfold within it, and we identify these events as distinct from one another, then the temporal transition from one present to another is in principle tied to the replacement of a given event by a different one. However, the fundamental association of the event itself with the time of its occurrence brings about an undecidable and tautological relationship between these two aspects, it being equally true that we conceive of the present time in terms of the event(s) it "contains," and that we conceive of the event in terms of the time of its unfolding. Doane quotes an appropriately chiastic aphorism from Ernst Bloch's *Philosophy of the Future* in this regard: "Time *is* only because something happens, and where something happens, there time is."[41] Our partitioning of time into past, present, and future is thus revealed to be inextricably connected to our perception of events as discrete and successive, ordered according to their categorization as what *has happened*, what *is happening*, and what *will happen*. As an alternative to this endless process of succession, Deleuze puts forward an image of the whole of time as a single event and draws upon a quote from Bernard Groethuysen to support this concept:

> It is quite different if we are established inside one single event; if we plunge into an event that is in preparation, arrives and is over; if for a longitudinal, pragmatic view we substitute a vision which is purely optical, vertical, or, rather, one in depth. The event is no longer confused with the space which serves as its place, nor with the actual present which is passing: "the time of the event comes to an end before the event does, so the event will start again at another time . . . the whole event is as it were in the time where nothing happens[.]"[42]

If we cease to index the passage of time according to the presence of successive events, then an utterly different perception of both phenomena emerges: time presents itself as aeonian—omnidimensional and substantive rather than linear and transitory—whereas the event presents itself as occurring *outside of* our spatiotemporal perspective. As with the unrepresentable and always already unmediated event of death—which was discussed in connection with *Benny's Video*—the event ultimately takes place within the void, exerting its influence on a given spatiotemporal situation without ever being counted among its elements.

Cinema presents us with a concept of time that is organized around the image, including, as Deleuze points out, the image of time itself. As such, cinema determines its own relations with time, forming a concept of temporality on which even philosophers and theorists outside of the realm of film studies draw.[43] As I have established, however, television as a medium is organized around not images but events themselves and thus accedes completely to the picture of time as a succession of events. This principle of succession, which is most clearly evident in news programming, irrevocably follows the unending process of presenting the viewer with the fact of the event only to immediately pass on to another event. This impression of "liveness" and the temporal sense of the passing present are conveyed at the expense of the fragmentation of its picture of the world and time into dissociated events and their locales, with the underlying implication that no event is of greater significance than the next, and what is current is always accorded precedence. Yet perhaps the medium of television offers a philosophically interesting perspective in emptying each event of its individual representational or political significance through this leveling process. To return briefly to *Benny's Video*, Benny's mother Anna's reply to her husband's question about what is happening in the news—"nothing"—is understandable in this regard. In sapping the energy and meaningful content of events through its informatic formalism and cyclical repetition, television ultimately presents a view of the event emptied of everything but its pure temporality, the medium's sense of "flow." There emerges an absolute equivalence between "something is happening" and "nothing is happening," an implicit acknowledgement of the void characteristic of the event, of the fact that—as Deleuze's quote from Groethuysen asserts—the event comes to pass "in the time where nothing happens."[44]

Let me return to Le Cain's interpretation of *71 Fragmente*, which posited a union of the filmic and televisual portrayals of the event of the bank shooting, to the mutual reinforcement of each medium's respective representational strengths. Thus far I have acknowledged an intermedial effect at work, with respect to the fact that the cyclical rhythm and temporal-discursive flow of the televisual are imparted to the fragmentary chronology of the film, though with the added effect of further fragmenting the filmic expression at the mimetic level. In this consideration, the film narrative represents the bank shooting as the culmination of a circumstantial "chronology of chance" with devastating consequences for nearly all of the major characters of the film. One of the final shots in the film is a static and sustained close-up of the face-down corpse of the slain security guard as a pool of blood slowly forms beneath it (see figure 7). Via its very duration—particularly in comparison with the suddenness and brevity of the shooting itself—the shot conveys the finality and tragic weight of the slaying.

By contrast, the news report represents the aftermath of the slaying in a succession of brief shots, the last of which is the stain left on the floor by the security guard's pool of blood (see figure 8). The news report thus registers only the indexical *signifiers* of the happening but simultaneously attests to a profound *absence* relative to the film image—the absence of the body itself, in this case. This is not only the absence of a *representation* of the event, then, but of its consequences, which are registered only as passing discursive information and audiovisual fragments set within a larger flow of the same. If one lends credence to Le Cain's assertion that the film's narrative duration, affective depth, and perceptual realism subtend the news segment, then these must be considered elements projected onto the latter by a viewer who cannot

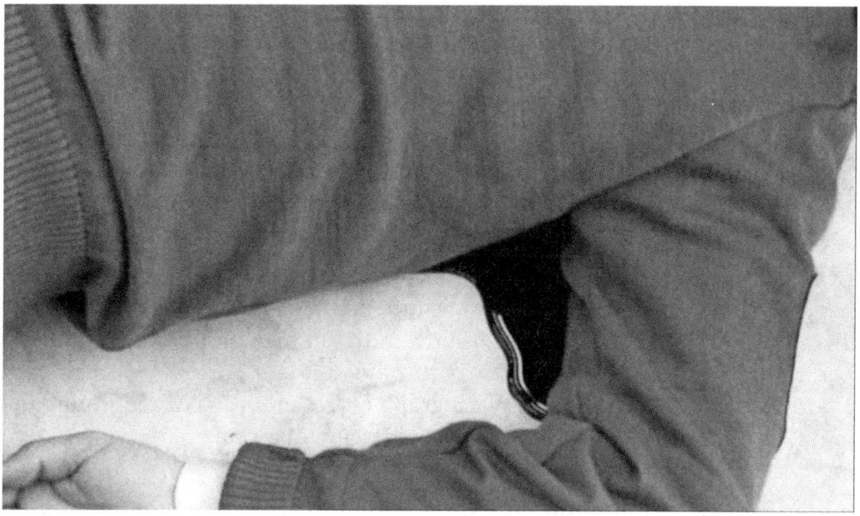

Figure 7: In a shot sustained for over a minute, we witness blood slowly pooling around the body of a slain security guard. *71 Fragmente einer Chronologie des Zufalls* (Michael Haneke, 1994).

Figure 8: The television news coverage of the mass murder registers the bloodstain that remains after the security guard's body has been removed. *71 Fragmente einer Chronologie des Zufalls* (Michael Haneke, 1994).

help but register their glaring absence in the televisual. However, through this very absence of the percepts and affects of the film image—which are completely overridden by television's informatic affective-perceptual force and its proximity to present time—a certain fundamental truth about the event is communicated: the profound spatiotemporal void of its ontological disposition.

In upholding the intermedial gaps between film and television that *71 Fragmente* displays, rather than seeking a conceptual-representational union of the two (as Le Cain proposes), one approaches a more complex and multifaceted perspective on the event than could be offered by either medium individually. Thus far, however, I have focused much more on television's mode of event-perception than on cinema's. In *Code inconnu*, though, we are presented with a consideration of film's—and photography's—own means of registering the event, and the role these properties play in defining cinematic realism.

Code inconnu: The Fragmented Real

As previously stated, *Code inconnu*, Haneke's first French-language film, is also his first cinematic work to eschew his strategy of detouring from filmic representation into video and television via close-ups on monitors that allow the other media to overtake the cinema screen.[45] While the film includes scenes of characters watching television, its adherence to a long-take aesthetic distantiates the viewer from these other media and their respective temporalities. Haneke's explanation for his approach in the film highlights this minimization of temporal manipulation:

> *Code Unknown* consists very much of static sequences, with each shot from only one perspective, precisely because I don't want to patronize or manipulate the viewer, or at least to the smallest degree possible. Of course, film is always manipulation, but if each scene is only one shot, then, I think, there is at least less of a sense of *time* being manipulated when one tries to stay close to a "real time" framework. The reduction of montage to a minimum also tends to shift responsibility back to the viewer in that more contemplation is required, in my view.[46]

Thus, even though, as in *71 Fragmente*, the individual scenes in *Code inconnu* are separated by black spacers, Haneke's general adherence to this long-take aesthetic—the hallmark, along with depth of field, of Andre Bazin's definition of postwar cinematic realism—as well as the greatly reduced role of other media in the film's discourse, lends this film a greater sense of internal coherence and cohesion as compared to the earlier film. Le Cain even goes so far as to state that the film actively works to overcome a sense of mimetic fragmentation: "*Code Inconnu* is as visually *anti*-fragmentation as the earlier films were defined by it."[47] Yet, as the subtitle of the film—which identifies the plot threads as "incomplete tales"—implies, the concept of fragmentation remains a prominent narrative and aesthetic concern in the film. This concern is attested to in a set of questions that Haneke drafted before beginning work on *Code inconnu*, which were included as part of the press notes upon the film's release. Among these one finds the following: "Is the fragment the aesthetic response to the incomplete nature of our perception?"[48] Indeed, *Code inconnu* offers several considerations regarding the limitations of film's inherently partial and fragmentary representation of reality, which is analogous, Haneke suggests, to a given subject's apprehension of actual events. The process of filmmaking itself is therefore deconstructed and fragmented through a series of scenes depicting various stages of production in the thriller in which Anne plays a role; in these scenes, the tenuous relationship between visual and sound-images in film is explored in particular. Anne's partner Georges's work as a photographer is also given developed consideration both within the dialogue and through two sequences in which a series of photographs are displayed on-screen as excerpts from Georges's letters to Anne are read in voice-over, sequences that constitute the most pronounced departures from cinematic representation in the film, yet also serve as an oblique inquiry into cinema's expression of the event.

While television elicits the event through a sense of temporal proximity, the cinematic event is linked more closely to the medium's capacity for expressing duration. Thus, Bazin, in his essay "Cinematic Realism and the Italian School of the Liberation" (1948), refers to the inherent power of the sustained shot as a means for realist filmmaking to free itself from the "tyranny of the *découpage*."[49] Significantly, the emergent neorealist narrative and aesthetic exemplified by Roberto Rossellini's *Paisà* (1946) is described by Bazin in the following terms: "The unit of *Paisà*'s narrative is not the shot, with its abstract perspective on the reality being analyzed, but the event—a fragment of raw reality, inherently multifarious and ambiguous, whose meaning becomes apparent only after the fact, through other events connected up in our minds."[50] This unit, which Bazin terms the "image-event," may be directly contrasted with the televisual event in that it arrives with no inherent informatic baggage: the image-event remains both "ambiguous" and initially empty of meaning, as opposed to information's being, as Walter Benjamin puts it, "already . . . shot through with explanation." Moreover, Bazin assigns to the image-event a function exceeding that of its role in the narrative, which is only assembled after the fact in the consciousness of the spectator: "The nature of the image-event, however, is not simply to connect with other image-events in ways invented by our minds. This in a sense is the centrifugal nature of the image, which makes it possible to create a narrative. Because each image, seen on its own, is only a fragment of reality and exists prior to this meaning, the entire surface of the screen must have the same concrete density."[51] As Bazin implies, the image-event's nonnarrative effect is to remain a self-contained fragment of space-time, "concrete" rather than illusory or fictive in relation to actuality, regardless of whether the image-event documents an actual occurrence or one that has been staged for the camera. The screen may be considered, in this reading, the site of an actual encounter with the event, an affirmation of objective reality that reinforces Deleuzian "belief in the world" via the cinematic image. Narrative coherence in cinematic realism is thus always threatened to some degree by the necessary fragmentation of our perception of the real, a tension that Haneke is explicitly concerned with preserving in *Code inconnu*. This mutual tension between the fictionality of the narrative and the reality effect of image-events increases the longer these shots are sustained, provided nothing occurs to prevent the investment of such images with the temporal character of actuality.

For this reason, the narrative of *Code inconnu* has a stake in preserving fragmentation even as it upholds continuity, if only to enhance its own realist agenda and aesthetic. Hence, although the individual scenes or segments present themselves as unitary in duration and spatial representation, the separate story lines that are initiated by the opening scene remain largely disconnected from one another. The individual plot paths of those involved in the opening incident—Anne, Jean (and his father and brother, by proxy), Amadou, and Maria—have completely diverged by the end of the film. In this respect, the narrative inverts the plot structure of *71 Fragmente*, in which the largely unrelated lives of the characters converge in the tragic event of the bank massacre that ends the narrative. Both films, though, reflect an increasingly familiar narrative model in which the lives of a largely unrelated group of characters converge in unexpected ways. However, most examples of this type of narrative film—which Roy Grundmann terms the "multistrain narrative" and Michel Cieutat refers to as a "subgenre called the 'choral film' "[52]—seem to present the idea of social and humanist interconnection. In the Cieutat interview, Haneke states that he is consciously working against such a narrative approach in his own films:

> *71 Fragments* and *Code Unknown* are different from *Short Cuts*, *American Beauty*, or *Magnolia*, a genre that's currently in vogue. These films have a tendency to tie up the strings of all the stories at the end. After finishing *71 Fragments*, I tried to do the opposite, or something much more complicated. I prefer to follow all the strings, in perfect continuity, without losing them, but without ever having to come back to them to tie them up in an explanatory way. That was my biggest worry during the elaboration of the structure of *Code Unknown*. It's very difficult to tell a story in that way.[53]

Without the sense of finality imparted to the plots of *71 Fragmente* or *Der siebente Kontinent* by their tragic turns of events, the overtly "incomplete tales" of *Code inconnu* remain unfettered by narrative closure or by any sense of the characters' enduring interrelationships.

This narrative structure, I have suggested, directly mirrors the mode of cinematic realism that characterizes the formal aesthetic of *Code inconnu* and stands in contrast to the overtly intermedial aesthetic that Haneke brings to bear on his previous films, with their bases in actual events widely reported in the mass media (*Funny Games* excepted). To be sure, however, Haneke is adamant about the fact that every plot point of *Code inconnu* is drawn directly from actuality, albeit in this case unfiltered by media reportage. In the 2004 documentary film on the director, *24 Wirklichkeiten in der Sekunde* (*24 Realities per Second*) by Nina Kusturica and Eva Testor, Haneke states the following: "In *Code inconnu*, everything that happens in the film, especially the things concerning Africans and Romanians, are things that I've seen or that I've been told. There's nothing invented. Sometimes reality is much more unbelievable than things you make up. A lot of things you'd like to show in a film would seem ridiculous or unbelievable. You've got to have a sort of instinct for what is believable and what isn't, but I like to be inspired by reality."[54] Later in the documentary, it is implied that one of the story lines in the film—that of Jean's unwillingness to inherit his father's farm and its attendant lifestyle—directly refers to the circumstances of Haneke's own adolescence: "My mother was an actress, but I grew up with my aunt. My aunt had a big farm and desperately wanted me take it over. Of course I didn't. That's the way it goes . . . ."[55] The narrative of *Code inconnu*, then, is oriented toward a mode of realism—the derivation of its events from actual experience—that is consonant with the formal gestures toward realism instituted by the long-take aesthetic. The fractures between the individual story lines may be read, in this sense, as a consequence of the story's adherence to the fragmentary structures of lived experience and human interrelationships in a multicultural urban environment, an aesthetic and narrative model that Scott Durham aptly refers to as "Haneke's realism of divergent series."[56]

Whereas *71 Fragmente* uses television footage as a negative medial correlate to its fragmented mode of cinematic realism, *Code inconnu* self-reflexively signals its representational construction by inserting scenes of film production that both parallel and depart from Haneke's film itself in important respects. The film-within-the-film is a conventional procedural thriller (*policier*) that Anne tentatively refers to as *Le collectionneur* ("The Collector"—the title, she notes, may be changed before its release), and the contrast between its approach to cinematic narrative and montage and the approach of *Code inconnu* itself is apparent. As Haneke notes in his interview with Cieutat, the use of *Le collectionneur* as an index of difference from his own approach to representational realism was intentional: "I used the long-take in *Code Unknown* for several reasons. First, in order to find a rigid structure for the fragments, as in a puzzle, but also to separate them from the scenes relating to the film-within-the-film, which are shown in the usual way."[57] Haneke's refusal to cut within scenes formally demarcates the images of the film from those of the film-within-the-film, which are not bound by this aesthetic choice.[58] This use of the film-within-the-film thus appears, on the surface, to be a relatively straightforward, self-reflexive strategy, a gesture toward an established trope of modern cinema utilized in works such as Michael Powell's *Peeping Tom* (1960) and François Truffaut's *Day for Night* (1973).[59] In fact, a review of *Code inconnu* by Andrew James Horton points out the seeming banality of this approach, in comparison with Haneke's use of fragmentation and nonfilmic media to greater effect in previous films: "[Haneke] is running out of mechanisms to force us to question the power of film as a medium. He resorts to tactics that are now seemingly commonplace in his films, such as suddenly cutting off the dialogue mid-sentence. Even worse, he employs techniques that are universally clichéd, such as showing the making of a film within the film we are watching and trying to confuse us as to which level we are looking at. This, quite frankly, is old hat."[60] Against such a reading, however, one can assert that the presentation of the film-within-the-film introduces into the diegesis two theoretically intriguing aspects of filmic representation itself: the temporal incongruities between the chronologies of production and narrative and the increasing distance from *Code inconnu*'s realist aesthetic that these incongruities imply; and the independence of visual and sound-images in cinematic mimesis.

In all, three scenes from *Le collectionneur* are depicted within the film: Anne's rehearsal, during the film's preproduction, of a scene in which her character realizes that she is a captive and is being threatened with murder;[61] the filming of a scene in which Anne's character is given a tour of a house by the realtor, just before being locked within the room that becomes her prison; and a scene in which her character cavorts in a rooftop pool with her husband and witnesses their child almost fall to his death when he climbs the railing to retrieve a balloon. This final scene ends with Anne's character telling her husband that they have to find a new home in order to avoid anything like this happening in the future (followed by a brief cut to the realtor character, her future captor, receiving a phone call). This footage is revealed to be situated at the postproduction stage of the film's chronology; Anne and the actor portraying the husband have been called to a studio in order to rerecord this scene's dialogue, which had been partially obscured by the noise from a passing airplane during the shoot. Thus, within *Code inconnu* the three scenes from *Le collectionneur* are presented in reverse order with respect to their places in the narrative of the film-within-the-film: Anne's character's imprisonment is followed by her tour of the house just before she is taken captive, which is in turn followed by the incident that leads to her decision to move and hence puts her into contact with her future captor. Yet, with respect to the narrative chronology of Haneke's film, each scene is depicted at a progressively later stage in the film's creation, from pre- to postproduction. Interestingly, this narrative regression corresponds to what

Figure 9: Anne's videotaped rehearsal for a scene in the film-within-the-film assumes its own independent affective power and spatiotemporal dimensions. *Code inconnu* (Michael Haneke, 2000).

is also presented as an aesthetic regression from *Code inconnu*'s high realist mode to that of mainstream cinematic convention.

The rehearsal scene is presented in a single shot via a video camera and thus resembles the long-take aesthetic of Haneke's film. However, the presence of the video apparatus within the scene is registered, both by Anne's gaze into the lens and by having the cameraman briefly move the camera as he acknowledges to the offscreen voice of the director that he is recording. Even with these overt acknowledgements of the scene being staged, though, as the duration of the scene and the emotional intensity of Binoche-as-Anne's performance increase, the perceptual-affective realism of the situation asserts itself more strongly (see figure 9).[62] Peter Brunette thus reads into the shot "a self-conscious ambiguity" with regard to its relationship to actuality: "[I]t's finally impossible to tell whether the character Anne is playing is frightened, or whether Anne herself has suddenly become genuinely afraid . . . and we can easily imagine [the offscreen voice's order to "show your real face"] as a command coming from Michael Haneke himself, directed not toward the actress character, Anne, but toward the actress Juliette Binoche herself." Brunette concludes that the scene demonstrates "the impossibility of ever fully distinguishing, at least in the context of the cinema, between reality and its representation, and thus of ever understanding the basic ontological status of any noncontextualized image."[63] However, whether one attributes this expression of fear and desperation to Binoche, Anne, or Anne's character in *Le collectionneur*—or, for that matter, attribute the offscreen voice to Haneke, an unseen actor portraying a director, or the character of the captor whose dialogue the director reads—is redundant. The performance's ambiguous ontological status arguably does not factor into its affective power; or, rather, the image's ontological status is destabilized *by* the sheer affective power of the image. In this reading, the sense of situational ambiguity is brought about through the sustained encounter with "faciality,"[64] the face as the very expression of the affection-image in Deleuze's cinema theory. This image finds its proper milieu in the ambiguous, fragmented, and delocalized territory of "any-space-whatever" (*un espace quelconque*): "We now say that there are two kinds of signs of the affection-image, or two figures of first-ness: *on the one hand the power-quality expressed by a face or an equivalent; but on the other hand the power-quality presented in any-space-whatever*. . . . The any-space-whatever would be the genetic element of the affection-image."[65] The affection-image embodied by the face of the actress is itself a decontextualizing force, then, in that it overcomes its relation to any one of the individual milieux accorded to it—that of a prison in *Le collectionneur*, that of a rehearsal space in *Code inconnu*, that of a scene recorded by Haneke and Binoche—and instead defines its own field of emergence as any-space-whatever, within an ambiguous status or level of representation. In this way, the spare and simplified staging of the scene, its very minimization of visual flourish, accords it a maximal affective force and almost paradoxical realism, though at the expense of the scene's narrative contextualization. In Bazinian terms, this image-event has temporarily broken free of its narrative connection to other image-events.

The second depiction of the film-within-the-film's production corresponds more directly with the aesthetic of *Code inconnu* itself. As the scene opens, the camera is static and positioned at a high angle in a darkened room with voices audible offscreen. The light is turned on, and Anne enters the room with another actor (playing the realtor) as well as a film camera and a small crew who track the movement of the two figures within the space. As Anne asks the man a question (why there are no windows in the room), the film cuts, startlingly, to the point of view of the camera filming within the scene. When there is a mistake in the filming, there is a cut to outside of the room and we remain aligned with the diegetic camera's perspective as the scene begins filming once again. The fact that the scene being filmed within the film is composed of a single tracking shot already implicitly mirrors the mode of production of *Code inconnu* itself, which would by necessity have used a similar crew, camera dolly, marks for the actors, and so on. But this reflexive gesture then becomes a recursive one, as the camera within the scene is appropriated by Haneke's film.[66] A firsthand account of the production of the film-within-the-film is thus supplied by the camera shooting the film itself, once again blurring the distinctions that can be made between the levels of representation in operation. The question of whether we are viewing the filming of *Le collectionneur* or of *Code inconnu* itself is undecidable, but within this ambiguity lies another realization: just as Haneke's employment of noncinematic media indexes an absolute difference in the perceptual and affective qualities these media bring to bear in comparison to film—as made apparent by *71 Fragmente*'s television news reports—here it is shown that there is a fundamental *equivalence* between the medium of film and itself, such that the film and the film-within-the-film become fully exchangeable entities within the scene. This relationship of equivalence is overturned, however, by *Code inconnu*'s final presentation of the filmmaking process.

Although the scene in which Anne is depicted cavorting in a swimming pool with an unknown man is presented without narrative context, having been immediately preceded by a spacer, its visual style—which captures the action through a series of brief shots and cuts—evinces that it is not at all stylistically continuous with Haneke's film. Several minutes into the scene, this difference is signaled diegetically by an offscreen voice, which requests that the film be stopped, at which point the image freezes and rapidly reverses as the projector's reel is rewound.[67] As this occurs, the camera pulls back to situate itself in a screening room, in which Anne and the male actor from the scene have been viewing the film. This gesture confirms the aesthetic differentiation from *Code inconnu* already apparent from the rapid editing and noncontiguous staging of the film clip. Whereas the long takes of the static camera in the rehearsal and the tracking shot of the filming express potential aesthetic equivalencies and ambiguities between *Le collectionneur* and *Code inconnu*, once the film-within-the-film is screened it evinces a clear stylistic break from the latter, to the point that an intermedial relationship between the two can be perceived. The film-within-the-film, in this sense, may be considered the negative coefficient of *Code inconnu*'s realist ambitions, functioning in this regard in a manner similar to that of the television news clips in *71 Fragmente*. Thus, the Cavellian concept of genre-as-medium emerges once again, as it did in connection with *Funny Games*: the orientation of the thriller toward action expressed through dynamic camera movement and rapid montage, as well as the manufacture of moments of extreme tension and character endangerment within the staging, presents an almost absolute fracture with *Code inconnu* itself that is tantamount to its belonging to a separate medium of expression. Following this line of consideration, it is possible to orient the three scenes of filmmaking not only in terms of production stages but also in terms of realism, with the degree of realism corresponding to the level of ambiguity each scene presents with respect to *Code inconnu*. The affective realism of Anne's videotaped rehearsal renders its context utterly ambiguous (in other words, as any-space-whatever); the tracking shot may be equally interpreted as a filming of the scene for *Le collectionneur* or as *Code inconnu*'s documentation of this filming; and the scene that is screened does not present itself, finally, as anything other than a decidedly nonrealist genre film displayed within *Code inconnu*'s diegesis, breaking completely from Haneke's own film.

Haneke's juxtaposition of his own film with the film-within-the-film posits a direct relationship between a shot's duration and the degree to which the cinematic medium conveys image-events via *temporal*, as opposed to representational, realism. In this respect, his own long-take aesthetic conforms more closely to Bazinian realism, with its focus on minimal temporal manipulation. The matching of unrelated shots and the acceleration of montage that are present in the footage of *Le collectionneur* assume the status of a negative correlate to this approach (recalling the role of television in *71 Fragmente*). The reverse chronology of this film's production relative to its narrative further enforces this temporal differentiation, which finally overcomes the profound ambiguity present in the initial departures into the film production process. Yet this screening also reflects an aspect of the film medium with implications for realism that impinge on *Code inconnu* itself, namely the fact of the actors overdubbing their original dialogue within the scene. Here, an overt fracture between cinema's image track and cinema's sound track is brought directly into relief, supplying a different vector for fragmentation.

Heautonomy and the Photographic Image

Thematically, it is possible to relate the divorce between the visible and the audible in *Code inconnu* to the film's meditation on the failure of the act of communication to vouchsafe understanding or to establish meaningful connections between individuals. Yet the differences between sound and visual image that are revealed in the overdub recording scene also bring into focus a specific medial configuration—one that Haneke consistently explores in his films—that is premised on a perceptual-affective separation of audible and visible amplitudes. Georg Seeβlen offers the following comment on the effect of this aural and visual segregation as it conforms to Haneke's overall strategy of perceptual fragmentation: "Through this limitation, the information systems of image and sound are further separated; especially in *71 Fragments* it happens again and again that we see something but hear nothing and vice versa."[68] Seeβlen's essay was published prior to the release of *Code inconnu*, and one could argue that the separation of these "information systems" (which I would prefer to refer to as "systems of sensation") has only increased in the later film. The overdub scene in particular presents sound and visual image in cinema as disparate medial entities by definition, the audio track being altered and recomposed in a completely different context than that of the filming.

Deleuze offers a particularly efficient means of conceptualizing this medial fracture between the audible and the visible. The fracture presents itself most overtly in what he refers to as the "second stage" of sound cinema, which came to the fore in the era of the time-image: "The sound image is born, in its very break, from its break with the visual image. There are no longer even two autonomous components of a single audiovisual image, as in Rossellini, but two 'heautonomous' images, one visual and one sound, with a fault, an interstice, an irrational cut between them."[69] The Kantian term "heautonomous"—which Rodowick concisely defines as referring to the fact "that image and sound are distinct and incommensurable yet complementary"[70]—indicates that the relationship between sound and picture that defines the "talkie" is preserved, but that the sound-image is no longer subordinate to the visual image in either a technical or an aesthetic-representational sense. In this way, the sound track is capable of its own expressive potentialities, which need not be considered equipollent with those of the visual track. Here, an audio-visual relation is posited that resembles that of television news, in which the continual vocal discourse on the sound track lends coherence and cohesion to the fragmented visual footage. In fact, in an extended parenthetical remark following the above passage, Deleuze states that audio-visual heautonomy would have been unthinkable without the influence of television and thus constitutes an overtly intermedial development:

> [U]ndoubtedly this second stage would never have arisen without television; it is television which made it possible; but, because television abandoned most of its own creative possibilities, and did not even understand them, it needed cinema to give it a pedagogical lesson; it needed great cinema authors to show what it could do and what it would be able to do; if it is true that television kills cinema, cinema on the other hand is continually revitalizing television, not only because it feeds it with films, but because the great cinema authors invent the audio-visual image, which they are quite ready to 'give back' to television if it gives them the opportunity[.][71]

In spite of Deleuze's extreme (indeed, Haneke-like) characterizations of television and film—the former selfishly sapping the vital energy of the latter, even as cinema's auteurs respond by altruistically offering television realizations of its own creative capabilities—the point is conceded that the newer medium's audiovisual configuration inspired novel potentialities for the use of cinematic sound (and thus, perhaps, spurred a decisive break from the audio-linguistic analogues to theater that characterized the first stage of sound cinema). Before exploring *Code inconnu*'s pairing of sound and visual images as it relates to Haneke's use of diegetic and extradiegetic music, let me turn to the two definably heautonomous audio-visual sequences in the film, in which Georges reads aloud his letters to Anne while photographs he has taken are displayed on-screen. In these sequences, the audio track assumes the narrative burden almost completely, while the visual track is literally fractured into a series of still images that enforce a greater degree of visual realism (though in a markedly different way than the cinematic long take).

Both photo sequences feature actual photographs taken by Luc Delahaye, an acquaintance of Haneke's whose work is presented within the film as that of the character Georges.[72] The first photo series uses Delahaye's images of conflict in Kosovo as indices of Georges's experience there, while the second series consists of portraits of passengers on the Paris Métro who have been photographed without their knowledge, in an act of image theft that the narrative depicts Georges performing. Although both photo series are identifiable as narrative content in the sense that they result from Georges's own off- and on-screen actions, the sequences simultaneously serve to introduce another representational medium into the film, and with it a non- or extracinematic perspective on actuality. Haneke makes this narrative and representational strategy clear: "I was interested in a character who was a photographer who specialized in war photography because it allowed me to integrate another reality by means of his photos."[73] Haneke is careful to note the fact that the two photo series were not staged or reproduced for the film, and thus that the photographs remain an utterly foreign element of the film's mimesis in a technical sense, albeit an element whose presence has been accounted for within the narrative context. While the significance of these sequences within the plot is fairly straightforward, then—particularly given that the dramatic associations with Georges's profession are further enforced by the character's voice-over narration—the medial relationship between these photographs and the film itself is extraordinarily complex. The photographic sequences institute radical departures from, and ruptures within, not only the film's diegesis—which shifts from fictionality to actuality—but also its spatiotemporal disposition, its mode of address to the spectator, and its overall representational strategy. Indeed, Raymond Bellour, whose insights into the differential relations between film and photographic media are profound, qualifies the insertion of photography's spatiotemporal "image-state" into that of cinema as productive of an irresolvable impasse to our recognition or identification of the two as independent media:

> [T]he effect of the photographic extends in a staggered fashion, going beyond photography itself, according to the greater or lesser degree of movement with which it affects the image, but without extending as far as its own self-contained, singular identity which might add up to the fiction of cinema itself . . . We are dealing, therefore, with *an art of confusion, an aesthetic of confusion*. As we might imagine, the word is only intended positively, contrary to any idea of specificity or authenticity of media, which have meaning only inasmuch as they mingle.[74]

The ontological-representational basis of the photographic and that of the cinematographic are so close as to be in many respects indistinguishable, apart from their temporal dispositions; yet, as Bellour points out, their respective medial properties assert themselves more directly through their very commingling, an interaction that also produces a uniquely engaging aesthetic effect. Haneke's use of these photo series thus invites a plethora of inquiries into the intermedial differences and medial commonalities between photography and cinema and into the degree to which these relations theoretically and thematically inform *Code inconnu*.[75] For my purposes, however, I will only examine in detail two aspects of the sequences: the perspective that these photo series, and photography as a medium, offer on the *event* in comparison to the perspective of film (and of television); and the use of voice-over as an aural supplement that simultaneously contextualizes and decontextualizes the images.

In a compelling piece of self-commentary, Haneke includes in his film a character—Georges and Anne's friend Francine—who questions the very premise of Georges's profession as a photographer of war and other atrocities. Francine's intellectual opposition to photojournalism appears to be focused on the obscenity inherent in visual representations of the victims of such events, as she frames her argument with Georges in the following terms: "[Y]ou have to photograph death and destruction so I know what war is? Starving kids so I know what famine is? What a dumb assumption!" Georges's counterargument to this position appears in his voice-over during the second series of photos, during which he refers to Francine and acknowledges that she may be right, but states, "It's easy to talk about the 'ecology of the image' and 'value of the non-transmitted message.' What matters is the end result." Georges's pragmatic justification of his occupation suggests an implicit faith in the power of the photographic image to overcome the banalization brought about by its very ubiquity and dissemination, a position strengthened by the evocative nature of Delahaye's photos relative to the film's own image system. The film thus appears to uphold both sides of this debate, as it refuses to suppress the images of war and human suffering that Delahaye has recorded but equally refuses to assign to them a specific context or representational referent. The photographs therefore seem to possess an *ontological* rather than a *representational* signifying function; as Haneke states in the above-quoted interview with Michel Cieutat, the photos introduce "another reality" into the film's diegesis, this additional reality being the perceptual field surrounding events in actuality.

Such an understanding of photography as a medium accords well with Stanley Cavell's work on this topic, particularly as interpreted by D. N. Rodowick. The latter states that, in Cavell's conceptualization, "the primary sense of the photograph is not to represent objects, but rather *to transcribe historical events*. This transcription is inseparable from the automated processes of a time-bound fixing of reflected light spatially organized by a lens. In other words, as an automated instrument, the camera is designed to register and preserve a profilmic event to which it was once present. The photograph has no sense apart from this function."[76] If, in Haneke's work, the photographic medium is to retain its autonomy relative to the film medium, then the photo series' presentation must express this relationship to the unstaged and unreproducible event indexed by the photographs.[77] In this sense, the photographs in *Code inconnu* realize an intermedial function similar to the news broadcasts punctuating *71 Fragmente*: each film layers its own gesture toward realism—which (especially in *Code inconnu*) proceeds in definably Bazinian terms, through fragmentary image-events represented in adherence to their proper milieux and durations—with that of another medium possessing an utterly different evental configuration. As was previously asserted with reference to Mary-Ann Doane, however, whereas television news registers the event informatically and through a temporal mode corresponding to the passing present, photography "embalms" the event, a term used by Bazin in "The Ontology of the Photographic Image" (1945): "for photography does not create eternity, as art does, it embalms time, rescuing it simply from its proper corruption."[78] The image-event in photography is arrested in a condition of timelessness, perfectly preserving the unrepeatable material state of affairs the event effects but robbing this state of its temporal vitality and forcing the suspension of the event's animation. Thus, the two photographic series in *Code inconnu* constitute gestures away from fictionality and representation and toward actuality, as do the news reports in *71 Fragmente*, but along a wholly different temporal and intermedial axis.[79] Furthermore, rather than presenting an intermedial fracture such as that between the filmic and televisual, the filmic and the photographic maintain a sense of continuity with one another, an overlap in their perceptual fields.[80] In spite of the differential temporalities and degrees of actuality with which each medium mediates an event, then, Haneke is able to integrate the photographic series into his film *in cinematic terms*, while the televisual is only admitted into the film *in televisual terms*. This cinematographic treatment of the photo series is evident in the heautonomous relationship they obtain with the vocal narration on the sound track.

In "The Pensive Spectator," Bellour states that works composed largely of still photographs, such as Chris Marker's *La Jetée* (1962), reveal a subtle truth about cinematic expression: "it isn't movement that defines most profoundly the cinema. . . . Rather, it is time: the concatenation, the unfolding of images in time, a time the spectator cannot control." Bellour then immediately goes on to note that in the absence of movement in the visual images themselves the sound track adopts the cinematic burden of expressing duration: "Music and voiceover harmonize particularly well in films composed of photographs. It isn't simply that the two audio tracks animate such films; it's rather that their respective manifestations (*defilements*) share the character of temporal movement, and that these movements reinforce each other."[81] In this regard, a major distinction presents itself between voice-over as an expression of informatic discourse in television news reports and voice-over as an expression of cinematic duration in the absence of on-screen movement. The voice-over in television vouchsafes both discursive and temporal flow, whereas the voice-over in cinema—in a heautonomous effect related to but also distinct from its narrational function—superimposes its image of duration onto that of the visual image (which, in this case, itself lacks temporal extension). Thus, *Code inconnu*'s two photo series are not "animated" or even explicitly "narrated" by Georges's voice-over but rather are simultaneously juxtaposed against and enfolded into the chronotope of its sound-image. As divergent as the photographs and the sound track are in content and effect,[82] then, they nonetheless retain a temporal and medial suture as heautonomous images upholding an affirmatively cinematic mode of expression. In what ways, however, is this effect altered when music rather than speech is employed on the sound track?

Haneke's films, on the whole, differ from most in their general eschewal of scoring and musical cues, with the result being that when music is presented as potentially altering the temporal and affective nature of a scene or as providing a thematic or conceptual bridge between scenes, the effect is noticeable and significant. For instance, Haneke's use of diegetic music in *Der siebente Kontinent* and *Benny's Video* at times suggests that a fragile and almost unthinkable sublimity has been accorded to the perceptions of children: Evi's vision of the passing ship in the *Der siebente Kontinent* is accompanied by Alban Berg's violin concerto "To the Memory of an Angel" playing, apparently, on a car's radio; and in *Benny's Video* televised organ music provides a musical accompaniment to Benny's view of ships in a harbor during his trip to Egypt and then continues through a montage of video footage from the trip. The fact that this music emanates, in both cases, from media *within* the film invests the music with a sense of ambiguity in terms of one's acceptance of its use as an artistic statement on Haneke's part. However, the very presence of music in such scenes—a presence that also manifests through the use of a personal cassette player in *Le temps du loup* and of a car stereo during the opening sequence of *Funny Games* (only to be violently supplanted on the sound track by the grindcore aggression of John Zorn's band Naked City)—effectuates what amounts to a tonal shift in cinema's medium of expression. As Michel Chion argues in a short essay focused on the utter absence of music in *Caché*, the presence of music in a film is equivalent to a linguistic shift into a poetic register: "[M]usic, in the classical sense, is perceived as a principle of association of sounds, which unfixes them from their origin, on the one hand (a sound is no longer just 'a sound of,' the sound of a piano, a voice, etc.), and, on the other, liberates them from language in the functional and everyday sense, from the 'chains' of language, as Valéry put it. This comes down to the difference between 'prose' and 'poetry.' "[83] The recognition of a heautonomous relation between visual and sound-images in Haneke's oeuvre, however, complicates one's understanding of such a shift in affective and expressive tone, to the extent that the "poetic" and "prosaic" modes of cinematic expression must be acknowledged simultaneously. Even as the music seems to impart an almost elegiac significance to the visual imagery, one may question whether the music itself, in its indifferent medial reproduction within the diegesis, is not thereby in turn stripped of its normal affective associations.[84] The anchoring of musical accompaniment within the diegesis thus maintains Haneke's mode of realism in such a way that the music's relation to the image is only ambiguously interpretable as a gesture toward aesthetic artifice. In *Code inconnu*, though, a different effect is achieved than in the aforementioned scenes and films.[85]

The first major distinction that presents itself is the fact that *Code inconnu*'s most significant instance of musical accompaniment does not underpin a child's quasi-Romantic encounter or vision but rather is produced by children themselves. At one point we are shown the class of deaf children, whom we had encountered at the opening of the film, practicing group drumming under Amadou's direction (it is later revealed that his younger sister is hearing-impaired and is a member of the class). Near the end of the film, the children and Amadou stage a public performance of their drumming in a city park, and the percussive and almost cacophonous rhythm first becomes audible over one of the black-screen spacers, cutting through the silence that has previously fragmented the sound track during these cuts. After a scene identifying the source of the drumming, there is a cut to black before we see a succession of scenes set at the same location as the long tracking shot that has introduced the main characters. The sound of the drumming remains continuously audible, dominating the sound track throughout all of these shots and the spacers that separate them, as first Maria, then Anne, and then Georges are depicted in separate tracking shots that register new stages in their individual stories or "journeys": Maria must abandon her former begging spot as it has been taken over by another group; Anne returns to her apartment alone after having been accosted by a teenager on the Métro; and Georges returns from another war zone to find that Anne has changed the entry code of her apartment building and effectively ended their relationship. The continuous presence of the drumming on the sound track of this last scene is particularly intriguing, as it appears to be set some time after the previous scenes with Maria and Anne (it is now raining outside), indicating that the music has long outlasted its ambient diegetic presence in the film and has assumed a different, identifiably structural function. The sound track becomes at this point the film's primary gesture toward temporal and narrative coherence, drawing the disparate fragments into a common relation that belies the spatial, temporal, and interpersonal isolation of the scenes themselves and the characters within them. Yet the medium of this relation is neither identifiably prosaic nor poetic, containing no words and no melody, but rather a purely percussive expression of rhythm, a propulsive force that lends no explicit meaning or significance to the characters' movements and actions.[86] The contrast between this sequence of shots and the long tracking shot that sets the entire narrative in motion is apparent: the establishing shot placed the characters (with Jean standing in for the absent Georges in this case) into a common space and recorded an event, a random encounter, the meaning and implications of which fail to cohere even when the actants attempt to account for their actions verbally to one another and to the authorities who intervene; whereas the final sequence is wordless, the spatiotemporal relationships and milieux of the characters are utterly fractured, and the drumming on the sound track seems less a potential medium for communication than an expression of the indefinable forces that propel these individual journeys on their divergent paths. In this case, then, the heautonomous relation between the drums on the sound track and the film's return to the locale of the opening enables the imposition of a virtual duration—expressed here by the sound-image of pure rhythm—onto these fractured temporalities, replacing the sustained duration of the single-take opening scene. Haneke thereby suggests, in an echo of the means through which the photo series are drawn into a common cinematic framework, that these disparate segments (and the film as a whole, perhaps) have unfolded as part of a single image-event. In his intermedial gestures away from audiovisual realism, Haneke thus affirms a more profound expression of realism that obtains beyond, and through, cinematic fragmentation itself.

The narratives of *71 Fragmente* and *Code inconnu* are equally structured around real events—in the former, an actual bank shooting provides the basis for an examination of individual lives that will be inexorably altered by tragedy, while the latter's similarly transversal approach to plot has a basis in what Haneke claims were actual occurrences he has restaged for the film. Both films are thus aesthetically invested in uncovering formal foundations for registering real events in a narrative context, and this project is realized through the films' respective gestures toward fragmentation. Haneke confronts the problem of cinema's inherently partial and disjointed representation of the real by introducing gaps into the very image systems of the films. Furthermore, the director implies that this approach is analogous to the necessarily delimited perception of a subject's lived experience: "If the cinema wants to be responsible—in other words, a true art—it's obligated to realize that our perception of the world is naturally fragmented. So we have to find the aesthetic means that will allow us to transfer this fragmented look onto the screen."[87] The modes of fragmentation that permeate these films, however, extend beyond the narrative and mimetic gaps instituted by the black-screen spacers. Like *Der siebente Kontinent* before it, *71 Fragmente* foregrounds a definably intermedial form of fragmentation by introducing television directly into its medial field and does so more consistently than the earlier film. *Code inconnu* does not visually register such a direct relationship with electronic or informatic media—apart from the use of video in Anne's rehearsal—but it likewise highlights a number of identifiably intermedial disparities: between the divergent aesthetics of artistic and commercial cinema; between cinematography and photography; and between sound and visual imagery. These modes of intermedial fragmentation—which one could characterize as "vertical" gaps imposed on the films' entire image systems—complement the "horizontal" gaps in narrative and image continuity signified by the spacers. Moreover, intermedial fragmentation impinges more directly on the question of realism than does narrative fragmentation, insofar as it problematizes the longstanding assumption that film—or any other medium—can assume the capacity to "represent" and preserve actual events.

More than any other function, the multiple modes and axes of fragmentation that inform the image systems of *71 Fragmente einer Chronologie des Zufalls* and *Code inconnu* serve to discompose the very structure of the mediated event. By factoring in the gaps obtaining between individual conceptions of events—including the image-events of the cinematic long take, the "live" events of television news's cyclical programming, and the arrested events of photography—the films make recourse to the definition of a given event as exceeding the parameters of any and all forms of mediation. If, as Haneke asserts, our perception of reality is fragmented by default, then this approach to the event constitutes the height of realism. Yet Haneke forces the issue still further, in that his intermedial fragmentation demonstrates that the incompatible percepts and affects each medium brings to bear on a given event serve not to enrich our apprehension of actuality but only to further alienate us from the fabric of the real. In this way, the void that inheres in the logic of the event (which occurs, as Deleuze states via Groethuysen, in "the time where nothing happens")[88] is made manifest in—or, more properly speaking, *between*—the very media through which the event is "represented." In *Code inconnu* especially, sound is utilized not as a medium in itself but as an *intermedium*, affectively and virtually suturing the fragmented image-events of the film to elicit the structure and register of events in actuality. The next chapter will extend this conceptualization of sound as intermedium to the idea of voice as well in the process of exploring another intermedial practice crucial to understanding Haneke's development as an auteur: his literary adaptations for television, and his sole cinematic adaptation, *La pianiste*.

Chapter 4

✦

Adaptation as an Intermedial Practice

Haneke's Television Adaptations, *Das Schloß*, and *La pianiste*

Before releasing *La pianiste*—an adaptation of Elfriede Jelinek's remarkable 1983 novel *Die Klavierspielerin*, which was released in English with the title *The Piano Teacher*, a translation also applied to the film—in 2001, Haneke adapted four literary works for Austrian television as a writer and director: Ingeborg Bachmann's short story *Drei Wege zum See* (*Three Paths to the Lake*; 1976), Peter Rosei's novel *Wer war Edgar Allan?* (*Who Was Edgar Allan?*; 1984), Joseph Roth's novel *Die Rebellion* (*The Rebellion*; 1993), and Franz Kafka's long fragment *Das Schloß* (*The Castle*; 1997). Interestingly, in an interview with Willy Riemer that was published before the release of *La pianiste*—and, presumably, prior to Haneke's attachment to the production—the director expresses what appears to be a general disdain for the practice of adaptation, a disdain that is seemingly inconsistent with his multiple forays into the genre. Haneke states that he considers adaptation the province of educational television rather than of cinema, which should strive for independent aesthetic value:

> In my view, film adaptations are not genuine works of art. And I don't really know of any film adaptation that really worked very well. . . . It is not possible to serve two masters at the same time. Thus one has to decide. Either I use a book as a quarry for ideas for something that I want to create myself, then it is a failed project as a film adaptation. Or it is to be a film or a television program that has a commitment to cultural standards. In that case I should attempt to convey the spirit of the book; that I can do more or less skillfully, but film adaptation will never be autonomous art.[1]

Haneke does not simply dismiss film adaptation as an artistic endeavor compromised by its own definition, however; indeed, his expression of what one might consider film adaptation's treasonous aesthetic disposition—its betrayal of either the literary merits of the source text, its own potential cinematic-artistic autonomy, or both—reflects concerns that have long shaped adaptation studies as a whole. As Robert Stam points out, film adaptations are consigned to a critical "double bind": "A 'faithful' film is seen as uncreative, but an 'unfaithful' film is a shameful betrayal of the original. . . . The adapter, it seems, can never win."[2] Haneke suggests that in his television adaptations he escapes this dilemma, intentionally subordinating his own artistic interests to those of the author and serving television's educational function over and above his own aesthetic concerns. For the acclaimed *La pianiste*, however—his sole cinematic adaptation—Haneke seemingly has no recourse to such a defense. Instead, he claims to have taken a number of liberties with the structure and tone of Jelinek's novel in order to translate it to cinema (an approach he would not have taken with Kafka):

> I would not have dared to turn "The Castle" into a movie for the big screen; on TV, it's OK, because it has different objectives. But with "The Piano Teacher," if you compare the structure of the novel to the structure of the film, it's really quite different, and I feel I've been dealing very freely with the novel and the way it was written. I would say that my version of looking at the story is pretty distanced and cool, while the novel itself is almost angry and very emotional. The novel is much more subjective and the film is much more objective.[3]

Although these differences are acknowledged, Haneke also points out that the film reflects Jelinek's sensibilities as much as or more so than his own, stating in an interview with Christopher Sharrett that the film's subject and themes are "a bit distant from me. For example, I couldn't have written a novel on the subject of female sexuality. The topic of the novel interested me, but my choice of other source material for a film will probably continue to be the exception."[4]

Such assertions on Haneke's part create an interrelated pair of critical distinctions: the first with respect to authorship—delineating Haneke as separate from Jelinek in the consideration of *La pianiste* as an artistic statement—and the second to media—delineating the adaptation of a literary text to television as opposed to cinema. If one attributes the narrative and thematic content of the television adaptations to the original author, with Haneke taking on the task of "translating" the narrative to a new medium as a *metteur en scène* rather than assuming the role of auteur in his own right, then the primary criteria for their assessment remain tied to the notion of fidelity, defined by the textual-representational logic of original and copy. Such a logic persists in connection to *La pianiste*, albeit complexified by the realization that Haneke has in this case applied his own sensibilities as a filmmaker to the source material more directly, thus seemingly presenting a hybrid text or puzzle for critical analysis. Such a perspective invites investigation into the changes made to Jelinek's narrative in the film and speculation on the motivations underlying these changes, their thematic implications, and their merits or shortcomings vis-à-vis the original novel.[5] In this chapter, however, I will seek to map out a different approach to the negotiation of the intermedial relationships emergent in adaptation, one focusing less on *narrative* as an underlying structure shared by these media and more on *voice* as a medium utilized by literature, television, and sound cinema, though possessing different configurations and modes of expression in each. Of particular interest in this consideration will be Haneke's use of a third-person voice-over narrator in his television adaptations and its reflection of television's status as a vococentric medium, in contrast with *La pianiste*'s lack of voice-over in any traditional sense and the implications of this absence on the presentation of Erika, as well as the role of music as a supplement or substitution for vocal expression. I will begin, however, by examining some of the most obvious problems inherent in the prospect of comparing a written work to a cinematic one, and will by extension address the overall difficulties involved in the analysis of film via writing.

Writing on Film

Any attempt to engage with the concepts of media and intermediality in and of themselves must by necessity already be mediated, if only by written language. As a discursive practice, then, intermediality must account for its reflexive relationship with its own object of study, a conceptual torsion that suggests that any theory of media is necessarily intermedial and moreover has already confronted the limits of its own capacity for mediation. Does this imply that intermediality—including the gaps and void spaces that one perceives therein—precludes any attempt to formulate a substantive notion of the (pure) medium? Jens Schröter seems to suggest as much in his own consideration of discursive models for intermediality: "What is important is to see that one should not start with definitions of media and then discuss intermediality but the opposite: The intermedial field (*including the intermedial processes on writing about intermediality*) produces definitions of media."[6] As a definably non-audiovisual medium, writing presents a particularly problematic intermedial association with film that is implicitly or explicitly confronted in any attempt at a structuralist or textual engagement with the medium of film itself.

Raymond Bellour's short essay "The Unattainable Text" (1975) remains the definitive statement on this inherent resistance of film to written analysis. While affirming that film is a text in the Barthesian sense, Bellour equally asserts that the film text is uniquely "unquotable."[7] Cinematic expression's absolute distance from written language, notation, and print reproduction forecloses the possibility of generating anything like the forms of logical and semiotic analysis that developed in relation to other types of nonlinguistic texts, for the moving image simultaneously presents both a temporal and a spatial aspect: "On the one hand it spreads in space like a picture; on the other it plunges into time, like a story which [in] its serialization into units approximates more or less to the musical work."[8] Such an image remains by definition semiotically unreproducible via either notational, linguistic, or graphic text, even if certain important aspects are communicable—for example, dialogue and on-screen text via writing, and certain elements of mise-en-scène via still photos or frame reproductions. As a structuralist scholar with extensive experience in the formal analysis of cinematic texts, Bellour affirms that the use of a combination of writing and photographic stills as analytic tools functions as both the only method available to the analyst and the implicit confirmation of the utter insufficiency of this method: "That is why [filmic analyses] are so difficult, or more accurately, so graceless to read, repetitive, complicated, I shall not say needlessly so, but necessarily so, as the price of their strange perversity. That is why they always seem a little fictional: playing on an absent object, never able, since their aim is to make it present, to adopt the instruments of fiction even though they have to borrow them."[9] This Quixotic element, which haunts even (or especially) the most rigidly formal and structural film analyses, seems to suggest that the practice and the discipline of film studies remains forever on the verge of losing its grasp on its own object of study. What can be gained, however, by conceiving of the vexed relationship between written (and graphical) analysis and the cinematic text as a uniquely illustrative intermedial problem?

In the introduction, I proffered a Deleuzian definition of the medium as the flesh-like "developer" for percepts and affects external to itself, but examples of this were confined largely to audiovisual media forms that precondition the production of sensation, *combining* disparate percepts (such as film's heautonomous combination of visual images and sound) and *overlayering* disparate affects (such as the *jouissance* experienced by the overcoding of one's immediate sense-data in the experience of playing a video game). Language in and of itself does not seem to obviously precondition percepts and affects in this sense and is therefore scarcely definable as a singular or unified medium, as a number of scholars have pointed out. For instance, Noël Carroll—in an essay entitled "Forget the Medium!" (2003)—uses linguistic text as a primary example in his argument against what he considers the classical notion that "each artform ha[s] its own distinctive medium, a medium that distinguishes it from other artforms and that determines the laws of the artform in question": "Literature, for instance, does not appear to have a medium at all."[10] This statement is qualified with reference to the fact that, firstly, speech and writing produce modes of expression that are not identifiable as art forms; and, secondly, that speech and writing play important roles in art forms not identifiable as literature, such as cinema and video games. Carroll's disproof of the notion that language itself constitutes an artistic medium is valid, and yet this fact alone does not deter one from applying the concept of the medium to primarily linguistic texts. Rather, it serves to clarify the fact that the definition of linguistic media must take directly into consideration the vast range of formal, genre-specific, and actantial structures or assemblages that emerge both in speech and in writing. It is possible, for example, to consider the novel, the short story, and the prose poem as relatively distinct media even though they appear at first blush to differ from one another only in length; each of these forms brings to bear distinct potentialities for perceptual and affective production and combination. Even if we tend to refer to literature as a "medium," then, we are in fact identifying it as a "media assemblage," the "content" of which would also be a multiplicity of established media forms and emergent medial potentialities based on the aesthetic and artistic choices informing its production. As Eckart Voigst-Virchow points out, the complexities of literature and cinema challenge the very concept of homogenous media and, for this very reason, invite intermedial consideration: "Films—and books for that matter—possess an 'impure' mediality and precisely this 'impurity' is the subject of studies in intermediality."[11]

This realization of the heterogeneous medial configurations that are enfolded into writing and film leads us back to Cavell's largely unqualified assertion, in *The World Viewed*, that "a genre is a medium."[12] Cavell's statement retains its validity whether one considers genre in formal terms—the novel as a distinct literary genre from the short story—or in narrative-stylistic terms—science fiction as a distinct genre from the western. Even as seemingly broad a category as cinematic or literary realism may be understood in specifically genre-based terms, as Deleuze points out: "[Realism] can include the fantastic, the extraordinary, the heroic and above all melodrama. It can include exaggeration and lack of moderation, as long as these are of its own type. What constitutes realism is simply this: milieux and modes of behavior, milieux which actualize and modes of behavior which embody."[13] The genre-dependent categories of setting (or milieu) and character action (or modes of behavior) are together the proper constituents of realism, provided simply that the former is self-actualized—i.e. that it is a consistent milieu that is maintained on its own terms, whether or not these terms correspond to lived reality—and that the latter provides a sense of embodiment within the milieu—something like a proper gravity and solidity of physical, affective, and social comportment with respect to the milieu. Haneke's realism—which is consistent throughout all of his films except for *Funny Games*, which, as we have already seen, is informed both by realism and by violent genre-specific and metafictional shifts away from realism—is itself an important medium of expression within his work and does not differ in principle from literary realism. Thus, while Carroll rightly objects to privileging the concept of medium over that of the artwork or art form, particularly in the case of literature, one may counter that there is by definition *no* fixed relationship between an art and its medium wherein the former is predetermined by the latter. There is no question that cinema has appropriated a great number of narrative techniques, genre-specific practices, and other conventions from literature, theater, and comics (to cite but a few examples) and thus that there are numerous affective and perceptual assemblages that cinema shares with literature, as well as with these other art forms. Yet cinematic scholarship still presents a different problem than literary scholarship, a problem directly connected to its particular intermedial relationship with other narrative-linguistic art forms.

Film studies as a discipline has generally moved away from a linguistic-semiotic conceptual model of film, an approach instituted and promoted by scholars such as Christian Metz and Peter Wollen. Metz and Wollen's influential work was motivated in no small part by a perceived need to establish a system of reference for cinematic works that opened these texts to forms of structural analysis derived from linguistic models, as practiced by Bellour, among numerous other scholars. As Rodowick points out, this approach yielded a number of critical insights into cinematic expression and developed a terminology and mode of discursive analysis that is still relevant in the field: "[O]ne of the curious consequences of structuralist film theory and narratology is their demonstration of film narration as a complex, highly elaborated, and codified system that nonetheless escapes notation."[14] The attempt to uncover an underlying "grammar" of filmic representation thus did not result in the attainment of a linguistic-cinematic "text," as Bellour makes clear. Cinema clearly generates and conveys meaningful structures of thought that invite or demand scholarly interest, but these structures are codified differently than literary media even though significant commonalities present themselves—for instance, in the media's shared openness to certain modes of narrativity and genre. At what level, then, do these relationships between cinema and literature obtain, if not on the basis of a shared linguistic or logical system? Turning yet again to the conclusion of *Cinema 2*, we find that Deleuze provides, at the very outset of his conceptualization of the film medium, a response to this state of affairs:

> Cinema is not a universal or primitive language system [*langue*], nor a language [*langage*]. It brings to light an intelligible content which is like a presupposition, a condition, a necessary correlate through which language constructs its own "objects" (signifying units and operations). But this correlate, though inseparable, is specific: it consists of movements and processes (pre-linguistic images), and of points of view on these movements and processes (pre-signifying signs). It constitutes a whole "psychomechanics," the spiritual automaton, the utterable of a language system which has its own logic. The language system takes utterances of language, with signifying units and operations from it, but the utterable itself, its images and signs, are of another nature.[15]

The conceptualization of cinematic expression as compositions of "utterables" rather than "utterances" relieves the film scholar of the duty of continually creating or uncovering correspondences between filmic and linguistic texts in order to justify cinema's intelligibility. There is, Deleuze avers, a semiotics of the cinema, but it is not a linguistic semiotics; Deleuze's position in this regard is stated much more concisely in "The Brain is the Screen": "Cinema should be understood not as a language, but as a signal-material."[16] Additionally, the fact that the utterable has "its own logic" implies that one cannot expect linguistic analysis to obtain in film studies in anything like the manner it does in literary studies, in which utterances are applied to other utterances. The attempt to forge utterances from utterables will always leave some potential expression untouched, resulting in what Bellour characterizes above as the ungraspable "absent object" of film analysis.

In what way, then, can a film adaptation be assessed in relation to its literary antecedent, given that cinema and literature diverge fundamentally as media, even to the extent of possessing different logical bases? Must one abstract from both the written work and its adaptation an ideal reconstruction of their prelinguistic, pre-signifying (but still narrative) "thought-material" in order to arrive at some basis of comparison and thereby come to a potential judgment as to the film's fidelity to the written work? Refraining from any such attempt, I will instead focus on conceiving of a theoretical framework for adaptation that provides avenues of departure from the overriding criterion of fidelity and its attendant literary bias, as well as providing the terms for comparisons between film or television and literature that are not defined solely by narrative. In this way, I will attempt to uncover a set of potential medial and intermedial negotiations between, on the one hand, film, literature, and television and, on the other, voice—which is a medium common to all three—as active and dynamic relationships rather than as predetermined schematics for the translation of a narrative from one medium into another. In particular, I will focus on the work of four French theorists who present distinctly different yet equally innovative concepts informing their respective approaches to the problem of film adaptation: André Bazin, André Gaudreault with Philippe Marion, and Félix Guattari.

Intermedial Transposition and Adaptation

The elaboration of alternatives to the conceptual strictures of "fidelity" is a persistent concern in contemporary adaptation studies, as Robert Stam makes clear in his selection of essays for the seminal three-volume collection *Literature and Film: A Guide to the Theory and Practice of Film Adaptation* (2005). Indeed, Stam concludes his introduction to the text with the following summation of the current discourse surrounding adaptation studies: "We can still speak of successful or unsuccessful adaptations, but this time oriented not by inchoate notions of 'fidelity' but rather by attention to 'transfers of creative energy,' or to specific dialogical responses, to 'readings' and 'critiques' and 'interpretations' and 'rewritings' of source novels, in analyses which always take into account the gaps between very different media and materials of expression."[17] The focus for adaptation studies, in other words, has shifted away from the regime of model-copy with respect to the film's literary precursor, and toward the conceptualization of the inescapable textual, authorial, and medial transformations adaptation entails as positive and academically interesting phenomena. Yet the alternative that Stam offers—a pseudosexual characterization of adaptation as a process of "transfers of creative energy"—appears just as "inchoate" as the fidelity model he is overturning.[18] The fact that Stam highlights the gaps between literature and other media is also significant, suggestive as it is of the relevance of intermedial perspectives on adaptation both in practice and as a subject for academic investigation. But, before fully renouncing the notion of fidelity to the source text—which, as I have stated, is consciously and consistently applied by Haneke in his television adaptations—let us see whether the approach yields any insights into the interrelationship between literature and film that do not automatically privilege the former above the latter as a narrative medium. One such approach is exemplified by André Bazin's concept of stylistics.

In two important essays—"*Le Journal d'un curé de campagne* and the Stylistics of Robert Bresson" (1951) and "Adaptation, or the Cinema as Digest" (1948)—Bazin presents a definition of "style" as an undifferentiated quality of both literature and film, one that forms the basis of a shared identity between the two art forms while simultaneously bringing their fundamental differences into relief. Hence, in the essay on *Le Journal d'un curé de campagne*, Bazin begins by reiterating and accepting Robert Bresson's stated "avowal of fidelity" to Georges Bernanos's 1936 novel (the basis for the 1951 film), but identifies the director's adaptation as being informed by a "most insidious kind of fidelity."[19] According to Bazin, rather than seeking a visual-cinematic equivalent for Bernanos's vividly descriptive prose, Bresson simply ignored those passages "that cried out for visualization," and as a result "it is the film that is literary while the novel teems with visual material."[20] Furthermore, rather than naturalizing or reinterpreting the novel's language in order to render it amenable to dramatic performance, both the voice-over narration and the dialogue consist of recitations of Bernanos's text precisely as written: "The cast is not being asked to act out a text, not even to live it out, just to speak it."[21] Yet Bazin does not see Bresson's film as thereby veering away from realism and toward mannered or expressionistic intentions; on the contrary, the film is said to attain a heightened degree of realism through this strategy:

> Of course the deliberate emphasis on their literary character can be interpreted as a search after artistic stylization, which is the very

> opposite of realism. The fact is, however, that in this case the reality is not the descriptive content, moral or intellectual, of the text—it is the very text itself, or more properly, the style. Clearly the reality at one stage removed of the novel, and that which the camera captures directly, cannot fit or grow together or become one. On the contrary the effect of their juxtaposition is to reaffirm their differences.[22]

In this manner, Bresson has, in Bazin's interpretation, purposely avoided anything like a "translation" of the content of the novel into a "cinematic language"—Bazin emphatically states that "[t]here is no question here of a translation, no matter how faithful or intelligent"—but has instead placed the novel and the film in a direct, even overdetermined, relationship. The novel is presented *qua* novel, as not only the precursor but also the material and existential foundation of the film, even as the film assumes its own status as a "new aesthetic creation."[23] Bazin perceives no aesthetic or mimetic contradiction in this state of affairs, and to Bresson he attributes the Pierre Menard-like function of upholding both repetition and difference with respect to the relation of novel to film: "*Le Journal* has just proved to us that it is more fruitful to speculate on their differences rather than on their resemblances, that is, for the existence of the novel to be affirmed by the film and not dissolved into it. It is hardly enough to say of this work, once removed, that it is in essence faithful to the original because, to begin with, it *is* the novel."[24] Medial difference is preserved by Bresson's film's *identicality with*, as opposed to its *resemblance to*, Bernanos's novel; in transposing the novel to the film without subjecting it to any intermediary process of transformation, however, the film can scarcely be conceived of as an adaptation. Instead, in a gesture toward both stylization and metanarrative realism, the film affirms the autonomy of the novel, which in turn affirms cinema's own aesthetic autonomy from literature.

This unique conceptualization of "style" as a quality transposable between media is also elaborated in "Adaptation, or the Cinema as Digest," which more generally develops Bazin's theory of adaptation. Here, Bazin is careful to avoid the association of style with purely formal considerations: "'Form' is at most a sign, a visible manifestation, of style, which is absolutely inseparable from the narrative content, of which it is, in a manner of speaking and according to Sartre's use of the word, the metaphysics."[25] To illustrate this point, Bazin points to André Malraux's film *L'Espoir* (*Man's Hope*; 1939, released 1945), codirected by the author and based on his own novel: "The *style* of Malraux's film is completely identical to that of his book, even though we are dealing here with two different artistic forms."[26] By defining style as the "metaphysics" of narrative and decoupling style from the formal dictates of the medium, Bazin proposes a trans-medial constant between the literary and cinematic poles of adaptation that is related both to narrative events and to linguistic form without being reducible to either. This stylistic overlap being granted, the essay goes on to outline its argument for the consideration of film adaptations as "digests" of their literary sources, a model based not on translation but on condensation and intensification, the emphasis of certain stylistic-narrative attributes of the novel over and above others. Bazin then distinguishes between two possible orientations or aims for adaptation: "To be sure, one must first know to what end the adaptation is designed: for the cinema or for its audience."[27] Interestingly, the distinction between the two types of adaptation correspond, roughly, to Haneke's own stated attitudes regarding adaptation: while adaptation for the cinema aims at creating an aesthetically independent work even as it retains specific elements of the source's style, adaptation for the audience constitutes a "digest" primarily intended to bring the literary work closer to a mass spectatorship. Like Haneke, Bazin emphasizes the fact that the second function is more aligned with the aims of broadcast media, although he refers to radio since his essay predates the ubiquity of television as a mass medium: "The problem of adaptation for the audience is much more evident in the case of radio. Indeed, radio is not quite an art like the cinema: it is first and foremost a means of reproduction and transmission. The digest phenomenon resides not so much in the actual condensing or simplification of works as in the way they are consumed by the listening public."[28] The sense in which Bazin employs the term "digest" links this form of adaptation directly to the idea of consumption, the audience-oriented film or television adaptation serving as an intentionally "pre-digested" fare—in Jean-Paul Sartre's words, "a literary chyle"[29]—which is thereby more easily absorbed by the public. Yet Bazin perceives nothing negative in this development, and at the close of his essay reflects on the possibility of such digests eroding scholarship's focus on form and its hierarchization of artistic media, which tends to privilege literature over theater and theater over cinema. Thus, apropos John Steinbeck's *Of Mice and Men*, which was adapted to all three media in quick succession, Bazin states the following: "[T]he (literary?) critic of the year 2050 would find not a novel out of which a play and a film had been 'made,' but rather a single work reflected through three art forms, an artistic pyramid with three sides, all equal in the eyes of the critic. The 'work' would then be only an ideal point at the top of this figure, which itself is an ideal construct."[30]

Although he is careful to distinguish his notion of style from the determinations of form and the structure of narrative, then, Bazin's theoretical approach to adaptation nonetheless resembles to some degree the narratological model initiated by the Russian Formalists, a model that posits that a given story—the *fabula*—may find expression through any number of particular narrative configurations or *syuzhets*, including those rendered in different media. In Bazin's formulation, the *fabula* would be roughly equivalent to the ideal point at the pyramid's apex, while each side would correspond to a separate but related *syuzhet*, and thus the entire figure would qualify as an intermedial structure. Yet, as André Gaudreault and Philippe Marion point out in an essay titled "Transécriture and Narrative Mediatics: The Stakes of Intermediality" (2004), such a structure would be asymmetrical by default, since each medium possesses its own "communicational energetics"—its own way of combining and multiplying what Gaudreault and Marion refer to as the "'familiar' materials of expression . . . rhythm, movement, gesture, music, speech, image, writing"—that fundamentally shapes and reshapes the narrative itself.[31] Indeed, Gaudreault and Marion argue that even when one accedes to the narratological terms proposed by Russian Formalists such as Boris Tomashevsky, one does not elude the influence of media: "But when the Formalists argue that the *fabula* is independent of the media, it does not mean it is possible to refer to that *fabula* without thinking of a medium. To think, or express, the *fabula* in its very independence in relation to media, we still need to express or think the *fabula* in relation to some medium. In most cases, the medium will be verbal language as a kind of integrated medium closely linked to our own thought processes."[32] Two distinct notions of the *fabula* are at play in this reading: the first is of the *fabula* as the ideal point in the narratological-intermedial framework that adaptation studies seem to presuppose, while the second is of the *fabula* as a literalized—and thus primarily linguistic—event sequence providing a common frame of reference for each medial permutation of the narrative. The former demands conceptualization independently of any formal medial elements; the latter seems to indicate the *impossibility* of escaping mediation even in the process of defining narrative in purely evental terms. Gaudreault and Marion thus go on to tentatively position narrative as a subset of media: "In a sense, narrativity is included within the larger category of mediativity; it is in this sense a particular modality of mediativity."[33] In the authors' reading, the realization that the only means we possess of conceptualizing or referring to narrative is mediated by default implies that considerations of medium should by rights always precede considerations of narrative.

In this account, then, the object of adaptation is less the pursuit of a means of transposing or translating a preestablished set of narrative events—a *fabula*—into another medium and more the establishment of an almost entirely new *fabula-syuzhet* relation founded on the respective exigencies of each medium. Thus, the seeming resistance to adaptation that one encounters with certain works is attributed by Gaudreault and Marion to the fact that the *fabula* is so inextricably tied to a particular *syuzhet*-medium that its essential integrity is threatened by its transposition into another medium:

> One might make the same point about the intimate confidences of Proust in *A la recherché du temps perdu*, the various adaptations of which have generally been seen as scandalous. We find the same situation with the *Adventures of Tintin*, whose *fabula* is of a body, almost literally, with its *syuzhet*, and its *syuzhet* with the medium, and whose adaptation in the form of an animated cartoon is criticized,

> somewhat paradoxically, for freezing its characters in place. Here we have a strange paradox, indeed, since the model, despite the intrinsic stasis of its fixed images, seems less static than its adaptation into moving images.[34]

The authors' reference to the "unadaptability" of Hergé's *Tintin* is telling, as it indicates the fact that the "communicational energetics" of the comic book medium are not tied to the figures' visual "stasis" (relative to the cartoon film); on the contrary, the drawn figures on the page possess more pictorial and narrative dynamism than their literally animated equivalents. In other words, the narrative (and even visual) energy of Hergé's *bandes dessinées* does not result from the *fabula* in itself—since the events of the story are presumably transposable to a film narrative—nor from the *syuzhet*-medium of comics, but from the specific and unique relation between the two. Animation's substitution of a moving image—created by projecting a rapid succession of drawn images—for the spatial rhythm of the comic book page founds a new *fabula-syuzhet* relationship that Gaudreault and Marion characterize as possessing less dynamic energy and spectatorial impact than that of the source. While this example is interesting, however—if only for the apparent paradox it introduces through the question of medial and narrative-visual stasis and motion—their first example of Marcel Proust is perhaps more illustrative of the intermedial pitfalls that adaptation brings to light, and their relevance to Haneke's literary productions.

Gaudreault and Marion state that Proust's "intimate confidences" are ineffective in nonliterary media, though they do not elaborate on this point.[35] If one emphasizes the "intimacy" of the relationship between Proust and his reader, one could perhaps conclude that his prose is generally ill-suited to mass audience address, which forces on the narrative an air of indiscretion relative to the aura of privacy and confidence privileged by the solitary act of reading. Thus, while the language of Proust's *À la recherché du temps perdu* could be theoretically preserved, its affects would be drastically diminished or transformed due to intrinsic qualities of the new medium of expression. Adaptation, then, becomes a matter not only of preserving the source's narrative structure and linguistic (or visual, as the case may be) style, but also of retaining the associated affective charges. In my own approach, which is centered around the idea of literary voice, this would entail capturing the *tone* as well as the *sense* of the literary antecedent in the cinematic adaptation. Accepting this, it is possible to consider the affective charge of a given work as being a relatively independent attribute, or at least one that does not emerge directly from a given *fabula*. As I posited in the introduction, after Deleuze and Guattari, affect is a product of the medium itself as much as or more so than the meanings signified at a narrative or representational level. However, Félix Guattari himself sought to produce a television program that harnessed Kafka's affects directly without relying on narrative and representational material as means of communicating or negotiating the affects' impact—a project with important implications for Haneke's *Das Schloß*. How did he propose to achieve such a transposition?

Guattari's notes for this ultimately unsuccessful endeavor were eventually published as "Project for a Film *by* Kafka" (2007), a title that captured the stated purpose of the television program: "The (inordinate) ambition of our project would then be not to make a film about Kafka's work, or a film on Kafka, but a film by Kafka; let Kafka's machine live within the coordinates of cinema, work within the oeuvre."[36] In a Deleuzo-Guattarian consideration, "Kafka" refers not simply to the author himself, but to the complex system of percepts and affects produced through his writing-machine; the system is initiated by the artist but tends to attain autonomy from authorship and even from the literary medium. Gary Genosko, in his essay on Guattari's Kafka project, describes such a system as follows: "The affects with which Kafka wrote may live in film and television because they are independent and survive their author."[37] The survival of such affects, furthermore, is for Guattari not limited to the literary corpus that Kafka left behind, according to Genosko: "Guattari sought in affect the autonomy necessary to stake the claim that his project was *by* Kafka. 'By Kafka' does not signal another auteur, but affect's distance from intention and the contagiousness of its channeling and passage through different media to a potential viewership."[38] Although Guattari was cognizant of the fact that television possesses its own medial affects—Genosko characterizes Guattari's view of television as being that of "a vivid machinic assemblage of subjectification and flickering sensory affects of all sorts"[39]—he was nonetheless convinced that Kafka's affects would not only survive but thrive in the newer medium. And yet Guattari's proposed film by Kafka is not strictly definable as an adaptation; in Guattari's own words, it was to be a nonnarrative that borrowed few story elements from Kafka's writings, aiming instead at capturing through various means certain affects—for example, "bureaucratic *jouissance*"[40]—that suffused the author's writing-machine: "What interested Kafka, and what should interest us in cinema, are not characters, plots, but systems of intensity, gestures, reflections, looks—for example a face behind a window, attitudes, sensations, changes in gravity, in space and time coordinates, and the dilations or retractions of all perceptual semiotics[.]"[41] Guattari's screenplay encompasses scenes directly derived from *Das Schloß*—even naming characters such as K., Frieda, and Klamm—as well as from *Der Prospekt* (*The Trial*) and the stories "Das Urteil" ("The Judgment") and "Ein Landarzt" ("A Country Doctor"). However, such elements do not stand as narrative fragments, nor do they appear to allude to a common theme. Such representations and derivations are instead utterly subordinate to the affective charges they carry, which in the newer medium become allied with the desubjectified televisual affects of *jouissance* as well as with what could be described as an intensification and inversion of television's very banality, as Genosko points out: "Guattari's television project by

Kafka is not only designed to unleash fabulation, but through television's boring formal machinic effects implant complex affects not in virtue of representational content alone . . . but in a way that pours out of the home viewing situation and turns its passivity inside out."[42] The project proposed by Guattari, then, sought to uncover affects particular to Kafka's work within a new medial assemblage—or what could be termed a new *fabula-syuzhet* interrelationship—by forcing on the affective structure of the television medium a stylistic encounter with Kafka's writing assemblage. While the potential success of such a venture remains indeterminate, Guattari's intended approach can be aligned with that of Bazin and that of Gaudreault and Marion in its eschewal of a strictly representational framework in favor of a complex and relational notion of adaptation as an active and unfolding process upholding considerations of mediality and intermediality.

In summary, in response to the theoretical models for adaptation conceptualized in terms of narrative fidelity, I have offered three separate but interrelated alternatives: Bazin's redefinition of style as a constant passed from literary work to film and vice versa; Gaudreault and Marion's reassessment of the formalist and narratological terms *fabula* and *syuzhet* as medial and intermedial phenomena, with the former term thereby assuming an even more abstract ideational constitution; and Guattari's assertion that affects are independent of considerations of representation and therefore are directly transposable between media. Each theoretical framework posits, in its own way, a counterargument to the longstanding perception of adaptation as being exclusively defined by an imperfect model-copy relation between a source text and its translation into film or television. Yet, even taken together, each of the alternatives presented does not appear to provide a substantive model for adaptation studies to follow. The theories of Bazin, Gaudreault and Marion, and Guattari complicate the text-film relation without offering terms through which it might be fully reconceptualized. In fact, Gaudreault and Marion's application of intermediality to adaptation would seem to undermine not only the "narrative fidelity" argument but also Bazin's and Guattari's assertions that certain aspects of the filmic work and the literary work are identical to one another, since Gaudreault and Marion position the medium as a primary consideration and imply that no facet of any work—whether style, *fabula*-event, or affect—is conceivable independently of its particular medium of expression. In other words, according to Gaudreault and Marion's criteria, literature and film or television *must* share a common medium of expression, in order that authorial style or affect may pass from one to the other without itself undergoing some intermediate process of change or translation. As already stated, for my present purposes I will posit that all of these media differentially "contain" (in McLuhan's sense of the word) the medium of voice.

Literary voice is, in the majority of fictional works, inseparable from the functions of narration and description, while also serving pseudotheatrical functions of drama and comedy in the form of dialogue.[43] The latter functions assimilate with sound cinema quite easily, although often with alterations to the textual dialogue made in order to suit the requirements of cinematic realism. As Theodor Adorno points out in "Transparencies on Film" (1966), "[e]ven when dialogue is used in a novel, the spoken word is not directly spoken but is rather distanced by the act of narration—perhaps even by the typography—and thereby abstracted from the physical presence of living persons," and hence, in the context of realism, "phrases justified by the diction of narrative . . . sound pompous and inauthentic in film."[44] Haneke admits to similar motivations in his colloquialization of the stylized secondhand dialogue of Jelinek's novel (which was also subsequently translated into French for the film) in his screenplay for *La pianiste*.[45] However, the dialogues in his television adaptations tend to adhere much more closely to the wordings of their source texts.[46] As in Bresson's adaptation of Bernanos (in Bazin's reading), the dialogue and the voice-over narration in Haneke's television films invoke less a naturalization of the novelistic voice than a recitation of the same. Furthermore, the fact that voice-over narrators are employed in the majority of his television adaptations, but not in *La pianiste*, is telling with regard to the utilization and disposition of literary voice in these media and their respective relations to the source texts. In the following sections, I will elaborate on this concept of voice as intermedium, paying special attention to certain effects of its relationship to the visual image in television and film, as well as to music and performance in *La pianiste*.

Haneke's Television Adaptations: Literary Voice and Voice-over

We have already alluded to the fact that Haneke views his television adaptations as serving educational rather than artistic functions, and thus as deferring to their literary sources in nearly every respect. In Bazinian terms, the four television adaptations—*Drei Wege zum See* (1976), *Wer war Edgar Allan?* (1984), *Die Rebellion* (1993), and *Das Schloß* (1997)—were conceived strictly as digests, as adaptations intended for the audience. Haneke himself could not have been clearer on this point, stating the following in his interview with Willy Riemer: "I consider [my television adaptations] to be an honorable enterprise that brings literature closer to an audience, not more than that."[47] Indeed, as Deborah Holmes notes with reference to a 1995 German-language interview with Haneke, the director tends to dissociate himself from these adaptations, referring to them as a form of "adult education" and dismissing their cinematic or protocinematic merits outright.[48] Haneke is quoted in the same essay as stating of his first three adaptations that "as films they are failed projects in the final instance. The question is of course on what level they fail. It is possible to fail in a primitive or in a relatively intelligent way."[49] Such an assessment is intriguing, both because it preceded *Das Schloß*, tempting one to wonder whether or not Haneke considered this film a failure as well,[50] and because it raises the question of whether *any* audience-oriented adaptation is capable of simultaneously holding up as an artistically successful film in its own right, and under what terms or conditions this would be possible. Haneke's comments highlight the idea that film and literature are mutually insupportable, but suggest that as "intelligent" failures the adaptations may at least serve an edifying function, even if they do not serve an aesthetic one. Yet according to what criteria is it possible to assess even the films' educational value without also assigning to the films those aesthetic qualities attributable to the literary works? In order to effectively convey or elucidate the inherent artfulness of the written texts on which they are based—a project that entails including not only the source materials' narrative content but also their language, which is rendered via voice-over in the majority of Haneke's adaptations—do the films not thereby also attain aesthetic value? To conclude that this is not the case, one would presumably have to argue on the bases of originality (the film cannot lay aesthetic claim to aspects derived from other works) and medial difference (what is of aesthetic value in a film is inherently incommensurable with what is of aesthetic value in a literary work). Both of these criteria are problematized, however, if one approaches adaptation as the process of uncovering voice as a common medium for both literature and sound cinema.

Up to this point, I have been concerned with negotiating intermedial gaps between cinematic and noncinematic audiovisual media (such as television or video), highlighting in the process the perceptual and affective differences that are revealed in their utilization by Haneke. Yet it has also been taken for granted that certain representational qualities are shared by these media—and shared to the point where many assume a relationship of equivalence between all "moving-image media"—in spite of their separate *dispositifs* and the different modes of engagement that they entail. In the case of the media of literature and film, though, significant medial differences *are* conventionally perceived, even to the point that it is easy to overlook the commonalities in the way that both art forms utilize voice as a mode of expression distinct from strictly narrative considerations. The fact that voice is conveyed through writing and thus experienced virtually or mentally in the work of literature, whereas in film and television it is explicitly recorded and transmitted aurally, is of course important to acknowledge, but this distinction does not necessarily preclude the acceptance of both manifestations of voice as existing on the same continuum or constituting permutations of a single medium.[51] The cinematic voice-over—and I will consider the use of voice-over in the television adaptations in primarily cinematic terms, since they differ in function and disposition from the use of voice-over in news reportage, as discussed in chapter 3—is regularly employed in literary adaptations in order to effect a sense of distantiation that corresponds to an act of storytelling in its overt addition of another level of narration to a film, one separate from its image track. Thus, it is arguable that the use of voice-over itself contributes a "literary" disposition to even nonadaptations.[52] In my examination of the use of voice-over in Haneke's oeuvre, however, I will focus not only on the manner in which voice-over narration helps forge a connection with the literary source, but also on the ways in which the voice-over diverges from the on-screen images and registers certain inconsistencies between literary voice and visual cinema. Before doing so, however, a brief definition of the voice as a concept—and of the relation of voice to written text and image, respectively—will be necessary.

There is no question that the voice constitutes a medium in and of itself, and that this medium remains, in myriad ways, completely distinct from language. Indeed, in his intriguing study *A Voice and Nothing More*, Mladen Dolar is able to affirm the existence of the "object voice"—the pure form of the voice itself, independent of the content of the verbal utterance—only by paradoxically positioning it *between* the symbolic register of linguistic expression and the ontological register of corporeality: "[T]he voice stands at . . . the intersection of language and the body, but this intersection belongs to neither. *What language and the body have in common is the voice, but the voice is part neither of language nor of the body*."[53] The seemingly impossible configuration held together by the voice raises the possibility that the voice could be considered *the* prototypical medium. Dolar suggests as much in his gloss on McLuhan's slogan: "'The medium is the message'—this notorious slogan should perhaps be twisted in such a way that the message of the medium pertains to its voice."[54] The fact that one can understand voice as a constitutive element of such seemingly diverse media as recorded speech and written text is accountable in this formulation, but not without introducing troubling questions regarding the voice's own phenomenological and ontological status. Where does the voice itself reside, if not in either of the systems it negotiates between? Dolar affirms that the "topology of the voice" is this very liminality, "the intersection, the void";[55] in other words, voice presupposes, and resides within, the intermedial gap that inheres within any instance of mediation, any compound of perceptual and affective relations that produces sensation or signification. Yet, even if one accepts that the object voice is definable as—and perhaps only as—an intermedial phenomenon, what specific configuration does this denote between literature and sound cinema?

In the previous section I circumvented both the model-copy logic of the fidelity theory of adaptation and the nebulous energetic and dialogical interactions that Stam characterized as the next wave of adaptation studies. By referring to theorizations that perceive direct continuities between literature and cinema—in stylistic, medium-formalist, and affective terms—I provided the context for my own assertion that we are able to refer to written voice and to audible voice without presupposing any essential difference between the two. If one applies the Lacanian concept of the "object voice," as Dolar does, sound recording and text present different expressions of a common medial and intermedial supplement that remains distinct from both systems. What is at stake is not the idea that priority should be given to either a spoken or a written utterance; rather, the stakes lie with the medial configurations that the voice is subject to in each mode of expression. This is precisely the issue that Michel Chion explores in his groundbreaking studies of cinematic voice. As Chion affirms in *The Voice in Cinema* (1982), the introduction of recorded sound into the cinematic apparatus was less a matter of linguistic integration and more a matter of accommodating the profoundly different *register* the audible voice inhabited, in comparison both to text and to the cinematographic image: "As film began to talk, the problem was not text; silent cinema had already integrated text through the bastard device of intertitles. It was the voice, as material presence, as utterance, or as muteness—the voice as being, double, shadow of the image, as a power—the voice as a threat of loss and seduction for the cinema."[56] The implications of this unstable configuration of the seen and the heard are significant and varied, and to some extent I have already broached the topic in discussing *Code inconnu*'s sound and visual image relationship in terms of heautonomy. Indeed, Chion describes the introduction of the audible voice into cinema in terms that reinforce both Dolar's definition of the object voice and Deleuze's concept of heautonomous images: "If the talking cinema has shown anything by restoring voices to bodies, it's precisely that it doesn't hang together; it's decidedly not a seamless match."[57] Of most interest to me in the present chapter is Chion's insight into cinema's use of voice-over as a "textual" mode of the utterance, just as Bazin perceived in Bresson's filmed dialogue nothing more or less than the text of Bernanos's novel.

Chion characterizes most voice-over narrative as a particular mode of the acousmatic voice—whose power is derived from the fact that its speaker, or *acousmêtre*, remains unseen—that retains a close relationship to the neutrality of third-person literary narration. Referring to it as the "I-voice," due to its serving as the "*pivot of identification*" for the filmgoer, Chion defines voice-over narration in the following terms: "A certain neutrality of timbre and accent, associated with a certain ingratiating discretion, is normally expected of an I-voice. Precisely so that each spectator can make it his own, the voice must work toward being a *written text that speaks* with the impersonality of the printed page."[58] Expanding on this comparison in a different study, Chion identifies cinematic "textual speech" as being "generally that of voiceover commentaries" and differentiates this form of voice from "theatrical speech" on the basis of its retaining priority over the film's images and diegetic sounds, which remain "at its mercy."[59] The latter phrase is not used lightly, as Chion considers voice-over narration to assume a fundamentally dominant, and therefore disruptive, role in the mimesis of a given film: "Textual speech has the power to make visible the images that it evokes through sound—that is, to change the setting, to call up a thing, moment, place, or characters at will. If textual speech can control a film's narration, of course, there no longer remains an autonomous audiovisual scene, no notion whatever of spatial and temporal continuity."[60] The narrative control conceded to impersonal or third-party voice-over is derived from the voice-over's acousmatic quality, and it can, of course, be employed by films with no literary antecedent; however, Chion's identification of voice-overs of this type with textuality is significant in that it indicates a mode of the voice that retains a basic structuring function. The textual voice is not a component of the visual imagery, nor is it completely independent of the image track (otherwise it could not affect or undermine the imagery so thoroughly). Yet the voice-over, when present, is always already the primary mediator between the body of the spectator and the "language system" of the audiovisual expression in precisely the same way that the narrative voice of a novel mediates between the body of the reader and the language of the text. Simply put, the I-voice is the primary residence of the object voice in cinematic and literary narrative alike.[61] Moreover, textual voice is a veritable intermedium in the sense that I have given the term throughout this text, in that it indexes both the relationality of the disparate systems—voice to written expression, and voice to audiovisual expression—and the void that obtains from the disjunction its presence inevitably introduces (the fracturing of spatiotemporal contiguity to which Chion refers in the quote above). In order to elaborate on this quality of voice-over narration, let me turn to an examination of Haneke's adaptations, beginning with the role of voice-over in his films for television.

As a number of Haneke scholars have pointed out, the director's television adaptations have generally adhered fastidiously to the wording of their literary sources. Holmes in particular highlights this "fidelity" to literary text: "[Haneke makes] minimal changes to the text he appropriates from the originals, both in the narrative voice-overs and the characters' dialogue. He makes no substantial textual additions to any of his three adaptations for television; *The Rebellion* and *Three Paths to the Lake* feature at most snatches of background conversation not to be found in the originals, and there are no additions at all to the texts taken from *The Castle*."[62] Like Bresson in his adaptation of Bernanos, then, Haneke adds virtually nothing to the source texts of his films, inviting the application of Bazin's theory that film adaptations are capable of upholding the style, and by extension the literary voice, of the source without resorting to any act of intervention or translation. In each of the three films, extended passages from the original text are recited by an impersonal and offscreen male I-voice—Axel Corti in *Drei Wege* and Udo Samel in *Die Rebellion* and *Das Schloß*—whose function corresponds almost exactly to that of the literary narrator. Yet we also assign other associations to the voice-over, as is made clear when Holmes cites Alexander Horwath's criticism of the use of Corti as a vocal "presence" in the film version of Ingeborg Bachmann's story: "Horwath is . . . dissatisfied with the fact that a male voice narrates a text written by a woman about a woman."[63] The overtly patriarchal overtones perceived in having a male voice provide the narration from the story verbatim arise directly from the expectations and associations made by the reader or viewer with regard to voice. One can imagine a story written by a female author with a male protagonist narrated by a male voice, and likewise one written by a male author with a female protagonist—in both of these cases, there is an element of the narration that supports a masculine voice. Of course, the narratorial I-voice is never directly identifiable with either the persona of the author or of the protagonist, but rather with *impersonality* itself, and Chion reluctantly notes in this regard that "*most acousmêtres are masculine.*"[64] One can attribute this to the majoritarian status of the unaccented male voice in traditional Western cultural practices. In the case of *Drei Wege*, however, the narrative itself possesses, like *La pianiste*, a feminine or feminist inflection, a quality apparently marginalized by the masculine voice-over. Even if Corti's voice retains the exact linguistic form and sense of Bachmann's narration, and technically speaks *of* rather than *for* the central character Elisabeth, it nonetheless presents the spectator with a problematic dissociation with or departure from the literary text that is neither semantic nor narrative-representational, but rather strictly *vocal*.

We have suggested that the voice is a specialized medium—or more properly speaking intermedium—unto itself that is utilized by both literature and film without belonging to either.[65] Rather than positing a relationship of equivalence between film and literature, then, I am positing a twofold intermedial relationship with a common term: literature-to-voice and picture-to-voice. How does this latter relation, and the gap it institutes in the overall terms of the relevant work's expression, manifest itself in Haneke's "literary" television films? As would be expected, Haneke's television adaptations' use of the third-person voice-over often institutes delays or disjunctions between voice and visual track—configurations intended both to evoke the act of reading and to highlight the independence of the audiovisual system from the vocal narration. Several scholars have noted this effect; Holmes, for instance, indicates an inconsistency in the vocal bridge from *Die Rebellion*'s opening montage of historical footage to the narrative proper:

> The novel's opening sentence, "The barracks of the war hospital number XXIV were situated on the edge of town" (Roth 1956: 289), is read by Udo Samel over the last archive image to be shown before the lap dissolve, a field gun firing repeatedly. This is a good example of a technique Haneke uses throughout his literary adaptations for television. Voice-over and images are not synchronized; one often anticipates the other, creating a tension which attracts the audience's attention to exactly which shots are juxtaposed and how.[66]

This approach is convincingly interpreted by Holmes as Haneke's "attempts to recreate the simultaneity of literary narrative," quoting the director in this regard: "As Haneke himself has said, 'Coordinating literature and film is difficult. In literature I can think up a sentence that unites three different times and locations. In film I have one image, I am here and now. Then the next image comes—and I am somewhere completely different. In film, there is an immediate contrast, whereas in a book I can create simultaneity' (in Diethardt 1995: 18)."[67] By this reckoning, the voice-over evokes not only a separate space-time than that pictured by the visual image, multiplying the number of referents the film narrative is able to draw together at a given moment; it also evokes a different notion of spatiotemporal representation, since vocal narration is capable of evoking separate representational coordinates in a single syntactic gesture. One could thus conclude that the film's relation of voice-over to audiovisual mimesis replicates the temporal disposition or "style" of literary narrative, in which voice necessarily precedes imagery because it is the vehicle of its conveyance. Narrative voice emerges from the storyteller's space-time, which is conventionally situated after the events of the narrative (which is why the simple past is the default grammatical tense for fiction); but in its act of enunciating the narrative, voice is inevitably "staged" before the visual scene, holding the latter temporarily in reserve. This effect is discernible even in mainstream films that make use of voice-over: the voice of the narrator, if present, is often the first element to assert itself, emerging over a black opening screen or static establishing shot, before any narrative action is visually foregrounded. In all such configurations of voice and diegesis, the former seems to take narrative precedence, composing and describing the scene from a removed spatial and temporal perspective, while the latter conveys a sense of immersion and presence. Indeed, although Haneke makes a valid point about the film image remaining tied to a spatiotemporal present, one can easily imagine a voice-over referring simultaneously to a number of space-times while the film image depicts them in succession, in much the same manner that the rhetorical flow of the voice of the reporter in a news segment maintains a sense of unity while a series of fragmented views are relayed via the image track. The voice-medium's tendency to retain temporal integrity in spite of its multiple referents thus both supplements and undermines the film image's tendency toward spatiotemporal immediacy. But what effects occur when the contents of the voice-over are absent from or contradicted by the contents of the visual imagery?

Let us begin with the latter case, which arises at one point early in *Drei Wege zum See*, during a montage of photographs over which the narrator describes Elisabeth's experiences as a photographer. Fatima Naqvi describes the image/voice contradiction in this way: "[T]he film brazenly juxtaposes a photograph of Marilyn Monroe and Arthur Miller when Corti's voice-over, citing directly from the written text, mentions Ernest Hemingway. The disjunction between the measured, neutral soundtrack and the incongruous picture calls into question any standards of judgment adhering to bygone notions of fidelity as a one-to-one transmission of content."[68] This disjunction is curious in a film that otherwise—and in accordance to Haneke's stated objectives—attempts to adhere to the referential-representational content of the source text as closely as possible. In this instance the voice-over is the element that maintains the "transmission of content," as Naqvi puts it, while the visual track offers an alternate referent. This gesture does not necessarily break with the notion of fidelity as an aim of adaptation, however, as Naqvi implies; the voice-over remains entirely consistent with the literary voice of the short story, and it is instead the intermedial relationship between voice and visual image that forms the locus of this disjunction. Once again the Deleuzian notion of sound and picture as heautonomous images is eminently applicable, particularly as discussed by Rodowick in connection with Alain Resnais's first collaboration with novelist Alain Robbe-Grillet, the film *Last Year at Marienbad* (1961): "[S]ound and image are synchronized yet autonomous. In fact, throughout the film, while the spoken *récit* does seem to drive the image, in fact the image refuses to 'cooperate' with the sound in any consistent way."[69] Because it is not an adaptation, *Last Year at Marienbad*'s voice-over and visual imagery enter a mutually falsifying interrelationship, whereby, in Rodowick's words, "[w]e may seek to unify sound and image in a single narration—a single character or consistent diegetic space—but we will be disappointed every time."[70] However, the natural tendency, in the case of an adaptation like *Drei Wege*, is to defer to the literary source and consider the film's departure as an intentional act of narrative or representational infidelity vis-à-vis the written work. Considering sound and image as heautonomous elements, though, it is possible to see the film as simultaneously *consistent with* literary voice, to the extent that voice is a medium independent from the film image, and *inconsistent with it*, to the extent that the visual representation puts forward a "false" image relative to the voice-over. If one defines voice as a shared medium between film and literature and also acknowledges film sound's partial discontinuity with its image analogue, then the entire notion of "fidelity" in adaptation is reframed. The "one-to-one transmission of content" that Naqvi describes as the old fidelity model is not repudiated, nor does it define the terms through which it is possible to evaluate film adaptations.

A different and much subtler effect occurs when the voice-over refers to events and imagery that are not visualized at all by the film, a technique utilized by Haneke most prominently in *Das Schloß*.[71] As Willy Riemer points out, the inherent challenges of adapting Kafka force a redefinition of the fidelity question: "[T]he question of fidelity is not particularly illuminating for writings rich in interpretative ambiguity. While Kafka's *Das Schloß* challenges the reader for interpretation, it also obstructs any approach to ready meanings. The ambiguity of this novel thus opens the possibility of adaptation without the benchmark of fidelity and with more weight given to the film as an autonomous work of art."[72] Guattari's seemingly abstract and piecemeal approach to adapting Kafka—wherein the affects themselves are the only aspects of the work that are carried over with any consistency—is understandable in this light. Kafka's oblique authorial perspective and fragmented or fractured approaches to character, setting, and narrative make any traditional cinematic staging of his works difficult. For his part, Haneke has embraced these aspects of the author's work, stating in an interview with Riemer that "Kafka's fragmentary, ambiguous perception of reality characterizes my work as well."[73] Along with his usual array of techniques—including delimited and severe framing, a nontraditional use of offscreen space and shot/countershot pairings, and the addition of black spacers to the montage—*Das Schloß* uses the relation between voice-over and visual image to imbue the narrative with a sense of internal disconnection and ambiguity reflected at the level of form. This nonsynchronization is particularly evident at points during which the actions described by the vocal narration and the actions performed by the actors are completely divergent. For example, when K. is visiting the home of the messenger Barnabas and his sister Olga, the voice-over states, in keeping with the novel, that the visitor forces open the door to the point that Olga is "scarcely able to keep him out," though the on-screen action shows her admitting K. without any visible struggle. The illogical disjunction between sound and image thus becomes yet another means of expressing Kafkaesque sensations of ambiguity and disorientation.

Furthermore, Haneke utilizes the copresence and relative independence of both textual voice and visual representation in order to uphold Kafka's gestures toward both realism and surrealism. As the director himself puts it, an enormous challenge of adapting Kafka consists in finding a means of expressing these simultaneous yet seemingly mutually insupportable modes or styles of writing: "In Kafka's narratives there is the element of the grotesque. But as soon as you transpose the grotesque into a scenic effect, it seems too theatrical. It loses its quality of realism. But Kafka is also at the same time the great realist. There is hardly anyone who can describe reality with such precision as Kafka does. Now if you become theatrical in film in order to transport the grotesque, then you lose the sense of reality."[74] As both Holmes and Riemer point out, *Das Schloß* preserves both the grotesque and the realistic elements of the original fragment largely by relegating the grotesque to the voice-over narration while preserving the realistic through staging and performance. In Holmes's words, Haneke "chooses not to extemporize on the aspects which could be given a psychological or surreal twist, preferring to leave them to the voice-over, and therefore ultimately still in the hands of Kafka."[75] The instance of this that she cites by way of example is the passage in which K. telephones the castle, and we are informed by the voice-over that K. hears a strange sound, "like the hum of innumerable children's voices," but Holmes correctly notes that "no attempt is made, either visually or acoustically, to illustrate the text of the voice-over."[76] The voice-over and image track, then, present not only noticeably divergent narratives but also divergent levels of reality or reality-perception, each referring to a separate milieu in which fantasy and actuality are differently negotiated. Indeed, the juxtaposition between the voice-over narration and the audiovisual diegesis of the film emphasizes the instability of any relation between the mundane and the grotesque, effectively communicating, one could argue, the affective charge with which Kafka imbues ambiguity itself: a pervasive sense of unreality that is nevertheless grounded in and suspended by a world that disallows any decisive recourse to supernaturalism or transcendence. (Guattari's implication that the medium of television itself possesses Kafkaesque qualities is perhaps understandable in this regard, television being at once the most mundane and the most uncanny of technologies.)

Haneke's television adaptations, then—and *Das Schloß* in particular—use voice-over narration and dialogue in order to forge direct textual connections with their literary sources via the shared intermedium of voice. However, the heautonomous relation between voice and visual image in cinematic narrative (a relation that the television films clearly respect) also becomes a means of conveying affects and elements of style that are not easily relayed through straightforward visualizations of text. In this way, the voice-over plays a central and multifaceted role in the film's acknowledgement and transmission of both style and content from the literary source. However, the instances wherein the visual track diverges from the vocal track also index the essential differences between literature's and film's respective mediations of voice itself, and consequently their disparate representational dispositions. As we turn to *La pianiste*, Haneke's sole cinematic adaptation—and his only adaptation apart from the little-seen *Wer war Edgar Allen?* that does not employ voice-over narration—we will encounter a completely different vocal disposition relative both to Jelinek's source novel and to the television adaptations, but one that nonetheless offers a highly intriguing configuration of textual voice (or, in this case, nonvoice) and cinematic narrative.

La pianiste: The Silent Voice

The most identifiable change that Haneke makes to the narrative of *La pianiste* in his adaptation is his overt dramatization of its core emotional and psychological conflicts, an approach that couches the story within the genre form of the melodrama. Elfriede Jelinek's novel is relentlessly and colorfully descriptive, presenting a panoply of grotesque and pseudosexual imagery denoting the uniquely warped and obsessive sensibilities of the three main characters: Erika Kohut (Isabelle Huppert), her mother (Annie Girardot), and Walter Klemmer (Benoît Magimel). The film, though, is pictorially spare and tonally subdued, even by the standards of Haneke's ascetic visual style. Yet in terms of character interaction and emotional expression, the relation is reversed: the novel contains virtually no dialogue and emphasizes the lack of intimacy and understanding that results from each verbal exchange;[77] the film, however, stages encounter after encounter between the three main characters in which the dialogue and the characters' comportments are infused with emotion, whether histrionic (Erika's mother), blithe (Klemmer), or barely repressed (Erika). Even as it abides by the form of the classical melodrama, however, Haneke's film—in typical fashion for his genre exercises—veers sharply toward dark parody and satire by its end. In Libby Saxton's words, the film "systematically breaks with the generic conventions of the melodrama":[78] the dashing and ardent male positioned to rescue Erika from the strictures of family, culture, and class instead rapes her (an act rendered even more twisted for its accordance with her stated masochistic desires), and even Erika's planned act of revenge against Klemmer is ultimately directed at herself instead. Haneke, in an interview with Scott Foundas, makes it clear that this subversion is necessary from the standpoint of artistic principle: "It's a parody of a melodrama. As a European filmmaker, you can not make a genre film seriously. You can only make a parody." When asked why this is the case, the director responds, "Because the genre film, by definition, is a lie. And a film is trying to be art, and therefore must try to deal with reality. It cannot do this by means of lies. If films are just business, then you can lie. You can sell the lie with a good conscience."[79] Georg Seeßlen, in an article preceding all of Haneke's French-language features, in fact perceives this rejection of melodrama as the director's statement of purpose; after asserting that any mature film aesthetic must be by definition antimythical, antipsychological, and antimelodramatic, Seeßlen gives the following account of Haneke's critical stance and its purpose:

> [A]t issue is an awareness with regard to delimitation and to the move of liberation, because myth, psychology, and melodrama are as much as ever the foundations of our communication, from every advertisement to the coverage of war. Taken together, they probably constitute the language whose boundaries are also the boundaries of our world. Hardly any filmmaker has found a film language that is so consequentially anti-mythical, anti-psychological, and anti-melodramatic as Michael Haneke has, whose works no less continue to critically examine myth, the psyche, and morality.[80]

Defining melodrama as "morality without transcendence and mercifulness," a superficial movement toward liberation and personal expression brought about by the introduction of an object of desire, Seeßlen's attribution to Haneke of an antimelodramatic authorial approach is applicable to *La pianiste* more so than to any of Haneke's other features.[81]

Haneke's choice to present the narrative as a parody of the emotionally charged and dramatically overwrought genre of melodrama has the further effect, however, of maintaining the critical and cynical distance from the characters' words and actions that the novel maintains through narrative voice. This distantiation is conveyed from the outset through one of Haneke's signature framings of a television screen, which in this case depicts a scene from a medical drama. The camera focuses on the TV program in the immediate wake of a violent confrontation between Erika and her mother (the scene that has served as our introduction to the characters); by association, the transparently artificial dramaturgy of the program cheapens the emotional impact of the conflict and of the tearful reconciliation that follows the intermedial detour. As with *Funny Games*, Haneke utilizes the conventions of genre film—of genre as a medium for narrative and affective expectations—in such a way as to warp their attendant affects, utterly undermining the characters' professed sentiments and denying them a means of vocalizing their emotions sincerely. Even more significantly, however, the television clip offers a figuration of Erika's central dilemma as being centered on a lack of means for vocal expression, as it features a (male) patient who clumsily attempts to speak through a mouthful of gauze and bandaged lips in order to engage in a debate about gender inequality. The film thus simultaneously signals and undermines its own themes, as well as Erika's psychosocial situation, via ironic juxtaposition. In Jelinek's novel this sense of ironic and cynical distance is conveyed via the overriding narrative voice, which systematically subverts the characters' statements and gestures and often attributes to them petty and pathetic motivations. For instance, Erika's confession to Klemmer at the recital that her father was committed to an asylum, an admission that spurs the sense of growing intimacy between the two in the film, is rendered in the text as follows: "Erika, in gentle music, tells Klemmer that her father lost his mind and died in the Steinhof Asylum. That is why people have to be considerate of Erika, she has gone through so much. . . . Because of her suffering, this woman deserves every ounce of male interest she can squeeze out."[82] Neither the novel nor the film, in other words, allows the characters themselves a voice as a vehicle for sincere and unproblematic self-expression; the novel subsumes all dialogue within its highly sardonic narration, while the film twists the characters' interactions into a genre parody that subsequently unravels in brutal fashion. Yet within both works a common undercurrent of genuine pathos persists and is arguably continuous between novel and film in the manner of Bazin's concept of style or Guattari's direct transposition of affect. Moreover, in this reading the adaptation relies on a reconfiguration of the novel's intermedial relationship to voice, but in this case it reproduces the novel's very *repression* of the voices of Erika and the other characters, an element of the text that is not communicable solely through either dialogue or voice-over narration. Let us examine the unusual configurations of dialogue in the film more closely as a vehicle for this mode of repression.

In visual-cinematic terms, *La pianiste* emblematizes Haneke's use of delimited framing and mise-en-scène to convey a sense of bodily entrapment, with an additional feature aligned with Erika's voyeurism. As Libby Saxton points out, "[t]he film visualizes Erika's psychological prison in terms of spatial relations"; however, the character is simultaneously presented as directing her gaze out of these spaces, through doorways and windows, but in a manner suggesting their inescapability: "Rather than liberating her from the networks of gazes and spaces that constrict her, Erika's penchant for voyeurism compounds her isolation."[83] When viewing figure skaters practicing, for instance, Erika is framed behind the bars of a fence, and she is consistently circumscribed by doorways and windows throughout the film.[84] This strategy of isolation also applies to the characters' voices, and Erika's in particular, which are similarly delimited and marginalized via editing and off-screen space. Haneke cuts between speakers during dialogue in ways that do not correspond to the rhythms of the conversations, "framing" vocal expression in a manner that relegates it to a space detached from faces and bodies, and that renders the exchanges more difficult for the audience to follow. As in *Das Schloβ*, where this technique is also employed, the visual image of *La pianiste* is never quite synchronized with the characters' voices, a subtle but telling effect that has been noted by Willy Riemer with regard to the Kafka adaptation.[85] An even subtler and more profound disjunction between voice and image, however, is accomplished through manipulations of the vocal track itself.

While many Haneke scholars have commented on the fact that *La pianiste* retains its setting in Vienna in spite of all of the characters speaking French—Roy Grundmann, for example, refers to the "distancing effect" produced by this disjunction between language and locale[86]—few in English-language scholarship have remarked on the film's extensive use of vocal overdub. Apart from the three main characters—Erika, her mother, and Klemmer—most of the film's cast is Austrian and includes Haneke mainstays such as Susanne Lothar in the role of Anna's mother and Udo Samel as Dr. Blonskij. These actors, along with many others in the film, have different voices technically superimposed onto their own, and hence the characters appear to speak in unaccented French, as though Haneke wished to populate the film with Austrian faces but French voices.[87] Consequently, the dialogue in the film exists at a perpetual remove from the images and actors, overlaying the expressions and actions of the latter but never quite assimilating with them. The overall effect is comparable to that which Bazin perceives in Bresson's *Le Journal d'un curé*, which is described as "a silent film with spoken titles" that reconfirms the fact that "[t]he spoken word . . . does not enter into the image as a realistic component."[88] Chion also comments on the phenomenon of postsynchronization and the consequent independence of dialogic vocal production: "In Fellinian extremes, when all those post-synched voices float around bodies, we reach a point where voices—even if we continue to attribute them to the bodies they're assigned—begin to acquire a sort of autonomy, in a baroque and decentered profusion."[89] One could suggest that in such cases, particularly where postsynchronization is most obvious, the dialogue can be considered to occupy the same acousmatic stratum as a voice-over, albeit without the intimate impersonality of a singular I-voice.

In other words, nonsynchronized dialogue—both in the sense of the vocal overdubs of *La pianiste*'s secondary characters and the arrhythmic editing of dialogue exchanges between its main characters—is understandable as a specifically *textual* mode of voice. While the film lacks a voice-over, it nonetheless renders all of its dialogue as a profusion of *voices-over* that retain many of the qualities and dispositions of the object voice.

These manipulations of sound and language allude not only to the vocal track's constituting a heautonomous medium in its relation to the cinematic image, but also to the problematic relationship the film establishes between verbal and emotional expression or, more precisely, between voice and face and their respective affective bearings. In this sense, Erika herself presents a reversal of Anne, the actor played by Juliette Binoche in *Code inconnu*. As pointed out in chapter 3, Deleuze's affection-image finds its purest expression when "faciality" overrides spatiality. The viewer's direct encounter with Anne's ambiguous performance of a state of desperation in *Code inconnu* produces an affective suture that actively undermines and destabilizes the representational and narrative context of the scene, reframing it topologically as an "any-space-whatever." *La pianiste* consistently presents the obverse of this effect: Isabelle Huppert's performance as Erika is restrained to such an extent that her face almost resembles an unchanging mask throughout most of the film, withholding all expected affective responses, while the milieu of Vienna—its musical heritage in particular—rarely ceases to assert the weight of its cultural authority, continually reinforcing the film's sense of place.[90] Haneke is quite clear on this relation, stating the following to Christopher Sharrett: "Vienna is the capital of classical music, and is therefore the center of something very extraordinary. The music is very beautiful, but like the surroundings can become an instrument of repression, because this culture takes on a social function that ensures repression, especially as classical music becomes an object for consumption."[91] If one perceives such a connection between the cultural context of Vienna and the repression of affect evident in Erika's faciality and vocality, then, it is qualifiable in terms of a twofold appropriation: The first, already mentioned above in the discussion of the opening scene's overwrought drama and its reflection in the television program, is the appropriation and banalization of emotional expression by mainstream narratives, including the genre of melodrama through which Haneke mediates the film; the second, perhaps more pernicious, appropriation is played out via the high-culture musical compositions that would supposedly present transcendent affective expressions but have also, as Haneke points out, become "objects of consumption" and thus forms of social capital defining power relations that reinforce class and gender inequalities. Seen through this second lens, the film's diegetic musical performances (which also function extradiegetically, since they bleed into subsequent scenes taking place in different locations) figure into the film's narrative and thematic content not only as bearers of affect but also as vehicles for the *suppression* of affect and emotional expression. In other words, music—Vienna's cultural milieu expressed in its most intense form—does not constitute a "voice" for Erika without also signifying her profound voicelessness. Let us explore this relation of music to voicelessness in more detail.

Critical accounts of *La pianiste* often note the significant roles that music plays in elucidating the film's narrative and in giving shape to its themes and characters, particularly in relation to Erika. Haneke is uncharacteristically forthright in this regard, telling Sharrett that the seventeenth song of Franz Schubert's *Die Winterreise*, which is performed several times in the film, "could be viewed as the motto of Erika and of the film itself."[92] Willy Riemer similarly singles out Schubert's *A Major Sonata*—the piece performed by Klemmer at the recital where he and Erika first meet, and in which his attempted seduction of her begins—as a motif for their affair, calling it "the musical emblem for [Erika] Kohut's infatuation with Klemmer. The movement begins and ends with slow melodic measures, but in extreme contrast the middle section erupts into powerfully disturbing, almost chaotic sonority." In this sense, Riemer goes on to say, the piece "anticipates the violence and rape at the end of the film."[93] The score has thus been charged with bearing a great deal of the thematic and narrative weight of the film, including standing in for Erika's motivations, which are obscured by the sheer reticence of the film's presentation—and Huppert's performance—of the character. Along with being perceived as an emblem for the character's unexpressed emotions, however, the music is also interpretable as an ironic counterpoint to Erika's perversions.[94] Christopher Sharrett strongly implies the equal validity of both readings in his comments on the film's score, stating both that "Schubert's *Winterreise* . . . seem[s] to occupy the healthiest space of Erika Kohut's consciousness and sensibility" and that "[c]ertain scenes of the film are grotesque parodies of Schubert, with Erika offered, it seems, as Schubert's traveler."[95] Such apparently contradictory interpretations of the music's significance—with the music standing as a signifier of Erika's situation, but Erika actively undermining this relation as the negative correlate of Schubert's traveler—would suggest that music tends toward a polyvalent status with respect to the film narration, and to its central character especially. Jean Ma thus aptly observes that music in the film resists any definitive reading of its supplementarity to character and action, even a reading positing an overall sense of "cognitive dissonance"; instead, Haneke's strategic employment of music introduces polyvalent modes of affective interplay, as though the score were a distinct voice or character: "Such a strategy does not reduce merely to a stylistic effect of ironic counterpoint, with sublime background music heightening the shock effect of base actions. Rather, music is foregrounded as a principal mechanism of enunciation, operating at multiple narrative levels throughout the film."[96] As a "mechanism of enunciation," music is in perpetual "dialogue" with the characters and the film itself, but a dialogue that is utterly virtual and metanarrational in nature since music remains incapable of responding to its listeners or performers, and hence speaks *for* rather than *with* them. Erika, who is similarly impassive and who rarely speaks about anything except music, appears to have had her own voice overcoded by the very music she performs. This lack of voice only becomes fully manifest, however, in the film's depiction of her relationship to Klemmer.

As already noted, Haneke's extensive use of vocal overdubs suggests a systematic separation of voices from bodies in the film, with Erika, her mother, and Klemmer among the only characters possessing "true" voices from an extradiegetic standpoint. Yet Erika's voice undergoes an even more profound alienation from her affective-expressive being in the two scenes in which Klemmer visits her house. The first time Klemmer enters (and disrupts) this domestic space, he brings with him an unopened letter Erika has written, in which (unbeknownst to him) she has confessed her masochistic desires and detailed the various scenarios she proposes for their fulfillment. She makes Klemmer read the letter aloud as she listens, seeming to become visibly aroused in the process and presenting to him her hidden collection of bondage gear—all this in spite, or because, of the apparent disgust and confusion her stated desires bring about in her paramour. Klemmer insults her and storms out after reading the letter's contents; when he returns at the film's climax (after their aborted sexual encounter at the hockey rink) he humiliates, beats, and rapes Erika, but as he does this he repeatedly quotes her letter back to her, reminding her that she had asked for these things specifically. Having already given voice to Erika's desires by reading the letter aloud, he now appropriates her words entirely, leaving her utterly bereft of vocal agency. This exploitation of Erika's voice of course compounds the atrociousness of Klemmer's actions rather than justifying them in any way—a particularly grotesque instance of the type of ironic subversion that Grundmann refers to, speaking about the film's verbal play, in general, as "language['s] . . . violation of its own structures."[97] Erika's words are used by Klemmer as a way of further demeaning and abusing her, but not through any distortion of their literal or textual definition; rather, he manufactures for Erika's written voice a horrific context wherein it is stripped of all agency and thus reinvested with an inverted affective charge, a return of the repressed in its most violent form. The rape is in fact all the more disturbing for this focus on the affection-image. The act is staged purely facially—in a single take that is framed, disturbingly, like a classical Hollywood two-shot—and through Huppert's extraordinary performance we witness Erika's mask of total composure give way to fear, pain, and despair.[98] Klemmer's appropriation of Erika's voice, and its "literal" expression of her desires, culminates in a brutal bodily violation. It is as though, having given voice to her desire, Erika has lost the shield of her silence. Her object voice, expressed in her letter and vocalized by Klemmer, has become the instrument for her abjection.

La pianiste's lack of a conventional voice-over does not disqualify it from consideration in terms of its sharing a vocal medium with Jelinek's novel. On the contrary, the film is largely interpretable as a meditation on the intermedial relationships the embodied subject obtains with different diegetic and extradiegetic manifestations of voice. In particular, it focuses on the myriad ways in which the voice—and specifically the voice as a vehicle for desire—is repressed or appropriated, including by mechanisms of cinematic expression such as desynchronized dialogue and music. This play of vocal structures of repression and, ultimately, violence transpose the affects and intermedial configurations of the novel directly to the film, where they discover divergent modes of expression that are nonetheless stylistically and structurally identical to the source text, offering new avenues for both enunciation and repression, or silence.

Beginning with the premise that voice is itself a specialized intermedium common to both literature and cinema, I hope to have uncovered a basis for conceptualizing adaptation not as a process of translation from textual to audiovisual medium but as a matter of divergent "vocological" orientations. Citing a German-language article on intermediality, Jens Schröter frames the issue as follows: "Joachim Paech suggests that 'there is no intermediality between literature and film; there is one only between media narrating literarily or cinematically.' "[99] The voice itself is a singularly important vector for these intermedial connections. Addressing as it does relational structures rather than objective identities, intermediality is uniquely capable of the recognition and treatment of literary voice in a film (and, presumably, vice versa). Though they do not evidence the same type of intermedial relations found between cinema and other audiovisual media in his other films, then, Haneke's adaptations provide a means of accounting for the voice's unique disposition by attending to specific qualities of both literary and audiovisual narrative. Above all, Haneke emphasizes the expressive and ironic void that the voice itself uncovers in both forms, a void that improbably provides a direct conduit between these disparate and complex medial systems. In the next chapter, the director's masterpiece of intermedial expression, *Caché*, will be interpreted as unfolding an even more direct relation than that of the vocal vector connecting film to literary text. Furthermore, the indiscernible intermedial relation between film and video becomes, in *Caché*, the site of a profoundly complex affective experience of shame.

Chapter 5

✦

The Intermediate Dynamics of Shame

Caché

The central question posed by the characters and the viewers of Michael Haneke's film *Caché* is the following: What are the source and the purpose of the videotapes delivered to Georges? The present chapter will directly confront, and posit an answer to, this very question, but my approach will not be based on a strictly narrative perspective. Instead, the existence of the videotapes will be accounted for in my inquiry through a simple yet highly problematic explanation: that the source of the tapes from the perspective of the characters and from that of the viewers is one and the same. The tapes are, in other words, a form of self-representation; they are video reproductions *of* the film itself that have been generated *within* the film narrative. Like the "instant video cassettes" in *Spaceballs*, these tapes are "impossible objects" that present a logical and representational paradox, as they destabilize the categories of reality and representation with respect to both the situations of the characters within the film and the situation of the viewing audience. While this interpretation compromises the spatial and temporal consistency of the film's narrative and diegesis, it introduces the possibility of understanding the film as uniquely staging an intermedial experience of shame, which in turn impinges on the visual system of the *film* in its very indiscernibility from that of *video*. In my close reading of *Caché*, then, shame will become relevant not simply as a thematic element of the film, vicariously experienced by the viewer through an identification with the protagonist's situation, but as an affective and tonal dominant around which the film is perceptually and temporally oriented. Haneke's film thus manifests, via its interplay of the recursive modes of representation of film and video, the effects of shame with respect to the act of spectatorship, as well as the specific temporalities that are initiated by subjective and collective experiences of shame. In this chapter, I will begin with a theoretical definition of shame as a reciprocal perceptual phenomenon with radical temporal implications, and then I will proceed to an extended reading of *Caché* that applies this definition first at the narrative and thematic level, then to the film's visual field and the system of surveillance manifested therein, and finally to the self-representational qualities of *Caché* that constitute, I argue, both a direct conceptualization of shame and an intermedial permutation of the Deleuzian-Bergsonian time-image.

To what extent can *Caché* be singled out among Haneke's filmography as the culmination of the director's use of intermediality—an assertion I have made a number of times so far—and to what extent can one differentiate it from his other films in this respect? On the whole, *Caché* remains largely consonant with his realist aesthetic and rigid representational ethos. For instance, it is unsurprising that Haneke leaves the audience with virtually no means of ascertaining the true source of the videotapes by the end of the film. This strategy of eliding explanatory gestures is consistent with the director's narrative approach in other films, as his commentators frequently point out: "The withholding of crucial narrative information, including flagrant use of ellipses, becomes the formal embodiment of a reluctant ethics framed largely through negation."[1] Stylistically, *Caché* shares a number of other traits consonant with Haneke's oeuvre: long takes are still favored over frequent cuts, the married couple is named Georges and Anne, and their home contains a rather imposing television set that almost continually displays news footage of wars and other international crises. However, *Caché* clearly distinguishes itself from Haneke's previous films in two key ways: through its use of clearly delineated flashbacks and its on-screen depictions of violence and nudity.

As Libby Saxton notes, "Haneke has rigorously eschewed flashbacks on the grounds that they are liable to assume an explanatory function which oversimplifies and diambiguates reality."[2] In this consideration, the director's realist aesthetic, which is invested in preserving ambiguity, precludes the use of the flashback as a plot device.[3] In *Caché*, several apparent flashbacks are included, yet they remain highly ambiguous, it being unclear whether they represent real events or are simply Georges's subjective dream- or memory-images. Still, the very fact that the audience is given a glimpse into the mind and memory of a character is quite unusual if one compares these moments to the rigorously impersonal and objective stance that Haneke's camera takes in his earlier films. Haneke's strategy of relegating representations of violence and nudity to the visual out-of-field is also apparently abandoned in *Caché*, since the film presents both Majid's act of self-inflicted violence and Georges's nude body on-screen.[4] Along with the presence of the flashback sequences, then, the framing of violence and nudity strongly suggests that the categories of the visible and the hidden, as developed in Haneke's other films, have been realigned in *Caché*. Furthermore, rather than mediating violence and nudity through television and video—as he has done in previous films, such as with the videotaped killing of the pig in *Benny's Video*, the pornography on a video screen in *La pianiste*, and various examples of televised violence—Haneke stages the acts directly for the film camera.

From these facts one might conclude that *Caché* stands as a departure from both Haneke's realist aesthetic and his stated ethics of cinematic representation. The visualization that is accorded to flashbacks or dream images suggests that Haneke is following an agenda other than strict realism, while his on-screen depiction of violence and nudity suggests that this agenda incorporates facets of sensationalist cinema—an identifiably different narrative medium, as I previously noted with reference to Stanley Cavell—whose representational strategies the director had demonstrably disavowed. *Caché* thus presents itself as a puzzle not only from the narrative perspective, where the plot is informed by a central mystery that remains unsolved by the film's end, but also from the perspective of a critical approach to the director's oeuvre. For what reasons does Haneke detour in this film from the auteurist style he upheld so rigorously in his previous work? In order to account for these strategies, which, in my estimation, point toward a specific and complex intermedial relationship, I will begin by defining the affective and existential condition that forms the core of the film's expression: the experience of shame.

Shame, Self-Image, and the Inescapable Past

In his video interview with Serge Toubiana, Haneke begins by stating that *Caché* was conceived as a "morality tale" dealing with "how one lives with guilt."[5] Certainly this is an acceptable interpretation of a main theme of the film and of the motivations of its main character, yet the interplay of surveillance and exposure that the film presents is arguably informed by the idea of *shame* more so than guilt, though of course the two are not mutually exclusive.[6] I will therefore begin by differentiating these two phenomena and by examining how a dynamics of vision brings these feelings to bear on Georges in a manner that also implicates the spectators of the film, and in doing so I will draw on a number of diverse definitions and theorizations of shame offered by the philosophers Bernard Williams, Jean-Paul Sartre, Giorgio Agamben, and Emmanuel Levinas, as well as on psychological definitions given to shame by Sigmund Freud and the Lacanian psychoanalyst Jacques-Alain Miller. By evoking these distinct methodologies in relation to the film, a common set of terms will emerge that will help to situate Georges's predicament within a specific historical and social context, yet with respect to a flexible concept of spectatorship that can be applied both within and to the film. Shame will be conceptualized as an affective experience rooted in the actual and virtual relationships of seeing and being-seen that constitute self-image, both individually and collectively, and carry profound implications on social, ontological, and temporal levels. Thus, though the theorists often differ significantly in their approaches to the idea and effects of shame, what can be traced through these works is an illumination of several fundamental affective qualities of shame that are realized in *Caché*. These qualities are profoundly applicable to the intermedial relationship between film and video that unfolds over the course of the film, and particularly to the capacity for self-representation that this relationship potentializes.

Bernard Williams's *Shame and Necessity* (1993) provides a convenient starting point for this inquiry, as his definition highlights the specifically visual nature of shame and opposes it to guilt with respect to agency and affective tenor. According to Williams, the basic difference between the experiences of guilt and shame stems from their respective connections to the morality of the agent: shame is considered to be morally "neutral," while guilt "is closely related to the conceptions of morality."[7] Williams's analysis of shame extends back to the Homeric concept of *aidos*, and he considers shame to be a fundamental element of Western sociocultural mores that continues, in a relatively unchanged form, to function as a regulating force in society. Indeed, both shame and guilt are considered essentially social phenomena, provoked by or experienced in relation to an other, though the nature of this other differs greatly between the two. Guilt is predicated on the existence of a *victim*, one who is potentially or realistically hurt or angered by the agent's action (or inaction), whereas in the experience of shame a *viewer*, either actual or imagined, is necessary, though the viewer is not the focus of the experience: "The viewer's gaze draws the subject's attention not to the viewer, but to the subject himself; the victim's anger, on the other hand, draws attention to the victim."[8] Shame, unlike guilt, can therefore be considered ultimately self-directed and autoaffective, even if the experience of shame involves an external agent. Williams also connects shame and guilt with different sense data: "The most primitive experiences of shame are connected with sight and being seen, but it has been interestingly suggested that guilt is rooted in hearing, the sound in oneself of the voice of judgement; it is the moral sentiment of the word."[9] Moreover, although another's gaze is essential to the experience of shame, "the imagined gaze of an imagined other will do"; this imagined other is subsequently identified as "the internalized other," a *potentially* real person who reflects a genuine social reality.[10] In the most basic manifestation of shame, the exposure of one's genitalia, this internalized other does not normally assert itself (otherwise, being nude would be shameful even if alone). However, other shameful—i.e. socially contemptible or disempowering—behavior may be held in check simply by one's own realization of how one *would* appear to the gaze of another, were that other present. Williams's study of archaic shame and its persistance in Western culture thus identifies several fundamental qualities of the experience of shame that persist in its other theorizations: its rootedness in visuality, its reliance on the gaze of an other (real or imagined), and its autoreflexivity, wherein the self is both the subject and object of the shame experience.

Though Freud did not devote specific attention to shame in his later work[11]—certainly it received less attention than that paid to his extensive theorization of guilt—*Three Essays on the Theory of Sexuality* (1905) includes shame as an important element in its analysis of perversion. In this work, Freud, like Williams, links shame specifically to the act of seeing, stating that shame is "[t]he force which opposes scopophilia, but which may be overridden by it."[12] As a check and a regulating influence on the libido, shame is likened to a "mental dam" acting as a normative force on human sexuality, and Freud focuses on the forms of behavior that result from its absence rather than its presence.[13] Thus, if shame is overridden by the scopophilic impulse, a form of perversion becomes manifest by means of which "the eye corresponds to an erotogenic zone."[14] Both the gazes of others and one's own gaze are implicated in this perversion, lending it active and passive counterparts that are identified, respectively, as exhibitionism and voyeurism. The active perversion is always accompanied by the passive: "anyone who is an exhibitionist in his unconscious is at the same time a *voyeur*."[15] Exhibitionists, according to this theorization, "exhibit their own genitals in order to obtain a reciprocal view of the genitals of the other person."[16] Freud thus considers the exhibitionist to be caught in what amounts to a visual feedback loop, whereby the other's view of *their* genitalia is substituted for—and at some level equivalent to—their own voyeuristic view of the genitalia of the other, in an affirmable instance of intersubjective indistinction. The gaze of the subject and that of the other—their very bodies in fact—are in this way rendered entirely exchangeable. The absence of shame thus brings about a fundamental change in the structure of the gaze that is tantamount to an alteration in subjectivity itself. Like a reverse Narcissus—one who misrecognizes the image of the other as his own reflection—the shameless exhibitionist-voyeur mistakes the other's gaze for his or her own, and his or her own genitals for the other's. At stake in the loss of shame, in Freud's view, is no less than the very structure of self-image, and thus of one's being itself. Sartre, in his well-known philosophical account of shame in *Being and Nothingness* (1943), connects the affect to precisely this existential problem of intersubjectivity.

The shame response is used by Sartre as a key part of the thought experiment describing a man looking through a keyhole, a demonstration of the distinction between reflective and unreflective consciousness, which respectively correspond to states of being (self) and nothingness (nonself). So long as Sartre (who writes his account in the first person) is fully absorbed in his action of peering into a keyhole, his existence is bound up fully with what he is doing: "My consciousness . . . is my acts."[17] However, when some background noise alerts him to the presence (or suspected presence) of another's gaze on him, he is instantly made aware, through his shame response, not only of the other but simultaneously of *himself*: "I see *myself* because *somebody* sees me."[18] This is not simply a consciousness of Sartre's humiliating situation, however, but a shift in the very state and status of his existence in such a way that a self emerges where before there was the nothingness of pure action. The ego is "discovered" in shame, for "shame . . . is shame of *self*; it is the *recognition* of the fact that I *am* indeed that object which the Other is looking at and judging."[19] The obverse of the shamelessness of Freud's exhibitionist is presented here: the passive *voyeur* (Sartre) is confronted with the possibility of exposure to another's gaze, and shame is the defining tonality of the irreconcilable, yet inescapable, consciousness of one's being simultaneously a viewing subject and a viewed object. Shame could be called the "flavor" of self-consciousness, at least insofar as self-consciousness is conceivable as *self-image*, i.e. as a visually structured phenomenon. Sartre goes on to define this Other of shame, then, not as an external consciousness or self that is recognizable by him in turn, but rather as a sort of precondition for the unfolding of one's self-image into a world that recognizes it and forces it to recognize itself: "the Other is the immense, invisible presence which supports this shame and embraces it on every side; he is the supporting environment of my being-unrevealed."[20] For Sartre, shame is conditioned on the same moments of self-consciousness as Being itself. Through shame, Being confronts itself as such: denuded, as it were, before the inescapable, irreducible, and fundamentally unknowable Other who "haunts" consciousness and ensures that the *cogito* "bears indubitable witness of itself and of its own existence."[21] Yet for Sartre this Other is conceived of not as an individual spectator—even one that is "internalized" (as in Williams's concept of the other of shame)—but rather as a pervasive sense of exposure to a disembodied and panoptic gaze.

Sartre's thought experiment attributes existential significance to the experience of shame, uncoupling it from a dyadic self-other relationship. Yet, even while Sartre's Other is diffused into an elementary presence, the philosopher nonetheless still premises his definition of shame on this presence's capacity for judgment. Sartre's Other is referred to as "looking at and judging" the subject, implying that it possesses an ethical-moral perspective, or at least reflects one's own moral values. By contrast, Jacques-Alain Miller, like Bernard Williams, draws a definite distinction between shame and guilt on this basis: "guilt is the effect on the subject of an Other that judges, thus of an Other that contains the values that the subject has supposedly transgressed," while "shame is related to an Other prior to the Other that judges . . . a primordial Other, not one that judges but instead one that only sees or lets be seen."[22] In order to assign the capacity for moral judgment to the Other there must be assumed a means of communication or shared basis for understanding; the other must embody what Williams terms the "voice of judgment."[23] Yet the Other of shame need only complete a circuit of vision through which the subject's potentially disempowering action, appearance, or gesture of concealment is reflected and exposed. Miller therefore eschews the notion of judgment in favor of a concept of limitation and trangression, modesty and shamelessness, wherein self and other are equally implicated at the level of being. Hence, he theorizes, with reference to Jacques Lacan's intriguing characterization of one pole of this opposition, the grounds for a collective experience of shame:

> Lacan describes this modesty . . . as being "amboceptive of the conjunctures of being." *Amboceptive* means that modesty is attached, that it takes hold, on the side of both the subject and the Other. It is attached to both subject and Other. As for the "conjunctures of being," the relationship to the Other constitutes the essential conjuncture of the subject's being and demonstrates itself as such in shame. Lacan makes this explicit when he says, "The shamelessness of one forms the veil for the shame of the other."
>
> In this inaugural relationship not only is there shame over what I am or what I do, but if the other goes beyond the limits of modesty, my own modesty is affected by this very fact.[24]

Shame is not only experienced in relation to oneself as a result of being subjected to another's gaze, but is also potentially experienced in relation to another who trangresses the limits of modesty. In Lacan's view, according to Miller, one is capable of experiencing shame solely by bearing witness to another's shamelessness. According to this model, if one were in the position of Freud's exhibitionist, one would not simply be relinquishing one's shame but rather *transferring* it onto the subject to whom one exposes oneself. The affect is generated intersubjectively, *between* viewer and viewed, as opposed to *within* one or the other, and either party may assume its affective-existential burden.

Miller goes on to identify a collective shamelessness that underpins the whole of contemporary society, a milieu that converts "reality into a spectacle": "Lacan never ceases telling the students of the day that they represent a world in which there is no shame anymore."[25] It is as though Sartre's Other (the pervasive gaze that forms the supporting environment of shame) has been "embodied" (or, to be more precise, "disembodied") by the systems of media that legislate the society of the spectacle's seeing and being-seen relationships via camera and screen. The contemporary subject's self-image—and Benny would be paradigmatic of this—has been displaced onto a mediated representation that attains its own status as object-image, one divorced from the subject's embodied self. Yet what this lack of shame implies, on a deeper level, is that "there is nevertheless shame at being alive behind the absence of shame."[26] A profound and collective sense of shame that we cannot even experience directly manifests itself "in the form of insecurity,"[27] the suspicion that there exists a lurking presence, a shame that threatens to engulf every act of spectatorship. It is as if shame is being continually displaced from the present situation only to be deferred to another temporality, when and where it will have to be reckoned with at some point. These atemporal dimensions of shame, as conceptualized by Agamben and Levinas, will next be explored.

Giorgio Agamben's interpretation of Kafka in *Idea of Prose* (1995) can almost be read as a response to Lacan's idea that we have lost touch with our collective shame, and hence with ourselves. As Agamben points out, at the moment of Josef K.'s death in *Der Process* (*The Trial*), we learn that it seemed as though "his shame would survive him," that shame was the one thing that could be abstracted from the character's ignoble life and death. In Agamben's view, Kafka "was faced with a kind of humanity—the world-wide middle-class—which had been expropriated of every experience except its shame—the pure, empty form of the most intimate sense of self"; hence, Agamben states, Kafka teaches us "not to liberate oneself from shame, but liberate shame."[28] Like Miller, Agamben discovers a collectively repressed "shame at being alive," but he identifies this shame as the self's final refuge from total dehumanization and locates it in the political conditions of modernity. In his extensive study of shame in *Remnants of Auschwitz* (2000), Agamben further argues that shame is not simply the limit-value of dignity, wherein one withholds from others' scrutiny that which is disempowering or degrading, but rather the limit-value of freedom itself: "[Shame is] produced in the absolute concomitance of subjectification and desubjectification, self-loss and self-possession, servitude and sovereignty."[29] As the foundation of the social experience as well as of the subject's self-recognition, shame is an unavoidable consequence of being. It presents itself, then, not simply in singular instances of exposure to another's gaze in a disempowered state, but also as a temporally unbounded and supersubjective precondition of free-willed existence. Thus, exploring the ethical consequences of living normally after the atrocity of Auschwitz, Agamben identifies a shame that transcends not only the actions and experiences of those directly involved in the Shoah—so that society and humanity at large are implicated—but also the historical and even spatiotemporal conditions of its occurrence. Nietzsche's idea of eternal recurrence assumes a horrific significance in the atrocity, which is defined by Agamben as "an event that returns eternally but that, precisely for this reason, is absolutely, eternally unassumable. Beyond good and evil lies not the innocence of becoming but, rather, a shame that is not only without guilt but even without time."[30] This is the aspect of shame that reveals itself most clearly in the atrocity or traumatic event, but remains a potential quality of any experience of shame: its defiance of temporality with respect to the subject, who is affixed to the shameful event, unable to internalize it and assimilate it into the fabric of remembrance in order to make it pass. This property of shame has in fact already been identified by Emmanuel Levinas, in his essay "On Escape" (1935).

Levinas offers one of the most concise definitions of shame—calling it "the representation we form of ourselves as diminished beings with which we are pained to identify"[31]—and then proceeds to point out the very insufficiency of this definition with respect to shame's ontological implications. Shame, he argues, is not merely a product of identity, arising from the impossibility of separating our ideal selves from our petty actions or disempowering appearance. Rather, shame results from the very consistency of being, the impossibility of denying or escaping the essential unity or tautology of one's existence: "What appears in shame is thus precisely the fact of being riveted to oneself, the radical impossibility of fleeing oneself to hide from oneself, the unalterably binding presence of the I to itself."[32] Nausea, which Levinas defines as "shame . . . purified of any admixture of collective representations,"[33] is the only other phenomenon that so uncompromisingly manifests this inescapability of being. Considered in this light, as a facet of ontology, shame can no longer be categorized positivistically as a mental or psychological state, and for Levinas its nature (like that of nausea) "is nothing other than its presence, nothing other than our powerlessness to take leave of that presence."[34] This "presence" can be understood in both an existential and a temporal sense: the inability to take leave of the present is an inability to let the present be subsumed in time's passing, just as it is an inability to retreat into the past (as memory) or project oneself into an alternative future. Jacques Rolland, in his annotations to the 1981 edition of *On Escape*, pursues this concept to its fullest metatemporal and metasubjective implications:

> That then is shame: the discovery—in this halting, in this deportation—of our own presence as unjustified and already possibly at fault. This is like a fracture in time, or in its projection toward the future, like the opening of a sort of present that seems no longer able to finish unless shame itself is lifted. But from this, for shame itself, grasped "in the moment in which it is experienced," we have a present that we must call without-end. . . . And from this, too, for the one who is halted in this halting of time, we have the perception of oneself as of one person *too many*.[35]

The inability to escape the present is accompanied by a virtual desubjectification, a subject whose self-image is that of "one too many," who occupies more than one present time. Shame can thus be defined as this very *fracturing*, both of time and of the subject; its pure presence adheres to, and persists in, the fact of being in such a way that it pushes linear time and the unity of the subject into crisis.

Before proceeding to a consideration of shame as a thematic dominant in *Caché*, let me summarize its characteristics as uncovered in the preceding analyses: Shame is a *primary*, *premoral affect* that is associated with the conjunction of seeing and being seen, and its most basic experience is finding oneself nude before another's gaze. It can thus be differentiated from guilt, which involves a moral (self-)judgment that can be expressed vocally. The *other's gaze* is essential to the experience of shame, though the imagined gaze of an imagined Other is enough to provoke a shame response. Furthermore, one's own perception of *another's immodesty or shamelessness* may be reciprocally experienced as shame—thus, both the viewing *and* viewed selves are susceptible to the affect, which is omnidirectional. As Sartre discerned, the viewing other need not be conceived of as an individual subject and may be instead a ubiquitous seeing "presence" that provokes self-recognition through the *idea* of having revealed oneself. At a deeper level, shame is *immanent in being*, formed from the inescapable fact of being subjected to the perception of others. In this regard it offers perhaps the most intimate sense of self. However, it is also a social phenomenon, and thus it may be experienced collectively, or collectively denied, particularly with respect to a historical trauma or atrocity. Finally, shame is *temporally unbounded* and thus capable of fracturing the self in its continuity of being in time, arresting the self in an unending, traumatic present, or one that recurs eternally. It is clear from these formulations that shame is fundamental to self-image, and that it is potentialized through all of the same trajectories or categories through which the self is posited: in one's self-conscious perceptions, in the perception of another or others, and as a historical and temporally continuous subject.[36] Shame exists in this sense as a *limit* that is placed on the self as it emerges along each trajectory, a limit as to how much of the self is exposed and how much it is exposed to. *Caché* presents us with an individual who is forced beyond this limit through an experience of surveillance, and thus shame can be considered as both an essential theme of the film and the defining quality of Georges's circumstances.

Shame as a Theme of *Caché*

At the level of plot, Georges's situation in *Caché* should at this point be clearly recognizable as a reckoning with shame more so than guilt, with shame the overriding affect implied in the character's unwilling exposure and his vain attempts to hide and keep hidden his petty actions and compromised appearance. It is necessary to recall that the videotapes in *Caché* are accompanied by drawings, but no written messages. The sole exception is the postcard that is sent to Pierrot at school, upon which is written, simply, "For Pierrot on behalf of his papa" ("*Pour Pierrot de la part de son papa*"). There is also at one point a telephone call answered by Anne, which may or may not be from the source of the videotapes, in which a male voice politely requests to speak with Georges, but will not answer when asked to identify himself. Whoever sends the tapes expresses no "voice of judgment" imparting the "moral sentiment of the word," which one would associate with guilt or conscience.[37] Instead, this entity resembles a Recording Angel—a remote, invisible, seemingly panoptic presence that does little more than observe and preserve Georges's actions. It is an absolutely passive observing force, its existence testified to solely by the videotapes and the drawings and postcards sent with them, and it demands only that Georges and his family realize that they are being observed. In this way it is akin to the Other that Sartre defines in *Being and Nothingness*; however, while for Sartre the mere *idea* of such a presence suffices to bring about the self-revelation necessary to the experience of shame, the horror of Georges's experience in *Caché* is that there is no possibility of discounting this other's existence. The gaze has generated evidence of itself in the form of the videotapes. Georges's pursuit of the person recording and sending the tapes is futile, however, serving only to confirm the utter elusiveness and unknowability of the source of the tapes.

It is perhaps best to approach the narrative operation of shame in the film, then, not through an attempt to define the qualities of the indefinable other whose gaze provokes the reaction, but to remain with the subject who has been exposed. We recall that, in its simplest definition, shame is brought about by a consciousness of one's diminished appearance to oneself as given via the gaze of another. Shame therefore implies a doubling wherein the subject is identifiable as the viewer and the viewed simultaneously, following a circuit of vision that begins and ends with the self, but requires another's vision (or that of oneself-as-another) to be completed. This conjunction of *viewing* and *being-viewed* implies a disposition in the subject that participates in the subject's own exposure to the gaze of another, to some extent at least. Without going so far as to label Georges an exhibitionist, then, is it possible to assign him an active role of some kind in the experience of surveillance? In the opening shot, the film's camera (and hence the viewer) occupies Georges's point of view and that of the video-*voyeur* within the film simultaneously, perfectly encapsulating the condition of simultaneously viewing and being-viewed described above. In this case, the conditions for the experience of shame are fully articulated within the video apparatus: here, Georges is both the viewing and the viewed subject, though with a temporal lapse between the recording of the tape and its viewing, a lapse of which the film spectator is initially unaware. We notice, moreover, that Georges isolates himself in the video by rewinding and pausing the tape over his own image (see figure 10). Though his wife Anne and son Pierrot are also seen exiting the house in the shot, Georges brings *himself* into focus as the subject of the tape, fixing the video on his self-image, and it is only after this gesture that it becomes clear that he is the intended receiver of the subsequent videos and pictures. This act of temporal manipulation of the video on Georges's part is mirrored in a later scene in the film, occurring after his profession, that of host of a weekly televised literary forum, has been revealed.

The fact that Georges regularly exhibits himself to potentially millions of viewers both clarifies and complicates our understanding of the character's reaction to the videotapes mailed to him. His video image is, in fact, his stock in trade—this is made apparent in a scene in an editing suite, in which Georges and an editor are manipulating his televised image and dialogue, along with those of other pundits, by similarly rewinding and freezing the video image. In this case, however, Georges is able to alter his image and that of others in such a way as to portray himself in the best possible fashion. This forms a marked contrast to his representation on the final videotape, viewed by Anne and also sent to Georges's agent, which shows him apparently intimidating,

Figure 10: Viewing the surveillance tape that has been sent to him anonymously, Georges freezes the video footage so as to "capture" himself as the person of interest. *Caché* (Michael Haneke, 2005).

threatening, and demeaning Majid. It is thus made abundantly clear that it is not the mere fact of being recorded that is a source of anxiety or shame for Georges but the loss of power that is associated with having no influence over the way he is filmed, the output on the tapes, the conditions under which he is presented, and, above all, with not being able to identify the position of the camera itself and thus realize when and where he is being filmed. What was formerly a source of empowerment for Georges becomes an agony as soon as the element of volition has been removed or reversed. There is a subtle yet highly disturbing sign of this loss of control early in *Caché*'s first act, when we see Georges finishing the taping of one of his programs. After he bids goodnight to his guests and to the viewers, addressing the television camera directly in close-up, the camera—in a gesture common to many talk shows—slowly begins to pull back as a voice offscreen instructs everyone to stay seated while the credits roll, then informs them that they may leave. An assistant enters the stage and tells Georges something, prompting him to move off the set, but the camera *continues to track him*. What was initially the television camera with which he interacted directly has been transformed into (or always was) a surveillance camera that now refuses to let him escape the frame, presumably the movie camera filming *Caché*. The camera to which Georges was exposing himself professionally is now exposing him privately, following him even as he goes behind the scenery of the talk show. The culmination of this cycle of exposure that engenders Georges's shame occurs near the close of the film, when Georges literally exposes himself—appearing naked on camera (*Caché*'s movie camera, that is) before getting into bed. However, to what purpose or effect is this display of nudity? Are we to interpret this as an act of exhibitionism for the benefit of the film viewer, and thus a final enactment of the character's shame, or is he simply undressing while we, like Sartre looking through the keyhole, are supplying the intrusive gaze (to *our* potential shame)?

Though the questions of shame and the act of film spectatorship will be touched upon more directly in the next two sections, even in this narrative-thematic approach to the film the distinction between Georges's shame and the viewer's may not be at all clear, in consideration of the collective form of shame identified by Miller. The fictional situation in *Caché* has been precipitated by an actual historical event that is directly referred to only once in the film, and briefly: the violent suppression by police of a peaceful protest of the Algerian war, which took place on October 17, 1961. This massacre, in which as many as two hundred people were shot or drowned in the Seine, is in the film cited as the event at which Majid's parents lost their lives, orphaning him and positioning him as Georges's adopted rival sibling. Haneke is clear as to the inspiration that this event provided for *Caché*'s story line: "I had been toying with the idea of writing a script in which someone is confronted with his guilt for something he did in childhood. I wanted to explore a character's reactions to this trauma. As chance would have it, around this time I saw a documentary broadcast on ARTE, which dealt with the events precipitated by this demonstration in October 1961. After watching that broadcast, all of these different elements coalesced."[38] Georges is of course not morally responsible for the murder of Majid's parents at the hands of Paris authorities, nor, indeed, is he morally responsible for having engineered Majid's removal from his home and placement in an orphanage, as the character himself points out: he was a child at the time and not a fully developed moral agent. Georges also asserts several times in the film, quite reasonably, that he cannot be made to feel guilty about Majid's suicide, which Majid invited him to witness. But while Georges is not necessarily *morally* responsible for having brought about the crime, he nonetheless has a stake—and in his case it is a particularly personal stake—in having covered it up and allowing it to remain hidden. Haneke implicates all of French society, and by extension all postcolonial national histories, for their complicity in such cover-ups: "I don't want my film to be seen as specifically about a French problem. It seems to me that, in every country, there are dark corners—dark stains where questions of collective guilt become important. I'm sure in the United States there are other parallel examples of dark stains on the collective unconscious."[39] The historical "stain" of the massacre—which finds its sublimation in the bloodstains present in the childish drawings, Georges's dream-flashbacks, and the stain left on the wall after Majid's suicide—can never be removed, ignored, or displaced.[40] The term "collective guilt" is often applied to such cases, but "collective shame" would be more appropriate, since the dynamics of suppression and exposure that follow such a historical trauma point more toward a legacy of shame than of guilt.

Indeed, Hannah Arendt has argued that the idea of "collective guilt" is in fact "a highly effective whitewash of all those who have actually done something, for where all are guilty, no one is."[41] Agamben supports this view, arguing convincingly in favor of Primo Levi's assertion that "it makes no sense to speak of collective guilt (or innocence) and that only metaphorically can one claim to feel guilty for what one's own people or parents did."[42] It is not implausible that Georges would feel guilty about what he did to Majid as a child, since his own actions, the lies he told, resulted in Majid's being sent to an orphanage (if, indeed, this is exactly what happened; the film is somewhat ambiguous as to the truth of the events themselves and we rely almost exclusively on Georges's impressions of them). Yet to interpret the main theme of the film, as Haneke himself does, as being connected with how one lives with guilt is limiting in several respects. Not only can Georges's guilt not be transposed directly onto society at large, but this interpretation does not properly account for the effect of the surveillance videos either within the story or as a part of the signifying structure of the film. It is instead an experience of shame (which is, of course, not exclusive of guilt) that the videotapes potentially bring about, and in which we as a viewing audience potentially participate. The film ultimately renders the question of Georges's true condition relative to his shame ambiguous, or even a moot point—we can neither consider Georges ashamed or shameless. Yet if Georges, like us, participates in what Lacan terms a "shameless culture" in which continual televisual and video surveillance produce "a gaze castrated of its power to shame," then his very shamelessness is profoundly shameful.[43] The theme of shame in *Caché* has thus brought us to a convergence of story and structure, the latter consisting of the visual strategies of the film that are in themselves invested with and determined by a sense of shame, relative to Georges and to the viewer. These strategies will be examined more directly in the next part of this analysis.

Seen and Unseen: Framing Spectatorial Shame

So far I have identified some of the possible effects of the *voyeur*-camera's gaze within the narrative of *Caché* relative to the characters and the viewer apropos the experience of shame, but little has been said about the agency behind this gaze, other than noting its silence and passivity.[44] The intermedial relationship between the videos and the film is deeply connected to the subjectivity of Georges, who embodies the seer and seen dichotomy at the heart of *Caché*'s visual system. However, it cannot be said that the videos emanate from Georges's psyche (since this interpretation risks throwing the entire mimetic status of the film into question), nor that the character's consciousness is incidental to the gazes of these cameras (since Georges's dreams and memories are represented to the viewer, among other reasons). What, then, is the nature of the representational agency operating in the film, both in terms of the content of the film and the content of the videotapes within the film; and how are these related to one another and to Georges? I proposed at the beginning of this chapter to demonstrate that these two modes of representation have a single source relative to film viewer and character alike, yet I also noted that this interpretation problematizes the spatial integrity of the film and simultaneously ruptures the space of viewership. Thus, neither a purely diegetic nor a purely extradiegetic status can be assigned to the sources of these overlapping camera gazes. As Libby Saxton points out in her examination of offscreen space in *Caché*, the film instead employs "a complex system of competing frames, cameras and image technologies which constructs a multiplicity of invisible spaces."[45] These spaces are permeated by a productive gaze that is at times associated with the point of view of the spectator, and at other times with Georges's, yet it seems in the final analysis to occupy the perspective of an unknown and seemingly unknowable agency that defies and exceeds both. In order to understand this disembodied gaze, which produces the tapes within the film in addition to the film itself, I will proceed by examining these tapes' contents and then attempting to infer its position or attitude relative to them.

Caché unfolds as what can be regarded as a double-visual game—we are expected to consistently identify both with Georges, the victim of voyeuristic intrusion, and with the unidentifiable *voyeur*. As mentioned already, this unsettling and circuitous play of subject and object of surveillance is evident from the establishing shot of the film. We are presented with a wide shot of the facade of Georges's home over which the title and opening credits are displayed. After the static shot has been held for several minutes, we hear Georges's voice from offscreen, and it becomes clear that we are actually watching a video, and that our point of view is identical with that of Georges and Anne, with the frame of the movie screen standing in for that of the TV screen. As Libby Saxton puts it, "We thus share, at least temporarily, the confusion and disorientation of a couple we encounter in the uncanny situation of watching themselves being watched. What is more, from the very outset of the film, we find ourselves already implicated, as spectators, in an economy of voyeurism and surveillance."[46] Not only are we, as spectators, not able to fully identify with either the victim or the victimizer, but we are often not even able to determine whether there is a difference between the surveillance of the characters *within* the film and our viewing *of* the film itself. In fact, in this opening shot, like many other shots in *Caché*, the video and the film are irreconcilable *precisely because they are exactly the same*. The intermedial difference between these media thus asserts itself most directly in its very imperceptibility—the video and the film image coalesce within a single shot while nonetheless remaining, at the mimetic level, mutually insupportable.

This is not a matter of overlapping images so much as it is a conflict of the conceptual statuses of the same image—an undecidability between whether it is a film image or an image *within* the film, whether the video picture is part of the film's representation of these objects and actions or is itself an "object" represented on film. The content of these images being indistinguishable, this medial difference can perhaps best be understood with respect to the concept of framing. In other words, is the video framed by the film, or is the film image framed by the video? Which medium assumes priority in determining the modes of exposure to which the audience and the film's characters are subjected, these being crucial to the film's affective expression of shame?

In *Cinema 1*, Deleuze categorizes two basic forms of framing, of delimitations of visual fields, both of which strongly come into play in *Caché*. Mathematical or geometrical frames are "preliminary to the existence of the bodies whose essence they fix," while dynamic or physical frames go "as far as the power of existing bodies goes" and hence assume the kinetics of the bodies they capture. Geometrical framing is constituted in relation to spatiotemporal coordinates; dynamic framing is constituted in relation to "selected variables," such as the body or bodies contained in the frame.[47] The first two videotapes sent to Georges are, like most video surveillance footage, framed geometrically: the camera is immobile and exterior shots of Georges's home (one during the day and one at night) are held for long periods of time with little or no on-screen action, as if patiently waiting for its objects to enter the frame. The next two videos are dynamic in their framing, consisting of forward-moving handheld shots that purposefully and methodically target the destination objects: Georges's childhood home in the first case, and Majid's apartment door in the second. Both these videos and the film itself employ clearcut examples of both types of framing. In some scenes the camera frames a space in a way that mirrors the presentation of the first videotapes, confusing, if not erasing, the distinctions that we can make between the tapes Georges receives and the film we are viewing. At other points the camera is fixed on Georges, panning to follow his every movement and refusing to let him escape the frame, though others such as Pierrot and Anne enter and exit the frame freely—the most extreme example of this phenomenon is the television camera that continues to film Georges after the taping of his show has ended.

Deleuze's approach to framing, furthermore, conceives of the film screen not in terms of content as such but as the selective delimitation of variables from an infinitely more extensive set of visual data. Hence, it puts forward the idea that the frame metonymically establishes a complex spatial and temporal multiplicity of objects and actions that are given in and by a film, and that do not necessarily appear as visual or auditory data. In this conception of film as an expansive spatiotemporal field, then, on-screen space has no more privileged an ontological claim than offscreen space. The "out-of-field" (*hors-champ*) is thus defined by Deleuze in *Cinema 1* as consisting of "what is neither seen nor understood, but is nevertheless perfectly present."[48] The terms "viewing a film" and "viewer" are to some extent reductive, for we accept that much more occurs in a given film than what we actually see, or hear, whether or not we are able to say exactly *what* has occurred. In a temporal sense, experiencing a film is akin to the Bergsonian experience of the "past in general," which Deleuze describes in *Bergsonism* (1966): "It is the past in general that makes possible all pasts. According to Bergson, we first put ourselves back into the past in general: He describes in this way the *leap into ontology*. We really leap into being, into being-in-itself, into the being in itself of the past."[49] This "leap" is necessitated by the fact that recollection is not a process of summoning individual images out of the past, but of repositioning ourselves with respect to the ontology of the past, which, in a very definite sense, is coextensive with the ontology of the present. As Rodowick notes, "Bergson argues that our entire past is preserved as a nonchronological coexistence in time. There is no 'natural' chronology or continuity to the past as remembered. Rather, the entirety of the past rests in a state of virtual and simultaneous coexistence that expands as time passes."[50] Cinematic time is likewise cotemporal with the being of the present, and when we immerse ourselves in a cinematic experience we "leap" into the milieu of the film with an implicit faith that much is transpiring, has transpired, and will transpire that will not be signified visually or aurally. There are two important consequences of this "leap": Firstly, our acceptance of this milieu allows for the spatial and temporal malleability of the images that are presented. In other words, a film does not need to articulate itself as a singularly unified, chronological entity coextensive with its running time or duration—our idea of the milieu as a whole enables the utilization of techniques such as flashbacks, parallel montage, the replaying of scenes from different spatial coordinates or perspectives, and so on. A film's milieu is a true multiplicity in both a temporal and spatial sense, and thus one can qualify as "offscreen" both objects and actions that are spatially present but never enter the frame, and interregnal actions or events that are not given a scenic representation. Secondly, there is a socio-ethical dimension that emerges in the form of an implicit contract between the film and the viewer, most apparent in "classical" or Hollywood cinema but present in all types of film, with regard to what may appropriately occur on- and offscreen. It is through this contract that an experience of shame is potentially introduced into the filmgoing experience, based on the terms it establishes with regard to the degree of visual exposure the audience is given to the cinematic field, and the genre type and affective tonality of this exposure (whether it is comedic or dramatic, for example).

Slavoj Žižek (drawing in turn on an analysis by Richard Maltby) refers rather amusingly to these often ambiguous visual politics in his analysis of a scene in *Casablanca*: Ilsa confronts Rick and then embraces him passionately, at which point the film dissolves to a three-and-a-half second shot of an airport tower. When we rejoin the pair, Rick is looking out the window, smoking, and he and Ilsa continue their conversation; we are left to wonder whether or not, in the interim implied by the dissolve, they had sex. Žižek maintains that an innocent interpretation and a lascivious interpretation of the scene are equally valid and both may be accepted simultaneously, even by a single viewer. What is important is simply that the decorum that defines what may be seen or even alluded to in the public domain is left intact: "This double reading is not simply a compromise on the part of the symbolic law, in the sense that the law is interested only in keeping up appearances, and leaves you free to exercise your dirty imagination on condition that it does not encroach upon the public domain. The law itself needs its obscene supplement, it is sustained by it."[51] These visual mechanics, then, are regulated by a law whose enforcer is shame, preserving what cannot be displayed or framed though it remains hidden from view. Even in less ambiguous examples than this one, there is present a tacit, mutually sustained agreement between the film and the viewer as to what should and should not be represented onscreen, and, of course, this code is variable depending on the type of film and its intended audience as well as the social mores and conventions informing the film. Haneke has been characterized as a provocateur because films like *Funny Games* and *La pianiste* are perceived of as transgressing these conventions both by sustaining, on-screen, discomforting scenes of intense emotional anguish, and by refusing to frame acts of violence, nude actors, or other scenarios associated with voyeuristic enjoyment. Catherine Wheatley describes the effects of Haneke's application of this approach to established film genres, including its relationship to spectatorial shame: "A thriller is thus revealed as an ordeal of intense suffering in which one should not want to take voyeuristic pleasure; an erotic melodrama, an excruciating exposure to more detail than we really want to know. The emotions that arise from these revelations are wide-ranging and differ from spectator to spectator: among them are discomfort, embarrassment, shame, sometimes anger."[52] Haneke's provocative auteurial style, broadly speaking, is largely derived from a fundamental shift in framing that is oppositional to more familiar or genre-specific film narratives: violent and erotic acts are relegated to offscreen space, while the traumatic aftermaths of such acts linger in the frame far longer than in typical genre films.

A different example of this type of uncomfortable revelation in *Caché* is perfectly demonstrated via the final videotape mailed to Georges's home, which captures and lingers on Majid's fit of sobbing following Georges's initial visit and confrontation. The video represents, first of all, a far greater violation of Majid's privacy than any video surveillance of Georges within the film—the camera (following Georges) has penetrated Majid's living space and has captured a moment of personal suffering. The shame of witnessing Majid's private display is, for Georges, compounded in several ways: his wife views it before he does, catching out his lie to her that no one was home when he went to the location shown on the previous tape; a copy of the tape is sent to his agent, and so he suffers the embarrassment of having his private confrontation exposed more widely; and he is forced to view his own domineering and unpleasant attitude from an external perspective. For the viewer, the video serves as an obscene supplement to the earlier scene of their confrontation, and its appearance, in addition to potentially provoking a shame reaction as described by Wheatley above, signals a change in the film's narrative trajectory. The economy and momentum of the story's development, the focus on Georges's perspective, and the premise that the mystery of the videos is in the process of being solved—all of these aspects of the film begin to unravel when this outpouring of emotion, which should have remained hidden, is rescued from the passing of time in the film and wedged into the narrative by whatever force is generating the videos. Haneke's strategy of revelation, which usually involves maintaining a scene well beyond the spectator's normal level of comfort, is thus expressed through a chronological reordering and through an intermedial relayering of the film's modes of representation. The viewing audience is not privileged above the characters with respect to the discomfort of witnessing Majid's anguish, and there is an excess of emotion displayed that cannot be accepted as cathartic, since we are distanced from it in a similar manner to Georges, temporally and through its mode of representation as a video within the film narrative. Like the murder in *Benny's Video*, when it is replayed for the parents, this medial supplement assumes a much different affective and perceptual disposition than that of the original scene itself.

The shift in Haneke's strategic use of on- and offscreen space in *Caché*, as compared to his previous films, orients the film more strongly toward a gaze generative of, and generated by, shame and in the process toward a more radical mimetic mode challenging not only narrative convention but also the limits of cinematic representation itself. By blurring the distinction that can be made between the film we are watching and the surveillance footage sent to Georges within the film, *Caché* promotes an undecidability between the footage obtained by the film-camera and by the *voyeur*-camera. This undecidability is almost certainly intentional, as Libby Saxton notes: "Haneke's decision to shoot the whole film in high definition digital video obscures the distinctions between the covertly filmed videotapes and the other images. The resulting confusion is aggravated by the preponderance of static sequence shots, many of which bear a disquieting resemblance to surveillance footage."[53] The intermedial relationship between the film and the videos seems to privilege indiscernibility over difference through the use of a single medium—digital video—and similar framing for both. However, the position occupied by the camera gaze that captures the on-screen space of the videotapes remains irreconcilable with the spatiotemporal field of the film. Saxton thus defines the surveillance camera's existence as being "at once a necessity and a tantalizing impossibility, a ghost-like glitch in time and space."[54] The camera gaze of the tapes emanates from an out-of-field that defies the spatiotemporal dimensions defining this field itself. It is a case in which, as Deleuze describes it, "the out-of-field testifies to a more disturbing presence, one which cannot even be said to exist, but rather to 'insist' or 'subsist,' a more radical Elsewhere, outside homogeneous space and time."[55] This "disturbing presence" is in *Caché* the gaze of the Other of shame (in the Sartrean sense); within the film it is at some points Georges's own gaze at his recorded image, at other times the gaze of Anne, or Georges's friends or agent, or anyone who watches the video. It is also at all points the gaze of the film spectator, whether or not this is doubled by the perspectives of those viewing the tapes in the film, as in the opening shot. The possibility is introduced, then, that we, the viewers of *Caché*, are the "others" whose collective gaze (which appears to Georges in the form of the videotapes) completes the circuit of vision that sublimates his shame and leads him to reveal what he has attempted to conceal his whole life, leaving him fully exposed, literally denuded, before our eyes by the film's end. The out-of-field that insinuates itself from "outside of homogeneous space and time" is, in this interpretation, the space the viewer occupies in relation to the film, and it is as though we "leap" into the film's milieu only to end up where we started, in our own spectatorial situation.

While this metacinematic dimension of the film must be acknowledged, it is an oversimplification to say that *we* are generating the videos that sublimate Georges's shame and motivate the plot of the film, or even that, as some have commented, "Haneke is stalking his own characters."[56] Our gazes stand in for the gaze of the other of shame by proxy only—just as in a comedy the viewer may assume the perspective of a "divine" witness to folly or misfortune, as argued in chapter 2 with respect to *Funny Games*—and we remain susceptible to the direct experience of shame that is generated by the film's interplay of real and virtual gazes. The film is in this sense demonstrative of a shame structure that brings together Sartre's and Lacan and Miller's concepts of the Other of shame. The gaze of Sartre's virtual Other, as pointed out in the previous section, is not an abstraction, but rather is embodied in the very system of videography that Georges subjects himself to professionally and that also begins to record his private actions (as in the example of the television camera that continues to film him after the taping has finished). As Lacan's comments suggest, though, the prevalence of this system of representation promotes not firsthand shame, but rather a collective shamelessness, as it produces images affectively independent of, and thus estranged from, their subjects.[57] Yet shame is reintroduced, in *Caché*, through the transmission of the images captured in the gaze of the absolutely passive and reflexive Sartrean Other to Georges and to the film viewer *simultaneously*. This allows for the "conjuncture of being" between self and (nonvirtual) other, the defining quality of shame for Lacan, to be established between Georges and the film viewer, albeit within a totally different visual structure than that of lived experience. Rather than the direct exchange of gazes that defines the affective experience of shame in actuality, it is instead the shared act of viewership that unites Georges and the film viewer with respect to shame, exposing both to the perspective of the Sartrean Other even if only Georges is (visually) exposed *by* its gaze. The film viewer is thus implicated in the visual circuit that produces shame, but as an Other in the Lacanian rather than the Sartrean sense. The Sartrean Other—the "supporting environment of [one's] being-revealed"[58]—remains an agency that is totally unknowable both to Georges and the viewer. This staging of shame is predicated, however, on the identicality of the visual material constituting the videos within the film and the film itself, both of which can be considered products of a common camera gaze that reproduces the spatiotemporal field of the film within the film, framing its own gaze in the process of staging the reflexive visual experience of shame that connects Georges and the filmgoer. The shift of violence and nudity from offscreen to on-screen space in *Caché* (relative to Haneke's previous films) results from this function of the camera gaze, which exposes Georges and exhibits these obscenities to Georges and the viewer. In the next section, the temporal implications of the film's representation of itself on video will be explored in more detail relative to the temporalities of shame defined by Agamben and Levinas and sublimated in the Deleuzian concept of the "time-crystal."

Intermediality and the Time-Crystal

I suggested in the introduction that a Deleuzian approach to intermediality is not only possible but has been proposed by the philosopher himself, who states in his "Letter to Serge Daney" that it is the mission of cinema to "stop 'being cinematic,' stop playacting, and set up specific relationships with video, with electronic and digital images, in order to develop a new form of resistance and combat the televisual function of surveillance and control."[59] I have proceeded to characterize this mode of resistance as integral to the development of Haneke's oeuvre and have singled out *Caché* as the film in which the director's engagement with noncinematic media reaches its apogee. In this section, I will argue that the film presents an intermedial permutation of the Deleuzian-Bergsonian time-image defined in *Cinema 2*, the coalescence of the videos and the film producing a crystalline thought-structure that simultaneously reflects present, past, and future. Presenting as it does "distinct yet indiscernible" modes of enunciation in continual exchange, *Caché* exhibits a visual schema of what Deleuze terms the "principle" of the crystal-image.[60] That is, if one considers the videos within the film and the film itself as mutually reflective manifestations of a common plane of immanence, each virtual with respect to the other but offering in the circuit of exchange between them a direct image of time itself, then the very fracture between these media forms the seed of a nonpsychological "pure recollection" or, in Deleuze's Proustian terms, "a little bit of time in the pure state."[61] Furthermore, I assert that the affective tonality of this brief yet evocative image, as well as its premise, is deeply connected to the film's expression of a direct experience of shame and the unique temporalities that emerge therefrom. Let me briefly examine the nature of these temporal gaps and reversals before suggesting the formation of a time-image at their core.

In *Caché*, I have affirmed, no overriding consciousness emerges that would order or explain the bizarre metaspatial and metatemporal nature of the videotapes, although most of the film narrative is concerned with locating the person or persons who would account for their existence. Deleuze, in *Cinema 2*, offers the following observation about films that, in expressing "a mode of the crystal-image," represent themselves within themselves: "It will be observed that, in all the arts, the work within the work has often been linked to the consideration of a surveillance, an investigation, a revenge, a conspiracy, or a plot."[62] The tapes that appear within the film are indeed indicative of a surveillance of Georges and his family, and Georges immediately deduces that they are a part of a revenge conspiracy or blackmail attempt and soon determines that their apparent source is Majid. The film then plays out as a *reversal* of the scenario constructed by the character: Georges begins to harass and threaten Majid and his son, making them the targets of his own campaign of intimidation. The videos are thus linked to a plot or conspiracy, yet its events are out of sequence—the videos *initiate* a plot rather than appearing as evidence of one that has already begun, and the character positioned as its engineer ultimately becomes its victim. This inversion of events at the level of story is reflected, moreover, in the modes of temporal manipulation that are revealed in the media objects that constitute the "works within the work" in relation to the work itself. Additionally, there is ultimately no particular consciousness, like that of Paul in *Funny Games*, with respect to which these diegetic manipulations of temporality are accountable at another level.

In fact, the notion of the "work within the work" does not serve to convey the degree of interdependence that the videos obtain with the film, and the temporal aporias that result from this intermedial relationship. The videos Georges receives, in other words, do not simply represent or reflect the film at the diegetic level, but often seem to comprise the actual film we are viewing. For example, the content of the second tape sent to Georges, a static exterior nighttime shot of the facade of his house, is identical to a scene from the film that occurred several minutes before; Georges and Anne are, in effect, watching a part of the film that we have just watched. Not only this, but when we first see the scene being (re-)played on their television it is being rewound, and so we see the shot of Georges driving up and exiting his car in reverse, before it once again unfolds in normal sequential time. The film itself—insofar as it has been rendered as video—is subjected to temporal manipulation, as is *Funny Games*, but in this case the effect is retroactive and recursive, and *Caché*'s primary mode of representation is undecidable. Its image is transposed not only from film onto videotape, as in *Spaceballs*, but also from videotape back onto film. The videos within the film thus obtain a direct correspondence to the visual field of the film itself, their contents flouting spatiotemporal contiguity on both the narrative and mimetic levels of the film. The intermedial relationship between film and video potentializes new temporal relationships that, as stated, constitute a new form of the Deleuzian time-image.

Let us examine the modes of temporality portrayed by the videos themselves in relation to the film. The two types of videos sent to Georges seem to correspond, roughly, to two forms of time: the recent past and the near future. The tapes that represent the past are the remote, geometrically framed shots, such as the first video (the opening shot of the film), the second video, and the final tape of Georges's confrontation with Majid in his kitchen. The other types of image that appear on the tapes are the dynamically framed handheld shots that steadily move forward, from the perspective of one either driving or walking. These tapes are connected with future actions for the simple reason that they represent what Georges will do before he does it: when a tape is sent of someone driving to Georges's childhood home, Georges drives to his childhood home; when one is sent of someone driving to Majid's apartment building and walking down the hallway to his apartment door, Georges again does exactly that. Of course it could be argued, quite correctly, that these tapes are directly leading Georges to perform these actions. However, just as the second tape was a replay of a shot that had occurred two scenes earlier in the film, the tape of the handheld shot moving down the hallway of Majid's apartment building is *identical* to the shot employed when Georges visits Majid's apartment later in the film. The basic form of this shot is repeated three times, in fact, each time with a different content: first the shot is utterly consistent with the video for several seconds, until Georges steps into the frame when it halts in front of Majid's door; the second time, Georges's back is in frame for the length of the handheld shot as the camera follows him down the hall and to the door to confront Majid for supposedly sending a tape to his agent (but Majid doesn't answer); the third and final time, the backs of Georges and two policemen are framed as they walk to the door in order to investigate Majid's possible involvement in Pierrot's disappearance (this time Majid's son answers). The tape that ostensibly has directed Georges to Majid's apartment can thus be considered a prochronic or proleptic representation of this repeated action, a transmission from later parts of the film to an earlier part. Deleuze comes closest to this idea in his discussion of the crystal-image, in connection with Alain Resnais's *Last Year at Marienbad* (1961). He proposes the existence of an "interplanetary narration":

> The essential point . . . appears if we think of an earthly event which is assumed to be transmitted to different planets, one of which would receive it at the same time (at the speed of light), but the second more

> quickly, and the third less quickly, hence before it happened and after. The latter would not yet have received it, the second would already have received it, the first would be receiving it, in three simultaneous presents bound into the same universe. This would be a sidereal time, a system of relativity, where the characters would be not so much human as planetary, and the accents not so much subjective as astronomical, in a plurality of worlds constituting the universe. It would be a pluralist cosmology, where there are not only different worlds (as in Minnelli), but where one and the same event is played out in these different worlds, in incompatible versions.[63]

The film *Caché* and the tapes within the film are narratively coexistent, but they are similarly incompatible for two reasons: because they are not (chrono) logically ordered, and therefore do not enter into a legitimate temporal or causal relationship with one another; and because the tapes are, impossibly, representations *of* the work which appear *in* the work. No objective or subjective perspective exists that would unify these images either spatially or temporally—their milieu encompasses more than one "world," but utilizing an intermedial, rather than interplanetary, mode of narration.

Continuing with a Deleuzian analysis, one can view the temporal and representational disjunctions in *Caché* as aspects of a singular gesture, the splitting-in-two that constitutes the crystal-image. Deleuze writes, in *Cinema 2*, that "[t]ime has to split at the same time as it sets itself out or unrolls itself: it splits in two dissymmetrical jets, one of which makes all the present pass on, while the other preserves all the past. Time consists of this split, and it is this, it is time, that we *see in the crystal*."[64] In Haneke's film, the videos serve as evidence and echoes of these splits, the static shots preserving the past, the handheld shots passing into the future, but a future that is not completely indeterminate but rather inextricably linked to the destiny of Georges. Quoting Jean Ricardou's study *Le nouveau roman*, Deleuze clarifies this splitting's effect on a narrative:

> What we see in the crystal is therefore a dividing in two that the crystal itself constantly causes to turn on itself, that it prevents from reaching completion, because it is a perpetual *self-distinguishing*, a distinction in the process of being produced; which always resumes the distinct terms in itself, in order constantly to relaunch them. "The putting into abyss [*mise en abyme*] does not redouble the unit, as an external reflection might do; in so far as it is an internal mirroring, it can only ever split it in two," and subject it "to the infinite relaunch of endlessly new splitting."[65]

Georges's nightmarish situation is brought about by his being caught within this internal mirroring, both his past and his future actions continually and disorientingly reflected back to him via the videos he receives. This is not a redoubling, as Ricardou points out, but a potentially infinite series of self-reflections, the sum total of whose divisions amounts to what Borges terms, in "The Garden of Forking Paths," "[a]n invisible labyrinth of time."[66] It becomes impossible to establish, in this scenario, a unitary and unidirectional chronology, or a logic of causality, since no lineal duration emerges that would order and encompass the temporally incompatible, yet simultaneous, existences of the film and the videos of the film. This is not to say that there is no form or structure to this process, however. There is, but instead of the linear form of "time's arrow," it is the crystalline form of a time-image, and one whose formation is conditioned or possibilized by shame's affective-existential amplitude.

Before I attempt to elaborate an account of these intermedial time-crystals in *Caché* with respect to an experience of shame—and connect these to the unfolding of the final and most profound time-image to emerge in the film—there remains one other order of image that must be mentioned: Georges's subjective memory-images. These images, which appear in the form of flashbacks in the film, correspond not to the images on the videotapes but rather to those depicted by the childish drawings that accompany them, one of which also appears on the postcards sent to Georges and to Pierrot. There are two such drawings: the first is of a boy coughing up blood, the second of a rooster being beheaded. The brief flashback of the boy, Majid as a child, coughing up blood is intercut with the image of the second tape that Georges is viewing (which has been accompanied by the drawing). A longer, more detailed flashback of the rooster being killed is presented as a dream sequence that occurs while Georges is spending the night in his childhood home, after having received the second drawing. As Haneke points out in his videotaped interview with Serge Toubiana, these sequences are not representations of actual events in Georges's past, but reflect rather the lies that Georges admits telling his parents and Majid as a child in order to have Majid removed from his parents' care.[67] Thus they are not "pure" recollection images, nor are they images of the actual (diegetic) past, yet they are nonetheless accorded visualization. Deleuze categorizes this type of recollection-image by contrasting it with Bergson's virtual image proper: "Bergson calls the virtual image 'pure recollection,' the better to distinguish it from mental images—recollection-images, dream or dreaming—with which it might be readily confused. In fact, the latter are certainly virtual images, but actualized or in the course of actualization in consciousnesses or psychological states. And they are necessarily actualized in relation to a new present, in relation to a different present from the one that they have been."[68] Such "mental images," then, enter into a dynamic relation with the present in their actualization; they are subject to the peregrinations of chronological time and psychological states, plastic rather than fixed in their ontology. As stated previously, these two sequences in *Caché* are practically the only images in Haneke's entire filmography that could be understood as breaking with objective realism and instead representing the contents of a character's psyche or memory (the other exception being the moving poster image from *Der siebente Kontinent*, the first time it is presented). The fact that these seemingly internal, wholly subjective images are introduced into the film's image system is problematic, once again raising questions of causality—do the drawings motivate or bring into being these recollection-images or dreams, or are they proleptic materializations of these images? If the latter is the case, then what is the nature of the force that would bring about their existence?

The atemporal interplay of images in *Caché*, I argue, is oriented around an experience of shame that binds one subject (Georges) to another (Majid) and also unites past and present irrespective of time's passing. The final videotape that Georges receives is the recording of his first confrontation with Majid and Majid's reaction after he has left. It is as though the videos have existed to bring about and to preserve this meeting and its devastating consequences, and are no longer necessary afterward. Their function has been to set the scene for Majid's shocking act of suicide, his slitting of his own throat, and Georges's witnessing of this act. The significance of Majid's suicide has been interpreted in different ways, with Haneke suggesting that it represents, among other things, "an act of aggression directed towards Georges," while Roy Grundmann places this event alongside other acts of actual or symbolic human or animal sacrifice in *La pianiste*, *Le temps du loup*, and *Code inconnu*, interpreting these as follows: "The desperate urge for catharsis conveyed in these scenes shows Haneke in search of a new kind of negative dialectic, one that proposes ritualized death as a signifier for the unobtainability of solutions."[69] Even if no (re)solution has been obtained by this act, though, there is a definite sense that with it something has been transformed. For instance, there is a synthesis between film and video implied in the scene's presentation. The suicide is shot in a manner strikingly similar to the final videotape sent to Georges, with a static camera occupying the same position as that of the video, and the shot being likewise held for several minutes after Majid's death, capturing Georges's reaction of stunned silence and nausea. It is as though we are still watching a surveillance video, but one that has finally merged with the film itself as a fully cotemporal medium. Indeed, immediately following the suicide there is a shot that is highly suggestive of a profound fracture in the cinematic character of the narrative: we do not see Georges walk out of Majid's kitchen or apartment; instead, we cut from him standing over Majid's corpse to a shot of him walking out of a movie theater. Though this is accounted for when he explains to his wife later that he went to see a movie in his state of shock, the matching of these shots carries the implication that Georges, and perhaps the film itself, has departed from the conventions of cinematic representation entirely, that the medium itself has shifted in nature.

Majid's suicide, the obscene act that Georges and the film audience are forced to witness, is at the heart of this shift. It is also, and not coincidentally,

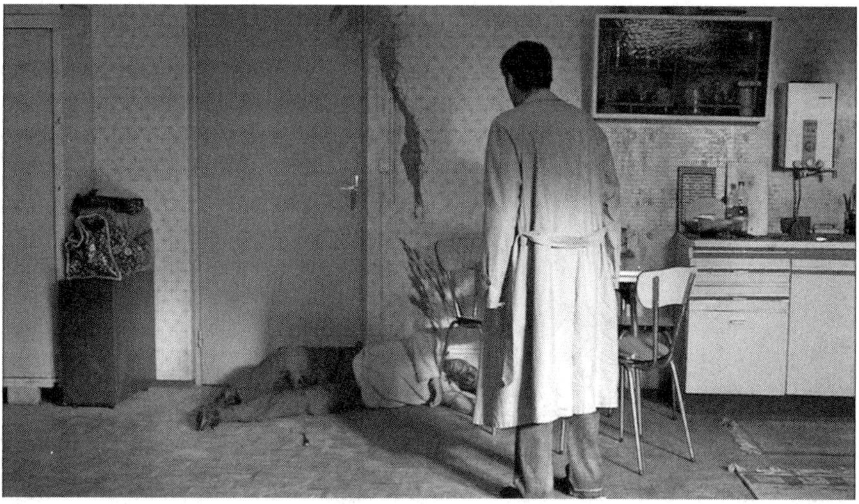

Figure 11: The bloodstain that remains on the wall following the event of Majid's suicide, which becomes a figure for the fracturing of representation and temporality that the film traces. *Caché* (Michael Haneke, 2005).

the sublimation of an undiluted shame that has inextricably connected the destinies of Georges and Majid. The intermedial dynamics of vision and representation have become—indeed, were always—structured by a gaze that is temporally unattenuated, the look of an Other of a shame that is unaffected by time's passing and unmediated by representation. If nausea is, in Levinas's definition, a form of shame "purified of any admixture of collective representations,"[70] then Georges's nausea in the aftermath of Majid's suicide is—like the nausea that Majid admits to having felt when he first saw Georges's image on television, even before recognizing Georges as a figure from his past—the index of a profound sense of shame unmitigated by temporal and social distance. The bloodstain Majid leaves on the wall is likewise a sublimation of this shame, its color so vivid that it seems, like a work of abstract art, to defy the very notion of representation (see figure 11). This bloodstain—which became an emblem of sorts for *Caché*, featuring on most of its posters and advertising materials—resembles in function Michel Chion's concept of the "screaming point": "The screaming point is a point of the unthinkable inside the thought, of the indeterminate inside the spoken, of unrepresentability inside representation. It occupies a point in time, but has no duration within. It suspends the time of its possible duration; it's a rip in the fabric of time."[71] The bloodstain constitutes a sort of visual "screaming point"—a "bleeding point," perhaps. The pure shock it delivers to the senses when it arrives marks, quite clearly and precisely, such a fracture in the film's narrative, visual, and temporal systems. The suicide also resonates

Figure 12: The penultimate shot of the film, consisting of impossible "surveillance footage" of Majid's removal from Georges's childhood home. The shot is a testament to an event that resonates between the actual atrocity that took the lives of his parents and his own eventual suicide. *Caché* (Michael Haneke, 2005).

with another event that, in the wake of Majid's death, is summoned out of the past in a perfectly preserved form, as though shame has prevented it from being subsumed in the passing of time. This image—the penultimate shot of the film—depicts Majid as a child being forcibly removed from the custody of Georges's parents and placed in an orphanage.

Majid's removal is presented in a shot that is not identifiable as either an actual or a virtual image, but may in fact be both; its form is identical to that of the videotapes, yet it occurs in the same chronotope as Georges's memory- or dream-images. In Deleuzian terms it is the heart of the film's time-crystal, which he describes—using a particularly fitting analogy for this shot—as a living "postcard": "It is as if an image in a mirror, a photo, or a postcard came to life, assumed independence and passed into the actual, even if this meant that the actual image returned into the mirror and resumed its place in the postcard or photo, following a double movement of liberation and capture."[72] Naked before the audience, Georges gets into bed and we cut to a shot of his childhood home from a perspective inside the barn, the site of Georges's dream about the death of the rooster. In a static shot, sustained for over three minutes, we witness Majid being led from the house by Georges's parents, then attempting to run away before being caught and forced into their waiting vehicle, kicking and screaming (see figure 12). As in the opening shot, there is no way to distinguish whether it is a remote, third-person perspective—a video of an event predating the existence of home video—or a point of view shot with the young Georges's gaze occupying the place of the camera. In this case, however, there is no technological or even temporal mediation of the image. The image is instead a Bergsonian "pure recollection," a "past" that has not passed and is liberated, for Georges and for the viewer, by shame. It is not a memory but rather a recurrence; not the *re*presentation but the presentation of an event that still persists. It is a moment of pure vision that is summoned forth by Georges's shame.

We recall that Jacques Rolland, in his commentary on Levinas, stated that shame's effect on the subject "is like a fracture in time, or in its projection toward the future, like the opening of a sort of present that seems no longer able to finish unless shame itself is lifted."[73] Shame, in other words, effectively—or, rather, affectively—sutures the subject to the event, forming the seed of a direct time-image. In this consideration, the image does not function like a flashback, a narrative technique that Haneke completely eschews in his films; it is instead a sliver of crystal. Its temporal mode is not one of pastness, then, but rather of the infinitely small and indefinitely present virtual time of the event. When Deleuze revisits the concept of the time-crystal in one of his final essays, "The Actual and the Virtual" (1995), this virtual aspect of the event is directly opposed to the actual, passing present of chronology: "[T]he virtual's ephemerality appears in a . . . period of time that is smaller than the smallest period of continuous time imaginable in one direction," but which is "also the longest time, longer than the longest unit of continuous time imaginable in all directions."[74] The de-actualized event that binds together the lives of Georges and Majid within the narrative introduces what Deleuze describes as "the possibility of treating the world or life, or simply a life or an episode, as one single event."[75] In Haneke's film, the shot of Majid's removal is a sliver of crystal reflecting in its facets two other aspects of the same event, one of which we witness—the suicide of the man the boy has later become—and the other of which we do not, as it is not given to be represented: the massacre of October 17, 1961. Although it is directly alluded to only once during the film, *Caché* is in a definite sense structured around a virtual encounter with this actual historical occurrence and is evocative of the shame inherent in the collective and official disavowal of this event. Furthermore, this atrocity is made manifest in the film through the very mechanisms of surveillance that seem to foreclose the possibility of an encounter with the actual event, and of our own collective shame. Surveillance stages and conditions this encounter, and does so by pushing the dynamics of visuality itself—that is, the visual exchange between viewing subject and viewed subject—to the edges of its limit-value and beyond.

In the second series of *The Logic of Sense*, Deleuze states the following: "Events are like crystals, they become and grow only out of the edges, or on the edge."[76] This edge indicates a properly Stoic concept of limit-values—surfaces as the limits of bodies, paradoxes as the limits of language, and, I would add, shame as the limit of self-image. In addition to rendering the actual and virtual indiscernible, the crystal of the event in the Stoic sense provides an image of thought for the reversible and interchangeable relation between active and passive effects: the event itself is neither active nor passive but rather their "common result . . . (to cut—to be cut)."[77] I wish to suggest that surveillance, as a condition of electronically mediated perception, similarly establishes an audiovisual limit forming an undecidable relation between active and passive modes of technological engagement: *to see* and *to be seen*, *to hear* and *to be overheard*, *to record* and *to be recorded*.[78] Each of Georges's attempts to find the source of the videos, and thus to stop their production, generates new and increasingly intrusive videos, and through this an image-idea of the event unfolds that is inseparable from the experience of shame. This is Haneke's concept of the event as it emerges within a regime of surveillance: the event persists, or finds the de-actualized present proper to it, in the shame of the witness, and crystallizes at the limit of visuality, the indiscernibility between seeing and being seen. The remarkable opening shot of the film, which places Georges in the uncanny position of watching himself being watched, initiates this relation, and the penultimate shot crystallizes it.

Ultimately, shame exposes us not only to the inescapability of the visual regime for the embodied subject but also to the inescapable *immediacy* of the event for the temporal subject. Georges's shame as a witness to the event of Majid's removal to an orphanage, as a witness to Majid's death, and as a witness *in effect* to the Parisian massacre, is made accessible to the viewer of the film, who is also called on as a witness, retaining an important role in the film's economy of surveillance. The spectator, in this sense, arbitrates between the *fictionality* of what is visualized on film and video and the *reality* of the unrepresented and unrepresentable event itself, which is summoned forth by the indiscernible but unavoidable void between these two media, and colored by the shame of its remaining hidden. For Deleuze, we recall, the cinema possesses an inherent Catholicism, "a special relationship to belief": "The modern fact is that we no longer believe in this world. We do not even believe in the events which happen to us, love, death, as if they only half concerned us. It is not we who make cinema; it is the world which looks to us like a bad film."[79] This latter is the an-aesthetic image of the world proliferated by electronic media, which Deleuze exhorts cinema to confront directly by creating new images or discovering new forms of the time-image. The intermedial and metarepresentational relationship between film and video in *Caché* provides both a visual and a temporal structure for this crystalline event. The indiscernibility between its modes of mediality evokes both the simultaneity of past, present, and future, and the exchangeability between the actual (historical reality) and virtual (a fictitious memory-image) reflected in the crystal's faces. Georges and the spectator, uncannily united in the opening shot of the film, are here reunited in an experience of shame, in a crystalline conjunction of beings: he is nude, we are "nude"; his eyes are closed, our "eyes" are "closed." A veritable time-image emerges in this impossible actualization of virtual vision, a transcendental video preconditioned by all of the impossible videos that have preceded it. *Caché* thus offers to restore our faith in the event by giving it a time-image that crystallizes within the very conditions of medial surveillance, and thus reveals to the collective witnesses of a historical atrocity, the worst possible kind of event, the shame proper to us.

It is in this film, then, that Haneke's practice of intermediality reaches its apex, and in the process opens up new possibilities for the cinematic image in the process. For if one defines a given medium as an assemblage of percepts and affects—in other words, as raw sensation—then in this intermedial time-image a unique compositional schema of these forces emerges. The indiscernibility between the medium of the film (*qua* video) and the medium of video (*qua* film) reveals, as I have demonstrated, a *void*, a fracture within the very fabric of perception such that cinema and video—and hence also image and non-image, viewing subject and viewed subject, the diegetic and the nondiegetic, actuality and virtuality—become impossible to distinguish. And yet this void itself assumes an intense and disquieting affective power *via this very fracture*, which is finally revealed to be nothing less than the structure of an experience of shame that is both personal and collective. While it is generally assumed that perception structures affect—the *I see* or *I hear* preceding the *I feel*—here the reverse is the case, with shame as an affect composing, or rather decomposing, the very experience of perception. As it does for Majid—who upon seeing Georges on the television experiences nausea before he even recognizes Georges as the boy who orchestrated his eventual fate—affect overrides and reconfigures percept for the spectator, to the point that time itself becomes dis- and reorganized by shame.

Conclusion

✦

Haneke's Intermedial Realism

Throughout this book I have presented Michael Haneke as an auteur who, in spite of his professed and demonstrable commitment to an aesthetic of sociopolitical realism, produces films that defy definition according to a framework of strictly realist-representational cinema. Indeed, Haneke's films even elude categorization as purely cinematic works; *Der siebente Kontinent*, *Benny's Video*, *71 Fragmente einer Chronologie des Zufalls*, *Funny Games*, *Code inconnu*, *La pianiste*, and *Caché* instead combine images with non-images, narrative coherence with fragmentation, genre tropes with artistic experimentation, and, above all, film with other media. It appears utterly counterintuitive to assert that these admixtures of modes of expression and media constitute a form of realism, yet Haneke's oeuvre nonetheless exemplifies such an aesthetic, perhaps more so than that of any other contemporary auteur. The perceived counterintuiveness of this categorization stems from the theoretical framework through which we are accustomed to viewing Haneke's cinema. If one annexes realism to questions of representation—-i.e., of the extent to which a given work, or medium, offers a correct or even "true" representation of actuality—then Haneke's fractured, multitextual, and intermedial films do not present themselves as realistic works in any sense, whether classical, modernist, or neorealist. His film-texts would instead seem to lend themselves to definition as exercises in impressionistic relativism, their play of signifiers lacking a stable referent. However, by applying intermediality as a theoretical framework to much of his oeuvre, what is revealed is a highly compelling portrait of contemporary lived experience, whereby the characters and spectators are aligned in terms of a shared and mutually fractured process of subjectification, one that reflects the profound ways by which media have affected our means of perceiving and engaging with the world at large on both personal and collective, sociopolitical levels. The primary aim of this book has been to explore such fractures less as evidence of our collective disaffection—prevalent though this theme is in Haneke's narratives—and to attend much more to the polyvalent modes of art-cinematic and otherwise-mediated realism that Haneke initiates, and the conceptual insights into contemporary subjectivity that these potentialize.

Before exploring Haneke's aesthetic in more depth, though, it will be necessary to recapitulate the theory of media and intermediality that Haneke's films inspired, and which Gilles Deleuze's philosophical concepts of sensation and the event provided a means of articulating.

Let us recall, for one final time, Deleuze's exhortation to contemporary filmmakers as expressed in his "Letter to Serge Daney":

> Cinema ought to stop "being cinematic," stop playacting, and set up specific relationships with video, with electronic and digital images, in order to develop a new form of resistance and combat the televisual function of surveillance and control. It's not a question of short-circuiting television—how could that be possible?—but of preventing television [from] subverting or short-circuiting the extension of cinema into the new types of image.[1]

Deleuze implies that cinema's relevance as both a medium and an art form depends on its response to the implicit challenge presented by the perceptual and affective structures of new media. This is not simply a matter of how these media respectively *represent* reality, but also a matter of how these media respectively stage the ontological and epistemological conditions that inform our engagement with the world. As D. N. Rodowick points out, Deleuze expressed a concern that informatic and mass-communicational media such as television would not only supercede the cinematic image, but, in a more profound sense, would "lay claim to the title of *concepteurs* as the creators of 'events.'"[2] Deleuze identifies a core shift in our mode of being in the world—a shared and constitutive realism—away from the perceptual and affective richness of cinema and toward the more immediate and compelling, but also more conceptually impoverished, world picture provided by informatic and electronic media. However, Haneke's intermedial realism does not resist this state of affairs by simply reasserting a "pure" cinematic image of the world; instead, Haneke's films destabilize both cinematic and noncinematic media by upholding the relations and nonrelations that obtain between their disparate sensational figures.

Deleuze's exhortation was used at the outset of this study to characterize the premise of Haneke's mode of intermedial practice; however, Deleuzian philosophy has informed my approach in more profound ways as well, having been utilized both as a means of analyzing Haneke's films and as a means of redefining media studies and intermediality as modes of relational thinking. With respect to the latter, I would assert that Deleuze's formula—"relations are external to their terms"[3]—deserves to be as influential for media studies as McLuhan's "the medium is the message." Relational thinking unfolds a world resembling, as Deleuze puts it, "a Harlequin's jacket or patchwork, made up of solid parts and voids, blocs and ruptures, attractions and divisions, nuances and bluntnesses, conjunctions and separations, alternations and interweavings, additions which never reach a total and subtractions whose remainder is never fixed."[4] Such is the perspective on contemporary lived experience that Haneke's intermedial films affirm, but this study has argued that it would be a mistake to characterize this as a cause for despair (in spite of what the comments of many Haneke scholars, and Haneke himself in certain interviews, may lead us to believe). Instead, I have preferred to treat such voids, gaps, and ruptures less as conditions of disaffection and lack of perceptual power and more as sites of emergent sensations, new configurations of percepts and affects. Intermediality has therefore been defined not in terms of mutually supportive modes of representation with a vast set of common referents—a diversely composed *mediascape*, in other words—but rather as a negative sensory plane or void that inheres *in between* different media. But at the same time it is asked: what kinds of sensational figures and potential modes of subjective perception and affection teem and swarm within these gaps or cracks?[5] What events traverse this plane of immanence, and what emergent spatiotemporal structures unfold around their margins?

This study has used the concept of the intermedial void to describe diverse phenomena in Haneke's films: the utopian non-place and non-image—on-screen and out-of-field—encountered by the suicidal family in *Der siebente Kontinent*, and intensified by televisuality; the impossible "representation" of pain and death possibilized by the temporal and subjective violence perpetrated by video itself in *Benny's Video* and *Funny Games*; the voice as an unstable configuration of heautonomous systems of bodies and language in literary adaptations for television, ultimately giving way to a decomposition of the voice-body paradigm in *La pianiste*; and the respective modes of fragmentation in *71 Fragmente einer Chronologie des Zufalls* and *Code inconnu* as they express the profound social and intersubjective reverberations preceding and following events, these being the traces remaining of phenomena that inherently resist photographic, informatic, and even cinematic mediation. Indeed, the Deleuzian notion of the event—"its irreducibility to the denotatum and to the signified, its neutrality in relation to the particular and to the general, or its impersonal and pre-individual singularity"[6]—is likewise crucial to one's understanding of the aesthetic effects and theoretical implications of Haneke's mode of intermediality. All of the above-mentioned films enforce multiple medial—and thus spectatorial—perspectives on their narrative events, only to have these events recede further from our capacity to understand them in potentially meaningful ways. Information does not complement image, just as sound does not complement visuality; instead, each system obliquely forces the other to its limits, and any common borders or planes that they seem to develop become annexed to perpetually deferred, virtual space-times where they remain inaccessible to us as such. *Caché*, once again, is the apotheosis of this strategy, as its intermedial interplay between film and video develops imperceptibly into a negotiation between actuality and virtuality as dimensions in themselves. The film thereby attains a veritable Bergsonian-Deleuzian time-crystal: the historical event defies temporal distance *because* it has been consigned to the unseen and unspoken-of, and it attains actualization via the surveillance milieu that constitutes a new virtual vector for collective shame.

As spectators of a Haneke film, our understanding of the on-screen milieu is predicated upon an engagement with multiple and irreconcilable media, and thus multiple and irreconcilable perspectives on events that elude assimilation by an integral and singular subject. This spectatorial situation is reflected by that of the films' characters, most of whom are themselves essentially spectators. The dramatic structures of Haneke's films often depend on these characters' utter subjectification by and subjugation to these mass-mediated modes of audiovisual perception and affective expression, as has been demonstrated throughout this study. Indeed, each of the above-mentioned intermedial voids resonates profoundly with a process of subjectification (or desubjectification) also present within the films: the family in *Der siebente Kontinent* tries to annihilate every trace of itself from the world, and at the moment of death the memories of its last surviving member are absorbed into television's signal-less void; Benny's sensorium and self-image are conditioned largely, if not entirely, by the video apparatus; Maximilian B. in *71 Fragmente* exchanges his own lived existence, and those of his victims, for a place within the repetitive cycles of the television news event; Paul in *Funny Games* is less a character than a player of a video game, and violently and relentlessly subjects the family of victims (as well as the film itself and its viewers) to its medial structures; in *La pianiste*, Erika's voice—overwritten by that of the narrator in the novel—rediscovers its own terrible silence as it is drowned out by her music, by her written words (appropriated by Klemmer), and by the cheap melodrama of a televised soap opera; Georges in *Caché* descends into a fissure in time brought about by his own shame, which simultaneously stands for the indiscernible difference between film and video; and so on. What these narrative and metanarrative actants present are not so much representations of being-in-the-world as they are cognitive mappings of subjectivities fundamentally altered and restructured by the perceptual and affective influence of diverse media. With these films, Haneke implies that it is no longer possible to create a unified and substantive "representation of reality," simply because there is no longer any equivalent to such a view of the world available to us, even in lived experience. Hence, he is not able to offer any definable perspective on actuality without also accounting for the fracturing of perception and affect brought about by audiovisual media, and he demonstrates this state of affairs by incorporating these media directly into his films. In this way, the question of the contemporary subject and the question of the event become indistinguishable facets of a pervasive intermedial condition, in a manner that has been aptly described by Samuel Weber in the following terms: "In the age of the media, things, people and places *come to pass*, in an *event* more sportive than any sporting event, and more spectacular than any spectacle."[7]

One final example might be cited to illuminate the manner in which Haneke's films are structured around events more so than subjects—or rather events-as-subjects and subjects-as-events—and it is expressed through a film that did not factor into my study directly: 2003's *Le temps du loup* (*Time of the Wolf*). Set immediately after some unspecified catastrophe has brought about the collapse of industrialized society, the film presents a near-future scenario in which there are no electronic media and thus no basis for presenting a sustained intermedial relationship between the film image and other modes of audiovisual expression.[8] While he had written the film much earlier—soon after *Der siebente Kontinent*, in fact—Haneke decided to release it following a world-altering occurrence: "After Sepember 11, I told myself that the moment had come to pull it out of the drawer, because the events had given it a new relevance."[9] In fact, as Haneke stated in a *Sight & Sound* interview at the time of the film's release, the film itself was reshaped by 9/11:

> The first hour was to have taken place in an indeterminate European capital in which things slowly start to go wrong. There are problems we don't quite understand: the water doesn't work and neither does the electricity. This was to have been set in a ghetto for rich people such as you find in some American and South American cities, enclaves with police protection. Then one of the families decides it would be easier to go to their countryhouse. And that's where the finished film picks up. After 11 September 2001 I felt it was no longer necessary to explain this build-up. It's now easily conceivable we could be faced with a similar catastrophe.[10]

The narrative of *Le temps du loup*, according to Haneke, is supplemented by the actual occurrence of 9/11; it obtains an implicit relationship with the globally disseminated television footage and print reportage of a real event. In this case, Haneke—somewhat naively, perhaps—had assumed an intermedial continuity between his fictional film and actuality itself, locating this relation in the perceptual and affective associations brought to bear by the spectators themselves. Though ostensibly a work of science fiction (a genre one can scarcely imagine Haneke embracing), *Le temps du loup* nonetheless adheres to a strictly realist aesthetic, albeit one that is founded not on representational considerations but on an unvisualized and unstated relationship to an utterly external and actual, albeit highly mediated, event. Indeed, the fact that the film's original opening was excised is a testament not only to Haneke's implicit faith in cinema to uphold associations with real (mediated) experience—as though the film were a kind of speculative sequel to 9/11—but also to the void character of this connection itself, its being premised on a *fracture* instituted by the actual event more so than a verifiable continuity with it.

Haneke's practice of intermediality and intermedial realism, I have asserted, is founded on precisely this confrontation with the void, which in turn indexes the profound gaps that different and irreconcilable media institute not only *between* one another—and between themselves and cinema—but also *within* the individual and collective processes of production of perception, affect, and subjectivity itself. Haneke's work thus reaffirms the power of cinema to sustain Deleuzian faith, a belief "in this world, as it is."[11] Intermedial realism suggests that "this world" can no longer be defined without making recourse to the audiovisual media that structure our perceptual and affective apprehension of it, and to the transformations these media effect on sensation itself. A new and necessary mode of realism, a Hanekean realism, is thus uncovered by an intermedial cinema that expresses the profoundly fractured and mediated reality of contemporary life.

Appendix

✦

Plot Summaries and Credits of Relevant Haneke Films

Der siebente Kontinent [*The Seventh Continent*] (1989)

Direction and Screenplay: Michael Haneke
Production: Veit Heiduschka, Wega Film
Cinematography: Anton Peschke
Editing: Marie Homolkova
Cast: Dieter Berner, Leni Tanzer, Birgit Doll
Country: Austria
Language: German

The film opens with a family of three—Georg (Berner), his wife Anna (Tanzer), and their nine- or ten-year-old daughter Evi (Doll)—sitting impassively in their vehicle as it goes through an automated car wash in an unnamed Austrian city. The first two of the film's three parts—the first set in 1987, the second in 1988—follow seemingly typical days in the life of the family but often with an emphasis on the objects used by the characters rather than the characters themselves. Letters to Georg's parents, read aloud in voiceover by Anna in the first two parts, portray the family's existence as a comfortable and unproblematic one, although there are hints in the film that not all is well: Evi pretends to be blind at school and is slapped by her mother when this is discovered; Anna's brother Alexander joins the family for dinner and begins to cry for no apparent reason; the family passes by a road accident and Anna breaks down and refuses to be consoled.

The third and final part of the film, which takes place over the course of three days in 1989, depicts the family's systematic destruction of all of their personal possessions and their subsequent group suicide. Shots of the destruction—clothes ripped apart, pictures smashed, furniture sawed into pieces, life's savings flushed down the toilet—match the close-ups and quick cuts through which their daily routines were presented in the first two parts of the film. The final scenes show the family ingesting or injecting lethal doses of sedatives and expiring in front of the television, seemingly the only appliance to escape destruction. Georg, the last survivor, dies while staring at a television without a signal, as flashbacks to previous parts of the film play in quick succession. The film ends with scrolling on-screen text that identifies the narrative as having been based on an actual event.

Benny's Video (1992)

Direction and Screenplay: Michael Haneke
Production: Veit Heiduschka, Michael Katz, Bernard Lang, Gebhard Zupan, Wega Film
Cinematography: Christian Berger
Editing: Marie Homolkova
Cast: Arno Frisch, Angela Winkler, Ulrich Mühe, Ingrid Stassner
Country: Austria
Language: German

The film opens with a video of a pig being killed by a farmhand with a bolt gun. The video is rewound and then played again in slow motion. Within the context of the film, the video was recorded by an adolescent boy named Benny (Frisch), whose interest in home video is depicted as somewhere between an intense hobby and an obsession—his bedroom contains multiple video cameras, monitors, editing equipment, and shelves full of videocassettes. While his parents are away for the weekend, Benny invites a teenaged girl (Stassner) to his apartment and shows her his equipment and the pig video. He then produces the bolt gun used to kill the pig and, after challenging her to shoot him with it, shoots and then kills her. After cleaning up the blood and storing her body in his closet, Benny seems to go about his weekend plans as normal, but certain actions of his betray the effects of this traumatic experience—he shaves his head, for example.

Benny plays the video of the girl's killing for his horrified parents (Mühe and Winkler) upon their return, then retires to his room as they discuss what to do. It is decided that Benny will travel to Egypt with his mother while his father will stay behind to dispose of the girl's body by dismembering it. We follow Benny and his mother to Egypt and view videos of their leisurely travels and tourism, but Benny's mother shows signs of experiencing an emotional breakdown. Upon their return, as life seems to be returning to normal, we are shown Benny at a police station playing video footage for law enforcement officials in which his parents can be heard discussing their plans to dispose of the girl's corpse. Walking out of the police station, Benny encounters his parents being escorted in, under arrest, and there is a wordless exchange of gazes before he excuses himself. The last shot is of the station's video surveillance monitors, which have recorded this brief confrontation.

71 Fragmente einer Chronologie des Zufalls [*71 Fragments of a Chronology of Chance*] (1994)

Direction and Screenplay: Michael Haneke
Production: Veit Heiduschka, Willi Seigler, Wega Film
Cinematography: Christian Berger
Editing: Marie Homolkova
Cast: Gabriel Cosmin, Urdes Luka Miko, Otto Grünmandl, Anne Bennent, Udo Samel, Branko Samarovski, Georg Friedrich, Claudia Martini

Country: Austria
Language: German

Opening with on-screen text detailing a mass shooting at a bank in Vienna in 1993, the film is composed of brief scenes from the lives of a number of seemingly unrelated individuals and families who will be killed or profoundly affected by this tragedy. The characters include the shooter himself, a sensitive and volatile university student named Max (Miko); a young homeless boy (Cosmin) who has illegally immigrated from Romania; a couple (Bennent and Samel) trying unsuccessfully to connect to a little girl they have adopted; a religious security guard (Samarovski) with an unhappy home life; and a pugnacious older man (Grünmandl) who is trying to maintain contact with his daughter, a bank teller, and his granddaughter. The origins and peregrinations of the gun used in the slaying are also accounted for in the film, from its theft from a military base to its sale to Max.

Like *Der siebente Kontinent*, *71 Fragmente* orders its narrative around presentations of events occurring on specific dates leading up to the shooting. However, in this case, each new day or section begins with a highly convincing replication of part of a television news program that details the worldwide events of the day. The film ends with one such news report, which includes a report on the bank shooting itself.

Funny Games (1997) and *Funny Games U.S.* (2007)

1997 version:
Direction and Screenplay: Michael Haneke
Production: Veit Heiduschka, Wega Film
Cinematography: Jürgen Jürges
Editing: Andreas Prochaska
Cast: Susanne Lothar, Ulrich Mühe, Arno Frisch, Frank Giering, Stefan Clapczynski
Country: Austria
Language: German

2007 version:
Direction and Screenplay: Michael Haneke
Production: Rene Bastian, Christian Baute, Chris Coen, Hamish McAlpine, Linda Moran, Jonathan Schwarz, Andro Steinborn, Naomi Watts
Cinematography: Darius Khondji
Editing: Monika Willi
Cast: Naomi Watts, Tim Roth, Michael Pitt, Brady Corbett, Devon Gearhart
Country: USA
Language: English

A family of three—mother (Lothar in the original / Watts in the remake), father (Mühe / Roth), and twelve-year-old son (Clapczynski / Gearhart)—is held hostage at their country cottage by a pair of polite-seeming but psychopathic young men who refer to each other as Paul (Frisch / Pitt) and Peter (Giering / Corbett). The young men put the family through a series of sadistic "games" that escalate as the film progresses and eventually lead to the deaths of first the child, then the father, and finally the mother. However, at certain moments throughout the film the character Paul acknowledges and even addresses the spectator directly, implying that the spectator is complicit in the violence occurring within the narrative. At one point, when Peter is shot dead by the mother, Paul grabs the family's remote control and "rewinds" the film itself, undoing the action and changing the course of events to suit his own agenda. The film ends just as another "game" begins, this time at a family home across the lake.

Code inconnu: Récit incomplet de divers voyages [*Code Unknown: Incomplete Tales of Several Journeys*] (2000)

Direction and Screenplay: Michael Haneke
Production: Yvon Crenn, Christoph Holch, Marin Karmitz, Thilo Keine, Titi Popescu, Michael Weber, Bavaria Film, Canal+, Filmex, France 2 Cinéma, Les Films Alain Sarde, MK2 Productions, Romanian Culture Ministry, Zweites Deutsches Fernsehen, arte France Cinéma
Cinematography: Jürgen Jürges
Editing: Karin Martusch, Nadine Muse, Andreas Prochaska
Cast: Juliette Binoche, Thierry Neuvic, Alexandre Hamidi, Ona Lu Yenke, Luminita Gheorghiu, Walid Afkir, Maurice Bénichou
Country: France / Germany / Romania
Language: French

After opening with a game of charades being played by a class of deaf children, the film's narrative is set in motion with a scene consisting of a single sustained shot set on a busy Parisian street: Jean (Hamidi), a frustrated teenager, appeals to his older brother's girlfriend, actress Anne (Binoche), to let him stay with her after running away from his home on the family farm. Jean then callously tosses a food wrapper into the lap of Maria (Gheorghiu), a Romanian woman begging for change, an action for which Jean is accosted and upbraided by a young Malian man named Amadou (Yenke). Jean and Amadou begin to fight, Anne returns, and the police are called over, at which point Amadou and Maria are arrested, and Maria is subsequently deported back to Romania.

The film then presents events from the lives of those involved in this incident over the next year or so, including Jean's older brother Georges (Neuvic), a photographer whose relationship with Anne is faltering. We also follow the making of a police thriller in which Anne is acting from pre- to postproduction; Maria spending time with her family in Romania—where the money she sends back from begging is being used to construct a home—and her eventual return to the streets of Paris; and the lives of Amadou and his family members, including his volunteering at the school for the deaf in which his much younger sister is enrolled. The final scenes of the film mirror the first, with the circumstances of some characters having changed—such as Anne and Georges having broken up, Jean's disappearance after having run away from home—and others remaining much the same—such as Maria's attempt to return to her original begging spot.

La pianiste [*The Piano Teacher*] (2001)

Direction and Screenplay: Michael Haneke (adapted from a novel by Elfriede Jelinek)
Production: Veit Heiduschka, Michael Katz, Christine Gozlan, Yvon Crenn, Bayerischer Rundfunk, Canal+, Centre National de al Cinématographie, Eurimages, Les Films Alain Sarde, MK2 Productions, P.P. Film Polski, Wega Film, arte France Cinéma, ORF
Cinematography: Christian Berger
Editing: Nadine Muse, Monika Willi
Cast: Isabelle Huppert, Benoît Magimel, Annie Girardot
Country: France / Austria
Language: French

Set in Vienna, the film is centered around the life of the virtuoso pianist and conservatory instructor Erika Kohut (Huppert), a woman still living at home with her domineering mother (Girardot). We follow Erika as she balances her time between her oppressive and conflictual home life, the mundane routines of her work, and her non-traditional modes of sexual gratification, which include cutting her genitals with a razor blade, visiting a public pornographic booth, and an act of voyeurism at a local drive-in theater. Erika's circumstances are then dramatically altered when she becomes the target of the lustful attention of a handsome and musically gifted, though much younger, man named Walter Klemmer (Magimel), whose attempts to engage her in a sexual liason are continually frustrated.

While the film presents itself as parodically melodramatic in tone and structure, Erika's burgeoning relationship with Klemmer has destabilizing and damaging consequences, including her mutilation of a student's hand in an act of apparent jealousy and several unconsummated and mutually frustrating sexual encounters, during which Klemmer refuses to cooperate with Erika's stated masochistic desires. Their disastrous relationship reaches a terrible culmination when Klemmer violently attacks and rapes Erika in her home. Erika prepares a knife and seems to be planning her revenge on Klemmer at a recital, but the opportunity passes, and instead she stabs herself in the upper chest and walk out of frame as the film ends.

Caché [*Hidden*] (2005)

Direction and Screenplay: Michael Haneke
Production: Valerio de Paolis, Veit Heiduschka, Michael Katz, Margaret Ménégoz, Michael Weber, Les Films du Losange, Wega Film, Bavaria Film, BIM Distribuzione
Cinematography: Christian Berger
Editing: Michael Hedecek, Nadine Muse
Cast: Juliette Binoche, Daniel Auteuil, Maurice Bénichou, Walid Afkir, Lester Makedonsky
Country: France / Austria / Germany / Italy
Language: French

The film opens with a static shot of a facade of a house, but as we hear a man and woman's voices commenting on the shot from offscreen, it is revealed that we are in the position of a bourgeois couple, Georges (Auteuil) and Anne (Binoche), viewing a surveillance video that has been left on their doorstep by an anonymous source. They are inclined at first to dismiss it, but their anxiety increases as more of these tapes are delivered, accompanied by what appear to be a child's drawings. Georges traces the tapes and drawings back to a figure from his childhood named Majid (Bénichou), a boy of Algerian descent whom Georges's parents had decided to adopt after Majid's parents, employees on Georges's family farm, were apparently killed during the Paris massacre of peaceful protestors of the Algerian war (October 17, 1961). We learn toward the end of the film that as a young boy Georges had told lies to his parents about Majid in order to have him expelled from the family and placed in a group home.

The adult Majid, when confronted, convincingly denies knowing anything about the videos. When Georges and Anne's adolescent son Pierrot (Makedonsky) goes missing, though, Georges has Majid and his son (Afkir) arrested as suspects, though it becomes clear that they had nothing to do with the disappearance when Pierrot returns the following day. Majid subsequently invites Georges to his apartment and commits suicide in his presence by slitting his own throat. There is a final confrontation between Majid's son and Georges in which the son reiterates that he and his father had no part in any surveillance of Georges and his family. The film ends with a nude Georges getting into bed and apparently dreaming of the young Majid being forcibly removed from his parents' home years before. There is a final shot, over which the credits play, of the front of the school Pierrot attends, and if one looks carefully one can see Majid's son approach Pierrot and have a brief, friendly conversation with him, the words of which are inaudible.

NOTES

Introduction

1. I have opted not to provide in the introduction an overview of Haneke's biography, education, and career—including the geopolitical context of his early life; his study of music and, later, philosophy; his work in theater and television; and his awards and accolades as a director—in the manner of most auteurist or director-specific studies, preferring to let such facts and details emerge within the body of the text itself where relevant. The best and most thorough account, in English, of Haneke's life and work can be found in Roy Grundmann's introduction to his edited collection on Haneke. See Grundmann, "Introduction: Haneke's Anachronism," 1–50.

2. It should be noted that the definition of intermediality put forward here is derived primarily from the interactions and presence of different media that are particular to Haneke's aesthetic practice rather than from the conceptual models and theories that are more commonly grouped under the term. In fact, in first drafting this approach to Haneke, the author of this book had no prior knowledge of the term "intermediality" and considered it his own coinage. However, this ignorance has since been remedied by an extensive and very enlightening critical investigation of the theory and its usage.

3. Haneke's films seem almost by definition to attract critical readings based upon French theory from the latter half of the twentieth century. D. I. Grossvogel, for instance, points out the susceptibility of Haneke's early Austrian films to such theoretical interpretations, if not to wider global recognition: "True, critic-philosophers (especially the French) were able to bring into their analyses [of the Austrian films] the theories of Marc Augé ('supermodernity': the superabundances of modern culture prevent rooting and doom us to endless transience), Gilles Deleuze ('actual/virtual': we are as affected by the 'image' of the world as by actuality [reality] itself), Jean Baudrillard ('simulacrum': the image has actually come to stand for reality), etc." Grossvogel, "Haneke: The Coercing of Vision," 37. Also, in his monograph on Haneke, Oliver C. Speck invokes Deleuze's film philosophy in a more general sense than I have done here: "Haneke is a Deleuzian filmmaker insofar as he subverts representational images. He goes beyond what Deleuze calls the 'movement-image' in order to bring up a 'time image,' a virtual image that has to be created." Speck, *Funny Frames*, 13. My own use of the above-mentioned theorists, therefore, is tempered by the understanding that their application to the director is well-established, and an attempt will be made to deepen and extend the connections and illuminations that have already been perceived between the aesthetic praxis of Haneke and the theoretical insights of these thinkers.

4. Deleuze, *Cinema 1: The Movement-Image*, 210.

5. Pointing out this troubling juxtaposition, along with the concomitant threat of undermining the cinematic image that the electronic image seemingly presents, generally characterizes the way Haneke scholars have discussed the presence of other media forms in his films. However, as will be shown later in this introduction and throughout this text, other scholars have recognized a deeper role and function in this intermedial schema.

6. Deleuze, *Cinema 2: The Time-Image*, 254 (italics added).

7. Ibid., 166.

8. My interpretation of Deleuze's film philosophy thus diverges from those that assert the applicability of his theory to other types of audiovisual media. Felicity Colman, for instance, states that "[t]he Deleuzian ciné-system is . . . applicable to any screen media that has the capacity for image, sound and movement," including video, television, computer games, and so on. While it is certain that there is a substantial, and growing, technical overlap between these, I take Deleuze's statements on television and video as the philosopher's designation of an aesthetic and conceptual rift between film and newer screen media forms and *dispositifs* that still persists and to which Haneke also adheres. This rift must be contended with before one can extend Deleuze's ideas beyond the cinema and into postcinematic "new media," just as I will argue that attending to this schism is crucial to understanding Haneke's mode of intermediality. Colman, *Deleuze & Cinema*, 6.

9. Deleuze, *Cinema 2*, 256, 259.

10. Rodowick, *Gilles Deleuze's Time Machine*, xiii.

11. Deleuze, *Cinema 2*, 166.

12. Haneke, "Violence and the Media," 579.

13. Haneke, "We Live in a Permanent State of War," 21.

14. Indeed, the definition of Haneke as a (or even "the last") "modernist" director is frequent in reviews and critical studies of his work. To cite a few examples: Christopher Sharrett states that "[w]ith each film . . . Haneke affirms his presence as one of the key modernist directors at a time when modernist ambitions seem defunct"; Brigitte Peucker that "Haneke's concern with spectator affect is conveyed by means of modernist strategies that privilege the materialities of his medium"; and Ian Johnston that "[l]ike any old-style modernist, Haneke likes to make the audience work." Haneke, "World That Is Known," interview by Sharrett, 581; Peucker, "Effects of the Real," *Kinoeye*; Johnston, "Children Are Watching You," *Bright Lights*.

The fact that Haneke utilizes divergent media and genres of cinema, however, has also led to a more general definition linking Haneke to postmodernist cinema, as is attested to by his being cited as such in the Wikipedia article titled "Postmodernist Film": "The Coen brothers, Michael Haneke, Woody Allen, David Lynch, Quentin Tarantino, Wes Anderson, Peter Greenaway, François Truffaut, Charlie Kaufman, Jean-Luc Godard, Alain Resnais, Federico Fellini, Paul Thomas Anderson, Spike Jonze, Jim Jarmusch and Christopher Nolan are a few of the most popular and well-known purveyors of postmodern cinema. The majority of their work demonstrates many of the principles of postmodernist film-making." While quite clearly not stemming from an authoritative source, the article's inclusion of Haneke within such a diverse group of filmmakers—and among those "modernist" auteurs such as Godard and Resnais whose work is perceived as crossing over into a postmodern sensibility—is telling with regard to the general reception of his films. "Postmodernist film," *Wikipedia*, accessed August 17, 2015, http://en.wikipedia.org/wiki/Postmodernist_film.

My own approach to Haneke's cinema in terms of media studies and intermediality, it is hoped, will circumvent this problem of identification, even if at the expense of Haneke's stated positioning of himself within the modernist cinematic tradition. As Haneke scholar Roy Grundmann rightly points out, "[n]otwithstanding Haneke's own modernist posturing and postmodern critics' eagerness to take him by his word, it may be his films' dual referencing of the modern and the postmodern that merits further interest in him." Extending this idea even further, one could justifiably argue that Haneke's films do not "reference" two identifiably different aesthetic approaches so much as problematize the very distinctions we make between them. Grundmann, "Introduction: Haneke's Anachronism," 2.

15. This notion is of course related to Marshall McLuhan's idea that the contents of a given medium are always another medium, a concept that will be dealt with in detail in the next section.

16. Spielmann, "History and Theory of Intermedia," 136.

17. Higgins, "Intermedia," 52.

18. Ibid., 49.

19. Voigst-Virchow, "Metadaptation: Adaptation and Intermediality," 147.

20. This statement is intended to echo Jay David Bolter and Richard Grusin's statement that "*all* mediation is remediation." Bolter and Grusin, *Remediation*, 55. For a brief investigation into the problems that arise from this overdetermined notion of media and media interaction, see endnote 72 of this introduction.

21. Seeβlen, "Structures of Glaciation," 327.

22. A number of analyses of specific intermedial relations that bear a great deal of similarity to those I sense in Haneke's work are offered by Ágnes Pethő in her text *Cinema and Intermediality* (2011). For example, Pethő sees the painting of the deceased title character in Hitchcock's *Rebecca* (1940)—which lingers onscreen at crucial moments in the film narrative as a sort of "spectral presence"—as utilizing the radical difference between the medium of painting and that of cinema in such a way. Thus, in an intermedial reading, the painted image becomes not simply a visual token of the dead first wife but also, in its very incommensurability with the cinematic image, a figure of an unbridgeable gap separating the living Mrs. de Winter (Joan Fontaine) from the dead one. The painting is, to cite a term I will expand upon in chapter 1, a *non-image* in relation to the film: "the painting itself in this way becomes a multiple sign of absence and uncertainty, a medium of the void." Pethő, *Cinema and Intermediality*, 185.

23. Luhmann, *The Reality of the Mass Media*, 8, 11.

24. Ibid., 4, 11.

25. McLuhan, "Media Log," 182.

26. Mitchell, "Realism and the Digital Image," 58.

27. Comolli, "Machines of the Visible," 124.

28. This perspective of course also accords exceedingly well with Stanley Cavell's characterization of cinema in *The World Viewed* (1971): "Film is a moving image of skepticism." Cavell, *World Viewed*, 188.

29. Manovich, *Language of New Media*, 187.

30. The conception of intermedial difference also obviously resonates quite strongly with Derrida's concept of *différance*; however, an elaboration of this connection is beyond the scope of the present inquiry.

31. This is not to say that Haneke avoids such an approach to realism, however. Indeed, the "long take" aesthetic which I refer to in most of his films—and which is especially prominent in *Code inconnu*—can be readily understood as a mode of image making that minimizes artifice and manipulation. Yet it must be acknowledged that this is not the sole, or even the primary, gesture toward realism in the majority of his films.

32. One critical approach that could be suggested as an alternative to intermediality is briefly mentioned by Deleuze in a footnote to his discussion of electronic media in the conclusion to *Cinema 2*. He refers to theorist and digital artist Edmond Couchot's definition of digital imagery as "immedia"—"because there is no longer a medium properly speaking"—and goes on to suggest that the same could be said for all electronic media: "already in television, there is no space or image either, but only electronic lines." Deleuze, *Cinema 2*, 321n. While a definition opposing image-based media to non-imagistic immedia is potentially productive (and accords well with my own discussion of television and video as "non-images" in chapters 1 and 2), a redefinition of electronic and digital informatics as "immedia" is not likely to be deemed critically acceptable at this stage in media and information studies, where these forms have long been accorded the status of media in their own right. Furthermore, the definition of a mode of expression as a form of media or immedia based upon whether or not it can be said to produce conventionally defined images is somewhat reductive.

33. Price and Rhodes, "Introduction," 7.

34. Ibid., 6. Price and Rhodes connect this strategy to questions regarding what can and cannot be ethically represented, though it may be more accurate to state that Haneke's images tend not only to mediate between the film's representation and the perceptions of the viewer but also to convey the *impossibility* of its investing this representation with truth, reality, or ethical meaning. Haneke's self-imposed image selectivity would thus not be, properly speaking, an ethical strategy, regardless of its highly relevant ethical or moral implications; it would be, rather, an acknowledgment of the radical *an*ethicality of media.

35. Deleuze, "Letter to Serge Daney," 72.

36. Ibid., 76.

37. Ibid.

38. Deleuze, *Cinema 2*, 255.

39. This is in contrast to Foucault's essay on Fromanger, "Photogenic Painting" (1975), which is reproduced alongside Deleuze's in a text that shares its title with Foucault's. Unlike Deleuze, Foucault immediately notes the historical antecedents for Fromanger's work, in particular its reflection of a period (1860–80) wherein "[p]hotographers made pseudo-paintings, painters used photographs as sketches." Foucault, "Photogenic Painting," in Deleuze and Foucault, *Gérard Fromanger*, 83–84.

40. Deleuze, "Cold and Heat," in Deleuze and Foucault, *Gérard Fromanger*, 71.

41. Ibid., 73–74.

42. McLuhan, *Understanding Media*, 36.

43. I do not personally subscribe to this potential criticism of Deleuze's use of McLuhan's terms "hot" and "cool" and would direct others in this regard to the almost Deleuzian inflection given to the terms by McLuhan in "The *Hot and Cool* Interview" (1967): "*Media, hot* and *cool* are not classifications. They are structural forms. These are slang terms from the musical world where they have high, structural meaning. . . . My own interest in studying media is a 'systems development' approach. 'Systems development' is a structural analysis of pressures and strains, the exact opposite of everything that has been meant by 'systems' in the past few centuries. 'Systems development' is the opposite of 'systems' in the philosophical sense. It is concerned with the inner dynamics of the form." McLuhan, "The Hot and Cool Interview," 74.

44. Deleuze and Guattari, *Anti-Oedipus*, 261.

45. Deleuze, it should be noted, also has no special interest in retaining literature's privilege as the preeminent philosophical medium, stating with Claire Parnet in *Dialogues* (1977) that "the good ways of reading today succeed in treating a book as you would treat a record you listen to, a film or a TV programme you watch; any treatment of the book which claims for it a special respect—an attention of another kind—comes from another era and definitively condemns the book." Deleuze and Parnet, *Dialogues*, 3–4.

46. Innis, *Empire and Communications*, 6.

47. Ibid., 169.

48. McLuhan, "Foreword," *Bias of Communication*, ix.

49. McLuhan, "Hot and Cool Interview," 71.

50. The contributions of McLuhan's Toronto School colleagues and contemporaries should not be underestimated, even if we tend now to refer to "McLuhan" as shorthand for the collective undertaking that constructed the foundations for media studies following Innis's initial forays. In fact, many of the concepts regularly attributed to McLuhan alone have their origins in the work of other thinkers. For instance, Edmund Carpenter—with whom McLuhan coedited the seminal journal *Explorations: Studies in Culture and Communication* (1953–59)—states the following in a 1956 essay, directly prefiguring McLuhan's famous dictum "the medium is the message": "For each communication channel codifies reality differently and thus influences, to a surprising degree, the content of the message communicated. A medium is not simply an envelope that carries any letter; it is itself a major part of that message." Carpenter, "The New Languages," 176. Also, the idea that media are extensions of the human senses is derived, by McLuhan's own admission, from a passage in Edward T. Hall's *The Silent Language* (1959): "Today man has developed extensions for practically everything he used to do with his body. . . . In fact, all man-made material things can be treated as extensions of what man once did with his body or some specialized part of his body." Quoted in McLuhan, "The Electronic Age—The Age of Implosion," 27–28. Hence, it is generally best to consider McLuhan as the leading figure in the emergent school of thought regarding media rather than as the originator of contemporary media studies.

51. McLuhan, "Hot and Cold Interview," 69.

52. Hall, "Encoding/Decoding," 163.

53. Ibid., 163–64.

54. Zielinsky, *Deep Time of the Media*, 33.

55. Paech, "Artwork—Text—Medium," accessed September 26, 2014.
56. McLuhan, "Myth and Mass Media," 12.
57. Kittler, *Optical Media*, 30.
58. Kittler, *Gramophone, Film, Typewriter*, xl–xli.
59. Winthrop-Young, *Kittler and the Media*, 122.
60. Deleuze and Parnet, *Dialogues*, 105.
61. Deleuze, *Foucault*, 89.
62. McLuhan, "Culture Without Literacy," 127.
63. Jones, "Senses," 88.
64. Deleuze and Parnet, *Dialogues*, 55.
65. Foucault, "Subject and Power," 295.
66. Deleuze, *Foucault*, 27.
67. Foucault, "Subject and Power," 293.
68. Ibid., 285.
69. Deleuze and Guattari, *Anti-Oedipus*, 2.
70. Ibid., 25.
71. McLuhan, *Understanding Media*, 8.
72. The distinction between production and reproduction—or between medial and representational effects—may best be made by examining an influential recent theory of media, namely that put forward in Jay David Bolter and Richard Grusin's text *Remediation: Understanding New Media* (1999). The subtitle of Bolter and Grusin's text quite clearly alludes to the conception of this work as an update—and perhaps a corrective one—of McLuhan's seminal text. Bolter and Grusin's account of new media can be read, generally, as a practical application of McLuhan's formula of media "content," albeit within what they identify as an accelerated process of medial exchange characteristic of a highly interconnected digital mediascape. Indeed, Bolter and Grusin cite McLuhan's abovementioned quote concerning media's "content," but label his illustrations of this phenomenon as "problematic"; they offer as an alternative example the manner in which "Dutch painters incorporated maps, globes, inscriptions, letters, and mirrors in their works." Their interpretation of mediatic "content" in explicitly representational terms carries over into their own terminology, as "remediation" is defined as "the representation of one medium in another." This definition assumes, by implication, that the material form of a medium (book, globe, or mirror) can unproblematically stand in for another medium as such. Bolter and Grusin, *Remediation*, 45.

Bolter and Grusin go on to assign a formal and functional "repurposing" and "refashioning" of older media in newer media, and vice versa—asserting, for example, that "television and the World Wide Web are engaged in an unacknowledged competition in which each now seeks to remediate the other": television borrows the windowed presentation of the web page for news broadcasts and other informational programming, and the web repurposes the temporal quality of "presentness" or "liveness" associated with television broadcasting. "Remediation" thus becomes a catchall term that is applied to any perceived representation or reproduction by a media text of any quality or qualities associated with different media or even with an older form of a given medium. Ibid., 47–48. For instance, film adaptations of novels are implied to be a form of remediation, and filmic, pictorial, and literary intertextuality is interpreted as "a special case of remediation"—the authors cite as examples the borrowing of elements from Hitchcock's *Vertigo* (1958) by Kathryn Bigelow's *Strange Days* (1995) and Tom Stoppard's use of *Hamlet* for *Rosencrantz and Guildenstern Are Dead* (1966). Ibid., 44–45, 49. The expansive applicability of the term leads almost inevitably to conceptual overdetermination, with Bolter and Grusin concluding that "*all* mediation is remediation" and that "a medium is that which remediates." Ibid., 55, 65. In a particularly puzzling formulation, the authors imply that remediation supplies a conceptual model for the relationship between a medium and immediate actuality: "Just as it remediates film or other media, television remediates the real." Ibid., 194. The need for a renovated definition of the medium and of intermediality should be clear from Bolter and Grusin's media theory alone, as should the fact that representation, intertextuality, the functional repurposing of older media forms, and the mediation of actuality or "the real" refer to highly individualized phenomena and practices that should not be subsumed under the single term "remediation."

73. Marrati, *Gilles Deleuze*, 95.

74. Deleuze, *Cinema 2*, 269.

75. Ibid.

76. Deleuze and Guattari, *What is Philosophy?*, 34.

77. Indeed, it is asserted in *What is Philosophy?* that concepts are generally created from other concepts: "In any concept there are usually bits or components that come from other concepts, which corresponded to other problems and presupposed other planes. This is inevitable because each concept carries out a new cutting-out, takes on new contours, and must be reactivated or recut." Ibid., 18. Cinema's concept of the image is not the same as Bergson's, but—as Deleuze presents them, in any case—they do share a history or plane of immanence, just as Kant's *cogito* shares a history with Descartes's. Ibid., 31–32.

78. Bergson, *Matter and Memory*, 31.

79. Deleuze, "Brain is the Screen," 285.

80. Deleuze and Guattari, *What is Philosophy?*, 164 (italics in original).

81. Ibid.

82. Deleuze, *Francis Bacon*, 28.

83. Ibid., 25.

84. Deleuze and Guattari, *What is Philosophy?*, 183.

85. McLuhan, *Understanding Media*, 3.

86. Deleuze and Guattari, *What is Philosophy?*, 178.

87. Cronenberg, *Videodrome*.

88. Jameson, *The Geopolitical Aesthetic*, 35.

89. Deleuze, "On *Sur et sous*," 127. This schema of informatics also appears, in more or less the same form, in Deleuze and Parnet, *Dialogues*, 22–23.

90. According to this model, the sheer speed and efficiency with which the informatic percepts of new media are generated and disseminated initiate an affective excitement or anticipation, a pure "flow," similar to what one would experience in the presence of an actual event in its unfolding. See the discussion of *71 Fragmente* in chapter 3 for further exploration of this notion of pseudo-eventalism.

91. Deleuze and Guattari, *What is Philosophy?*, 166.

92. Ibid., 165. In a typical Deleuzo-Guattarian gesture, this passage first qualifies a phenomenon in terms of another—"the void is sensation"—and then

immediately posits a wholly different constitutional relation between them—"sensation is composed with the void in composing itself with itself"—that seems to apply the relation to a different plane of consistency. For my purposes, I interpret the passage, with its resemblance to pre-Socratic atomism, as an assertion that the void's *in*existence does not prevent it from emitting or facilitating percepts and affects, and, furthermore, that the void introduces a crucial element of emptiness into sensation's mix of percepts and affects. In this regard, Deleuze and Guattari refer to the paintings of the insane as "holding up" (unlike the paintings of children or those created under the influence of hallucinogens) in a manner similar to the work of artists, but "on the condition of being crammed full, with no empty space remaining." Ibid. The emptiness of the void enables sensation to circulate as such—and to be received as such—in the same way that television's rhythmic flow of injunction and information is sustained by non-audiovisual forces.

93. I must also note that this philosophical concept of sensation has been applied to an intermedial framework, though rather generally, by Henk Oosterling, who writes that many avant-garde media artists produce works that are "intermedially 'sensational' in a Deleuzian sense, as introduced in Deleuze's books on Francis Bacon and on philosophy. Artists think in percepts and affects, i.e. sensations. They think in and with their medium: enveloped in and by means of it, i.e. immediately mediated mediating immediacy." Oosterling, "Sens(a)ble Intermediality and *Interesse*," 42.

94. Flaxman, "Introduction," 12.

95. Deleuze and Guattari, *Anti-Oedipus*, 246.

96. Ibid., 240.

97. Ibid., 251.

98. In the most obvious instance of intermediality in practice, video has long overtaken film as the primary means of spectatorial engagement with any given work of cinema. This shift is implied in much of Haneke's work: for example, in the rewinding of the action in the *Funny Games* films, during which VHS tracking lines appear in the original 1997 version (the 2007 U.S. version of the film depicts this as a digital picture's reversal, consistent with DVD technology). However, this fundamental shift in cinema's milieu toward intermediality has remained virtually unacknowledged both critically and within cinematic works. Rodowick is clear on this point: "For film scholars, only a few short years marked the transition from scarcity to an embarrassment of riches, though at a price: *film had become video*." Rodowick, *Virtual Life of Film*, 26 (italics in original). Rather than replacing film studies as a discipline with video studies, though, one hopes that the effects of this interrelationship may be integrated into a new medial schema for contemporary cinema, the current model being badly in need of conceptual renovation.

99. See chapter 1, section 1, for an extended discussion of these "spacers."

100. Fredric Jameson, *Postmodernism*, 16.

101. Catherine Wheatley, for instance, sees the episodic portrayal of family routine in *Der siebente Kontinent* as a portrayal of the family's collective disaffection. See Wheatley, *Michael Haneke's Cinema*, 57. See also Christopher Sharrett's discussion of Benny and his father as being equally subject to such a phenomenon: "the affectless present embodied in Benny is the legacy of western civilization." Sharrett, "Michael Haneke and the Discontents," 12. It should be

noted that neither Wheatley nor Sharrett perceives Haneke as carrying this lack of affect through in his own work, the latter stating in his interview with Haneke that the director "rigorously eschews the snide humor, affectlessness, preoccupation with pop culture, movie allusions, and moral blankness of postmodern art." Haneke, "World That Is Known," 582.

102. Jameson, *Postmodernism*, 16.

103. This idea will be elaborated on in the discussion of *Benny's Video* in chapter 2.

104. Kristeva, "Word, Dialogue, and Novel," 66.

105. Ibid.

106. Pethő, *Cinema and Intermediality*, 67.

107. Ibid., 69.

108. Cooper's project records high-definition video of children in their early teens or younger during gameplay, from which he derives digital photos and video montages. In nearly every subject, the face reaches a state of seeming affectlessness utterly disproportionate to the intensity of violent action represented on-screen (with the exception of exchanges with other players during multiplayer sessions). A collection of photos from the project and a short video can be viewed in a profile on the artist's project on *The New York Times Magazine*'s website. See Robbie Cooper, "My Game Face," *New York Times Magazine*, November 18, 2008, accessed August 2, 2016, http://www.nytimes.com/slideshow/2008/11/18/magazine/20081123-games_index.html; Robbie Cooper, "Immersion," *New York Times Magazine*, November 21, 2008, accessed August 2, 2016, http://www.nytimes.com/video/magazine/1194833565213/immersion.html.

109. While applicable to film and television studies, and to media studies in general, this doubling of the self or subject has been explored more directly in video game scholarship, perhaps because of the more apparent division of agency and subjectivity that occurs in the latter. David Surman, for instance, argues that the break between player and player-character impinges upon the ontological and referential status of the subject in a manner unknown to the film spectator: "To make a useful distinction between videogames and film, no matter the degree of identification, the majority of spectators recognise the status of the *filmed* subject as 'other'; an expectant desire to 'be' is not to be confused with real-time 'embodiment' per se. In videogames, a radically different system of subject association is constructed, in which players partially collapse on-screen characters with the first-person referent 'I', and (in an admittedly simplistic account) player-characters become a surrogate second self (Surman 2005). I don't want to recount the broader socio-cultural implications of this positioning, save to say that we might begin to think of embodiment as a central force in the formal analysis of videogames, a peak state or experience to which designers of gameplay aspire." Surman, "Pleasure, Spectacle and Reward in Capcom's *Street Fighter* series," in *Videogame, Player, Text*, ed. Barry Atkins and Tanya Krzywinska (Manchester: Manchester UP, 2007), 211.

110. Catherine Wheatley convincingly characterizes Haneke's films—and in particular the self-reflexive antagonism of the viewer by "Paul" in *Funny Games*—as generative of spectatorial "unpleasure" in the same manner as countercinematic works such as those by Jean-Luc Godard and Chantal Akerman. Wheatley, *Michael Haneke's Cinema*, 85–88. This affective strategy could also

be understood in terms of medial immersion though. Paul's evident *jouissance* seems intended as an appropriation of spectatorial affect that is intensified by his seeming role as a player-character—a subjectivity embodied both within the film, as actant-antagonist, and outside of the film, as commentator on and controller of the film itself as a medial text, specifically a video that can be paused and rewound. His immersion trumps that of the viewer, forcing the latter into a different affective relationship to the film that is clearly experienced by many viewers as intense dis- or unpleasure; it even initiated walkouts during the film's premiere at Cannes. See the description of the screening in Haneke, "The Discreet Harm of the Bourgeoisie," 10. This aspect of the film is explored further in the discussion of *Funny Games* in chapter 2.

111. Shame is a highly specialized affective experience that carries dynamic and complex perceptual-ontological implications with individual, dual, and collective manifestations. For this reason, shame is given an extensive philosophical and psychological definition in the first section of chapter 4.

112. Schröter, "Discourses and Models," 6.

113. Gaudreault and Marion, "A Medium is Always Born Twice . . . ," 12.

114. Ibid., 13.

115. Deleuze and Parnet, *Dialogues*, 57.

116. Virilio, *The University of Disaster*, 41.

117. Vogl, "Becoming-Media: Galileo's Telescope," 627.

118. Sloterdijk, "*Actio in Distans*," 637. It is no coincidence that both Vogl's and Sloterdijk's remarkable essays were included in Chang and Butchart's phenomenal collection *Philosophy of Communication*, a repository of highly interesting theoretical reconsiderations of media and communications.

119. Ibid., 640.

120. Herzogenrath, "Travels in Intermedia[lity]: An Introduction," 3. Square brackets in original.

121. Meier, "Genuine Thought is Inter(medial)," 125.

122. Virilio, *Polar Inertia*, 83.

123. Deleuze and Parnet, *Dialogues*, 90. This approach is echoed by the intermedial theorist Joachim Paech, who in applying Luhmann's systems theory to media studies points out that "media analysis is dependent upon the observation of configurations of media conditions of form processes which 'occur' in the breaks, gaps, and intervals of the form processes." Paech, "Artwork—Text—Medium." Qualities invisible to one still enmeshed within a given medial system become observable and analyzable only when one locates the operational margins and limits of the system, where breakdowns and gaps occur.

Chapter 1

1. Brunette, *Michael Haneke*, 10.

2. Haneke, "Beyond Mainstream Film," 168.

3. I will refer to Haneke's works for television throughout the text where relevant, and *Das Schloß* and the other literary adaptations for television will be examined in some detail in chapter 4. However, for the most part his works for television do not evidence the intermedial concerns found in the majority of his theatrical films, and therefore remain outside of the scope of this study.

4. Haneke, "World That Is Known," 585.

5. Austrian state television imposes fewer restrictions on the subject matter and imagery of its sponsored programming than most other countries, and is certainly far less restrictive than network television in the United States. For instance, as Brunette notes, Haneke's television productions from the 1970s feature "full frontal female nudity and [a] self-consciously, resolutely downbeat Weltanschauung." Brunette, *Michael Haneke*, 3.

6. Haneke, "World That Is Known," 587; Haneke, "Collective Guilt," 51; Haneke, "Interview: Michael Haneke, the Bearded Prophet," *Indiewire*.

7. Haneke, "Minister of Fear," interview by John Wray. Please refer to appendix A for a full overview of the plot structure of the film, as well as for synopses and cast names for the other films discussed in detail in subsequent chapters. I will provide such information in the text only where necessary for the purposes of analysis.

8. Haneke, "World That Is Known," 585.

9. Grundmann, "Auteur de Force," 9.

10. Wheatley, *Michael Haneke's Cinema*, 57.

11. Ibid.

12. Haneke, "World That Is Known," 586.

13. McLuhan and Fiore, *The Medium is the Massage*, 128.

14. Williams, *Television*, 91. Williams's concept of television's flow—which directly informs Jameson's conceptualization of television and video as well—bears a number of similarities to Deleuze's idea of the nonlinguistic force that underpins televisual expression, which is referenced in the introduction, a force "which would flow under redundancy and information, which would make language flow and still make itself understood." Deleuze, *Cinema 2*, 127.

15. An illustration of television's aversion to any element that would even minimally or momentarily disrupt the flow of audiovisual material is evident in the presentation of the closing credits of primetime network television shows: the text of the credits is relegated to a window in a small corner of the screen and the music to the background of the sound track, while the majority of the on-screen space and audio is occupied by teasers or previews for the program that will immediately follow, the continuation of the flow of entertainment having to be vouchsafed even during this minute-long interim.

16. Saxton, "Close Encounters," 95.

17. See Brunette, *Michael Haneke*, 143.

18. Wheatley, "Spectator as Moral Agent," 67.

19. There remains a tendency to associate the black screen with temporal manipulation, although longer spacers separate shots that occur within moments of one another in the time frame of the narrative. Adam Bingham thus relates the function of the spacer specifically to questions of temporality even while acknowledging that its presence does not necessarily denote a leap or gap in time: "The essence of this method is to suggest that a temporal ellipsis could well have taken place between the scenes we see of the daily lives of the three characters. The point is that their existence is such that they have very little difference or variety in their lives from day to day, year to year." Bingham, "Life, or something like it," Kinoeye.

The difficulty of dissociating the black screen with temporal effects is understandable considering its relation, on one hand, to the received grammar of cinema, which uses the fade and the black screen as indicators of time's passage between scenes, and, on the other hand, the fact that the black screen highlights the primacy of time itself—as opposed to movement or even the visual or aural image—as the constitutive signaletic material of postwar film, as Deleuze makes clear in his conceptualization of the time-image. See Deleuze, *Cinema 2*, xii.

20. Haneke, "Interview with Michael Haneke: 'The Fragmentation of the Look,'" 143.

21. Bellour, "Pensive Spectator," 10. Bellour, it should be noted, makes it clear in the essay that the insertion of photographs is not the sole or even the most powerful means through which film may achieve such effects, thus allowing for the possibility of the same or similar effects being achieved via other cinematic techniques or intermedial interventions. See ibid.

22. Ibid., 9.

23. Saxton, "Close Encounters," 95.

24. Carpenter, "New Languages," 165.

25. See Haneke, "Interview with Michael Haneke by Serge Toubiana." Segments from this 2005 interview series appear as extra features in the Kino Video DVD editions of Haneke's films. Henceforth, they will be referred to as "Toubiana Interview," followed by the title of the film with which it appears.

26. Augé, *Non-Places*, 95.

27. Haneke, "World That Is Known," 581.

28. Grundmann, "Auteur de Force," 9; Lebeau, "The Arts of Looking," 40.

29. It should be noted that the spectator does occupy the point of view of Evi, who can later be glimpsed in the rear middle seat of the car as it pulls out of the car wash in a frontal shot. This carries some interesting implications in consideration of the fact that Evi, unlike Georg and Anna, is presented as retaining the capacity for genuine perception. Robin Wood's essay on Haneke contains an eloquent interpretation of Evi's character in these terms. See Wood, "Michael Haneke: Beyond Compromise," 48.

30. Baudrillard, *Simulacra and Simulation*, 76.

31. Ibid., 92.

32. Virilio, *The Vision Machine*, 62.

33. Ibid., 62–63.

34. Ibid., 72–73.

35. Grundmann, "Auteur de Force," 9.

36. Le Cain, "Do the Right Thing." Cavell's assertion of the fact that "human beings are not ontologically favored over the rest of nature" in photography and postphotographic media is of course relevant to this state of affairs. Cavell, *World Viewed*, 37. Photographic and filmic representations are indifferent to questions of subjective or objective status relative to their views of the world. It is arguable, however, that much of television and new media—and particularly advertising—pushes this relation to a further extreme, offering a situation in which commercial products *are* in fact ontologically favored over human beings.

37. Haneke, "Interview: Michael Haneke, the Bearded Prophet."

38. Haneke, "World That Is Known," 586.

39. Carpenter, "New Languages," 175.

40. Jameson, *Postmodernism*, 76.

41. Baudrillard, *Simulacra and Simulation*, 51.

42. While one finds assertions of a similar effect with regard to cinematic spectatorship—from Hugo Münsterberg's psychological study *The Photoplay* (1916) to Deleuze's assertion that "the brain is the screen"—one could contrast this to television via the extremity of its desubjectifying effect. Television does not appeal to a preexisting mind or nervous system beyond the one that it installs informatically; it is thus nonpsychological and non-sensational to the extent that it does not presuppose a preexisting subject in possession of a mind or even of a central nervous system. As an informatic medium, it delivers not percepts and affects that can be composed into image-ideas, either psychological or aesthetic, but only irritants and anaesthetic.

43. Marshall McLuhan, who asserted the absolute equivalency of medium and message, could thus be considered one of the first theorists to approach an understanding of television as such. Moreover, considering the fact that his ideas came to prominence soon after television had come to dominate radio and film as the definitive medium of the age, it could reasonably be asserted that TV defined McLuhan's theories just as much as his theories defined the medium.

44. Cavell, "Fact of Television," 59–60.

45. Ibid., 72.

46. Ibid. (italics in original). I will return to the relationship between television and the event in chapter 3, since it constitutes an essential aspect of *71 Fragmente*.

47. The subjective approach evidenced in this final scene is most likely derived from the original conception of the film, in which the narrative took the form of a series of flashbacks Georg had after ingesting a lethal dose of sedatives. See Brunette, *Michael Haneke*, 11. In his video interview with Serge Toubiana, Haneke explains the reason why he changed the narrative structure during the screenwriting process: "I worked for six weeks without success, because each flashback ended up being an explanation. Eventually, I understood that I couldn't tell the story that way if I wanted the secret to remain troubling. I decided I would give myself a sort of framework. Three years, one day [each year], and we see what happens. And it's up to the viewer to find his or her own answers. . . . After that, it was very easy to write the script. It went very quickly. I finished it in about four weeks." Haneke, "Toubiana Interview," *Seventh Continent* DVD.

48. Haneke, "World That Is Known," 586.

49. Virilio, *A Landscape of Events*, 51.

50. Sutherland, "Death, with Television," 172.

51. An example of a mise en abyme effect brought about by a coincidence of screens and frames would be the opening shot of *Caché*, where the contents of the film screen and the couple's television screen within the film are undecidable. David Cronenberg's 1983 film *Videodrome* (a film that, like *Der siebente Kontinent*, expresses a sophisticated formal and thematic consideration of television as a medium) utilizes such an effect in a much different way: the ending of the film is displayed on a television screen within the film just before occurring in the film itself. Mel Brooks's *Spaceballs* (1987) also contains an example of an explicitly intermedial mise en abyme effect that will be examined in greater detail early in chapter 2.

52. Deleuze, *Cinema 1*, 17.

Chapter 2

1. See Doane, "Information, Crisis, Catastrophe," 222. This temporal quality of television will be explored in greater detail in chapter 3, with respect to *71 Fragmente*.

2. Virilio, *Polar Inertia*, 1.

3. Brooks, *Spaceballs*.

4. Interestingly, a similar interrogation of the effect of video representation upon the subject's sense of the temporal present is the focus of a very different work: Lynda Benglis's experimental short video *Now* (1973). Benglis's piece consists of the artist in profile mirroring the actions of video recordings of herself on monitors and then appearing to perform erotic interactions with her video selves. Throughout, the artist's voice can be heard on the sound track repeating the word "now" and asking, "Is it now?" As Rosalind Krauss states, "what is far more arresting in *Now* than the technological banality of the question 'which "now" is intended?' [i.e., the time of the video or the time of a video within the video] is the way the tape enacts a collapsed present time." Krauss, "Video: The Aesthetics of Narcissism," 55. In other words, the presence of the video within the video precludes any unified temporal perspective that its subject could identify as "now." There is no evidence that Benglis's short influenced the instant video scene in *Spaceballs*, which Mel Brooks states was conceived by himself and co-screenwriters Ronny Graham and Thomas Meehan. See Brooks, "Commentary," *Spaceballs*, directed by Mel Brooks (Los Angeles: Fox Video, 2004), DVD.

5. Other oft-cited examples of this subgenre include Terrence Young's *Wait Until Dark* (1967), Sam Peckinpah's *Straw Dogs* (1971), Michael Cimino's *Desperate Hours* (1990), and David Fincher's *Panic Room* (2002).

6. Benny's father Georg's care in disposing of the girl's body and her possessions—cutting the former into small enough pieces to be flushed down the toilet and incinerating the latter at their country home—is wasted, since he overlooks the most dangerous evidence of his and Benny's guilt: that recorded by the video medium itself. While the tape of the murder is presumably destroyed by Georg, Benny's video camera captures the incriminating conversation Georg and Anna have about how to cover up the crime, folding the original representation into a subsequent one.

7. This realist effect that we tend to associate with video media is also utilized for a key scene in *Code inconnu*—that of Anne's rehearsal during the preproduction of the film within the film—and is discussed in these terms in chapter 3.

8. Brunette, *Michael Haneke*, 23.

9. Several scenes in *Benny's Video* are markedly similar in style and presentation to *Der siebente Kontinent*, though. Most notable are those involving the McDonald's restaurant where Benny goes for lunch and the video rental store he frequents; transactions there are presented in a series of tight close-up shots of money changing hands and cash register displays in a manner strongly echoing scenes from Haneke's debut.

10. Spielmann, *Video: The Reflexive Medium*, 1–2.

11. Haneke's eschewal of flashbacks is noted, among other places, in Saxton, "Secrets and Revelations: Off-screen Space," 10.

12. Krauss, "Video: The Aesthetics of Narcissism," 57. Interestingly, Krauss's mode of understanding video in subjective-structural—rather than purely

technical—terms has been extended by Stephen C. Foster to artistic intermedia (in Dick Higgins's sense) more generally and to those works involving a video component more specifically. He writes: "Video is an extension of ourselves because we can no longer distinguish between ourselves and TV-type technology without what McLuhan has called an anti-environment. . . . The proper terms of a description (as well as evaluation) of intermedia might closely parallel how we would go about describing or evaluating a human being. Indeed, the effectiveness of intermedia isn't unlike the effectiveness of a human being and this is why video, especially, has been characterized as an extension of the nervous system. The nervous system is the co-ordinator, the enabler, and is more significantly described in terms of its use and structure, in terms of its efficaciousness, than it is in terms of its physiological being." Foster, "Video and Intermedia: Remarks," 64.

13. Spielmann, *Video: The Reflexive Medium*, 4.

14. Ibid.

15. Ibid., 8.

16. Manovich, *Language of New Media*, 100.

17. Spielmann, *Video: The Reflexive Medium*, 8. Video's representational output is "written" onto the monitor in much the same way we write words onto a page, left to right and top to bottom, though obviously at far greater and thus imperceptible speeds. However, the monitor cannot be considered a *tabula rasa* in the same way as a blank page (or canvas, or film screen), as the information is transmitted via rhythmic breaks in the audiovisual noise that marshal the chaos into discernible visual and aural material: "video's form requires . . . signals that are discontinuous, shift linearly, and are synchronized into image forms by horizontal and vertical scanning gaps, which are simultaneously written and broadcast and do not form a series of image frames separated in space and time." Ibid., 131. Video representation is thus based on *absences* rather than presences; it denotes the electronic imposition of specific gaps onto undifferentiated audiovisual noise rather than the presence of (photo)graphic images on a strip or other surface.

18. Ibid., 134.

19. Hediger, "Infectious Images," 92. Hediger goes on, however, to assert that ultimately "video is contained within film," a claim that is also put forward by others examining the relationship between film and video in *Benny's Video*. Ibid. Brigitte Peucker, for instance, states that the final shot of the multiple surveillance monitors in the police station implies that "finally Haneke's film subsumes Benny's video," while Catherine Wheatley, citing Peucker, affirms that the closing shot and similar shots of monitors throughout enable the film to "frame and control the [video] images that they contain." Peucker, "Fragmentation and the Real," 185; Wheatley, *Michael Haneke's Cinema*, 65.

20. Haneke, "We Live in a Permanent State of War," 17–18.

21. Haneke does not comment upon the medial significance of Benny having recorded the act on video, but he does emphasize elsewhere the replaying of the video for Benny's parents in terms of its impact upon the viewer: "The audience has witnessed the murder once already, but this second viewing, with the parents themselves now a de facto part of the audience, is vastly more affecting. Why, I asked Haneke, was the experience so different the second time? 'When you see the killing first, you're too shocked and bewildered to let the fact of it sink in,' he replied. 'But the moment that the parents, with whom one naturally identifies,

sit down to watch the video, one begins to see the murder in its social context: the discrepancy between the act we are witnessing and normal social behavior becomes clear.' He smiled. 'It's always important to keep in mind who's watching.' " Haneke, "Minister of Fear."

22. It is significant that the first shot we see of the room in which Schorschi's offscreen murder has taken place in *Funny Games* is a close-up of a blood-spattered television screen showing an auto race, though. This will be touched on in the third section of this chapter.

23. Lawrence, "Haneke's Stable," 72.

24. Brunette, *Michael Haneke*, 28.

25. Ibid., 29. Haneke is aware of this quality of sound, claiming in one interview that his strategy in *Benny's Video* was to "destabilize" the viewer by using the sound of the murder as an emotional manipulation while effecting a simultaneous "distantiation" through the focus on the screen within the film. Haneke, "Toubiana Interview," *Benny's Video* DVD.

26. As we will see in the next chapter, the premise of *71 Fragmente* could be considered a counter-program to this reception of television news reportage, the film acting to retroactively reinvest the televisual representation of the event—a shooting at a bank—with a connection to actual individuals and circumstances.

27. Wheatley, *Michael Haneke's Cinema*, 63.

28. Brunette, *Michael Haneke*, 24.

29. Speck, *Funny Frames*, 24.

30. Scarry, *Body in Pain*, 4. This highly interesting study was brought to my attention following Brian Price's application of it to Haneke in an essay titled "Pain and the Limits of Representation." Price's essay will be referenced directly in the third section of this chapter.

31. Scarry, *Body in Pain*, 9.

32. It can indeed be argued that any sensation addressed to or primarily experienced through the central nervous system—including any form of bodily discomfort, physical pleasure, sensations of heat or cold, etc.—is fundamentally unrepresentable and incommunicable. However, the relatively common (and thus shared) experiences of such sensations may be drawn upon via sense memory, or even via pure observation, and hence "read" with relative ease by means of their attendant indexical signs: vocalizations, for example, or perceptible physical reactions, such as sweating or shivering, as well as verbal descriptions. Intense pain, however, marks the point at which articulation breaks down not only on the part of the subject in pain but on the part of the observer; various signs may present themselves, but the relationship between signified and signifier is utterly insufficient. It is impossible for one who has experienced intense pain to recall it even to oneself after it has passed, much less to communicate it to another or obtain a means of representing it. Scarry quotes Virginia Woolf on this point: "The merest schoolgirl when she falls in love has Shakespeare or Keats to speak her mind for her, but let a sufferer try to describe a pain in his head to a doctor and language at once runs dry." Ibid., 4.

33. For example, how can one best account for the diverse affective responses to representations of violence from different genres, such as those found in comedies, action movies, horror movies (including "torture porn"), and dramas? This question will be revisited in connection to *Funny Games*.

34. Sobchack, *Carnal Thoughts*, 235.

35. This position differs radically not only from the common cultural perspective but also from that of most other theorists of violence in visual media, whose reasonings are usually based on the assumption that simulation, in principle, carries less sacred symbolic value than a representation of a real event. Sobchack, for instance, outlines a conception of the representation of violence that is diametrically opposed to that which I have derived from Haneke: "In sum, when death is represented as fictive rather than real, when its signs are structured and stressed so as to function iconically and symbolically, the spectator understands that only the *simulacrum* of a visual taboo has been violated. When death is represented as real, however, when its signs are structured and inflected so as to function indexically, a visual taboo has been violated, and the representation must find various ways to justify the violation." Ibid., 242.

36. Bazin, "Death Every Afternoon," 30.

37. Ibid.

38. Sobchack, *Carnal Thoughts*, 234.

39. Wood, "Michael Haneke: Beyond Compromise," 51.

40. Spielmann, *Video: The Reflexive Medium*, 4.

41. Deleuze, *Logic of Sense*, 165 (italics added).

42. Price and Rhodes, "Introduction," 6.

43. Bazin, "Death Every Afternoon," 30.

44. Le Cain, "Do the Right Thing."

45. Peucker, "Fragmentation and the Real," 179; Frey, "Supermodernity, Capital, and Narcissus," 7; Wood, "Michael Haneke: Beyond Compromise," 51; Grossvogel, "Haneke: The Coercing of Vision," 17.

46. The character Alex in Stanley Kubrick's *A Clockwork Orange* (1971), interestingly, does imagine himself in this exact role upon reading the New Testament in prison, and Kubrick subsequently withdrew the film from circulation in the United Kingdom after a number of crimes were committed by young males apparently imitating Alex. It is as though the film had offered a very specific commentary on a phenomenon that it ironically provoked in turn. For information on this withdrawal and the circumstances surrounding it see Alan Travis, "Retake on Kubrick film ban," *The Guardian*, September 11, 1999, accessed August 2, 2016, https://www.theguardian.com/uk/1999/sep/11/alantravis.

47. Grundmann, "Auteur de Force," 10.

48. Jameson, *Postmodernism*, 74.

49. Krauss, "Video: The Aesthetics of Narcissism," 55.

50. Frey, "Supermodernity, Capital, and Narcissus," 12.

51. Ibid., 8.

52. McLuhan, *Understanding Media*, 41.

53. Ibid., 42–43.

54. It remains an ambiguous point as to whether or not Benny intends to kill the girl when he fires the shot from the bolt gun. He has initially put the gun to his own chest and asked the girl to fire, which she refuses to do. His firing the gun when their positions are reversed is spontaneous, and he expresses first surprise, then terror, at the result of his actions. His confession to Georg that he wanted "to see what it feels like," then, could refer either to his being shot himself, to firing the gun, or to committing murder. In my interpretation of this response, the emphasis

is placed on Benny's desire for an actual experience, as opposed to a secondhand representation, of the event of pain and death, whether his own or another's.

55. A number of commentators have expressed confusion about this crowded display of prints on the wall, which seems completely at odds with the understated and bourgeois décor of the rest of the apartment. The explanation for the presence of the prints is revealed near the end of the film, when Benny identifies the name and address of his mother's place of business to the police. Her store is called "Kunstrepro" ("Art-repro") and it can be assumed that the framed pictures are examples of prints that have been produced for sale by her business. Even Benny's mother, then, is caught up within a regime privileging representation over actual objects, albeit one with definably cultural and commercial interests.

56. While the angle of Benny's initial eyeline matches the position of the Magritte print (upper left), it is never made clear that this is the particular painting that has affected him as the wall of art in his point-of-view shot is presented at a medium range, such that most of the wall is framed. When he lowers his gaze, we are presented with his viewpoint once more in a closer shot of the lower part of the wall, but no painting stands out at this viewing angle.

57. I am, of course, here positing on Haneke's part yet another intermedial encounter, or more precisely two: between painting and cinema at a mimetic level, and between this Magritte painting and video in an intellectual sense. While this aspect of the relation of the painted image to the technical apparatus will not be explored in great detail in this text, it does offer an interesting opportunity to pursue the question of Haneke's intermedial use of painting both here and in *Amour*. In the latter film, a sequence of close-ups focused on the paintings decorating the couple's apartment provides a highly innovative figure for the passage of time within close confines, the very stasis of the painted image evoking a particular subjective experience of time.

58. Spielmann, *Video: The Reflexive Medium*, 301(italics added).

59. Following this psychological account of Benny's emergent subjectivity, it could be suggested that he departs from his narcissistic phase and enters an Oedipal one. Frey, for instance, cites Benny's trip to Egypt with his mother, and singles out the scene in which Benny videotapes her on the toilet as having explicitly Oedipal overtones. See Frey, "Supermodernity, Capital, and Narcissus," 12n. However, Haneke preemptively undermines such interpretations by having them expressed within the film by the close-minded Georg, who, before discovering his son's crime, apparently sees Benny's act of shaving his head as an Oedipal gesture: "Who are you trying to impress? Not me, I hope. Perhaps you think your mother likes it."

60. Schwartz, "The Void at the Center of Things," 338–39.

61. Sobchack, *Carnal Thoughts*, 7.

62. The scene in which Benny reveals the corpse thus involves a phenomenological doubling of reality and representation, since he "views" the corpse's face through the video camera even as he touches it.

63. Haneke, "Toubiana Interview," *Benny's Video* DVD.

64. I refer throughout to the original Austrian version of *Funny Games*, from 1997; the English-language remake that was produced ten years later will be designated *Funny Games U.S.*

65. Haneke, "Toubiana Interview," *Funny Games* DVD.

66. Wheatley, *Michael Haneke's Cinema*, 46.

67. Ibid., 96.

68. Haneke, "Toubiana Interview," *Funny Games* DVD.

69. Haneke, "Minister of Fear."

70. Wheatley, "Spectator as Moral Agent," 69–70.

71. Jameson, "Allegorizing Hitchcock," 112.

72. Ibid. Walter Benjamin's oft-cited assertion that "[t]he audience's identification with the actor is really an identification with the camera" also points toward this realization. Benjamin, "Work of Art," 228. Character and spectator do not relate to each other, in other words; rather, like the camera, "identification" is an apparatus that draws viewing subject and viewed subject into a common relation with the cinematic apparatus without facilitating any veritable communication or exchange between the viewing and the viewed themselves.

73. Vernet, "Look at the Camera," 48.

74. Ibid.

75. Wheatley refers to a similar violation in her account of the film's generation of viewer discomfort and the viewer's self-reflexive moral objection to this strategy: "The impact on the spectator that occurs at the junctions between the differing stylistic and narrative modes results in an emotional experience of unpleasure, the source of which the spectator seeks within the film." Wheatley, *Michael Haneke's Cinema*, 105.

76. Cavell, *World Viewed*, 36.

77. Haneke, "Minister of Fear." Wheatley notes this similarity to *Tom Jones* as well and states that the primary differences between it and *Funny Games* are that in the former film it is the antagonist who addresses the spectator and that in the latter film the characters make it clear that they are performing for the viewer. See Wheatley, *Michael Haneke's Cinema*, 96.

78. Vernet, "Look at the Camera," 52. The seemingly risible practice of attaching an artificial "laugh track" to television sitcoms in lieu of a live audience response can be understood as a medial phenomenon in this sense. This disembodied laughter is not merely a stand-in for that of the television viewer—a secondhand *jouissance*—but also functions as a signifier of the presence of a collective, but abstract, "Third Party" to which the on-screen antics are addressed.

79. Durham, "Codes Unknown," 248–49.

80. Frampton, *Filmosophy*, 141.

81. Speck, *Funny Frames*, 10.

82. Price, "Pain and the Limits of Representation," 44.

83. Ibid., 42.

84. Galloway, "Origins of the First-Person Shooter," 65.

85. Speck, *Funny Frames*, 32.

86. Wheatley, *Michael Haneke's Cinema*, 94.

87. "Localizing" is a term used to describe the process of changing a video game for release in a foreign market; many Japanese games released in English-speaking countries have been localized. However, localization does not simply involve dialogue and text translation; visual, story, and gameplay elements can also be changed to suit the other cultural milieu. *Funny Games U.S.* similarly not only translates the original film but transposes it to another milieu through its recasting of actors, changes in location and prop design, and so on.

88. Price, "Pain and the Limits of Representation," 43. Here, Price also aptly points out that *Funny Games U.S.* does not actually match the original shot-for-shot and edit-for-edit, even though this was Haneke's stated intention for the production, as the director has repeatedly said in interviews.

89. A study of Haneke's film in this regard would be an interesting undertaking. It might resemble in certain respects Jan Simons's text *Playing the Waves: Lars von Trier's Game Cinema* (2007), which analyzes the Danish director's films in terms of game theory.

Chapter 3

1. The family as a site of medial and physical violence is a narrative and thematic constant in Haneke's subsequent films as well, including of course *Caché*, in which the "home invasion" motif of *Funny Games* plays out solely through the medium of video surveillance. *La pianiste* and *Le temps du loup* present forces of social and psychological violence that assault the nuclear family in the absence of the father, *Das Weiße Band* presents a village's violent punitive response to its collective and repressive patriarchal structure, and *Amour* poignantly follows the final undoing of a marital-familial structure ravaged by illness and senescence.

2. Michael Haneke, "*71 Fragments of a Chronology of Chance*: Notes to the Film," 175.

3. Ibid.

4. Ibid., 171.

5. See Haneke, "Interview with Michael Haneke: 'The Fragmentation of the Look,' " 139–40.

6. Haneke, "*71 Fragments of a Chronology of Chance*: Notes to the Film," 172.

7. Grundmann, "Between Adorno and Lyotard," 376.

8. Ibid., 372.

9. This reading corresponds in certain respects to D. N. Rodowick's definition of new media as articulations of the *figural* (Lyotard's term, though inflected by Rodowick with Deleuzian concepts as well). An understanding of media as figural constructs is resistant to the application of established aesthetic and representational binaries such as form/content or signifier/signified. Instead, medial phenomena are conceived of as expressions opposed to such categorical definitions both in nature and in principle: "What I call the figural is not synonymous with a figure or even the figurative. It is no more proper to the plastic than to the linguistic arts. It is not governed by the opposition of word to image; spatially and temporally, it is not bound to the logic of binary oppositions. Ever permutable—a fractured, fracturing, or fractal space, ruled by time and difference—it knows nothing of the concept of identity. The figural is not an aesthetic concept, nor does it recognize a distinction between the forms of 'high' and 'low' culture. It describes the logic of mass culture itself; or rather a culture of the mass." Rodowick, *Reading the Figural*, 46.

10. In German: "Am 23.12.93 erschoβ der 19-jährige Student Maximilian B. in der Zweigstelle einer Wiener Bank drei Menschen und tötete sich kurz darauf selbst mit einem Schuβ in den Kopf." Studies of Haneke often note the similarity of this text to that confirming the actuality of the incident of destruction of property and familial suicide in *Der siebente Kontinent*. Significantly, in Haneke's

debut feature this text appears at the end of the film rather than the beginning, indicating a retroactive rather than proleptic relation to the event that inspired the film.

11. Le Cain, "Do the Right Thing."

12. Ibid.

13. Haneke, "*71 Fragments of a Chronology of Chance*: Notes to the Film," 173–74.

14. In this reading, *71 Fragmente* shares a connection with the otherwise stylistically and thematically dissimilar *Funny Games*, since both seem intended to manipulate the expectations and assumptions of a spectator acclimated to commercial media.

15. Le Cain, "Do the Right Thing."

16. Indeed, if one enumerates the fragments composing the film so that they total seventy-one, each excerpt from the television news broadcast is counted as a single fragment even though each one generally encompasses several individual segments or reports.

17. Haneke, "Beyond Mainstream Film," 162.

18. Morse, "Talk, Talk, Talk," 3. As Morse suggests here, the distinction between story and discourse, as she employs the terms, is not dependent upon whether the content of either is fictional or factual with respect to actuality.

19. Ibid., 15. We recall from the introduction Deleuze's assertion that television addresses us injunctively, from a position of command. It could be argued that Morse's insight reveals the discursive mask worn by this injunction, which is that of an appeal to the spectator as an equal. Morse's identification of the viewer's "desire for mastery" over the medium is thus exploited and transformed, in Deleuze's reading, into its opposite: an acceptance of enslavement. Edmund Carpenter suggested as much long ago by rather amusingly reversing the owner/pet relationship with respect to television: "Some people who have no one around talk to cats, and you can hear their voices in the next room, and they sound silly, because the cats won't answer, but that suffices to maintain the illusion that their world is made up of living people, while it is not. Mechanized mass media reverse this: now mechanical cats talk to humans. There's no genuine feedback." Carpenter, "New Languages," 172.

20. Morse, "Ontology of Everyday Distraction," 206.

21. The vocal bridges between even fictional shows, which encourage the viewer to "stay tuned for more," are of course an extension of this phenomenon to televisual discourse as a whole.

22. Grundmann, "Introduction: Haneke's Anachronism," 21.

23. It should be noted that these conjoined scenes are counted as a single fragment among the seventy-one enumerated by the film's title. No other transition between locations within the film occurs without being marked by a spacer.

24. Morse notes a similar effect in cinematic works displayed on television with commercial interruptions: "[S]uch alternation of story and discourse is perceived as interruption by all sorts of extraneous material and an incessant disruption of the psychological mechanism of disavowal." The continual suspension of this mechanism of disavowal is perceived as affecting the viewer's immersion within the continuous story space of the narrative film: "Segmentation imposed on continuity editing is a mismatch of principles of coherence and dramatic unity

of character, plot and setting, and editing, as well as conditions of viewing which promote fairly concentrated attention, and identification can only suffer thereby." Morse, "Ontology of Everyday Distraction," 220n. *71 Fragmente* intentionally enforces this disruptive effect as part of its overall strategy of fragmentation.

25. Durham, "Codes Unknown," 248.

26. See Benjamin, "The Storyteller," 88.

27. Ibid., 89.

28. The admission of false and misleading relationships into the field of possibility surrounding an event in this latter model is of course inevitable. The Deleuzian concept of the positive "powers of the false" (in chapter 6 of *Cinema 2*), as they relate to the film image, is relevant here and will be examined in more detail in the discussion of *Caché*. Haneke's acknowledgement of this concept of truth's proximity to falsehood is given in his subversion of Godard's oft-quoted aphorism that cinema is "truth at twenty-four frames per second": "I've adapted Godard's observation to read, 'Film is a lie at twenty-four frames per second in the service of truth.'" Haneke, "Collective Guilt," 50.

29. There are, of course, a wide array of fictional films that present themselves as documentary texts, including comedic "mockumentaries," of which Rob Reiner's *This is Spinal Tap* (1984) is the paradigmatic example. A number of fictional horror films also present themselves as "found footage": *The Blair Witch Project* (Daniel Myrick and Eduardo Sánchez; 1999) is one such film that was able to convince much of its audience that it was a nonfictional text because of its clever marketing campaign, including a television special and simulated news articles disseminated via its website. Perhaps the most significant example of the effect of a fictional text presenting itself informatically, however, is Orson Welles's 1938 radio broadcast of the H. G. Wells novel *The War of the Worlds*, which is alleged to have caused widespread panic due to its highly verisimilar simulation of emergency news reports of an alien invasion.

30. Bellour, "Concerning the Photographic," 262.

31. Doane, "Information, Crisis, Catastrophe," 222.

32. Ibid., 228.

33. Ibid., 225.

34. Ibid., 229.

35. Cavell, "Fact of Television," 72.

36. Rodowick, *Gilles Deleuze's Time Machine*, 172.

37. Williams, *Television*, 43.

38. Baudrillard, *Simulacra and Simulation*, 53; Doane, "Information, Crisis, Catastrophe," 228.

39. See Doane, "Information, Crisis, Catastrophe," 222–23.

40. Deleuze, *Cinema 2*, 97.

41. Quoted in Doane, "Information, Crisis, Catastrophe," 222.

42. Deleuze, *Cinema 2*, 97.

43. Take, for example, Ludwig Wittgenstein's use of the cinematic apparatus as a means of distinguishing between two seemingly incommensurable ideas of time in his posthumously published *Philosophical Remarks* (1964): "Perhaps this whole difficulty stems from taking the time concept from time in physics and applying it to the course of immediate experience. It's a confusion of the time of the film strip with the time of the picture it projects. For 'time' has one meaning

when we regard memory as the source of time, and another when we regard it as a picture preserved from a past event." Wittgenstein, *Philosophical Remarks*, 81. Wittgenstein similarly draws on the image offered by the film strip/screen dichotomy as a means of differentiating two perspectives on time at numerous other points in this text.

44. The unique temporality of the event is, I argue, also implied by the return of historical trauma in *Caché* and will be explored in further detail in the discussion of that film.

45. The sole exception, in *Code inconnu*, to this adherence to the photographic and film image is a sequence shot on video, in which Anne rehearses a scene from the film in which she is acting. As this video follows the same long-take aesthetic as the rest of the film, however, it does not connote as drastic a departure from cinematic representation as the presence of television and video in Haneke's previous films. Certain aspects of video representation will be noted in the forthcoming discussion of this scene, though.

46. Haneke, "World That Is Known," 587.

47. Le Cain, "Do the Right Thing."

48. Quoted in Wheatley, *Michael Haneke's Cinema*, 115.

49. Bazin, "Cinematic Realism," 234.

50. Ibid., 241.

51. Ibid., 241–42.

52. Grundmann, "Between Adorno and Lyotard," 371; Haneke, "Interview with Michael Haneke: 'The Fragmentation of the Look,' " 141.

53. Haneke, "Interview with Michael Haneke: 'The Fragmentation of the Look,' " 141–42.

54. Kusturica and Testor, *24 Realities per Second*.

55. Ibid.

56. Durham, "Codes Unknown," 258. Christopher Sharrett describes another pronounced theme of the film that is directly related to the circumstances of contemporary urban existence, and is suggested by the title: the film's exploration of the "collapse of language" and "of the end of communication, and that failure's relationship to racism and economic/social injustice." Haneke, "World That Is Known," 582. While not directly bearing on my reading of the film, the concept of communication breakdown as a polarizing force—between social strata, ethnic groups, young and old, and so on—is directly tied to the divergence of the characters and story lines traced by the film narrative.

57. Haneke, "Interview with Michael Haneke: 'The Fragmentation of the Look,' " 142.

58. It should be noted that not all of Haneke's scenes are filmed in a single take. In the restaurant scene, for instance, there is at least one almost imperceptible cut as a customer passes in front of the camera.

59. Indeed, Brigitte Peucker compares *Code inconnu* to Powell's film in several respects, particularly to the extent that *Le collectionneur* mirrors certain central aspects of *Peeping Tom*'s plot and theme, which also concern the efforts of a sadistic murderer to "capture on film the quintessential image of (female) fear." Peucker, "Games Haneke Plays," 21. The dialogue during Anne's rehearsal suggests similar motivations on the part of that film's antagonist: Anne's character is told that she must show her tormentor (whose voice in the rehearsal seems to be

that of *Le collectionneur*'s director, significantly) her "true face," a "true expression" of her terror.

60. Horton, "Locked out!: Michael Haneke's *Code inconnu*," *Central Europe Review*.

61. Although it is generally referred to as a rehearsal, this scene may in fact depict Anne's audition for the role, or a screen test; its context is never made explicit.

62. The scene's presentation via the medium of video also contributes to the effects detailed here, both in the way that it divorces the representation from that of the film itself—situating the scene outside of the filmic mimesis and thus opening it up to an ambiguous status—and in the sense that video offers a "raw" and seemingly unmediated index of actuality (as I argued in chapter 2, in connection with the presentations of pig slaughter and murder in *Benny's Video*).

63. Brunette, *Michael Haneke*, 76.

64. The term "faciality" itself does not appear in Deleuze's *Cinema* books, but a similar concept to the affection-image is presented in this reconsideration of the face, which appears in chapter 7 of Deleuze and Guattari's *A Thousand Plateaus*.

65. Deleuze, *Cinema 1*, 110 (italics in original).

66. This appropriation is similar to a shot in *Caché* in which a television camera continues filming the protagonist, Georges, after the program taping has ended. This shot is discussed in more detail in chapter 5.

67. This gesture of suddenly rewinding the image recalls that of *Funny Games*, though in this case the gesture is given a realistic context to orient and explain it. Also, the viewing situation, in which what appears to have been the film itself is revealed by an offscreen voice to actually be a screen within the film's diegesis, prefigures the opening shot of *Caché*.

68. Seeßlen, "Structures of Glaciation," 329.

69. Deleuze, *Cinema 2*, 241.

70. Rodowick, *Gilles Deleuze's Time Machine*, 145.

71. Deleuze, *Cinema 2*, 241–42.

72. See Haneke, "Interview with Michael Haneke: 'The Fragmentation of the Look,'" 145.

73. Ibid.

74. Bellour, "Concerning the Photographic," 261 (italics in original). Bellour's primary example of this aesthetic and medial confusion between the photographic and cinematographic is that of Chris Marker's *La Jetée*, which the spectator accepts as a work of cinema even though only one shot frames a moving image. One could also point toward the justly celebrated shot in *Citizen Kane* in which the camera closes in on a photograph of a group of men—the rival newspaper staff that Kane covets—only to have it appear to come alive as it makes the barely perceptible medial-ontological transformation from a photograph within the film into a frame of the filmstrip itself.

75. A number of scholars, for instance, have read the photo sequences as adding a layer to the film's exploration of how meaning is encoded and communicated not only in linguistic acts but also between distinct media. In this regard, several scholars have pointed out the relevance of Roland Barthes's assertion—expressed in both "The Photographic Message" (1961) and "Rhetoric of the Image" (1964)—that the paradox of the photographic text lies in the fact of

its combining a coded message (the photograph as rhetorical act) with a message without a code (the photograph as bare visual analogue of reality). See, for example, two very strong readings of the film in Grundmann's *Companion to Michael Haneke*: Conley, "Tracking *Code Unknown*," 114–15; and Peucker, "Games Haneke Plays," 137–39.

76. Rodowick, *Virtual Life of Film*, 55.

77. This transcriptive function of photography—which remains, if not definably nonrepresentational, utterly indifferent to representation—equally applies to the candid portraits constituting the second series of photographs, even if they are not immediately associated with a definable event in the manner of the war photos. These Métro portraits, which were taken by Delahaye without the knowledge of the subjects, under the same conditions as those represented in the film, were originally published in a collection titled *L'Autre*. Apropos their display in the film, Haneke states the following: "We thought of having [Delahaye] retake the photos, but that would have produced photos consciously taken and would have been totally different. It's better to photograph beings who aren't conscious of having their picture taken." Haneke, "Interview with Michael Haneke: 'The Fragmentation of the Look,'" 145. This lack of conscious agency on the part of the subject—the inability to pose for the shot—emphasizes the ontological gesture of the photograph over and above any sense of identification or self-reflection that the subject might bring to bear on the photographic representation. Instead, no conscious control is exerted on the subject's part.

This premise accords with Rodowick's Cavellian definition of photographic portraiture: "A painted portrait is a representation in which the artist makes a likeness, after her or his own vision of the subject represented. A photographic 'portrait,' however, is first an assertion of existence: that the subject, human or not, was present to the camera in past space-time." Rodowick, *Virtual Life of Film*, 58. The notion of a photo as a representation of *this* person—his or her subjective attributes and identity—is superseded by that of a photo as testimony to the objective existence of *a* person. Rather than expressing any sense of identity, the figures in Delahaye's photos project only their anonymity and bare existence as Others, and hence the portraits convey the indexical power of the photographic medium over and above any representational qualities of the figures therein. Baudrillard similarly emphasizes this anonymity in his foreword to *L'Autre*: "Between reality and its image, exchange is impossible. There is at best a figurative correlation. 'Pure' reality, if it exists, remains a question without an answer. And this is what these photographs express: a question to the Other which expects to remain unanswered." Baudrillard, "Foreword: Poetic Transference," 1. The anonymous figures in the photographs are registered as indefinably "real" due to their very *inability* to participate, as subjects, in a reflexive relationship with their own images.

78. Bazin, "Ontology of the Photographic Image," 14.

79. It is notable that Ágnes Pethő reads these sequences from *Code inconnu* as a paradigmatic case study of a film narrative introducing an "intermedial metalepsis" in order to open up a conceptual space of self-reflection on its own construction of reality: "[metalepsis] can perform in itself a leap onto a metanarrative, self-reflexive level within the film, or it can point to the existence of such a meta-narrative level due to the fact that it always introduces a level of

'otherness' into the cinematic medium that can serve as a platform through which a reflexive point of view over cinema can be activated." Pethő, *Cinema and Intermediality*, 129. In the case of *Code inconnu*, "the whole film can be interpreted as a (fragmented) meta-narrative over the possibilities of (photographic) representation in the cinema." Ibid., 130.

80. This medial commonality may be understood in terms of the shared material-medial origins of photography and cinema—photochemical film—and also in terms of what Cavell identified in *The World Viewed* as the shared automatism of the two media, the ability of both to "manufacture . . . an image of the world" and to do so, moreover, "by removing the human agent from the task of reproduction." Cavell, *World Viewed*, 20, 23.

81. Bellour, "Pensive Spectator," 9.

82. The effect of the semantic juxtaposition of a personal missive with traumatic imagery would also have to be considered quite unsettling. Libby Saxton thus directly contrasts the voice-over accompaniment to the first photo series to the voice-over conventionally employed by television: "The disjunctive relationship between word and image in this sequence is disconcerting for viewers accustomed to the horrors of distant suffering being explained, contained and made more digestible by a televisual voice-over." Saxton, "Close Encounters," 91. Peter Brunette also signals this disjunction but reads into it a nascent sociopolitical commentary: "[A]fter a while the content of the letter suddenly veers over into the personal while the visual track is still occupied by the horrific photographs, creating a disturbing, obviously intentional juxtaposition that begins to raise questions, albeit indistinct, about the relation of the personal and the political." Brunette, *Michael Haneke*, 75.

83. Chion, "Without Music: On *Caché*," 164. Chion goes on to state that *Caché* presents the viewer with a "world . . . entirely 'in prose' " that constitutes an "inescapable reality." He reads this as an alternate form of reality in comparison to our world, which is no less saturated with mediatized music than it is with visual images as vehicles for escapism. He goes on to connect this absence of music to the overall indiscernibility of the different forms of image within *Caché*—including the film's diegesis, the videos, Georges's television broadcast, and Georges's dream-images: "The absence of music from all of these images helps to unify them: They all belong to a single world." Ibid., 165.

84. Another scene from *Benny's Video* stages a juxtaposition along these lines, when Benny uses his school choir's stirring rendition of Johann Sebastian Bach's "Trotz dem alten Drachen," from *Jesu meine Freude*, as a setting for the collection of cash and prescription drugs as part of his pyramid scheme.

85. Again, Haneke's use of music in *Code inconnu* also ties directly to the theme of miscommunication, with music standing in as a form of exchange that escapes the inherent constraints of language yet in itself does not offer any comparable system of signification, as Haneke points out in an interview: "Nonverbal communication is often more intense than language with its plethora of meanings. Communication is more immediated in music and sex. But they are also full of potential misunderstandings." Haneke, "We Live in a Permanent State of War," 23.

86. Peter Brunette offers an alternative interpretation of this use of drumming, connecting it to the film's thematic concerns as follows: "Through the use of

drums, Haneke seems to be suggesting that the only real communication possible in a multicultural context such as contemporary urban French society is through the visceral and nonverbal." Brunette, *Michael Haneke*, 78.

87. Haneke, "Interview with Michael Haneke: 'The Fragmentation of the Look,'" 139–40.

88. Deleuze, *Cinema 2*, 97.

Chapter 4

1. Haneke, "Beyond Mainstream Film," 165.

2. Stam, "Introduction: The Theory and Practice of Adaptation," 8.

3. Haneke, "Interview: Michael Haneke, the Bearded Prophet."

4. Haneke, "World That Is Known," 589.

5. Indeed, a number of analyses of *La pianiste*—as well as of Haneke's television adaptations—have been written in this specific vein. Willy Riemer offers the most thorough account of the textual differences between Jelinek's novel and Haneke's film, while Fatima Naqvi and Christophe Koné focus on specific changes Haneke made to the source narrative and its central character Erika, although the authors are careful to note from the outset that the film suffered less from comparisons to the novel than most adaptations: "[Critics'] reactions, on the whole, lent testimony to the maturity of the discourse surrounding films based on literary predecessors, in that few were interested in the film's supposed 'fidelity' to the original novel's contents." See Riemer, "Michael Haneke, *The Piano Teacher*," 273–75; Naqvi and Koné, "Key to Voyeurism," 127.

In the case of Haneke's television adaptations, analyses have generally stressed the adaptations' close adherence to the narrative events and dialogue of the literary texts, with few exceptions. For detailed textual comparisons between the television adaptations and their sources, see the following: Holmes, "Early Haneke," 117–28; Holmes, "Literature on the Small Screen," 107–122; Naqvi, "Melancholy Labor of Love," 205–22; and Riemer, "Tracing K," 129–38.

6. Schröter, "Discourses and Models," 6 (italics added). To further complicate these reflections: Schröter implies in a different essay that not only does the notion of a homogenous medium presuppose a concept of intermediality, but intermediality in turn presupposes the existence of "'pure media' (a notion which seems to be implied by 'intermediality', otherwise one would not know between what entities the 'inter' takes place)." Schröter, "Politics of Intermediality," 107.

7. Bellour, "Unattainable Text," 21–22.

8. Ibid., 25.

9. Ibid., 26.

10. Carroll, "Forget the Medium!," 3. It should be clear that Carroll's definition of the medium is in no way the one that I'm putting forward here. It may be noted, though, that in his essay Carroll in fact affirms much of what I have stated already about intermediality, arguing that media are rarely composed of homogeneous material or substances: "artforms generally involve a number of media, including frequently overlapping ones." Ibid., 5. However, the ambiguity, variability, and heterogeneity that inform my definition of mediality become, in Carroll's view, reasons for "discourag[ing] us from relying on the notion of the medium as a theoretically useful concept." Ibid., 6.

11. Voigst-Virchow, "Metadaptation: Adaptation and Intermediality," 147.

12. Cavell, *World Viewed*, 36.
13. Deleuze, *Cinema 1*, 141.
14. Rodowick, *Virtual Life of Film*, 22.
15. Deleuze, *Cinema 2*, 251 (square brackets in original). The affinities between Deleuze's film theory and that of Andrei Tarkovsky are quite apparent in this formulation. Tarkovsky's ideas in *Sculpting in Time* (1986) regarding the poetic aspect of cinematic art are laid out in a very similar fashion to Deleuze's concept of the alternate "logic" of utterables: "But film material can be joined together in another way, which works above all to lay open the logic of a person's thought. This is the rationale that will dictate the sequence of events, and the editing which forms them into a whole. The birth and development of thought are subject to laws of their own, and sometimes demand forms of expression which are quite different from the patterns of logical speculation. In my view poetic reasoning is closer to the laws by which thought develops, and thus to life itself, than is the logic of traditional drama." Tarkovsky, *Sculpting in Time*, 19–20.
16. Deleuze, "Brain is the Screen," 286.
17. Stam, "Introduction: The Theory and Practice of Adaptation," 46.
18. It is as though adaptation studies were seeking to replace the idea of a staid and dutiful avowal of fealty to the source with that of an adventurous and passionate *affair de coeur* (an "infidelity model"?), but in the process moved the discipline no closer to a state of analytical or conceptual rigor.
19. Bazin, "*Le Journal d'un curé*," 126.
20. Ibid., 128.
21. Ibid., 133.
22. Ibid., 136.
23. Ibid., 142.
24. Ibid., 143. In the preface to *Difference and Repetition*, Deleuze similarly perceives in Jorge Luis Borges's short story, which he quotes, an affirmation of the fact that repetition and difference are not mutually exclusive but rather covalent powers: "In this case, the most exact, the most strict repetition has as its correlate the maximum of difference ('The text of Cervantes and that of Menard are verbally identical, but the second is almost infinitely richer . . .')." Deleuze, *Difference and Repetition*, xxii.
25. Bazin, "Adaptation, or the Cinema as Digest," 42.
26. Ibid. Bazin asserts, in the final sentence of the essay, that "Malraux made his film of *Man's Hope* before he wrote the novel of the same title, but he was carrying the work inside himself all along." Ibid., 50. However, it should be noted that all other references to the film's production state that the novel was in fact published a year previous to the beginning of production on the film in 1938—see, for example, the biographical timeline on the following website: "Biographie détaillée," accessed January 12, 2017, Malraux.org, http://www.malraux.org/biographie/biographie-detaillee/. Bazin's point—the fact that the literary form of a narrative need not chronologically or conceptually precede the cinematic form—is certainly not invalidated by this seeming error, though, and its application extends beyond those literary works and films created by a single individual. An oft-cited example in adaptation studies is the existence of novelizations of many works of film, some of which are considered to match or even exceed the artistic merit of the films themselves—playwright David Rabe's novelization of

Sean Penn's *The Crossing Guard* (1991), for instance, or Isaac Asimov's novelization of Richard Fleisher's 1966 film *Fantastic Voyage*. In the latter case, the cover of Asimov's novel directly announces the story's convoluted authorial provenance: "Based on a screenplay by Harry Kleiner. Adaptation by David Duncan. Based on a story by Otto Klement and Jay Lewis Bixby."

27. Ibid., 43–44.

28. Ibid., 44. The similarities between Bazin's characterization of radio and Haneke's of television are apparent. Indeed, television is a vococentric broadcast medium, and as such is much more closely related to radio than to cinema, as Michel Chion avers: "Television is fundamentally a kind of radio, 'illustrated' by images. Television sound already has its established place, which is fundamental and mandatory (silent television is inconceivable, unlike cinema)." Chion, *Audio-Vision*, 165.

29. Quoted in Bazin, "Adaptation, or the Cinema as Digest," 49.

30. Ibid., 50.

31. Gaudreault and Marion, "Transécriture and Narrative Mediatics," 65.

32. Ibid., 62. Gaudreault and Marion's rereading of Formalism thus privileges voice as the principle mediator of any given narrative *fabula*. This notion of voice as the irreducible—and to some extent inescapable—component of a story is deeply relevant to my own approach to voice as a narrative intermedium common to literature and film, as will be further developed in the two sections that follow.

33. Ibid., 67.

34. Ibid., 68.

35. Bazin also identified an author who could be considered effectively unadaptable, referring to "those never-ending 'adaptations' of Balzac, which seem to have more than amply demonstrated that the author of *The Human Comedy* is the least 'cinematic' of all novelists." Bazin, "Adaptation, or the Cinema as Digest," 43. Given the significant stylistic and narrative differences between Proust and Balzac, further investigation into the "noncinematic" qualities of the latter would be highly interesting.

36. Guattari, "Project for a Film," 152.

37. Genosko, "Guattari TV, By Kafka," 211.

38. Ibid., 222.

39. Ibid., 212. Expanding on this notion of television as subjectification machine, Genosko notes that Guattari perceived the television viewer—including himself—not as a subject but as an interstice between television's vivid intensities and the viewer's own phantasms and modes of desire, both of which attain mutual expression via television's incessant technospiritual refrain: "Guattari is no more than a 'fluctuating intersection' or constellation of relatively heterogeneous components, and inchoate affects, held in place by a stabilizing, existentializing refrain, which is a non-ordinary, nonsemiotic, repetitive motif (a hypnotic feature), holding together different kinds of worlds (marked existential territories and universes of reference whose emergence refrains catalyse)." Ibid., 221.

40. Guattari, "Project for a Film," 152.

41. Ibid., 151. Diverse images and motifs derived from Kafka's work are employed to this end, but sparingly and in combination with Kafkaesque elements not identifiable as the author's invention. Examining Guattari's unfinished

draft screenplay, for instance, one finds that most of the program was to have taken place with a gray wall alternating as the foreground or backdrop for the visuals, while the sound track would have consisted, in the first scenes, of "rapidly flowing speech" (identified as a confession by Karl Rudels during the Moscow trials) that gradually "transforms itself into muffled music," and subsequently "transforms itself very progressively into the whistling of the wind which in turn will extinguish in reaching a perfect silence." Ibid., 157. At another point, the image dissipates and gives way to a white screen, accompanied by the sound of "the projector in which the film stock is cut." Ibid., 159.

42. Genosko, "Guattari TV, By Kafka," 219.

43. I would argue that theater was repurposed, along with the epic, in the development of novelistic discourse. The novel utilizes dialogue for very different effects than did the epic, and certainly many of these effects are comparable to those of dramatic theater. Thus, although Mikhail Bakhtin characterizes his concepts of dialogism and polyphony as new developments particular to Dostoyevskian novelistic discourse, having only had their "earliest budding" in Shakespeare, from a media studies perspective one could attribute to Dostoyevsky's long and involved passages of dialogue a pseudotheatrical "staging" of polyphonic discourse. See Bakhtin, *Problems of Dostoevsky's Poetics*, 33–34.

44. Adorno, "Transparencies on Film," 200.

45. See Riemer, "Michael Haneke, *The Piano Teacher*," 274.

46. See Holmes, "Literature on the Small Screen," 116.

47. Haneke, "Beyond Mainstream Film," 165.

48. Holmes, "Early Haneke," 119.

49. Ibid., 118.

50. This assessment also preceded *La pianiste*, but Haneke tends not to refer to the theatrical feature in the same terms as his television films, as previously noted.

51. The acceptance and increasing popularity of audiobooks as a literary medium is one indicator of the idea that written and recorded manifestations of voice share a common medium. One should also consider the fact that, as scholars such as Alberto Manguel have pointed out, the phenomenon of "silent reading" was unknown for much of the history of Western literacy. Before this, it was common for scholars to read scrolls and even, in the Middle Ages, early codices aloud, vocalizing the texts purely for their own benefit, an actual voice being considered a necessary medium for the act of reading. See Manguel, *A History of Reading*, 41–53.

Speaking from personal experience, I am often struck—sometimes distractingly so—by the seeming paradox of silent reading, which lies in the fact that I mentally "hear" the voices of the narrator and characters at a rate corresponding to spoken communication, in the tones and rhythms of human speech. However, in the act of silently reading the text I am absorbing the words at a speed greatly exceeding the rate of normal human speech. Voice is thus made internally manifest, for me as reader, even though in the time frame of silent reading vocalization itself would seem to be impossible.

52. In this sense, it would be possible to consider *Das Weiße Band*, an original narrative conceived by Haneke, as falling within the genre category of "adaptation" even though it has no actual literary source. The film's extensive use of voice-over—which, in this case, is spoken by the schoolteacher as an old man

(Ernst Jacobi) reflecting back on the events that transpired in 1913 and 1914—adds an additional level of vocal narration that is distanced from the action and thus corresponds to a "literary" narrational voice. This impression has been pointed out by many critics; for instance, Ian Johnston writes that "Haneke's screenplay gives every impression of being the adaptation of some little-known German novel from the early years of the last century. It's a tremendous act of artistic ventriloquy, and Haneke has spoken of how he took Theodor Fontane, the late-nineteenth-century social realist novelist, as a conscious model." Johnston, "Children are Watching You," *Bright Lights*. Thus, the voice-over narration of *Das Weiße Band* performs a stylistic function as well as a narrative one; while not technically an adaptation, the film utilizes the *genre* of adaptation as a medium of expression.

53. Dolar, *Voice and Nothing More*, 73 (italics in original).

54. Ibid., 191n.

55. Ibid., 121.

56. Chion, *Voice in Cinema*, 12.

57. Ibid., 125.

58. Ibid., 51, 54 (italics in original).

59. Chion, *Audio-Vision*, 172.

60. Ibid.

61. It is significant that both Chion and Dolar refer to the voice of the mother as a basis for the I- or object voice's mediating power. The former remarks that "[t]he very first image presenter is the mother; before the child learns any written signs, her voice articulates things in a human and linear temporality. In every master of ceremonies and storyteller as well as every movie voiceover, an aspect of this original function remains." Chion, *Voice in Cinema*, 49. Chion also refers in this study to the Lacanian theorist Denis Vasse's text *The Umbilicus and the Voice* and its assertion that in the immediate wake of the severing of umbilical connection "bodily contact with the mother becomes mediated by the voice." Ibid., 61. Dolar evokes exactly this concept as well, asking the following: "And is not the mother's voice the first problematic connection to the other, the immaterial tie that comes to replace the umbilical cord, and shapes much of the fate of the earliest stages of life?" Dolar, *Voice and Nothing More*, 39. Interestingly, Dolar also refers at length to Chion, and in particular to the latter's highly evocative reading of the voice of Norman's mother in *Psycho*. Ibid., 65–66. It is as though the two are engaged in a common project in separate disciplines: that of giving voice to the concept of the voice itself.

62. Holmes, "Early Haneke," 120. Holmes does not include Haneke's adaptation of Peter Rosei's *Wer war Edgar Allen?* among the films she examines. Being that this film lacks voice-over and has little or no exposure or video distribution, I will similarly not be attending to it in this chapter.

63. Ibid., 119.

64. Chion, *Voice in Cinema*, 55 (italics in original).

65. If one took a properly historiological approach to voice as a medium unto itself, one would surely have to contend with the fact that narrational voice in the form of oral storytelling predates any form of what could be defined as literature by a significant, and in fact unknowable, length of time. Audible vocalization, then—captured in the recording and transmission of speech in media such as

radio, sound recordings, cinema, and television—could arguably be considered to have stronger affinities with "textual voice" as a mode of storytelling than with literature itself.

66. Holmes, "Early Haneke," 124.

67. Ibid., 124–25.

68. Naqvi, "Melancholy Labor of Love," 219.

69. Rodowick, *Gilles Deleuze's Time Machine*, 102.

70. Ibid., 103.

71. The technique of intentionally relaying many or even most of the narrative's events via voice-over without any accompanying visual referents is not unknown. One particularly pertinent example of this technique may be found in Rainer Werner Fassbinder's adaptation of Theodor Fontane's *Effi Briest* (1974). In this film, the voice-over narrator (Fassbinder himself) at points describes key events from the narrative while the film's image track registers only seemingly mundane actions, such as the titular character lounging on an outdoor swing. Fassbinder, *Effi Briest*.

72. Riemer, "Tracing K," 131–32.

73. Haneke, "Beyond Mainstream Film," 166.

74. Ibid.

75. Holmes, "Literature on the Small Screen," 116. *Das Schloß* retains certain elements of the surreal through on-screen performance as well; in particular, the roles of K.'s two assistants Artur (Frank Giering) and Jeremias (Felix Eitner) are so broadly and farcically interpreted that they are almost totally out of step with the naturalistic and reserved performances of the other actors. The pair almost seem to be characters from a different film, like the pair of boys in *Funny Games* (one of whom, "Peter," was also played by Giering).

76. Ibid.

77. In fact, the text lacks quotation marks almost entirely, and the characters' utterances are distanced by the narratorial voice, which consistently speaks for the characters rather than letting them speak for themselves. Each act of personal expression, which the film melodramatically stages as having tragic or romantic emotional resonance (however ambiguous its presentation) is, in the novel, undercut by the vocal distance—and the relentless cynicism—of the authorial voice.

78. Saxton, "Close Encounters," 100.

79. Haneke, "Interview: Michael Haneke, the Bearded Prophet." It should be noted that Haneke's literary adaptations for television also function, albeit to a lesser extent than *La pianiste*, as subversions of conventional—and distinctly German—genre films. Deborah Holmes remarks that "*Das Schloß* can be seen as a kind of 'anti-Heimatfilm,' complete with ubiquitous folk music, either badly played or canned, and a stifling village community." *Heimatfilme* constituted a popular film genre dating from the 1940s and 1950s that focused on sentimental and idealized portrayals of rural life, and it later became a staple of German television. *Das Weiße Band* could also be considered in many respects a subversion of *Heimatfilm*. Holmes continues, "Similarly, critical parallels can be drawn between *Die Rebellion* and the Habsburg nostalgia films of the 1950s," noting particularly a growing resemblance of the lead character Andreas to Emperor Franz Josef as the film progresses and his circumstances become more squalid and depressed. Holmes, "Literature on the Small Screen," 122.

80. Seeßlen, "Structures of Glaciation," 324.

81. Ibid. One could perceive the film as "melodramatic" in the strictly literal sense, though, as the term etymologically means "music and drama." While music is used to enrich and reinforce the emotional texture of the narrative in traditional melodrama, however, in *La pianiste*—as I shall discuss in greater detail further down—the music is juxtaposed against the imagery ambiguously, neither consistently lending the imagery dramatic or emotional leverage, nor providing a consistent sense of ironic counterpoint.

82. Jelinek, *The Piano Teacher*, 71–72.

83. Saxton, "Close Encounters," 97, 99.

84. Erika does experience moments of reprieve from this visually claustrophobic environment, the first arriving when she flees onto the ice rink herself after being confronted by Klemmer's devastating verbal assault, with her figure temporarily occupying a field of pure white; her ambiguous visual liberation occurs again at the end of the film, when she walks out of field after leaving recital hall following her aborted revenge on Klemmer, the camera unwilling or unable to track her.

85. See Riemer, "Tracing K," 134.

86. Grundmann, "Introduction: Haneke's Anachronism," 32.

87. In his interview with Christopher Sharrett, Haneke is asked about his use of the French language in an Austrian setting, but his reply addresses only the practical motivations behind this choice: "This is to accommodate the producers and actors. My principal source of support has come from France, and my casts have been largely French." Haneke, "World That Is Known," 589.

88. Bazin, "*Le Journal d'un curé*," 138.

89. Chion, *Voice in Cinema*, 129.

90. The foregrounding of setting in *La pianiste* sets it apart from Haneke's other features, which tend to convey a sense of ambiguity with regard to place. For example, Haneke decided to set *Der siebente Kontinent* in Linz even though it was filmed in Vienna, explaining to Serge Toubiana in their video interview that he made this decision "because I wanted [the setting] to remain completely neutral. I didn't want to have elements that were typically Viennese, because I really think that the film must look like it could take place anywhere. . . . In my films I always try . . . to be specific without being local." Haneke, "Toubiana Interview," *Piano Teacher* DVD. *La pianiste* (and also, perhaps, much of *Code inconnu*, in which Paris itself plays a role in the exploration of communication breakdowns) presents a clear exception to this approach.

91. Haneke, "World That Is Known," 584.

92. Ibid. *Die Winterreise* is a cycle of twenty-four songs for piano and voice, each of which is a setting for a different poem by Wilhelm Müller. The seventeenth song, "Im Dorfe" ("In the Village")—as well as a portion of the eighteenth song, "Der stürmische Morgen" ("The Stormy Morning")—is performed several times in the film by Erika's acutely nervous student Anna Schober and a student tenor. The lyrics of the piece describe a lone traveler who reflects on his own solitude and restlessness as he passes through a sleeping village, a situation seemingly intended to reflect Erika's own state of alienation. This association is made clear through the use of the song in the film, where Erika speaks part of the lyrics during a lesson with Anna, and the first time we hear them sung on the sound

track the music accompanies an image of Erika viewing a pornographic video in a booth at a sex store, sniffing a tissue left behind by a previous male occupant.

93. Riemer, "Michael Haneke, *The Piano Teacher*," 278.

94. This disposition is also hinted at within the film, as Erika tells Anna during practice that the mood of Schubert's "Im Dorfe" "switches to irony" at the point when the traveler dismisses the peaceful existence of the villagers ("So what, so what? / They've had their pleasure"), adding that this attitude reflects "the obstinacy of the complacent middle class." One could interpret this scene as invoking yet another level of irony, as Erika could be understood as commenting on her own attitude, or on the attitudes of her patrons.

95. Sharrett, "Michael Haneke and the Discontents," 209.

96. Ma, "Discordant Desires, Violent Regrains," 512.

97. Grundmann, "Introduction: Haneke's Anachronism," 31.

98. As with the rewind scene and Paul's address to the camera in *Funny Games*, this fracture of Erika's composed visage seems to be at least partially a counter-spectacle intended as a reprimand to the viewer. The character's withholding of emotion throughout the film—in spite of the director's use of frequent close-up shots and staging of pseudomelodramatic scenarios that almost demand an affective payoff—is no longer possible, but instead of transportations into joy or tenderness, or even tragic catharsis, we are offered only squalid despair and unrelieved emotional and physical torture.

99. Schröter, "Discourses and Models," 3.

Chapter 5

1. Arthur, "Endgame," 28.

2. Saxton, "Secrets and Revelations," 10.

3. I previously noted this fact in connection to Haneke's original conception of the plot of *Der siebente Kontinent*, in which the events of the film took place entirely in the form of flashbacks by the dying Georg. Haneke told Serge Toubiana in their interview that this story structure was abandoned for exactly the reasons cited here by Saxton. Haneke, "Toubiana Interview," *Seventh Continent* DVD.

4. *La pianiste*, which Haneke made several years before *Caché*, also featured on-screen violence and nudity during Klemmer's attack on Erika. One could suggest, following this line of inquiry, that Haneke similarly incorporates a departure from realism into *La pianiste*, though to a lesser extent than in *Caché*: the scene represents both the harrowing "realization" of Erika's masochistic fantasies and the climax of the film's dark parody of melodramatic narrative. It is also notable that the story in this case does not originate with Haneke himself but is adapted from Jelinek's novel.

5. Haneke, "Toubiana Interview," *Caché* DVD.

6. In *Michael Haneke's Cinema: The Ethic of the Image*, Catherine Wheatley titles the chapter on *Caché* "Guilt and Shame," observing, as I do in this chapter, the distinction between these two phenomena and the presence of both in the film. I wish to note that my approach to the film was developed before her text was published, and hence was not influenced by her reading of the film.

7. Williams, *Shame and Necessity*, 92.

8. Ibid., 222. Christopher Cordner points out the fact that for Williams guilt is associated exclusively with action, while shame derives from and refers to

self-image only: "Shame directs us back to a sense of ourselves, while guilt directs us outwards towards the impact on others of what we have done." Cordner, "Guilt, Remorse, and Victims," 442. This important distinction also appears in the cognitive-psychological approach of Melvin Lansky, whose "incompatible idea model . . . keeps a firm focus on the balance between what one *is* (or is exposed as being) and what one *does* or *fails to do*. Such a perspective gives us a splendid balance between moral judgments that involve shame and those that involve guilt." Lansky, "Hidden Shame," 872.

9. Williams, *Shame and Necessity*, 89.

10. Ibid., 82, 84.

11. See Lansky, "Hidden Shame," 875.

12. Freud, *Three Essays on Sexuality*, 23.

13. Ibid., 44.

14. Ibid., 35.

15. Ibid., 33.

16. Ibid., 23.

17. Sartre, *Being and Nothingness*, 259.

18. Ibid., 260.

19. Ibid., 261.

20. Ibid., 269.

21. Ibid., 273.

22. Miller, "On Shame," 13.

23. Williams, *Shame and Necessity*, 89.

24. Miller, "On Shame," 13. Miller's strict opposition of modesty to shamelessness could be considered somewhat overdetermined, given that modesty is not necessarily a direct manifestation of shame. Yet the terminology employed here is necessary given the fact that, as Lansky points out, "[t]he English language lacks the distinction readily drawn in many languages between the affective state itself (e.g., French *honte*) and behavior or comportment that obviates the danger of the affect (in French, *pudeur*, something like modesty or the obverse of shamelessness)." Lansky, "Hidden Shame," 866.

25. Miller, "On Shame," 15, 25.

26. Ibid., 26.

27. Ibid.

28. Agamben, *Idea of Prose*, 85.

29. Agamben, *Remnants of Auschwitz*, 107.

30. Ibid., 103. Agamben here argues that shame compels us to confront history not as a "chain of events" but rather—as it is for Walter Benjamin's angel in "Theses on the Philosophy of History" (1940)—as "one single catastrophe which keeps piling wreckage upon wreckage." Benjamin, "Theses on the Philosophy," 257. The event remains immediate to us and lacking any temporal distantiation; it is continually unfolding, but never recedes, and shame is one of the primary affective avenues for our intuition of this Bergsonian dimensionality.

31. Levinas, *On Escape*, 63.

32. Ibid., 64. Deleuze's analysis of shame in his essay "The Shame and the Glory: T.E. Lawrence" is markedly similar to Levinas's ontological definition: "[Lawrence] has shame because he thinks the mind, though distinct, is inseparable from the body; the two are irremediably linked. In this sense, the body is

not even a means or a vehicle for the mind, but rather a 'molecular sludge' that adheres to all the mind's actions. When we act, the body lets itself be forgotten. But when it is reduced to a state of sludge, on the contrary, one has the strange feeling that it finally makes itself visible and attains its ultimate aim." Deleuze, "The Shame and the Glory," 123. It is in this state of abjection that the self "attains" shame as an affect, as though shame were a quality of matter that is passed, like an infection, from material reality itself to the body's deepest faculties for self-perception.

33. Levinas, *On Escape*, 67.

34. Ibid., 68. John Llewelyn clarifies this unusual tautological definition of nausea in terms of a lapse by the subject into a form of existence that precedes knowledge: "In the sickness of nausea there is not knowledge, reflective or pre-reflective, of one's state. One is not in a state. Not yet. As yet there is nothing to constate. There is only the pure there is, the pure being of being oneself." Llewelyn, *Emmanuel Levinas*, 19. Bettina Bergo, however, goes further still, arguing that these definitions of shame and nausea were facets of an ontological inquiry that Levinas abandoned and left ultimately undefined: "Levinas' attunements of shame and nausea 'give' us Being as seamless, untranscendable, and neuter." Bergo, "Ontology, Transcendence, and Immanence," 145.

35. Levinas, *On Escape*, 83n.

36. While it remains outside of the parameters of this study, one can also infer an evolutionary dimension of the shame experience, as Peter Sloterdijk does in his reading of prehistoric communities as localized media networks or assemblages: "[T]hese early human groups were already pure mediamatic formations. This was the case even in archaic 'shame cultures,' where the individual suffered from the exposure of his affect and wanted to conceal his interiority. It seems likely that the affect of shame is itself an evolutionary sedimentation, produced by the impossibility of hiding one's interiority from the penetrating empathetic gaze of others." Sloterdijk, "*Actio in Distans*," 639.

37. Williams, *Shame and Necessity*, 89.

38. Haneke, "Collective Guilt," 50.

39. Ibid.

40. Max Silverman significantly connects the bloodstains depicted in the film with the image of the Algerian and its connection to blood sacrifice in the collective French psyche, as identified by Frantz Fanon in *The Wretched of the Earth*. See Silverman, "The Empire Looks Back," 245.

41. Arendt, "Personal Responsibility Under Dictatorship," 21.

42. Agamben, *Remnants of Auschwitz*, 95.

43. Miller, "On Shame," 15.

44. Although *Caché* was shot on high-definition video, I use the term "film-camera" to refer to the camera used to shoot the film, while the camera that produces the videotapes within the film is referred to as the "*voyeur*-camera," "video camera," or "surveillance camera." Following this, the images received by Georges will be consistently referred to as "videos," and *Caché* itself as the "film."

45. Saxton, "Secrets and Revelations," 7.

46. Ibid., 8.

47. Deleuze, *Cinema 1*, 13.

48. Ibid., 16.

49. Deleuze, *Bergsonism*, 56–57. We ought to recall that Deleuze's concept of the cinematic time-image is in large part derived from this Bergsonian concept of the ontological disposition of time relative to actuality and virtuality. Deleuze's "time crystals"—which render actuality and virtuality indiscernible and exchangeable according to this temporal relation—will be discussed in the section that follows.

50. Rodowick, *Gilles Deleuze's Time Machine*, 99.

51. Žižek, *How to Read Lacan*, 84.

52. Wheatley, "Spectator as Moral Agent," 68.

53. Saxton, "Secrets and Revelations," 14.

54. Ibid., 12. The apparent impossibility of the video camera's existence within the diegesis—for instance, in Majid's apartment during Georges's initial visit—cannot be confirmed, and it appears to have been Haneke's intention to leave the notion of whether or not a camera is present ambiguous. In one interview, then, Haneke denies that there could be no camera in Majid's apartment, but also states that the fact of its presence does not implicate any agent: "If you could search the frame, you would see that a little camera has been placed there, against that wall, hidden right in the middle of all the clutter. A camera put there by anybody. But it's there! You could even think that the whole suicide is also a trick!" Haneke, "Interview with Michael Haneke: You Never Show Reality," 151. Haneke thus remains concerned with asserting his adherence to strict representational realism even as he points out the highly ambiguous status of the imagery itself relative to reality.

55. Deleuze, *Cinema 1*, 17.

56. Saxton, "Secrets and Revelations," 12. Saxton does not herself subscribe to this view of Haneke as tormentor; rather, she draws attention to its assertion by other scholars before proceeding to push her own interpretation further, while acknowledging the fact that "[o]n one level, the logic of such a reading is irrefutable." Ibid., 13.

57. Walter Benjamin's comments on the film actor's lack of aura in "The Work of Art in the Age of Mechanical Reproduction" are pertinent to this idea of self-estrangement and the neutering of shame: "The feeling of strangeness that overcomes the actor before the camera, as Pirandello describes it, is basically of the same kind as the estrangement felt before one's own image in the mirror. But now the reflected image has become separable, transportable. And where is it transported? Before the public. Never for a moment does the screen actor cease to be conscious of this fact." Benjamin, "Work of Art," 230–31. This nonpresence of the film actor to the audience and to him- or herself becomes a common condition of existence as human interaction and self-image are increasingly mediated and determined by video, photography, and other forms of digital reproduction.

58. Sartre, *Being and Nothingness*, 269.

59. Deleuze, "Letter to Serge Daney," 76.

60. Deleuze, *Cinema 2*, 101, 76.

61. Ibid., 79.

62. Ibid., 77.

63. Ibid., 102.

64. Ibid., 81.

65. Ibid., 81–82 (square brackets in original).

66. Borges, "Garden of the Forking Paths," 124.
67. Haneke, "Toubiana Interview," *Caché* DVD.
68. Deleuze, *Cinema 2*, 79.
69. Haneke, "Collective Guilt," 50; Grundmann, "Auteur de Force," 14.
70. Levinas, *On Escape*, 67.
71. Chion, *Voice in Cinema*, 77.
72. Deleuze, *Cinema 2*, 68.
73. Levinas, *On Escape*, 83n.
74. Deleuze, "The Actual and the Virtual," 151.
75. Deleuze, *Cinema 2*, 97. One might also cite the fact that Walter Benjamin, in *The Arcades Project*, advocates the application of the cinematic principle of montage to historical research, using such means "to discover in the analysis of the small individual moment the crystal of the total event. And, therefore, to break with vulgar historical naturalism." Benjamin, *The Arcades Project*, 461. As in Deleuze's philosophy, Benjamin's conception seriously considers the possibility of perceiving each individual moment of time as a facet of the crystalline structure of the event as a universal temporal singularity—the "total event."
76. Deleuze, *Logic of Sense*, 12.
77. Ibid.
78. One could also once again note, in this regard, Baudrillard's idea of advertising and television as presenting an exchange of gazes that is reminiscent of the actual-virtual exchange the time-crystal instantiates: "These billboards, in fact, observe and surveil you as well, or as badly, as the 'policing' television. The latter looks at you, you look at yourself in it, mixed with the other, it is the mirror without silvering (*tain*) in the activity of consumption, a game of splitting in two and doubling that closes this world on itself." Baudrillard, *Simulacra and Simulation*, 76.
79. Deleuze, *Cinema 2*, 165–66. And what better institutional arbiter of shame could be conceived of than the Catholic Church?

Conclusion

1. Deleuze, *Cinema 2*, 76.
2. Rodowick, *Gilles Deleuze's Time Machine*, 172.
3. Deleuze and Parnet, *Dialogues*, 55.
4. Ibid.
5. It should be specified that these potentialized and emergent perceptual and affective modes need not be defined solely in terms of human subjective experience, and instead enable all manner of non-human becomings: becoming-media, becoming-machine, or becoming-animal. Jussi Parikka's highly interesting text *Insect Media*, which employs the philosophy of Deleuze and Guattari throughout, thus uses the figure of the swarm to dedifferentiate affective and biological-architectural phenomena: "The swarm is a becoming that expresses potentialities that are always situated and yet moving. The affects that trigger the swarming and the birth of the new collective are related to communication in Maeterlinck's view. This mode of communication happens not on the level of consciousness, human language and concepts, but as affects of murmur, whisper, and a refrain that even the bees might not hear but sense in some uncanny way." Parikka, *Insect Media*, 49–50.

6. Deleuze, *Logic of Sense*, 164–65.

7. Weber, *Mass Mediauras*, 7 (italics in original).

8. There are a couple of significant scenes in which noncinematic media factor into the diegesis, however, including one in which the girl Eva encounters some photographs, upon which the camera lingers in close-up, and another in which she listens to a recording of Beethoven's "Sonata for Piano and Violin No. 5, Op. 24 in F Major" on a portable cassette player. The owner of this device shows Eva how they must rewind the tape by hand to conserve battery power, a gesture that serves to underscore the centrality of the film's speculations regarding the conditions of life in a world in which media technology has largely ceased functioning.

9. Haneke, "You Never Show Reality," 148.

10. Quoted in Wheatley, *Michael Haneke's Cinema*, 145.

11. Deleuze, *Cinema 2*, 167.

BIBLIOGRAPHY

Adorno, Theodor. "Transparencies on Film." Translated by Thomas Y. Levin. Special issue, *New German Critique* no. 24/25 (1981–82): 199–205.

Agamben, Giorgio. *The End of the Poem: Studies in Poetics.* Translated by Daniel Heller-Roazen. Stanford: Stanford University Press, 1999.

———. *Idea of Prose.* Translated by Michael Sullivan and Sam Whitsitt. Albany: State University of New York Press, 1995.

———. *Remnants of Auschwitz: The Witness and the Archive.* Translated by Daniel Heller-Roazen. New York: Zone Books, 2002.

Arendt, Hannah. "Personal Responsibility Under Dictatorship." In *Responsibility and Judgment*, edited by Jerome Kohn, 7–48. New York: Schocken Books, 2003.

Arthur, Paul. "Endgame." *Film Comment* 41, no. 6 (2005): 24–28.

Augé, Marc. *Non-Places: Introduction to an Anthropology of Supermodernity.* Translated by John Howe. London: Verso, 1995.

Bakhtin, Mikhail. *Problems of Dostoevsky's Poetics.* Edited and translated by Caryl Emerson. Minneapolis: University of Minnesota Press, 1984.

Barthes, Roland. *Image-Music-Text.* Translated by Stephen Heath. New York: Noonday Press, 1977.

———. "The Photographic Message." In Barthes, *Image-Music-Text*, 15–31.

———. "Rhetoric of the Image." In Barthes, *Image-Music-Text*, 32–51.

Baudrillard, Jean. "Foreword: Poetic Transference of Situation." In *L'Autre*, by Luc Delahaye, 1–4. Translated by Chris Turner. London: Phaidon Press, 1999.

———. *Simulacra and Simulation.* Translated by Sheila Faria Glaser. Ann Arbor: University of Michigan Press, 1994.

Bazin, André. "Adaptation, or the Cinema as Digest." Translated by Alain Piette and Bert Cardullo. In *Bazin at Work: Major Essays & Reviews from the Forties & Fifties*, edited by Bert Cardullo, 41–51. New York: Routledge, 1997.

———. "Cinematic Realism and the Italian School of the Liberation." In *What is Cinema?*, translated by Timothy Barnard, 215–49. Montreal: Caboose, 2009.

———. "Death Every Afternoon." Translated by Mark A. Cohen. In *Rites of Realism: Essays on Corporeal Cinema*, edited by Ivone Margulies, 27–31. Durham, N.C.: Duke University Press, 2003.

———. "*Le Journal d'un curé de campagne* and the Stylistics of Robert Bresson." In Bazin, *What is Cinema?*, 125–43.

———. "The Ontology of the Photographic Image." In Bazin, *What is Cinema?*, 9–16.

———. *What is Cinema?*, Volume 1. Translated and edited by Hugh Gray. Berkeley: University of California Press, 2005.

Bellour, Raymond. "Concerning the Photographic." Translated by Chris Darke. In *Still/Moving: Between Cinema and Photography*, edited by Karen Beckman and Jean Ma, 253–76. Durham, N.C.: Duke University Press, 2008.

———. "The Pensive Spectator." Translated by Lynne Kirby. *Wide Angle* 9, no. 1 (1987): 6–10.

———. "The Unattainable Text." Translated by Ben Brewster. *Screen* 16, no. 3 (1975): 19–27.

Benjamin, Walter. *The Arcades Project*. Translated by Howard Eiland and Kevin McLaughlin. Cambridge, Mass.: The Belknap Press of Harvard University Press, 1999.

———. *Illuminations*. Edited by Hannah Arendt, translated by Harry Zohn. New York: Schocken Books, 1968.

———. "The Storyteller: Reflections on the Works of Nikolai Leskov." In Benjamin, *Illuminations*, 83–109.

———. "Theses on the Philosophy of History." In Benjamin, *Illuminations*, 253–64.

———. "The Work of Art in the Age of Mechanical Reproduction." In Benjamin, *Illuminations*, 217–51.

Bergo, Bettina. "Ontology, Transcendence, and Immanence in Emmanuel Levinas' Philosophy." *Research in Phenomenology* 35, no. 1 (2005): 141–77.

Bergson, Henri. *Matter and Memory*. Translated by N. M. Paul and W. S. Palmer. New York: Cosimo, 2007.

Bingham, Adam. "Life, or something like it: Michael Haneke's *Der siebente Kontinent* (*The Seventh Continent*, 1989)." *Kinoeye* 4, no. 1 (2004). Accessed October 10, 2015. http://www.kinoeye.org/04/01/bingham01_no2.php.

Bolter, Jay David, and Richard Grusin. *Remediation: Understanding New Media*. Cambridge, Mass.: MIT Press, 1999.

Borges, Jorge Luis. "The Garden of the Forking Paths." Translated by Andrew Hurley. In *Collected Fictions*, 119–27. New York: Penguin, 1998.

Breder, Hans, and Klaus-Peter Busse, eds. *Intermedia: Enacting the Liminal*. Dortmund: Dortmunder Schriften zur Kunst, 2005.

Brooks, Mel, dir. *Spaceballs*. DVD. Los Angeles: Fox Video, 2004.

Brunette, Peter. *Michael Haneke*. Urbana: University of Illinois Press, 2010.

Carpenter, Edmund. "The New Languages." In Carpenter and McLuhan, *Explorations in Communication*, 162–79.

Carpenter, Edmund, and Marshall McLuhan, eds. *Explorations in Communication: An Anthology*. Boston: Beacon Press, 1960.

Carroll, Noël. "Forget the Medium!" In *Engaging the Moving Image*, 1–9. New Haven, Conn.: Yale University Press, 2003.

Cavell, Stanley. "The Fact of Television." In *Cavell on Film*, edited by William Rothman, 69–85. Albany: State University of New York Press, 2005.

———. *The World Viewed: Reflections on the Ontology of Film*. Enlarged Edition. Cambridge, Mass.: Harvard University Press, 1979.

Chang, Briankle G., and Garnet C. Butchart, eds. *Philosophy of Communication*. Cambridge, Mass.: MIT Press, 2012.

Chion, Michel. *Audio-Vision: Sound on Screen*. Translated by Claudia Gorbman. New York: Columbia University Press, 1994.

———. *The Voice in Cinema*. Translated by Claudia Gorbman. New York: Columbia University Press, 1999.

———. "Without Music: On *Caché*." Translated by T. Jefferson Kline. In Grundmann, *A Companion to Michael Haneke*, 161–67.

Colman, Felicity. *Deleuze & Cinema: The Film Concepts*. Oxford: Berg, 2011.

Comolli, Jean-Louis. "Machines of the Visible." In *The Cinematic Apparatus*, edited by Teresa de Laurentis and Stephen Heath, 121–42. New York: St. Martin's Press, 1980.

Conley, Tom. "Tracking *Code Unknown*." In Grundmann, *A Companion to Michael Haneke*, 113–23.

Cordner, Christopher. "Guilt, Remorse, and Victims." *Philosophical Investigations* 30, no. 4 (2007): 337–62.

Cronenberg, David, dir. *Videodrome*. DVD. New York: Criterion, 2004.

Deleuze, Gilles. "The Actual and the Virtual." Translated by Eliot Ross Albert. In Deleuze and Claire Parnet, *Dialogues II*, 148–52. New York: Columbia University Press, 2007.

———. *Bergsonism*. Translated by Hugh Tomlinson and Barbara Habberjam. New York: Zone Books, 1988.

———. "The Brain is the Screen." Translated by Ames Hodges and Mike Taormina. Interview by Pascal Bonitzer et al. In *Two Regimes of Madness: Texts and Interviews 1975–1995*, edited by David Lapoujade, 282–91. New York: Semiotext(e), 2006.

———. *Cinema 1: The Movement-Image*. Translated by Hugh Tomlinson and Barbara Habberjam. London: Athlone Press, 1986.

———. *Cinema 2: The Time-Image*. Translated by Hugh Tomlinson and Robert Galeta. London: Athlone Press, 1989.

———. *Difference and Repetition*. Translated by Paul Patton. New York: Columbia University Press, 1994.

———. *Foucault*. Translated by Seán Hand. Minneapolis: University of Minnesota Press, 1988.

———. *Francis Bacon: The Logic of Sensation*. Translated by Daniel W. Smith. London: Continuum, 2003.

———. "Letter to Serge Daney: Optimism, Pessimism, and Travel." In *Negotiations, 1972–1990*, translated by Martin Joughim, 68–79. New York: Columbia University Press, 1995.

———. *The Logic of Sense*. Translated by Mark Lester with Charles Stivale, edited by Constantin V. Boundas. London: Continuum, 2004.

———. "On *Sur et sous la communication*: Three Questions on *Six fois deux*." In *Cahiers du Cinéma*, Vol. 4, *1973–1978: History, Ideology, Cultural Struggle*, edited by David Wilson, 124–31. London: Routledge, 2000.

———. "The Shame and the Glory: T. E. Lawrence." In *Essays Critical and Clinical*, translated by Daniel W. Smith and Michael A. Greco, 115–25. Minneapolis: University of Minnesota Press, 1997.

Deleuze, Gilles, and Michel Foucault. *Gérard Fromanger: Photogenic Painting*. Translated by Dafydd Roberts. London: Black Dog Publishing, 1999.

Deleuze, Gilles, and Félix Guattari. *Anti-Oedipus: Capitalism and Schizophrenia*. Translated by Robert Hurley, Mark Seem, and Helen R. Lane. London: Continuum, 2004.

———. *A Thousand Plateaus: Capitalism and Schizophrenia*. Translated by Brian Massumi. Minneapolis: University of Minnesota Press, 1987.

———. *What is Philosophy?*. Translated by Hugh Tomlinson and Graham Burchell. New York: Columbia University Press, 1994.

Deleuze, Gilles, and Claire Parnet. *Dialogues*. Translated by Hugh Tomlinson and Barbara Habberjam. London: Athlone Press, 1987.

Doane, Mary Ann. "Information, Crisis, Catastrophe." In *Logics of Television: Essays in Cultural Criticism*, edited by Patricia Mellancamp, 222–39. Bloomington: Indiana University Press, 1990.

Dolar, Mladen. *A Voice and Nothing More*. Cambridge, Mass.: MIT Press, 2006.

Durham, Scott. "Codes Unknown: Haneke's Serial Realism." In Price and Rhodes, *On Michael Haneke*, 244–65.

Fassbinder, Rainer Werner, dir. *Effi Briest*. DVD. New York: Wellspring, 2003.

Flaxman, Gregory. "Introduction." In *The Brain is the Screen: Deleuze and the Philosophy of Cinema*, edited by Gregory Flaxman, 1–58. Minneapolis: University of Minnesota Press, 2000.

Foster, Stephen C. "Video and Intermedia: Remarks on their Relationship." In Breder and Busse, *Intermedia*, 63–65.

Foucault, Michel. "The Subject and Power." In Chang and Butchart, *Philosophy of Communication*, 285–301.

Frampton, Daniel. *Filmosophy: A Manifesto for a Radically New Way of Understanding Cinema*. London: Wallflower Press, 2006.

Freud, Sigmund. *Three Essays on Sexuality*. Translated by James Strachey. New York: Basic Books, 1962.

Frey, Mattias. "Supermodernity, Capital, and Narcissus: The French Connection to Michael Haneke's *Benny's Video*." *Cinetext: Film & Philosophy* (September 27, 2002): 1–15. Accessed October 28, 2015. http://cinetext.philo.at/magazine/frey/bennys_video.pdf.

Galloway, Alexander R. "Origins of the First-Person Shooter." In *Gaming: Essays on Algorithmic Culture*. Minneapolis: University of Minnesota Press, 2006.

Gaudreault, André, and Philippe Marion. "A Medium is Always Born Twice . . . ." *Early Popular Visual Culture* 3, no. 1 (2005): 3–15.

———. "Transécriture and Narrative Mediatics: The Stakes of Intermediality." Translated by Robert Stam. In *A Companion to Literature and Film*, edited by Robert Stam and Alessandra Raengo, 58–70. Malden, Mass.: Blackwell, 2004.

Genosko, Gary. "Guattari TV, By Kafka." *Deleuze Studies* 6, no. 2 (2012): 210–23.

Grossvogel, D. I. "Haneke: The Coercing of Vision." *Film Quarterly* 60, no. 4 (2007): 36–43.

Grundmann, Roy. "Auteur de Force: Michael Haneke's 'Cinema of Glaciation.'" *Cineaste* 33, no. 2 (2007): 6–14.

———. "Between Adorno and Lyotard: Michael Haneke's Aesthetic of Fragmentation." In Grundmann, *A Companion to Michael Haneke*, 371–419.

———, ed. *A Companion to Michael Haneke*. West Sussex: Blackwell, 2010.

———. "Introduction: Haneke's Anachronism." In Grundmann, *A Companion to Michael Haneke*, 1–50.

Guattari, Félix. "Project for a Film *by* Kafka." Translated by Jakub Zdebik. *Deleuze Studies* 3, no. 2 (2009): 150–61.

Hall, Stuart. "Encoding/Decoding." In *Media and Cultural Studies: Keyworks*, Revised Edition, edited by Meenakshi Gigi Durham and Douglas M. Kellner, 163–73. Malden, Mass.: Blackwell, 2006.

Haneke, Michael, dir. *Caché*. DVD. Sony Pictures, 2006.

———, dir. *The Films of Michael Haneke: "The Piano Teacher," "Code Unknown," "Franz Kafka's Castle," "Funny Games," "71 Fragments of a Chronology of Chance," "Benny's Video," "The Seventh Continent."* DVD Box Set. Kino Video, 2007.

———, dir. *Funny Games* [U.S.]. DVD. Warner Video, 2008.

———, dir. *Time of the Wolf*. DVD. Palm Pictures, 2004.

———, dir. *The White Ribbon*. DVD. Sony Pictures Classics, 2010.

Haneke, Michael. "Beyond Mainstream Film: An Interview with Michael Haneke." By Willy Riemer. In Riemer, *After Postmodernism*, 159–70.

———. "Collective Guilt and Individual Responsibility: An Interview with Michael Haneke." By Richard Porton. *Cineaste* 31, no. 1 (2005): 50–51.

———. "The Discreet Harm of the Bourgeoisie." By Richard Falcon. *Sight & Sound* 8, no. 5 (1998): 10–12.

———. "Interview: Michael Haneke, the Bearded Prophet of *Code inconnu* and *The Piano Teacher*." By Scott Foundas. *Indiewire*, December 4, 2001. Accessed October 20, 2015. http://www.indiewire.com/article/interview_michael_haneke_the_bearded_prophet_of_code_inconnu_and_the_piano_.

———. "Interview with Michael Haneke by Serge Toubiana." DVD special feature. *Benny's Video* et al. Dir. Michael Haneke. New York: Kino Video, 2007.

———. "Interview with Michael Haneke: 'The Fragmentation of the Look.'" By Michel Cieutat, translated by Peter Brunette. In Brunette, *Michael Haneke*, 139–47.

———. "Interview with Michael Haneke: You Never Show Reality, Just Its Manipulated Image." By Michel Cieutat and Philippe Rouyer, translated by Peter Brunette. In Brunette, *Michael Haneke*, 148–56.

———. "Minister of Fear." By John Wray. *New York Times*, September 23, 2007. Accessed October 21, 2015. http://www.nytimes.com/2007/09/23/magazine/23haneke-t.html.

———. "*71 Fragments of a Chronology of Chance*: Notes to the Film." In Riemer, *After Postmodernism*, 171–75.

———. "Terror and Utopia of Form Addicted to Truth: A Film Story about Robert Bresson's *Au hasard Balthazar*." Translated by Robert Gray. In *Robert Bresson*, edited by James Quandt, 551–59. Toronto: Toronto International Film Festival Group, 1998.

———. "Violence and the Media." Translated by Evan Torner. In Grundmann, *A Companion to Michael Haneke*, 575–79.

———. "'We Live in a Permanent State of War': An Interview with Michael Haneke." By Franz Grabner. In *Fascinatingly Disturbing: Interdisciplinary Perspectives on Michael Haneke's Cinema*, edited by Alexander D. Ornella and Stefanie Knauss, 13–33. Eugene, Oregon: Pickwick Publications, 2010.

———. "The World That is Known: An Interview with Michael Haneke." By Christopher Sharrett. In Grundmann, *Companion to Michael Haneke*, 580–90.

Hediger, Vinzenz. "Infectious Images: Haneke, Cameron, Egoyan, and the Dueling Epistemologies of Video and Film." In Grundmann, *Companion to Michael Haneke*, 91–112.

Herzogenrath, Bernd, ed. *Travels in Intermedia[lity]*. Hanover: Dartmouth College Press, 2012.

———. "Travels in Intermedia[lity]: An Introduction." In Herzogenrath, *Travels in Intermedia[lity]*, 1–14.

Higgins, Dick. "Intermedia." *Leonardo* 34, no. 1 (2001): 49–54.

Holmes, Deborah. "The Early Haneke: Austrian Literature on Austrian Television." In McCann and Sorfa, *The Cinema of Michael Haneke: Europe Utopia*, 117–28.

———. "Literature on the Small Screen: Michael Haneke's Television Adaptations of Josef Roth's *Die Rebellion* and Kafka's *Das Schloβ*." In *New German Literature: Life-Writing and Dialogue with the Arts*, edited by Julian Preece, Frank Finlay, and Ruth J. Owen, 107–22. Oxford: Peter Lang, 2007.

Horton, Andrew James. "Locked out!: Michael Haneke's *Code inconnu: Récit incomplet de divers voyages*." *Central Europe Review* 3, no. 19 (2001). Accessed October 23, 2015. http://www.ce-review.org/01/19/kinoeye19_horton.html.

Innis, Harold A. *The Bias of Communication*. Toronto: University of Toronto Press, 1968.

———. *Empire and Communications*. Edited by David Godfrey. Victoria/Toronto: Press Porcépic, 1986.

Jameson, Fredric. "Allegorizing Hitchcock." In *Signatures of the Visible*, 99–127. London: Routledge, 1992.

———. *The Geopolitical Aesthetic: Cinema and Space in the World System*. Bloomington: Indiana University Press, 1992.

———. *Postmodernism or, The Cultural Logic of Late Capitalism*. Durham, N.C.: Duke University Press, 1991.

Jelinek, Elfreide. *The Piano Teacher*. Translated by Joachim Neugroschel. New York: Grove Press, 1988.

Johnston, Ian. "The Children Are Watching You: Michael Haneke's *The White Ribbon*." *Bright Lights Film Journal* no. 68 (2010). Accessed October 28, 2015. http://brightlightsfilm.com/the-children-are-watching-you-michael-hanekes-the-white-ribbon/.

Jones, Caroline. "Senses." In *Critical Terms for Media Studies*, edited by W. J. T. Mitchell and Mark B. N. Hansen, 88–100. Chicago: University of Chicago Press, 2010.

Kittler, Friedrich. *Gramophone, Film, Typewriter*. Translated by Geoffrey Winthrop-Young and Michael Wutz. Stanford: Stanford University Press, 1999.

———. *Optical Media: Berlin Lectures 1999*. Translated by Anthony Enns. Cambridge: Polity Press, 2010.

Krauss, Rosalind. "Video: The Aesthetics of Narcissism." *October* no. 1 (1976): 50–64.

Kristeva, Julia. "Word, Dialogue, and Novel." Translated by Thomas Gora, Alice Jardine, and Leon S. Roudiez. In *Desire in Language: A Semiotic Approach to Literature and Art*, edited by Leon S. Roudiez, 64–91. New York: Columbia University Press, 1980.

Kusturica, Nina, and Eva Testor, dirs. *24 Realities per Second: A Documentary on Michael Haneke*. DVD. New York: Cinema Guild, 2005.

Lansky, Melvin R. "Hidden Shame." *Journal of the American Psychoanalytic Association* 53, no. 3 (2005): 865–90.

Lawrence, Michael. "Haneke's Stable: The Death of an Animal and the Figuration of the Human." In Price and Rhodes, *On Michael Haneke*, 63–84.

Lebeau, Vicky. "The Arts of Looking: D. W. Winnicott and Michael Haneke." *Screen* 50, no. 1 (2009): 35–44.
Le Cain, Maximilian. "Do the Right Thing: The Films of Michael Haneke." *Senses of Cinema* 26 (May 2003). Accessed October 20, 2015. http://sensesofcinema.com/2003/michael-haneke/haneke/.
Levinas, Emmanuel. *On Escape*. Translated by Bettina Bergo. Stanford: Stanford University Press, 2003.
Llewelyn, John. *Emmanuel Levinas: The Genealogy of Ethics*. London: Routledge, 1995.
Luhmann, Niklas. *The Reality of the Mass Media*. Translated by Kathleen Cross. Cambridge: Polity Press, 2000.
Ma, Jean. "Discordant Desires, Violent Regrains: *La Pianiste (The Piano Teacher)*." In Grundmann, *Companion to Michael Haneke*, 511–31.
Manguel, Alberto. *A History of Reading*. New York: Penguin, 1996.
Manovich, Lev. *The Language of New Media*. Cambridge, Mass.: MIT Press, 2001.
Marrati, Paola. *Gilles Deleuze: Cinema and Philosophy*. Translated by Alisa Hartz. Baltimore: Johns Hopkins University Press, 2008.
McCann, Ben, and David Sorfa, eds. *The Cinema of Michael Haneke: Europe Utopia*. London: Wallflower Press, 2011.
McLuhan, Marshall. "Culture Without Literacy." In McLuhan, *Media Research*, 126–38.
———. "The Electronic Age—The Age of Implosion." In McLuhan, *Media Research*, 16–38.
———. "Foreword." In Innis, *The Bias of Communication*, vii–xvi.
———. "The *Hot and Cool* Interview (With Gerald Emanuel Stearn)." In McLuhan, *Media Research*, 45–78.
———. "Media Log." In Carpenter and McLuhan, *Explorations in Communication*, 180–83.
———. *Media Research: Technology, Art, Communication*. Edited by Michael A. Moos. Amersterdam: G+B Arts International, 1997.
———. "Myth and Mass Media." In McLuhan, *Media Research*, 5–15.
———. *Understanding Media: The Extensions of Man*. Cambridge, Mass.: MIT Press, 1994.
McLuhan, Marshall, and Quentin Fiore. *The Medium is the Massage*. Middlesex: Penguin, 1967.
Meier, Julia. "Genuine Thought is Inter(medial)." In Herzogenrath, *Travels in Intermedia[lity]*, 125–36.
Miller, Jacques-Alain. "On Shame." In *Jacques Lacan and the Other Side of Psychoanalysis*, edited by Justin Clemens and Russell Grigg, 11–28. Durham, N.C.: Duke University Press, 2006.
Mitchell, W. J. T. "Realism and the Digital Image." In Herzogenrath, *Travels in Intermedia[lity]*, 46–62.
Morse, Margaret. "An Ontology of Everyday Distraction: The Freeway, the Mall, and Television." In *Logics of Television: Essays in Cultural Criticism*, edited by Patricia Mellancamp, 193–221. Bloomington: Indiana University Press, 1990.
———. "Talk, Talk, Talk: The Space of Discourse in Television News, Sportscasts, Talk Shows, and Advertising." *Screen* 26, no. 2 (1985): 2–15.

Naqvi, Fatima. "A Melancholy Labor of Love, or Film Adaptation as Translation: *Three Paths to the Lake*." In Grundmann, *A Companion to Michael Haneke*, 205–26.

Naqvi, Fatima, and Christophe Koné. "The Key to Voyeurism: Haneke's Adaptation of Jelinek's *The Piano Teacher*." In Price and Rhodes, *On Michael Haneke*, 127–50.

Oosterling, Henk. "Sens(a)ble Intermediality and *Interesse*: Towards an Ontology of the In-Between." *Intermédialités* no. 1 (2003): 29–46.

Paech, Joachim. "Artwork—Text—Medium: Steps En Route to Intermediality." Translated by Thomas La Presti. Accessed September 26. 2014. http://www.uni-konstanz.de/FuF/Philo/LitWiss/MedienWiss/Texte/interm.html.

Parikka, Jussi. *Insect Media: An Archaeology of Animals and Technology*. Minneapolis: University of Minnesota Press, 2010.

Pethő, Ágnes. *Cinema and Intermediality: The Passion for the In-Between*. Newcastle: Cambridge Scholars Publishing, 2011.

Peucker, Brigitte. "Effects of the Real: Michael Haneke's *Benny's Video* (1993)." *Kinoeye* 4, no. 1 (2004). Accessed October 28, 2015. http://www.kinoeye.org/04/01/peucker01.php.

———. "Fragmentation and the Real: Michael Haneke's Family Trilogy." In Riemer, *After Postmodernism*, 176–88.

———. "Games Haneke Plays: Reality and Performance." In Price and Rhodes, *On Michael Haneke*, 15–33.

Price, Brian. "Pain and the Limits of Representation." In Price and Rhodes, *On Michael Haneke*, 35–48.

Price, Brian, and John David Rhodes. "Introduction." In Price and Rhodes, *On Michael Haneke*, 1–11.

———, eds. *On Michael Haneke*. Detroit: Wayne State University Press, 2010.

Rajewsky, Irina. "Intermediality, Intertextuality and Remediation: A Literary Perspective on Intermediality." *Intermédialités* no. 6 (2005): 43–64.

Riemer, Willy, ed. *After Postmodernism: Austrian Literature and Film in Transition*. Riverside: Ariadne Press, 2000.

———. "Michael Haneke, *The Piano Teacher* [*Die Klavierspielerin*]: Repertoires of Power and Desire." In *Elfriede Jelinek: Writing Woman, Nation, and Identity: A Critical Anthology*, edited by Matthias Piccolruaz Konzett and Margarete Lamb-Faffelberger, 270–84. Madison: Fairleigh Dickinson University Press, 2007.

———. "Tracing K: Michael Haneke's Film Adaptation of Kafka's *Das Schloß*." In McCann and Sorfa, *The Cinema of Michael Haneke: Europe Utopia*, 129–38.

Rodowick, D. N. *Gilles Deleuze's Time Machine*. Durham, N.C.: Duke University Press, 1997.

———. *Reading the Figural, or, Philosophy after the New Media*. Durham, N.C.: Duke University Press, 2001.

———. *The Virtual Life of Film*. Cambridge, Mass.: Harvard University Press, 2007.

Sartre, Jean-Paul. *Being and Nothingness*. Translated by Hazel Estella Barnes. London: Routledge, 1969.

Saxton, Libby. "Close Encounters with Distant Suffering: Michael Haneke's Disarming Visions." In *Five Directors: Auteurism from Assayas to Ozon*, edited by Kate Ince, 84–111. Manchester: Manchester University Press, 2008.

———. "Secrets and Revelations: Off-screen Space in Michael Haneke's *Caché* (2005)." *Studies in French Cinema* 7, no. 1 (2007): 5–17.

Scarry, Elaine. *The Body in Pain: The Making and Unmaking of the World*. New York: Oxford University Press, 1985.

Schröter, Jens. "Discourses and Models of Intermediality." *CLCWeb: Comparative Literature and Culture* 13, no. 3 (2011): 2–8. Accessed October 28, 2015. http://docs.lib.purdue.edu/clcweb/vol13/iss3/3/.

———. "The Politics of Intermediality." *Acta Universitatis Sapentiae: Film and Media Studies* no. 2 (2010): 107–24.

Schwartz, Peter J. "The Void at the Center of Things: Figures of Identity in Michael Haneke's Glaciation Trilogy." In Grundmann, *A Companion to Michael Haneke*, 337–53.

Seeβlen, Georg. "Structures of Glaciation: Gaze, Perspective, and *Gestus* in the Films of Michael Haneke." Translated by Timothy Dail. In Grundmann, *A Companion to Michael Haneke*, 323–36.

Sharrett, Christopher. "Michael Haneke and the Discontents of European Culture." *Framework* 47, no. 2 (2006): 6–16.

Silverman, Max. "The Empire Looks Back." *Screen* 48, no. 2 (2007): 245–49.

Simons, Jan. *Playing the Waves: Lars von Trier's Game Cinema*. Amsterdam: Amsterdam University Press, 2007.

Sinnerbrink, Robert. *New Philosophies of Film: Thinking Images*. London: Continuum, 2011.

Sloterdijk, Peter. "*Actio in Distans*: On Forms of Telerational World-Making." In Chang and Butchart, *Philosophy of Communication*, 635–48.

Sobchack, Vivian. *Carnal Thoughts: Embodiment and Moving-Image Culture*. Berkeley: University of California Press, 2004.

Speck, Oliver C. *Funny Frames: The Filmic Concepts of Michael Haneke*. New York: Continuum, 2010.

Spielmann, Yvonne. "History and Theory of Intermedia in Visual Culture (Manuscript of the Paper Presentation)." In Breder and Busse, *Intermedia*, 131–36.

———. *Video: The Reflexive Medium*. Translated by Anja Welle and Stan Jones. Cambridge, Mass.: MIT Press, 2008.

Stam, Robert. "Introduction: The Theory and Practice of Adaptation." In *Literature and Film: A Guide to the Theory and Practice of Film Adaptation*, edited by Robert Stam and Alessandra Raengo, 1–52. Malden, Mass.: Blackwell, 2005.

Surman, David. "Pleasure, Spectacle and Reward in Capcom's *Street Fighter* series." In *Videogame, Player, Text*, edited by Barry Atkins and Tanya Krzywinska, 204–21. Manchester: Manchester University Press, 2007.

Sutherland, Meghan. "Death, with Television." In Price and Rhodes, *On Michael Haneke*, 167–89.

Szabados, Béla, and Christina Stojanova. "Introduction." In *Wittgenstein at the Movies: Cinematic Investigations*, edited by Béla Szabados and Christina Stojanova, ix–xix. Lanham, Md.: Lexington Books, 2011.

Tarkovsky, Andrey. *Sculpting in Time: Reflections on the Cinema*. Translated by Kitty Hunter-Blair. London: Bodley Head, 1986.

Vernet, Marc. "The Look at the Camera." Translated by Dana Polan. *Cinema Journal* 28, no. 2 (1989): 48–63.

Virilio, Paul. *A Landscape of Events*. Translated by Julie Rose. Cambridge, Mass.: MIT Press, 2000.

———. *Polar Inertia*. Translated by Patrick Camiller. London: Sage Publications, 2000.

———. *The University of Disaster*. Translated by Julie Rose. Cambridge: Polity Press, 2010.

———. *The Vision Machine*. Translated by Julie Rose. London: British Film Institute, 1994.

Vogl, Joseph. "Becoming-Media: Galileo's Telescope." In Chang and Butchart, *Philosophy of Communication*, 627–34.

Voigst-Virchow, Eckart. "Metadaptation: Adaptation and Intermediality—Cock and Bull." *Journal of Adaptation in Film & Performance* 2, no. 2 (2009): 137–52.

Weber, Samuel. *Mass Mediauras: Form, Technics, Media*. Edited by Alan Cholodenko. Stanford: Stanford University Press, 1996.

Wheatley, Catherine. *Michael Haneke's Cinema: The Ethic of the Image*. New York: Berghahn Books, 2009.

———. "The Spectator as Moral Agent: Kantian Ethics and the Films of Michael Haneke." In *From Plato's Cave to the Multiplex*, edited by Barbara Gabriella Renzi and Stephen Rainey, 61–72. Newcastle: Cambridge Scholars Press, 2006.

Williams, Bernard. *Shame and Necessity*. Berkeley: University of California Press, 1993.

Williams, Raymond. *Television: Technology and Cultural Form*. London: Routledge, 2003.

Winthrop-Young, Geoffrey. *Kittler and the Media*. Cambridge: Polity Press, 2011.

Wittgenstein, Ludwig. *Philosophical Remarks*. Translated by Raymond Hargreaves and Roger White, edited by Rush Rhees. Chicago: University of Chicago Press, 1975.

Wood, Robin. "Michael Haneke: Beyond Compromise." *CineAction* no. 73–74 (2007): 44–55.

Zielinski, Siegfried. *Deep Time of the Media: Toward an Archaeology of Hearing and Seeing by Technical Means*. Translated by Gloria Custance. Cambridge, Mass.: MIT Press, 2006.

Žižek, Slavoj. *How to Read Lacan*. New York: Norton, 2007.

INDEX

Page numbers in **boldface** refer to illustrations.